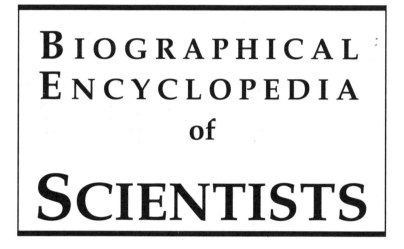

BIOGRAPHICAL ENCYCLOPEDIA of SCIENTISTS

BIOGRAPHICAL ENCYCLOPEDIA of SCIENTISTS

Volume 1
Abbott – Copernicus

Editor
RICHARD OLSON

Associate Editor
ROGER SMITH

Marshall Cavendish
New York • London • Toronto

Project Editor: Tracy Irons-Georges
Research Supervisor: Jeffry Jensen
Acquisitions Editor: Mark Rehn
Photograph Editor: Karrie Hyatt
Production Editor: Cynthia Breslin Beres
Proofreading Supervisor: Yasmine A. Cordoba
Layout: James Hutson

Photograph Researcher: Susan Hormuth, Washington, D.C.

Published By
Marshall Cavendish Corporation
99 White Plains Road
Tarrytown, New York 10591-9001
United States of America

Library of Congress Cataloging-in-Publication Data

Biographical encyclopedia of scientists / editor Richard Olson, associate editor Roger
  Smith.
    p. cm.
  Complete in 5 v.
  Includes bibliographical references and index.
  1. Scientists—Biography—Encyclopedias. 2. Science—Encyclopedias. 3. Science—
Dictionaries. I. Olson, Richard, 1940-   . II. Smith, Roger, 1953 Apr. 19-   .
ISBN 0-7614-7064-6 (set)
ISBN 0-7614-7065-4 (vol. 1)
Q141.B532 1998
509'.2'2—dc21   97-23877
                                                    CIP

First Printing

PRINTED IN THE UNITED STATES OF AMERICA

Publisher's Note

Science offers an ever-expanding and seemingly ever-changing array of facts and theories to explain the workings of life and the universe. Behind its doors, we can explore fascinating worlds ranging from the tiny—the spiral ladder of DNA in every human cell and the particle zoo of quarks and mesons in every atom—to the unimaginably vast—the gradual, often catastrophic shifting of continents over the globe and the immense gravitational fields surrounding black holes in space. Unfortunately, the doors of science often remain shut to students and the general public. The *Biographical Encyclopedia of Scientists* seeks to serve as a key. Its goal is to introduce many notable people and concepts, sparking interest and providing jumping-off points for gaining further knowledge. To this end, this encyclopedia offers a select survey of scientists and their accomplishments across disciplines, throughout history, and around the world. The life stories of these individuals and the descriptions of their accomplishments will prove both informational and inspirational to budding scientists and to all those with inquisitive minds.

This five-volume encyclopedia profiles 472 representative figures in the history of scientific investigation, arranged alphabetically by name from medical researcher Maude Abbott to inventor Vladimir Zworykin. Entries are usually 750 or 1,250 words in length, with some longer essays covering individuals who made numerous significant contributions to the development of science, such as Aristotle, Albert Einstein, Galileo, Louis Pasteur, and Sir Isaac Newton. In addition to celebrating famous names who made great strides in scientific inquiry and paved the way for others to follow, the encyclopedia gives credit to individuals and groups who have gone largely unrecognized, such as women and minority scientists and many contemporary researchers.

The lives and achievements of many notable figures in the history of science are covered in the *Biographical Encyclopedia of Scientists*—from ancient Greeks to today's working scientists. Efforts have been made to create a balance in era, nationality, race, gender, and scientific discipline. The focus is on the "hard" sciences, as opposed to such "softer" social sciences as anthropology or psychology. Thus, many scientists in the fields of physics, biology, immunology, chemistry, genetics, physiology, and astronomy are included, as well as some researchers in the fields of bacteriology, botany, cell biology, cosmology, earth science, medicine, pharmacology, virology, and zoology. Also featured are individuals who made their mark for inventing techniques, such as Joseph Lister and Jonas Salk, or technologies, such as Thomas Alva Edison and Edward Teller; those who won a popular reputation, such as Rachel Carson and Carl Sagan; and those who are also known as mathematicians in addition to their contributions to natural science, such as Archimedes and René Descartes. (A two-volume supplement, the *Biographical Encyclopedia of Mathematicians*, will follow.)

Every article begins with a list of the scientist's areas of achievement, a brief statement of that individual's contribution to science, and a time line listing birth and death dates, major awards and honors, and milestones in the scientist's education, research, employment, and private life. The entry then details the struggles and triumphs that characterize the lives of many who pursue knowledge as a career. One or more boxes within the article provide further coverage of the featured scientist's achievements—theories, research, inventions, or discoveries—and direct readers to further sources about the topic. For example, included in the encyclopedia are clear explanations of the big bang, evolution, relativity theory, genetic engineering, the hydrogen bomb, and quarks. A bibliography of works both by and about the scientist concludes each entry, and all articles are signed by the author. Photographs, drawings, and diagrams offer an important visual element and reinforce the information presented. To help readers pronounce foreign or difficult names of profiled scientists, a phonetic guide has been provided following the first mention of the name in that individual's entry; a Key to Pronunciation, listing the letters used in these guides to represent various sounds and examples of words in which those sounds appear, can be found at the beginning of all five volumes.

Volume 5 contains a Glossary that offers clear definitions of crucial terms and concepts; a Country List of the profiled scientists arranged by nationality and including headings for such traditionally underrepresented groups as *African Americans*, *Asian Americans*, *Latinos*, and *Women*; and an Areas of Scientific Achievement list arranged by discipline. To give readers a larger context in which to view the history of science, volume 5 also offers a general Time Line listing all the featured scientists in chronological order by birth date and providing information about country and field of research. In the back of all five volumes can be found a comprehensive Index that allows readers to locate information about the people, concepts, organizations, and topics covered in the encyclopedia.

Much gratitude must be expressed to Richard Olson, the editor of the set, for his dedication to this project, particularly his work on the Glossary, and to Roger Smith, the associate editor, for his help with the list of contents. Their combined expertise and knowledge were crucial to the success of this encyclopedia. We would also like to thank the many academicians and researchers whose belief in science education and the dissemination of knowledge fueled the engine behind this effort; their names and affiliations are listed at the beginning of volume 1.

Contributors

Amy Ackerberg-Hastings
Iowa State University

Richard Adler
University of Michigan, Dearborn

Drew L. Arrowood
American Institute of Physics

Grace A. Banks
Chestnut Hill College

Harold Belofsky
University of Akron

Peter K. Benbow
Oxford University, England

Raymond Benge
Richland College

Cynthia Berger
Independent Scholar

Christopher J. Biermann
Oregon State University

Terry D. Bilhartz
Sam Houston State University

Ann Binder
Independent Scholar

B. Christiana Birchak
University of Houston, Downtown

Bonnie Ellen Blustein
Foreman High School, Chicago

Paul R. Boehlke
Wisconsin Lutheran College

Kenneth H. Brown
Northwestern Oklahoma State University

Laurie M. Brown
Northwestern University

Louis Brown
Carnegie Institution of Washington

Helen M. Burke
Chestnut Hill College

Laurence M. Burke II
Independent Scholar

Dan Burton
Indiana University

Laura M. Calkins
University of Michigan, Ann Arbor

Doug Campbell
Texas Tech University

Ranes C. Chakravorty
University of Virginia

Peggy Champlin
Independent Scholar

Monish R. Chatterjee
State University of New York, Binghamton

Dennis W. Cheek
Rhode Island Department of Education

David L. Chesemore
California State University, Fresno

Francis P. Chinard
New Jersey Medical School

David E. Connolly
Ohio State University

Raymond D. Cooper
Academy of Senior Professionals at Eckerd College

Albert B. Costa
Duquesne University

Arlene R. Courtney
Western Oregon State College

John A. Cramer
Oglethorpe University

Ralph D. Cross
Independent Scholar

Keay Davidson
San Francisco Examiner

Thomas Drucker
University of Wisconsin

Kathleen Duffy
Chestnut Hill College

David Allen Duncan
Tennessee Wesleyan College

Val Dusek
University of New Hampshire

Thomas H. Eberlein
Pennsylvania State University

H. J. Eisenman
University of Missouri, Rolla

Derek W. Elliott
Tennessee State University

J. Eric Elliott
Independent Scholar

Jessica O. Ellison
Clarkson University

Linda Eikmeier Endersby
Massachusetts Institute of Technology

Amy England-Beery
University of Notre Dame

Sibel Erduran
Vanderbilt University

L. Fleming Fallon, Jr.
Columbia University School of Public Health

Loren Butler Feffer
University of Pennsylvania

David G. Fenton
Connecticut College

K. Thomas Finley
State University of New York, Brockport

Richard D. Fitzgerald
Onondaga Community College

George J. Flynn
State University of New York College at Plattsburgh

Donald R. Franceschetti
University of Memphis

C. George Fry
Lutheran College

Janet Bell Garber
Independent Scholar

Leonard J. Garigliano
Salisbury State University

Roberto Garza
San Antonio College

Sander J. Gliboff
The Johns Hopkins University

Martin A. Gold
University of Florida

Pamela J. W. Gore
DeKalb College

Robert R. Gradie III
University of Connecticut

Hans G. Graetzer
South Dakota State University

Hugh L. Guilderson
Boston College

Wendy Halpin Hallows
Chestnut Hill College

Jacob D. Hamblin
Independent Scholar

James G. Hanley
Yale University

C. James Haug
Mississippi State University

Robert M. Hawthorne, Jr.
Independent Scholar

Mark Gray Henderson
Harvard University

Charles E. Herdendorf
Ohio State University

Tom R. Herrmann
Eastern Oregon State College

Carl W. Hoagstrom
Ohio Northern University

John L. Howland
Bowdoin College

Stephen Huber
Custom Software, Inc.

Randy Hudson
Independent Scholar

Cecil O. Huey, Jr.
Clemson University

Tom Hull
South Umpqua High School

Tracy Irons-Georges
Independent Scholar

Paul Israel
Rutgers University

Jerome A. Jackson
Mississippi State University

Peter L. Jakab
National Air and Space Museum

Albert C. Jensen
Central Florida Community College

Jeffrey A. Joens
Florida International University

Richard C. Jones
Texas Woman's University

Karen E. Kalumuck
The Exploratorium

Sachi Sri Kantha
Japan Institute for Control of Aging

Armand M. Karow
Medical College of Georgia

George B. Kauffman
California State University, Fresno

Kyle L. Kayler
Kayler Geoscience, Ltd.

Christopher Keating
Angelo State University

Kenneth W. Kemp
University of St. Thomas

Firman D. King
University of South Florida

Steve Kirkpatrick
Blinn College

Robert Klose
University College of Bangor

Jeffrey A. Knight
Mount Holyoke College

Christopher S. W. Koehler
University of Florida

Lillian D. Kozloski
Independent Scholar

Joseph R. Lafaro
Gannon University

Lyndall Baker Landauer
Lake Tahoe Community College

Manfred D. Laubichler
Princeton University

Ronald W. Long
West Virginia University, Institute of Technology

Jeff Loveland
University of Cincinnati

Craig Sean McConnell
University of Wisconsin

Darbie L. Maccubbin
Villa Maria College of Buffalo

Mark R. McCulloh
Davidson College

Linda L. McDonald
North Park College

Francis P. Mac Kay
Providence College

Emerson Thomas McMullen
Georgia Southern University

Margaret H. Major
DeKalb College

Marjorie C. Malley
Independent Scholar

Joseph T. Malloy
Hamilton College

Nancy Farm Mannikko
Virginia Polytechnic Institute and State University

Bill R. Martin
Oregon State University

Ronald E. Mickens
Clark Atlanta University

Randall L. Milstein
Oregon State University

Martha J. Mitchell
Roy F. Weston, Inc.

John Panos Najarian
William Paterson College

Peter Neushul
California Institute of Technology

Anthony J. Nicastro
West Chester University of Pennsylvania

Brian J. Nichelson
Independent Scholar

Maureen H. O'Rafferty
Rutgers University

Lawrence K. Orr
Independent Scholar

Joseph C. Palais
Arizona State University

Robert J. Paradowski
Rochester Institute of Technology

Gordon A. Parker
University of Michigan, Dearborn

Lynda Stephenson Payne
University of California, Davis

Paul D. Peterson, Jr.
North Carolina State University

Alvin M. Pettus
James Madison University

John R. Phillips
Purdue University, Calumet

George R. Plitnik
Frostburg State University

George W. Rainey
*California State Polytechnic University,
  Pomona*

Richard E. Rice
University of Montana

Connie Rizzo
Pace University

Linda E. Roach
*Northwestern State University of
  Louisiana*

Charles W. Rogers
*Southwestern Oklahoma State
  University*

Robert Rosenberg
Rutgers University

Marc Rothenberg
Smithsonian Institution

Milton H. Saier, Jr.
University of California, San Diego

Virginia L. Salmon
*Northeast State Technical Community
  College*

Elizabeth D. Schafer
Independent Scholar

Kenneth J. Schoon
Indiana University Northwest

John Richard Schrock
Emporia State University

Joel S. Schwartz
*City University of New York
  College of Staten Island*

Rose Secrest
Independent Scholar

Philip N. Seidenberg
Georgia Institute of Technology

John H. Serembus
Widener University

Patricia Joan Siegel
*State University of New York
  College at Brockport*

Martha A. Sherwood
University of Oregon

Todd A. Shimoda
Independent Scholar

Beth Anne Short
Collin County Community College

R. Baird Shuman
*University of Illinois
  at Urbana-Champaign*

Sanford S. Singer
University of Dayton

Paul P. Sipiera
Harper College

Peter Skiff
Bard College

Roger Smith
Independent Scholar

Katherine R. Sopka
Four Corners Analytic Sciences

Joseph L. Spradley
Wheaton College

Grace Marmor Spruch
Rutgers University, Newark

Joan C. Stevenson
Western Washington University

Martin V. Stewart
Middle Tennessee State University

Anthony N. Stranges
Texas A&M University

Robert B. Sullivan
University of Wisconsin, Madison

Zeno G. Swijtink
Sonoma State University

William Tammone
Indiana University

Paul C. L. Tang
California State University, Long Beach

Nicholas C. Thomas
Auburn University at Montgomery

Nigel J. T. Thomas
California State University, Los Angeles

Rosa Alvarez Ulloa
Independent Scholar

David A. Valone
Quinnipiac College

Thomas E. Van Koevering
University of Wisconsin, Green Bay

Lee Venolia
Independent Scholar

Charles Vigue
University of New Haven

Michael J. Wavering
University of Arkansas

Jane Carter Webb
Christopher Newport University

Jack H. Westbrook
Brookline Technologies

Russell Williams
*University of Arkansas
  for Medical Science*

George Wilson
Independent Scholar

A. David Wunsch
University of Massachusetts, Lowell

Robinson M. Yost
Iowa State University

Kristen L. Zacharias
Albright College

Benjamin S. Zibit
*City University of New York
  Graduate Center*

Contents

Introduction

When I sat down to draft this introduction on January 20, 1997, my *Time* magazine arrived with the cover story "Where the Jobs Are." "From Silicon Valley to the Research Triangle," it proclaims, "companies are having a difficult time finding skilled workers to keep their businesses humming. The high-tech economy demands high-tech workers with high-tech training." The boom in jobs requiring scientific and technological training—jobs in biotechnology, pharmaceuticals, health care, software development, and high-tech manufacturing and design—produces jobs in service industries. But a huge and growing disparity exists in compensation between high-tech jobs (in 1997, some jobs in software design and computer animation offered starting salaries of around $70,000 per year for holders of bachelor's degrees) and the fast-food, domestic service, and retail sales jobs which they support (in 1997, salaries in these areas averaged less than $15,000 per year). As the *Time* article says, "A fault line divides the workers with the knowledge and credentials to get good jobs from those individuals . . . who lack the basic education to cash in."

If the shortage of technically educated workers and the increasing divergence in economic opportunities between those who are scientifically and technologically literate and those who are not were a short-term problem limited to the United States, it would be serious enough to be a matter of public concern in America. But it is neither. It is an international problem which will be with us all for the foreseeable future. Furthermore, studies of scientific and mathematical knowledge among grade-school and high-school students show that English-speaking nations in general are achieving lower levels of scientific literacy than students in Japan, Taiwan, Korea, Switzerland, Sweden, the Netherlands, Hungary, the former Soviet Union, Finland, and Israel. (Though the many international tests do not give completely consistent results, this claim is made on the basis of the comparative discussion of international science and mathematics tests in chapter 3 of David Drew's *Aptitude Re-*

visited: Rethinking Math and Science Education for America's Next Century, 1996).

This news is of critical concern because, as Sandra Harding, author of *The Science Question in Feminism* (1986) points out, "During the last century, the social uses of science have shifted: formerly an occasional assistant, it has become the direct generator of economic, political and social accumulation and control." Since it is likely that economic, military, and political success in the highly competitive high-tech global culture which is now emerging will depend heavily on a pool of technically educated and talented workers, it would seem that improving the quality, appeal, and inclusiveness of science education should be a national imperative everywhere, and especially among English speakers.

The reform and improvement of science education *is* currently attracting great effort and attention almost everywhere on the globe; we hope that the *Biographical Encyclopedia of Scientists* constitutes a worthwhile contribution to this effort. By linking the discussion of basic scientific principles with the biographies of those scientists involved in their formulation, development, and utilization, we hope to fuse scientific knowledge with human stories in a way that will allow greater numbers of students to relate to and retain that knowledge.

Just as it is important to the well-being of a nation and to the economic prospects of individuals to increase the overall percentage of students with an interest in and knowledge of science and technology, it is important to make certain that access to high-tech jobs via high-quality scientific and mathematical education is widely distributed across boundaries of gender and ethnicity. This is the case both because we need the collective talent of all members of society and because intentionally or unintentionally excluding members of any groups from the sources of wealth and power represented by scientific knowledge is certain to amplify existing intergroup social and economic disparities and encourage destructive intergroup conflict. There is every reason to believe that the disproportionate participation of white males in science is an historical accident, and not based on inherent talents or aptitudes. So, those of us responsible for choosing the persons to be included in the *Biographical Encyclopedia of Scientists* have made a special effort to acknowledge the contributions of outstanding women and members of different ethnic groups so that all students can identify with scientific activities.

Given the undeniable centrality of science and technology to our culture and the undeniable power which scientific knowledge has provided to create, sustain, destroy, or otherwise transform entities in the world, the role of the scientist and the scientifically trained worker is becoming increasingly important and increasingly deeply integrated into our social, political, and economic institutions. Again, according to Harding,

> No longer is the scientist—if he ever was—an eccentric and socially marginal genius spending private funds and often private time on whatever purely intellectual pursuits happen to interest him. Only rarely does his research have no foreseeable social uses. Instead, he (or, more recently, she) is part of a vast work force, [and] is trained from elementary school on to enter academic, industrial, and governmental laboratories where 99+ percent of the research is expected to be immediately applicable to social projects.

As the biographies in this encyclopedia will demonstrate, much of what Harding says about recent science is true.

Contemporary "big science" not only depends upon the cooperation of many scientists in most work but because it demands the investment of big money, also depends upon directing scientific activities toward problems which attract public or private support. And this means that scientific activities must offer the prospect of some critical public benefit—for example, improved defense or public health—or some private profit. This was not always so. As the biographies will also show, however, throughout most of the distant past scientists have been keenly aware of the need for patronage and thus have been concerned with satisfying the wants of those who could offer support.

Even the most ancient developments in mathematics and astronomy—developments which predate the assignment of credit to particular individuals—were often associated with commercial and other social activities. Astronomy developed independently in China, India, Mesopotamia, Egypt, and Central America in connection with the establishment of calendars for religious rituals; geometry developed to solve problems with allocating plots of land to individuals and with assessing the taxes attributable to different plots; and arithmetic and what we call algebra were developed for keeping commercial accounts and for solving engineering problems.

In ancient Greece, natural knowledge became associated with an aristocratic elite which prided itself on its ability to devote time to pursue pure knowledge and on its freedom from the need for doing manual labor. Thus, for a time the pursuit of natural knowledge was largely divorced from applications to productive and reproductive activities. But even in this context, some scientific knowledge was closely linked to societal needs. The works of Hippocrates and Galen of Pergamum, for example, were aimed at improving medical practice. The hydrostatic and mechanical works of Archimedes were aimed at solving military problems and questions such as whether objects were made of pure gold or of adulterated materials. Though public intellectual life in the ancient world was dominated by men, there were some women in the scribal classes in Mesopotamia and Egypt. In Greece, women played a substantial role in health care, while a few, including the Alexandrian mathematician Hypatia, managed to stand out in the exact sciences.

Within the Christian culture of late antiquity and early medieval Europe, scientific knowledge continued to be largely divorced from productive activities other than medicine. It was preserved and extended primarily for religious purposes, including the interpretation of biblical texts, and thus it was carried on largely in monastic communities and cathedral schools which were open only to men, as were the later medieval universities. Only a handful of women such as Hildegard of Bingen, who were abbesses responsible for the education of nuns and monks, became involved with scientific knowledge.

The most advanced science of the medieval period was done within the Islamic empire, which extended from India on the East, through the Near East and North Africa, into the Iberian Peninsula. Drawing on mathematical, medical, and technological traditions from ancient Greece, India, and Persia, Islamic scholars developed a vital synthesis, the primary characteristics of which were the revival of interest in applied knowledge among intellectuals and an emphasis on direct observation and experimentation, especially in alchemy, medicine, and the navigational arts. As medieval European universities developed and as Europeans came into contact with Islamic knowledge, the technical level of European science rose rapidly and scholars such as Roger Bacon introduced experimental science into Europe.

Throughout the early modern period, European natural knowledge became increasingly oriented toward applications as mathematics and mechanics were focused on military and architectural development, astronomy and chronometry were oriented toward navigation, and chemistry and anatomy were developed to improve medical practice. There remained an important tradition of science for its own sake—especially among wealthy amateurs—and some of the greatest early modern scientists, including René Descartes and Isaac Newton, are often identified with this tradition. Newly developing scientific institutions, however, such as the Royal Society of London (founded in 1662) and the French Académie des Sciences (founded in 1666) emphasized the production of "useful knowledge." The provision of salaries for members of the academy by the French government in return for scientific investigation of problems raised by the government established a new pattern of relationships between scientists and governments which would increase in importance over time.

Although many seventeenth century scientists hoped that their knowledge would lead to the improvement of human life and to their own enrichment, it was probably not until the application of chemistry to textile dyeing and bleaching processes toward the end of the eighteenth century that a new and continuously accelerating pattern of direct application of scientific knowledge to commercially significant activities began. This pattern accelerated through the nineteenth century with the creation of the electrical industry based on Michael Faraday's discoveries and the creation of the coal tar dye and chemical pharmaceutical industries in Germany. By the end of the nineteenth century, science had become the chief engine of economic change and military power.

While space limitations force the omission of many important scientists, the nearly 500 scientists and science-dependant inventors whose works are discussed here represent the broad spectrum of scientific activity—from the almost purely descriptive work of natural historians to the highly mathematical work of theoretical fundamental-particle physicists and cosmologists and the highly involved and collaborative experimental work associated with the Human Genome Project. The works discussed in the *Biographical Encyclopedia of Scientists* also span the globe and the chronological period from the emergence of what we call science in classical antiquity to the present, with greater emphasis on recent developments because as one of the founders of quantitative science studies, Derek Price, was fond of saying, more than 85 percent of all scientists who ever lived are alive today.

Richard Olson
Professor of History
Willard W. Keith Fellow in the Humanities
Harvey Mudd College

Key to Pronunciation

As an aid to users of the *Biographical Encyclopedia of Scientists*, guides to pronunciation for profiled scientists with foreign names have been provided with the first mention of the name in each entry. These guides are rendered in an easy-to-use phonetic manner. Stressed syllables are indicated by capital letters.

Letters of the English language, particularly vowels, are pronounced in different ways depending on the context. Below are letters and combinations of letters used in the phonetic guides to represent various sounds, along with examples of words in which those sounds appear and corresponding guides for their pronunciation.

Symbols	Pronounced As In	Spelled Phonetically
a	answer, laugh	AN-sihr, laf
ah	father, hospital	FAH-thur, HAHS-pih-tul
aw	awful, caught	AW-ful, kawt
ay	blaze, fade, waiter	blayz, fayd, WAYT-ur
ch	beach, chimp	beech, chihmp
eh	bed, head, said	behd, hehd, sehd
ee	believe, leader	bee-LEEV, LEED-ur
ew	boot, loose	bewt, lews
g	beg, disguise, get	behg, dihs-GIZ, geht
i	buy, height, surprise	bi, hit, sur-PRIZ
ih	bitter, pill	bih-TUR, pihl
j	digit, edge, jet	DIH-jiht, ehj, jeht
k	cat, kitten, hex	kat, KIH-tehn, hehks
o	cotton, hot	CO-tuhn, hot
oh	below, coat, note	bee-LOH, coht, noht
oo	good, look	good, look
ow	couch, how	kowch, how
oy	boy, coin	boy, koyn
s	cellar, save, scent	SEL-ur, sayv, sehnt
sh	issue, shop	IH-shew, shop
uh	about, enough	uh-BOWT, ee-NUHF
ur	earth, letter	urth, LEH-tur
y	useful, young	YEWS-ful, yuhng
z	business, zest	BIHZ-ness, zest
zh	vision	VI-zhuhn

BIOGRAPHICAL ENCYCLOPEDIA of SCIENTISTS

Maude Abbott

Area of Achievement: Medicine
Contribution: An acclaimed medical researcher and educator, Abbott was a pioneer in congenital heart disease research.

Mar. 18, 1869	Born in St. Andrews East, Quebec, Canada
1890	Receives a B.A. and the Lord Stanley Gold Medal from McGill University
1894	Earns an M.D. from Bishop's College Medical School
1894-1897	Studies in England, Germany, Austria, and Switzerland
1897	Sets up a private practice in Montreal
1898	Appointed assistant curator of the McGill Medical Museum
1901	Becomes curator of the McGill Medical Museum
1905	Appointed a research fellow in pathology at McGill
1907	Organizes the first meeting of the International Association of Medical Museums
1912	Appointed a lecturer in pathology at McGill
1915-1918	Helps edit the *Canadian Medical Association Journal*
1923-1925	Serves as Visiting Professor of Pathology and Bacteriology at the Woman's Medical College of Pennsylvania
1925	Returns to McGill University
1932	Named curator of the Medical Historical Museum at McGill
1936	Given honorary membership in the all-male Osler Society
Sept. 2, 1940	Dies in Montreal, Quebec, Canada

Early Life

Maude Elizabeth Seymour Abbott, born shortly after her father abandoned the family and only months before her mother died, grew up in the care of her maternal grandmother in St. Andrews East, Quebec, about 30 miles west of Montreal. An eager learner and a hard worker, Maude won a scholarship and entered McGill University in 1886, the third year that women were admitted. She decided to study medicine and hoped to remain at McGill, from where she would soon graduate with distinction.

Because McGill still denied admission to women as medical students, on receiving her bachelor's degree Abbott reluctantly accepted an invitation to join the medical faculty of Bishop's College in Montreal. Fortunately, Bishop's students took their hospital training at the Montréal General Hospital under McGill professors, and Abbott made contacts among the McGill faculty. In 1894, after taking the senior anatomy prize, she received her M.D. from Bishop's College and spent three years in Europe pursuing postgraduate studies in obstetrics, gynecology, and pathology.

(National Library of Medicine)

Congenital Heart Disease

Congenital heart disease, which results from disease or arrested development before birth, leads to alterations in the structure of the heart or its major vessels. This condition can place excessive strain on the heart or interfere with oxygenation of the blood.

Abbott classified patients with congenital heart disease as cyanotic (those with a bluish discoloration of the skin) or noncyanotic. She showed that cyanosis arises from reduced oxygenation of blood in the lungs, the mixing of arterial (oxygenated) and venous (unoxygenated) blood, or increased consumption of oxygen in the tissues, rather than solely from obstructed blood flow, as some researchers had believed.

In the noncyanotic group, into which the majority of cases fall, cyanosis is either entirely absent or only episodically present. Abbott distinguished between those cases in which a mechanical defect interferes with circulation and those in which an abnormal opening in the heart permits venous and arterial blood to mix. Such structural defects can result in endocarditis, bacterial inflammation of the lining of the heart.

Abbott systematically and exhaustively cataloged the host of defects and deficiencies that characterize congenital heart disease. She also insisted on the importance of distinguishing between lesions occurring congenitally and those acquired after birth when making diagnoses and prescribing treatment.

Abbott's work on congenital heart disease helped pave the way for advances in cardiac surgery, which was still in its early stages in the 1920's and 1930's.

Bibliography

Congenital Heart Disease. F. J. Macartney, ed. Boston: MTP Press, 1986.

Congenital Heart Disease in Adults. Joseph K. Perloff and John S. Child. Philadelphia: W. B. Saunders, 1991.

The Heart of a Child: What Families Need to Know About Heart Disorders in Children. Catherine A. Neill, Edward B. Clark, and Carleen Clark. Baltimore: The Johns Hopkins University Press, 1992.

Research, Organization, and Innovation

Back in Montreal in 1897, Abbott was soon appointed assistant curator of the McGill Medical Museum. A trip to Washington, D.C., in 1898 led to her lifelong association with the eminent physician Sir William Osler, formerly of McGill.

Preferring research to medical practice, Abbott gained notice in 1899 for her paper on functional heart murmurs. The presentation of this paper before the Montréal Medico-Chirurgical Society led the organization to open its membership to women.

Promoted to full curator in 1901, Abbott developed a method for organizing museum specimens and introduced a system for using them to teach medical students. She also helped found the International Association of Medical Museums (later called the International Academy of Pathology), an organization of curators that set museum standards.

Her growing prominence in cardiac pathology prompted Osler in 1905 to commission her

to contribute the essay "Congenital Cardiac Disease" to Osler and Thomas McRae's classic medical textbook *Modern Medicine, Its Theory and Practice* (1908). Abbott's authoritative presentation of hundreds of cardiac anomalies made her one of the first Canadian physicians with an international reputation. Three decades later, her text *Atlas of Congenital Heart Disease* (1936) would include a thousand such cases.

Stature Beyond Status

In addition to her clinical pursuits, Abbott had become an authority on Osler and his voluminous writings. By 1932, she had also published a dozen works on medical history. Material from her lectures on the history of nursing appeared in nursing school curricula throughout Canada.

Despite Abbott's achievements and international renown, McGill University denied her the academic status that a man of her stature would have received. Even at her retirement, the university that Abbott revered refused her request for promotion to full professor. In partial consolation, however, McGill awarded her an honorary M.D. in 1910 and an honorary LL.D. in 1936; she became the only person to receive two honorary degrees from that institution. Abbott died in 1940.

Bibliography
By Abbott
"On So-Called Functional Heart Murmurs," *Montréal Medical Journal*, 1899
"The Museum in Medical Teaching," *Journal of the American Medical Association*, 1905
"Congenital Cardiac Disease" in *Modern Medicine, Its Theory and Practice*, vol. 4, 1908 (William Osler and Thomas McCrae, eds.)
"Lectures on the History of Nursing," *Canadian Nurse*, 1916-1923
"The Clinical Classification of Congenital Cardiac Disease," *International Clinics*, 1924
"The Pathological Collections of the Late Sir William Osler at McGill University" and "Classified and Annotated Bibliography of the Publications of Sir William Osler, Bart." in *Sir William Osler Memorial Volume of the International Association of Medical Museums*, 1926 (Abbott, ed.)
"On the Clinical Classification of Congenital Cardiac Disease," *Lancet*, 1929
History of Medicine in the Province of Québec, 1931
"Congenital Heart Disease" in *Nelson's Loose Leaf Medicine*, 1932
Atlas of Congenital Cardiac Disease, 1936
Classified and Annotated Bibliography of Sir William Osler's Publications, 1939
"Autobiographical Sketch," *McGill Medical Journal*, 1959

About Abbott
"The Heart of the Matter: Maude E. Abbott, 1869-1940." Margaret Gillett. In *Despite the Odds: Essays on Canadian Women and Science*, edited by Marianne Ainley. Montreal: Véhicule Press, 1990.
Maude Abbott: A Memoir. H. E. MacDermot. Toronto: Macmillan Company of Canada, 1941.
"Maude Abbott: Pathologist and Historian." Kathleen Smith. *Canadian Medical Association Journal* 127, no. 8 (October 15, 1982).

(Robert B. Sullivan)

Louis Agassiz

Areas of Achievement: Earth science and zoology

Contribution: Agassiz, a leading American geologist and naturalist in the nineteenth century, studied glacial action on topography and showed that, in geologically recent times, widespread glaciation had resulted in an ice age.

May 28, 1807	Born in Môtier-en-Vuly, Switzerland
1829	Earns a doctorate in philosophy from the Universities of Munich and Erlangen
1830	Receives a doctorate in medicine from Munich
1832	Accepts a professorship at the College of Neuchâtel and begins studies of glaciers and glacial landforms
1837	Addresses the Swiss Society of Natural Sciences with his revolutionary theory of glaciation
1840	Publishes *Études sur les glaciers* (*Studies on Glaciers*, 1967)
1847	Publishes *Système glacière*
1847	Accepts a professorship at the Lawrence Scientific School, Harvard University
1855	Begins work on the four-volume study *Contributions to the Natural History of the United States*
1859	Establishes the Harvard Museum of Comparative Zoology
1863	Helps establish the National Academy of Sciences
Dec. 14, 1873	Dies in Cambridge, Massachusetts

(Library of Congress)

Early Life

Jean Louis Rodolphe Agassiz (pronounced "AG-uh-see") was born in Môtier-en-Vuly, Switzerland, in 1807. His father was a Protestant pastor, and, while Agassiz would never identify with any sectarian religious persuasion, his scientific studies were infused with an idealistic romanticism that attributed the wonders of the natural world to the power of a benevolent Creator. Agassiz attended the Medical School of Zurich and the Universities of Heidelberg and Munich. He earned his doctorate in philosophy in 1829 and his medical degree in 1830. After publishing a monograph on the fishes of Brazil, Agassiz came to the attention of Baron Georges Cuvier. After two years of study under Cuvier, Agassiz accepted a professorship at the College of Neuchâtel.

In 1832, he married Cécile Braun, with whom he had three children. In 1846, Agassiz moved his family to Boston, where he had accepted a lectureship at the Lowell Institute. Upon the death of his wife in 1847, he accepted a professorship at the Lawrence Scientific School of Harvard University, where he taught until his death. Agassiz's decision to stay in the United States was influenced by his second wife, Elizabeth Cabot Cary, who helped rear the three children from his first marriage and who was his constant companion during his explorations and studies.

Scientific Studies

Agassiz was initially interested in the study of ichthyology, and his first published works involved taxonomy of the fish of Brazil and central Europe. His interest in this field led to a ten-year research project in the area of fossil fishes and resulted in a five-volume series on fossil fishes of Europe published between 1833 and 1843.

Concurrent with his study of fish, Agassiz was researching the glaciers of Switzerland's Jura Mountains. In 1836, he visited the Diablerets Glaciers and as a result of this trip conceived a theory of "a great ice period" caused by climatic changes and marked by a vast ice sheet extending from the North Pole to the Alps and to central Asia.

Scientific Conflicts

Although Agassiz's theory of massive, cyclical ice movement was monumental in scope, it proved insufficient to convince the prominent geologists Charles Darwin and Charles Lyell that recent glaciation was the cause for the global distribution of diverse species of flora and fauna.

Agassiz was philosophically and scientifically unprepared to accept the theory of natural selection when it was proposed in 1859. He interpreted glaciation in metaphysical terms, crediting the "Deity" for creating ice ages to keep species of the past from those of the present. He insisted that extinct creatures within the fossil record were "prophetic types" and that creatures suggesting little change through geological history were evidence of a Creator's wisdom in inspiring perfect forms from the beginning of time. Unfortunately, Agassiz extended his concept to humankind, asserting that humans were of distinct species with different physical and intellectual traits. These ideas were used as rationalizations for the proponents of slavery and social class structuring.

Agassiz's "Discourse of Neuchâtel"

Agassiz's concept of an "ice age" was revolutionary for its scale of generalization and its level of supporting field data. While not the first to observe and record glacial phenomena, he was the first to integrate wide-ranging field observations and measurements of local geology into a theory explaining continental geomorphology and natural history.

On July 24, 1837, Agassiz presented his far-reaching scenario of ice age conditions before the Swiss Society of Natural Sciences. He pointed out that the Alps are littered with boulders completely unlike the bedrock on which they rest and that bedrock scratches and alpine topographic configurations could be linked to the movement of vast ice sheets. He argued that these "erratic" boulders must have been transported to their locations by glaciers—the same glaciers that presently existed in nearby high alpine regions—once extending beyond their present limits. Agassiz's address became known as the "Discourse of Neuchâtel" and is recognized as a landmark in the annals of science.

His radical theory of an ice age in the recent geologic past resulted in a furor among scientists. While most believed that the planet had undergone catastrophes in the past, few could accept ice as an agent of global change. According to the conventional wisdom of the time, evidence of geological change simply authenticated biblical flood narratives. Agassiz challenged the doctrine that geological devastation could be simply explained in terms of a "Great Flood."

Bibliography

"Flaws in a Victorian Veil." Stephen J. Gould. In *The Panda's Thumb*. New York: W. W. Norton, 1980.

Glacial and Quaternary Geology. Richard Foster Flint. Toronto: John Wiley & Sons, 1971.

Ice Ages. Windsor Chorlton. Alexandria, Va.: Time-Life Books, 1983.

Bibliography

By Agassiz

Selecta genera et species piscium quos in intinere per Brasiliam, 1817-1820, 1829
Études sur les glaciers, 1840 (*Studies on Glaciers, Preceded by the Discourse of Neuchâtel*, 1967)
Système glacière, 1847
Contributions to the Natural History of the United States, 1857-1862 (4 vols.)
Essay on Classification, 1859
"Evolution and Permanence of Type," *Atlantic Monthly*, 1874

About Agassiz

"Agassiz in the Galápagos." Stephen J. Gould. In *Hen's Teeth and Horse's Toes*. New York: W. W. Norton, 1983.
Louis Agassiz, a Life in Science. Edward Lurie. Baltimore: The Johns Hopkins University Press, 1988.
Louis Agassiz, His Life and Correspondence. Elizabeth C. Agassiz. Boston: Houghton Mifflin, 1885.

(*Randall L. Milstein*)

Georgius Agricola

Areas of Achievement: Earth science, medicine, and pharmacology

Contribution: Agricola described the mining and metallurgical industries of the sixteenth century in his many books on the subject. He also studied the pharmaceutical use of minerals and smelting products.

Mar. 24, 1494	Born in Glauchau, Saxony (now Germany)
1514	Enters the University of Leipzig
1515	Receives a B.A. from Leipzig and becomes a lecturer in elementary Greek
1520	Becomes principal at the Municipal School in Zwickau
1523	Returns to Leipzig to study medicine
1527	Works as the town physician at Joachimstal
1530	Publishes an account of Saxon minerals, particularly bismuth
1531-1533	Publishes books on politics and economics
1534-1554	Works as the historiographer for the court of Saxony in Chemnitz
1536-1555	Writes *De Re Metallica Libri XII*
1542	Marries his second wife, Anna Schutz, the daughter of a local guildmaster
1546	Elected burgomaster of Chemnitz
1546	Writes *De Natura Fossilium*, a systematic classification of minerals
1554	Publishes a medical book entitled *De Peste Libri III*
Nov. 21, 1555	Dies in Chemnitz, Saxony

Mining and Mineral Processing

Agricola studied mining, the process of extracting materials from the earth. Earth materials can be extracted in surface mines, wells, or underground mines.

Surface mines are appropriate for near-surface mineral deposits, while underground mines are generally more suited to deeper deposits. Both types of mines can be used to extract a variety of mineral types, both metallic and nonmetallic.

Wells are appropriate for mining liquid or gaseous materials such as natural gas and petroleum. They may also be used to mine salt and trona, an impure form of hydrous sodium carbonate.

Mineral processing includes all mechanical and chemical actions that are necessary to produce a mineral product from ore that has been mined. Processing may involve nothing more than hand sorting to select the most desirable pieces of ore from among those mined, or it may require additional steps to yield the desired product. These steps may include crushing, grinding, chemical digestion, filtration, extrusion, firing, and blending.

Mining is the primary means of obtaining raw materials used to manufacture the products that are used on a daily basis. Cars, homes, and computers all require earth materials for their manufacture. Cosmetics, pharmaceuticals, paint, paper, plastics, and a variety of other products also depend on the availability of earth materials.

Bibliography

Industrial Minerals and Rocks. Stanley J. Lefond, ed. 5th ed. 2 vols. Littleton, Colo.: Society of Mining Engineers, 1983.

Surface Mining. B. A. Kennedy, ed. 2d ed. Littleton, Colo.: Society for Mining, Metallurgy, and Exploration, 1990.

Underground Mining Methods Handbook. William A. Hustrulid, ed. Littleton, Colo.: Society of Mining Engineers, 1982.

Early Life

Georgius Agricola (pronounced "a-GRIHK-oh-luh") was born Georg Bauer on March 24, 1494, in Glauchau, Saxony. He later adopted the Latinized name Agricola, which means "peasant farmer."

Agricola entered the University of Leipzig in 1514 and received a B.A. the next year. He remained at the university as a lecturer in elementary Greek until moving to Zwickau. While in Zwickau, he authored his first book, *De Prima ac Simplici in Stitutione Grammatica* (1520). He taught classics at the Municipal School and eventually became its principal in 1520. Agricola returned to Leipzig in 1523 to study medicine and later visited Italy, spending three years in Bologna and Venice. His travels continued after he received his M.D. Agricola then returned home to study mining and related industries, living for a short while in a mining area in Bohemia.

Medical Career

Agricola became the town physician at Joachimstal around 1527. Joachimstal was an important European mining center during the early part of the sixteenth century, and Agricola's position gave him the opportunity to study the pharmaceutical use of minerals and smelting products.

Miners and smelter workers frequently suffered from occupational diseases. Agricola

(Library of Congress)

studied the workers' diseases, their lives, and the equipment and technologies that they used. He recorded his impressions and observations in *Bermannus Sive de re Metallica Dialogus* (1530), an account of Saxon minerals. It was his first book on mining.

Politics and Economics

Agricola published several books on politics and economics between 1531 and 1533. He moved to Chemnitz in 1534 and became the court historiographer. He held this position for twenty years, documenting the genealogy of all the rulers of Saxony.

Agricola had invested in a local copper smelter upon his arrival in Chemnitz, and he had become one of the richest men in town by 1542. It was in that year that he married Anna Schutz, the daughter of a guildmaster and smelter owner.

Mining

Agricola had developed a strong interest in mining and mineral processing early in his medical career as a physician in Joachimstal. His observations in Saxony provided a wealth of information, much of which was published in his books on mining and mining technology.

De Natura Fossilium, published in 1546, may have been the first publication to classify minerals systematically. Agricola wrote on the origin of rocks, mountains, and volcanoes in later publications, which included *De Animantibus Subterraneis* (1549).

Agricola's most significant work was *De Re Metallica Libri XII* (1556), which was published four months after his death. The book contains eleven sections dealing with mining and smelting and a final section providing an account of the chemical technology of the time. It is illustrated with woodcuts that were used for the next 101 years in seven editions. Agricola took twenty years to write *De Re Metallica*.

Bibliography

By Agricola

De Prima ac Simplici in Stitutione Grammatica, 1520

Bermannus Sive de re Metallica Dialogus, 1530

Oration, Anrede und Vermanung . . . widder den Türken, 1531

Medici Libri de Mensuris et Ponderibus, 1533

De Natura Fossilium, 1546 (*Textbook of Mineralogy*, 1955)

De Animantibus Subterraneis, 1549

De Peste Libri III, 1554

De Re Metallica Libri XII, 1556 (English trans., 1912)

Sippschaft des Hausses zu Sachssen, 1555

About Agricola

Collins Biographical Dictionary of Scientists. Trevor Williams, ed. New York: HarperCollins, 1994.

Dictionary of Scientific Biography. Pierre Abailard and L. S. Berg, eds. New York: Charles Scribner's Sons, 1970.

Great Engineers and Pioneers in Technology. Roland Turner and Steven Goulden, eds. New York: St. Martin's Press, 1981.

(Kyle L. Kayler)

Hannes Alfvén

Areas of Achievement: Astronomy, cosmology, and physics

Contribution: Alfvén made contributions to the development of several modern fields of physics, including plasma physics, the physics of charged particle beams, and interplanetary and magnetospheric physics. He was the first to propose a galactic magnetic field and was codiscoverer of the source of astronomical radio waves. He is considered the founder of magnetohydrodynamics.

May 30, 1908	Born in Norrköping, Sweden
1934	Awarded a doctorate from the University of Uppsala
1934-1940	Conducts research at the University of Uppsala and the Nobel Institute, Stockholm
1940	Appointed to a professorship at the Royal Institute of Technology, Stockholm
1945	Elected to the Royal Institute of Technology's newly created chair of electronics
1950	Publishes *Cosmical Electrodynamics*
1963	The chair of electronics is renamed the chair of plasma physics
1967	Condemns Sweden's nuclear program and moves to the Soviet Union
1967	Accepts a professorship at the University of California, San Diego
1970	Awarded the Nobel Prize in Physics
1974	Satellite measurements confirm Alfvén and Kristan Birkeland's theories about magnetospheric physics
1990	The Alfvén Laboratory is founded at the Royal Institute of Technology
Apr. 2, 1995	Dies in Djursholm, Sweden

Early Life

Hannes Olof Gösta Alfvén (pronounced "al-VAYN") was born in the town of Norrköping, Sweden, in 1908. His father was a practicing physician with a strong interest in the sciences, and his mother was one of the first female physicians in Sweden. Additionally, one of Alfvén's uncles, Hugo Alfvén, was a famous composer. Another uncle was an inventor, and a third was an agronomist with an interest in astronomy.

According to Alfvén, two experiences during his childhood would later determine his professional career. The first was a gift of a book on astronomy that resulted in a lifelong interest in the subject. The second was involvement in his school's radio club. While in the club, he built a radio and picked up signals from a station in Aberdeen, Scotland. His doc-

(The Nobel Foundation)

Magnetohydrodynamics

Alfvén argued that the behavior of plasma in an electromagnetic field is similar in many respects to the way in which fluids behave in a gravity field; therefore, this behavior can be calculated mathematically.

In addition to the three well-known states of matter—solid, liquid, and gas—there is a fourth state of matter called plasma. Plasma is a very thin gas in which the electrons have been stripped from their atoms. As a result, plasma is made of charged particles, ions and electrons, but its total charge is zero because the negative charge of the electrons is balanced by the positive charge of the ions. This fact causes plasmas to behave in ways unlike other forms of matter.

Plasmas occur only in very thin or very hot atmospheres, which explains why humans do not experience them directly. Nevertheless, plasma is actually the most common form of matter in the universe. High-altitude atmospheres and the gases between stars and planets are plasmas, and stars are made of plasma gases.

Prior to Alfvén's work, it was thought that an electromagnetic field would not penetrate into plasma because the electrons and ions would arrange themselves to cancel the field. Alfvén found, however, that it was possible to propagate an electromagnetic wave through plasma. When Alfvén first proposed this theory in 1942, it was rejected by the scientific community. After the highly respected physicist Enrico Fermi listened to a lecture by Alfvén in 1948 and concurred, however, acceptance of the theory quickly spread.

In 1950, Alfvén described this theory and his other ideas in *Cosmical Electrodynamics*. In this book, Alfvén showed how plasma in the presence of an electromagnetic wave would behave in a manner similar to the way in which fluids (gases and liquids) behave when experiencing the force of gravity. As a result, this theory is called magnetohydrodynamics (MHD) to signify the equivalent behavior of plasma to that of moving fluids. MHD provided scientists with a mathematically explicit way to calculate the way in which plasmas behave in the presence of a electromagnetic field. Alfvén's accomplishment gave scientists a very powerful new tool in the field of space physics.

MHD has become the foundation for the study of all plasmas. This theory not only has had a profound effect on the study of space, thin atmospheres, and stars but also has had a great impact on the work on hot, dense atmospheres, such as the study of fusion reactions. Fusion is the process of combining small atoms to make larger atoms, releasing energy in the process. It is hoped that fusion will be used someday as an unlimited power source. When that day arrives, it will be done with the understanding provided by Alfvén's theory of magnetohydrodynamics.

Bibliography

Introduction to the Space Environment. Thomas F. Tascione. Malabar, Fla.: Orbit, 1988.
Plasma Physics. Francis F. Chen. Vol. 1 in *Introduction to Plasma Physics and Controlled Fusion*. New York: Plenum Press, 1984.

toral thesis, "Ultra-Short Electromagnetic Waves," was an extension of his work in the radio club.

Scientific Pursuits

Alfvén received his doctorate from the University of Uppsala in 1934 and was appointed a docent of physics at both the University of Uppsala and the Nobel Institute for Physics in Stockholm. In 1940, he became a professor of electromagnetic theory and electrical measurements at the Royal Institute of Technology in Stockholm. In 1945, he was elected to that

school's newly created chair of electronics, which was converted to the chair of plasma physics in 1963.

Alfvén had strong objections to Sweden's nuclear program, and in 1967 he issued a strong condemnation of the program and left the country. He was immediately offered positions in both the Soviet Union and the United States, and, after spending two months in the Soviet Union, he moved to San Diego and accepted a position at the University of California, San Diego. He resolved his differences with the Swedish government, however, and, for the next twenty-three years, he would spend his winters in San Diego and work in Stockholm from April until October.

The Dispute with Chapman
When Alfvén became involved with magnetospheric physics, his views coincided with those of the great Norwegian scientist Kristan Birkeland, the founder of magnetospheric physics. Birkeland's theories had fallen out of favor, however, and the British-American geophysicist Sydney Chapman put forward a theory contrary to that of Birkeland (and hence, of Alfvén) that would become the predominant theory and make Chapman the leader of the space science community.

As a result, Alfvén was continuously disputed by the senior scientists in the community, and he was forced to publish his theories in obscure journals. The debate between Alfvén and Chapman was finally settled in 1974, four years after Chapman's death, when satellite measurements confirmed that Birkeland and Alfvén were correct.

Alfvén had the ability to take simple observations and deduce much larger principles. Because of his dispute with Chapman and his colleagues, however, Alfvén was unable to communicate his ideas to the science community at large. Finally, he collected his works and published them in *Cosmical Electrodynamics* in 1950. It was this work that made Alfvén known to the community and that would win for him the Nobel Prize in Physics in 1970.

Approach to Physics
Alfvén's approach to physics was based on intuition. He was equipped with a thorough understanding of how nature works, which enabled him to explain new observations by placing them into a larger context. In this way, Alfvén was able to acquire an understanding of large-scale physics more quickly than many other scientists were. As a result, his theories were frequently based on a great leap of creative intuition. This provided an opportunity for critics to question his theories, but in the end he was usually proved correct.

One story concerns Alfvén's discovery of hydromagnetic waves in plasmas. At first, he was highly criticized for this theory, which was dismissed. In 1948, however, Alfvén gave several lectures on the subject, one of which was attended by the great physicist Enrico Fermi. As Alfvén described his work, Fermi nodded his head and said "Of course." The next day, the entire physics community also said "Oh, of course."

Legacy
Although he would receive many awards and gain international recognition, becoming one of the few foreign members of both the U.S. and Soviet academies of sciences, many of Alfvén's ideas were initially dismissed by the scientific community. Today, many of his ideas are crucial to several areas of modern physics, frequently without researchers being aware of the originator of these theories.

Hannes Alfvén died in his home in Djursholm, Sweden, on April 2, 1995.

Bibliography
By Alfvén
Cosmical Electrodynamics, 1950
Magnetic Storms and Aurorae, 1954
On the Origin of the Solar System, 1954
Varlden-Spegelvarlden: Kosmologi antimateria, 1966 (*World-Antiworlds: Antimatter in Cosmology*, 1966)
Sagan om den stora datamaskinen: En vision, 1966 (as "Olof Johannesson"; *The Tale of the Big Computer: A Vision*, 1968)
Atomen, mannisken, universum, 1966 (*Atom, Man, and the Universe: The Long Chain of Complications*, 1969)
M-70, 1969 (with Kerstin Alfvén; *Living on the Third Planet*, 1972)
Structure and Evolutionary History of the Solar System, 1975 (with Gustaf Arrhenius)
Evolution of the Solar System, 1976 (with Arrhenius)
Cosmic Plasma, 1981

About Alfvén
"Hannes Alfvén." In *The Nobel Prize Winners: Physics*, edited by Frank N. Magill. Pasadena, Calif.: Salem Press, 1989.
"Hannes Alfvén (1908-1995)." C.-G. Falthammar. *Eos* (September 25, 1995).

(Christopher Keating)

Alhazen

Areas of Achievement: Astronomy, cosmology, mathematics, medicine, and physics

Contribution: Alhazen, one of the greatest scientists of the Middle Ages, revolutionized the study of optics with important new ideas and experiments on reflection and refraction. These made possible the theory of the lens, which in turn made possible the invention of the telescope and the microscope.

965	Born in Basra (now Al Basra, Iraq)
c. 1000	Travels to Cairo to the court of the Fatimid caliph al-Hakim
c. 1005	Forced to feign madness in order to escape the wrath of the caliph
1021	Emerges from obscurity upon the death of al-Hakim
1039	Dies in Cairo, Egypt
1270	His major work, *Kitab al-Manazir* (book of optics), is translated into Latin as *Opticae Thesaurus Alhazeni libri vii* and becomes an important influence on European thought

Early Life

Abu ʿAli al-Hasan ibn al-Haytham, known in the West as Alhazen (pronounced "al-ha-ZEHN"), was born in Basra, in what is now Iraq, in 965. Basra was a major center for the brilliantly thriving Islamic intellectual culture of the time, and Alhazen was educated there. He soon acquired a reputation as a mathematician and engineer.

A Colorful Career

Having boasted that he could design a scheme to control the flooding of the Nile, Alhazen was summoned to Cairo by the caliph al-Hakim. The caliph received him graciously and treated him generously. When Alhazen realized that his flood control plan was impracticable and

that al-Hakim was a tyrant and perhaps insane, he found it necessary to feign madness himself in order to avoid the caliph's wrath. Maintaining this pretense, he sank into deliberate obscurity for a number of years.

During these years, he continued his research, supporting himself by jobs such as copying mathematical manuscripts. When al-Hakim died in 1021, Alhazen was able to drop his counterfeit madness. He lived quietly in Cairo until his death in 1039.

A Great Scholar

Despite the perils of his later career, Alhazen maintained a large and diverse scholarly output. He is known to have produced more than two hundred works on subjects as varied as optics, astronomy, mathematics, mechanics, and medicine, as well as commentaries on classical philosophers.

This frontispiece from a 1572 translation of Alhazen's Opticae thesaurus *illustrates various aspects of optics, such as heat energy (mirrors used to set a ship on fire), the spectrum (a rainbow), perspective (elephants crossing a bridge), refraction (a man standing in water), and reflection (a man looking in a mirror). (Library of Congress)*

Spherical and Parabolic Mirrors

Mirrors with curved surfaces can be used to bring light rays together at a point, thereby concentrating their energy. Light rays striking the mirror from slightly different directions are brought together (focused) at slightly different points, forming images of extended sources.

The most common mirror shapes used for these purposes are spherical, where the mirror's surface is a part of a sphere, and parabolic, where the surface has the shape of a paraboloid formed by rotating a parabola around its axis. Both cases were studied and described by Alhazen.

It is a property of a spherical mirror that when parallel rays of light are incident on it, they are concentrated on the axis of the mirror. This axis points in the direction from which the rays came and intersects the mirror's surface at the point where the rays strike it perpendicularly. When a source of light is distant— compared to the radius of curvature of the mirror, the distance from the center of the sphere to its surface—the rays arrive at the mirror almost parallel to one another.

Although all rays are concentrated on the axis of a spherical mirror, they are not all concentrated at the same point on the axis. Those rays that strike the surface close to the axis are concentrated at a point that is half the radius of curvature from the surface; this point is called the focus of the mirror. Rays that strike the surface farther from the axis are brought together farther out along the axis. This inability to form a true focus of all incident rays is called spherical aberration and is an important factor in reflecting telescope design.

Spherical aberration can be minimized by using a mirror whose diameter is much smaller than its radius of curvature—in other words, a mirror that is only slightly curved. In this case, all rays striking the mirror are near the axis (paraxial) to a good approximation and are brought to a good focus.

Alhazen found another solution to this problem. For a parabolic mirror, all rays incident parallel to the axis are brought together at the focus of the parabola, precisely. Although aberration again occurs for rays not parallel to the axis, unlike a sphere, a paraboloid does not appear the same from all directions. The optical performance of a parabolic mirror is excellent for many purposes.

It is difficult, however, to form a precise parabolic surface, so most optical instruments built before the 1980's used spherical mirrors. Today, advanced manufacturing techniques have made parabolic mirrors practical even for large astronomical telescopes.

Bibliography

Geometric Optics: An Introduction. A. Nussbaum. Reading, Mass.: Addison-Wesley, 1968.

Geometrical and Instrumental Optics. D. Malacara, ed. Boston: Academic Press, 1988.

Geometrical Optics and Optical Design. P. Mouroulis. New York: Oxford University Press, 1996.

Optics I: Lenses, Mirrors, and Optical Instruments. J. W. Blaker. New York: Barnes & Noble, 1969.

In astronomy, he proposed a physical mechanism for the (erroneous) Earth-centered cosmology of Ptolemy. In mathematics, he studied geometry, particularly the conics. In mechanics, his ideas on inertia partially anticipated those of Galileo Galilei by five centuries. In medicine, he wrote about the function and diseases of the eye. The great work for which he is primarily remembered, however, is in optics.

A New Optics

Alhazen was the first important student of optics since the ancient Greeks, and he would be the last for several centuries. Ancient writers such as Euclid, Hero, and Ptolemy described vision in terms of rays from the eye to the object perceived. Alhazen realized that this was backward. When an object is illuminated, rays are reflected from every point of the object in all directions. Some of these rays enter the eye, which permits vision. He went further with this new idea, producing the text that became the foundation of modern optics.

In contrast to most scholars of his era, Alhazen was an active experimenter. He had a lathe on which he made mirrors and lenses for his experiments, and he conducted quantitative experiments on refraction by immersing graduated cylinders in water.

In addition, he applied the methods of geometry to optics, analyzing spherical and parabolic mirrors. By calculation and by geometric construction, he was able to discover and prove the important properties of these mirrors, which permitted the later development of reflecting telescopes. He worked out approximations for refraction at small angles of incidence (when the rays of light are almost perpendicular to the surface) that are correct and that can be used to understand thin lenses, such as those used in simple telescopes and microscopes. Alhazen also analyzed the optical phenomena of sunrise and sunset.

An Enduring Influence

After Alhazen's death, the study of optics declined in the Islamic world, not to recover for several centuries. His most important work, *Kitab al-Manazir* (book of optics), however, proved to be a lasting and critical influence in the revival of science in the West. This text was perhaps the most modern scientific work, in terms of method and thought, to be published in the Middle Ages. It was translated into Latin in 1270 and in this form became widely known to scholars in Western Europe.

The thirteenth century English Scholastic philosopher Roger Bacon incorporated many of Alhazen's ideas into his scientific writings; indeed, many of Alhazen's discoveries are often incorrectly ascribed to Bacon. Bacon also embraced—and transmitted to the reawakening philosophical community of the West—

Alhazen's methods and belief in the use of mathematics and experimentation to resolve scientific problems.

In this way, Alhazen not only left to the world his own substantial discoveries but also sowed one of the most critical seeds of the Renaissance, thus opening the way for modern scientific thought.

Bibliography

By Alhazen

Kitab al-Manazir, tenth or eleventh century (commonly known as *Optics*; Latin trans. as *Opticae Thesaurus Alhazeni libri vii*, 1270, and partial English trans. as *The Optics of Ibn al-Haytham: Books I-III, on Direct Vision*, 1989)

Al-Maqaalah fai Tamaam Kitaab al-Makhrauotaaot, tenth or eleventh century (*Completion of the Conics*, 1983)

Maqaalah fai Hay'at al-ʿAalam, tenth or eleventh century (*On the Configuration of the World*, 1990)

About Alhazen

Ibn al-Haitham: Proceedings of the Celebrations of the Thousandth Anniversary Held Under the Auspices of Hamdard National Foundation, Pakistan. H. M. Said, ed. Karachi, Pakistan: Hamdard Academy, 1970.

Ibn al-Haytham's Optics: A Study of the Origins of Experimental Science. S. B. Omar. Minneapolis: Bibliotheca Islamica, 1977.

Optics, Astronomy, and Logic: Studies in Arabic Science and Philosophy. A. I. Sabra. Brookfield, Vt.: Variorum, 1994.

(Firman D. King)

Sidney Altman

Areas of Achievement: Cell biology, chemistry, and genetics

Contribution: An esteemed molecular biologist, Altman won the Nobel Prize in Chemistry for his discovery of the catalytic properties of ribonucleic acid (RNA).

May 7, 1939	Born in Montreal, Quebec, Canada
1960	Earns a B.S. in physics from the Massachusetts Institute of Technology (MIT)
1967	Earns a Ph.D. in biophysics from the University of Colorado, Boulder
1969-1971	Works with the Medical Research Counsel in Cambridge, England
1971	Appointed assistant professor of biology at Yale University
1980	Named professor of biology at Yale
1985-1989	Serves as the dean of Yale College
1988	Elected a member of the American Academy of Arts and Sciences
1989	Wins the Nobel Prize in Chemistry
1990	Appointed Sterling Professor of Biology at Yale
1990	Elected a member of the National Academy of Sciences
1990	Elected a member of the American Philosophical Society
1990-1995	Serves on the Board of Governors of the Weizmann Institute of Science
1991-1994	Named a Fellow of the Whitney Humanities Center at Yale
1993	Appointed to the UNESCO International Committee on Bioethics

Early Life

Sidney Altman was born in Montreal, Canada, to parents who were recent immigrants from Eastern Europe. He grew up in Montreal's Jewish community, where learning and education were considered to be the highest goals and Albert Einstein was a hero and role model. Through books, Altman discovered his early interest in science. Reading Selig Hecht's *Explaining the Atom* (1947), he was struck by the simplicity and beauty of the periodic table.

Consequently, he enrolled as a physics major at the Massachusetts Institute of Technology (MIT). He also played ice hockey on the MIT team. During his senior year, Altman discovered the charm of laboratory work in physics. He also attended Cyrus Levinthal's course on molecular biology, which provided him with an introduction to this emerging field.

Altman was graduated with a B.S. in physics and went on to do graduate work in physics at Columbia University but dropped out after one year, depressed by the death of a close

(The Nobel Foundation)

Catalytic RNA and the RNA World

Several ribonucleic acid (RNA) molecules have catalytic properties and can function as enzymes. RNA has both essential properties of a self-replicating system: information storage and enzymatic activities.

The discovery of catalytic properties of RNA by Altman and Thomas R. Cech radically changed two areas of biological knowledge: The long-held assumption that all enzymes are proteins was overturned, and the problem of the origin of life has been seen in a different light.

All life on Earth is based on chemical reactions that take place within cells and organisms. These biochemical reactions are regulated by catalysts, called enzymes. The complex biochemical machinery of a cell cannot function without the presence of specific enzymes for every single reaction. Up to the early 1980's, it was accepted scientific knowledge that every enzyme could be identified with a particular protein. Altman showed that this paradigm no longer holds for all catalysts.

In 1983, he and his coworkers identified a RNA molecule that had all the properties of an enzyme—biological origin, catalysis in the chemical sense, and specificity with respect to its reaction—except that it was not a protein. They found that the RNA component of the enzyme RNase P catalyzes a reaction that cuts a precursor transfer RNA (tRNA) molecule at a specific site. At the same time, Cech demonstrated that another RNA molecule can catalyze a reaction that cuts out a specific segment of itself in the absence of any other enzymes. As a consequence, the standard definition of an enzyme had to be changed. Enzymes could no longer be identified with a specific class of molecules, proteins, but had to be defined in strictly functional terms.

The discovery of catalytic properties of RNA also effected theories about the origin of life on Earth. Previously, the first self-replicating systems were considered to have RNA to store information and proteins to provide all the enzymatic activities needed for reproduction. Such systems are already very complex.

With the discovery of catalytic RNA, a simpler system can be envisioned. An initial RNA world consisting of self-replicating RNA molecules would have been the first stage in the evolution of life. These RNA molecules were capable of a variety of complicated reactions. They could remove parts of their sequence—precursors of the introns in the molecular structure of modern genes—and insert them again. This mechanism already allowed for different combinations of sequences to evolve, an equivalent to the effects of sexual recombination.

At the next step, these RNA molecules began to synthesize proteins, and later deoxyribonucleic acid (DNA) replaced RNA as the molecule of choice for information storage. The enzymatic properties of RNA molecules today as well as the peculiar exon/intron structure of modern genes are a residual of the original processes in the RNA world.

Bibliography
Steps Towards Life: A Perspective on Evolution. Manfred Eigen and Ruthild Winkler-Oswatitsch. Oxford, England: Oxford University Press, 1992.

friend and Columbia's emphasis on classroom courses in the early years of graduate studies. He then worked as poetry and science editor for the Collier Publishing Company. His interest in literature and the humanities continued throughout his career.

Return to Academia
A position as science writer at the National Center for Atmospheric Research brought Altman to Boulder, Colorado, in 1963. There, he met George Gamow, who encouraged him to pursue graduate studies in biophysics. This was one of many lucky coincidences in Altman's career; as he explained, "I always met the right people at the right time." In 1967, he received his Ph.D. and left Boulder for Harvard University and later Cambridge University, where he pursued postdoctoral work with the top scientists in the field of molecular biology—Matthew Meselson, Sydney Brenner, Francis Crick, and Frederick Sanger.

Cambridge and Early Work on RNA

In Cambridge, Altman started a line of work for which he would eventually be awarded the Nobel Prize in Chemistry. Working with John Smith, he found a mutant ribonucleic acid (RNA) transcript that contained the genomic sequence for one of the transfer RNA (tRNA) molecules, tRNA-Try, that was much longer than the regular tRNA molecule. He also found that after treatment with an extract of normal cells of *Escherichia coli*, the longer transcript could be trimmed to its regular length. The identification of immature tRNA and its processing got him an appointment as assistant professor in the department of biology at Yale University in 1971.

The Detection of Catalytic RNA

At Yale, Altman continued his studies on tRNA processing. He was able to identify an enzyme, called RNase P, that is involved in cutting the original transcript. While investigating the question of how this enzyme could cut the initial transcript of tRNA at a specific position, Altman and his coworkers discovered that RNase P has a protein and a RNA component. This was a major discovery, as until then no enzyme was known to have a RNA component. Further studies revealed that the catalytic subunit of the enzyme RNase P is the RNA component.

This result was met with considerable skepticism. Conventional biological wisdom held that any enzyme is a protein. Altman's discovery that RNA can function as an enzyme as well led to the revision of this long-held principle. At the same time, Thomas R. Cech identified a large RNA molecule that could cut itself without any protein involved in the process. For their discoveries of the catalytic properties of RNA, Altman and Cech were awarded the Nobel Prize in Chemistry in 1989.

The discovery of the catalytic properties of RNA led to new avenues of biological research. The chicken-and-egg problem of the origin of life—deoxyribonucleic acid (DNA) is necessary to make proteins, and proteins are necessary to copy DNA—no longer seemed to be inevitable. A world of RNA molecules is now considered to be the first stage in the evolution of life on Earth. In addition, on the medical front, promising developments inhibiting the replication of human immunodeficiency virus (HIV) resulted from the application of RNA enzymes.

Dean of Yale College

From 1985 until 1989, Altman served as dean of Yale College. Under his leadership, the faculty revised the core curriculum to strengthen the science requirements. He also established a tutorial program in science and mathematics. In the 1990's, he was elected to several prestigious organizations and served on many committees.

Bibliography

By Altman

"Aspects of Biochemical Catalysis," *Cell*, 1984

"Ribonuclease P: An Enzyme with a Catalytic RNA Subunit," *Advances in Enzymology and Related Areas of Molecular Biology*, 1989

"Enzymatic Cleavage of RNA by RNA," *Angewandte Chemie*, 1990

"RNA Enzyme-Directed Gene Therapy," *Proceedings of the National Academy of Sciences*, 1993

"RNase P in Research and Therapy," *Biotechnology*, 1995

About Altman

Nobel Laureates in Chemistry, 1901-1992. Laylin K. James, ed. Washington, D.C.: American Chemical Society, 1993.

"Sidney Altman." In *The Nobel Prize Winners: Chemistry*, edited by Frank N. Magill. Pasadena, Calif.: Salem Press, 1990.

(Manfred D. Laubichler)

Luis W. Alvarez

Areas of Achievement: Astronomy, earth science, and physics

Contribution: Alvarez, a Nobel Prize-winning physicist, worked on the atomic bomb project, developed techniques for the detection of high-energy particles, and linked the impact of a 10-kilometer asteroid to the extinction of the dinosaurs.

June 13, 1911	Born in San Francisco, California
1928-1936	Studies physics at the University of Chicago
1936	Marries Geraldine Smithwick
1936	Joins the faculty of the University of California, Berkeley (UCB)
1938	Discovers the K-capture mode of radioactive decay
1940	Leaves UCB to join the radiation laboratory at the Massachusetts Institute of Technology (MIT)
1940-1943	Works on the development of microwave radar
1944-1945	Serves as a team member on the Manhattan Project
1945	Flies on the observer aircraft for the dropping of an atomic bomb on Hiroshima, Japan
1945-1978	Serves as a professor of physics at UCB
1964-1968	Searches for a hidden chamber in the Chephren pyramid
1968	Awarded the Nobel Prize in Physics
1980	Discovers iridium at the Cretaceous-Tertiary boundary, linking an asteroid impact to the extinction of the dinosaurs
Sept. 1, 1988	Dies in Berkeley, California

(The Nobel Foundation)

Early Life

Luis Walter Alvarez was born in 1911 in San Francisco, California. His father, a physician, worked as a research physiologist at the Hooper Foundation in the mornings and maintained a private medical practice in the afternoons. Alvarez spent many Saturdays with his father at the Hooper Foundation, developing an interest in scientific research. The family moved to Rochester, Minnesota, in 1925, when his father accepted a position at the Mayo Clinic.

Alvarez attended the University of Chicago, beginning in 1928. He married Geraldine Smithwick, a senior at the University of Chicago, a few days after completing his oral examination for the Ph.D. degree in physics. They moved to California, where he joined the faculty of the University of California at Berkeley in 1936.

The Impact of a Giant Asteroid and the Extinction of the Dinosaurs

Alvarez discovered a high concentration of iridium at the Cretaceous-Tertiary boundary and linked an asteroid impact to the extinction of the dinosaurs.

Early in Earth's history, the planet melted and the high-density metals settled into its core, a process called differentiation, leaving the surface with only low concentrations of those elements. Iridium is one of the elements that is concentrated in the earth's core. Most meteorites are pieces of asteroids that were small enough that they did not differentiate; therefore, meteorites contain much more iridium than do surface rocks. For this reason, iridium is frequently used to monitor the amount of meteoritic material falling to Earth.

Alvarez, working with his son Walter, a geologist, and two chemists, Frank Asaro and Helen Michel, found an unexpectedly high concentration of the element iridium in a layer of clay marking the boundary between the Cretaceous and the Tertiary eras. Because this iridium was distributed worldwide, a large amount of extraterrestrial matter must have been delivered to Earth in a short period of time. They suggested that the iridium was delivered to Earth by the impact of a giant asteroid, 10 kilometers in size, and that this impact caused the extinction of the dinosaurs.

Bibliography

The Nemesis Affair: A Story of the Death of the Dinosaurs and the Ways of Science. David M. Raup. New York: W. W. Norton, 1986.

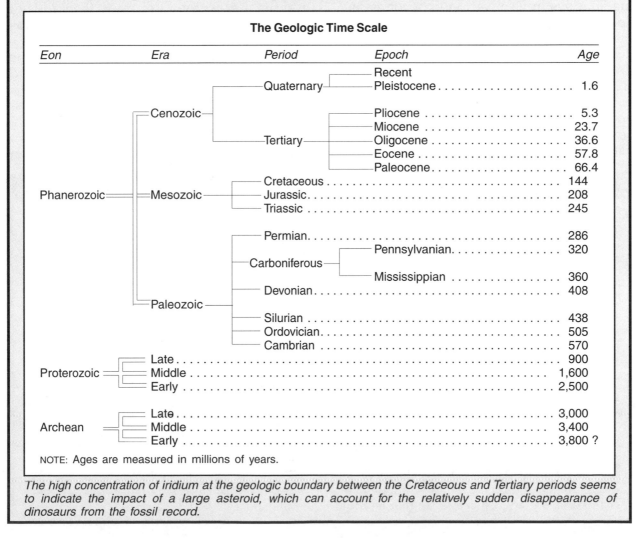

The Geologic Time Scale

Eon	Era	Period	Epoch	Age
		Quaternary	Recent	
			Pleistocene	1.6
	Cenozoic		Pliocene	5.3
			Miocene	23.7
		Tertiary	Oligocene	36.6
			Eocene	57.8
			Paleocene	66.4
Phanerozoic	Mesozoic	Cretaceous		144
		Jurassic		208
		Triassic		245
		Permian		286
		Carboniferous	Pennsylvanian	320
			Mississippian	360
		Devonian		408
	Paleozoic	Silurian		438
		Ordovician		505
		Cambrian		570
	Late			900
Proterozoic	Middle			1,600
	Early			2,500
	Late			3,000
Archean	Middle			3,400
	Early			3,800 ?

NOTE: Ages are measured in millions of years.

The high concentration of iridium at the geologic boundary between the Cretaceous and Tertiary periods seems to indicate the impact of a large asteroid, which can account for the relatively sudden disappearance of dinosaurs from the fossil record.

In 1938, Alvarez demonstrated that some radioactive elements decay by K-capture, a process in which an orbital electron is captured by the nucleus, decreasing the charge of the nucleus by one unit and thus transforming the element into the next lower element in the periodic table.

World War II Research

Just after the birth of his first child, Walter, in October, 1940, Alvarez left Berkeley to work at the radiation laboratory of the Massachusetts Institute of Technology (MIT) in Cambridge, Massachusetts. He participated in the development of a ground control approach (GCA) radar system so that a controller on the ground can monitor the approach path of an incoming aircraft and radio directions to the pilot, allowing landings in weather too poor for a visual approach.

He then joined the Manhattan Project, which developed the atomic bomb. He worked with Enrico Fermi at the University of Chicago for six months, then moved to the Los Alamos Laboratory, in New Mexico. Alvarez developed exploding-wire electronic detonators to ignite the high-explosive lenses critical to detonating the plutonium-type atomic bomb.

Alvarez had developed a technique to measure the explosive power of the first atomic bomb dropped on Japan, a uranium-type bomb never previously tested, and arranged to fly on the *Great Artiste*, the B-29 observer aircraft that accompanied the *Enola Gay* on the Hiroshima bombing mission.

Postwar Research

After World War II, Alvarez worked at the Berkeley Radiation Laboratory (now the Lawrence Berkeley National Laboratory) in California. The focus of his research was the study of resonance particles, short-lived subatomic particles. With his research group, he built huge bubble chambers, devices revealing the paths of charged particles, and developed data analysis techniques to identify one rare event in a background of many thousands of common events. For this work, Alvarez was awarded the Nobel Prize in Physics in 1968.

In 1964, Alvarez became intrigued with the Egyptian pyramids. Hidden chambers had been discovered in two of the three largest pyramids. Alvarez devised a technique for using cosmic rays to probe the interior structure of the third pyramid. Because cosmic rays can penetrate a large chamber more easily than

An Improved Bubble Chamber for Particle Physics

Alvarez improved the design of the bubble chamber, thus allowing its use in high-energy physics experiments.

In 1952, Donald Glaser, a physicist at the University of Michigan, invented the bubble chamber, a device that produces a trail of bubbles along the path of a charged particle. Glaser filled a container with diethyl ether that had been heated above its boiling point. The passage of a charged particle through the fluid forms ions, producing a trail of small bubbles along the path of the particle.

After meeting Glaser in 1953, Alvarez recognized the value of the bubble chamber in particle physics and set about improving on Glaser's design. Alvarez replaced the diethyl ether with liquid hydrogen and built a demonstration bubble chamber about an inch across. So that he could

follow the paths of high-energy particles, Alvarez developed ever-larger bubble chambers, until by 1959 he had built one measuring 72 inches. Alvarez and his research group used these large bubble chambers to study the behavior of resonance particles, very short-lived subatomic particles.

Alvarez was awarded the 1968 Nobel Prize in Physics for his development of large bubble chambers and the data analysis techniques to interpret the bubble chamber records.

Bibliography

"Evidence for a T=0 Three-Pion Resonance." B. C. Maglic, L. W. Alvarez, A. H. Rosenfeld, and M. L. Stevenson. *Physical Review Letters* 7 (1961).

"Resonance Particles." R. D. Hill. *Scientific American* (January, 1963).

A bubble chamber at Caltech in 1959. (California Institute of Technology)

solid rock, Alvarez "X-rayed" the pyramid by mapping the number of cosmic rays reaching the interior from each direction. No secret chamber was found, but Alvarez was pleased to have discovered a practical application for cosmic rays.

Alvarez also studied Abraham Zapruder's film of the assassination of President John F. Kennedy. He was able to establish the time sequence of the shots that were fired by noting streaks of movement in the individual frames when the photographer's muscles responded to the noise of the gunshots.

Alvarez would become known for yet another discovery. His son Walter, a geologist, was interested in determining how long a time interval elapsed in the formation of a layer of clay in a sedimentary rock from Italy. Alvarez recalled that iridium carried to Earth by extraterrestrial materials could be used as a chronometer. They found such a huge concentration of iridium in this clay sample, however, that they proposed, in a 1980 article, that it was the signature of an impact of a 10-kilometer-wide asteroid on the earth approximately 65 million years ago.

Luis Alvarez died of cancer in Berkeley, California, in 1988.

Bibliography
By Alvarez

"A Quantitative Determination of the Neutron Moment in Absolute Nuclear Magnetons," *Physical Review*, 1940 (with F. Bloch)

"Neutral Cascade Hyperon Event," *Physical Review Letters*, 1959 (with P. Eberhard, M. L. Good, W. Graziano, H. K, Ticho, and S. G. Wojcicki)

"Resonance in the $\Lambda\pi$ System," *Physical Review Letters*, 1960 (with M. Alston, Eberhard, Good, Graziano, Ticho, and Wojcicki)

"Evidence for a T=0 Three-Pion Resonance," *Physical Review Letters*, 1961 (with B. C. Maglic, A. H. Rosenfeld, and M. L. Stevenson)

"Spin and Parity of the ω Meson," *Physical Review*, 1962 (with Maglic, Rosenfeld, and Stevenson)

"Extraterrestrial Cause for the Cretaceous-Tertiary Extinction," *Science*, 1980 (with W. Alvarez, F. Asaro, and H. Michel)

Alvarez: Adventures of a Physicist, 1987

About Alvarez

"Luis W. Alvarez." In *The Nobel Prize Winners: Physics*, edited by Frank N. Magill. Pasadena, Calif.: Salem Press, 1989.

The Making of the Atomic Bomb. Richard Rhodes. New York: Simon & Schuster, 1986.

The Nemesis Affair: A Story of the Death of the Dinosaurs and the Ways of Science. David M. Raup. New York: W. W. Norton, 1986.

"Resonance Particles." R. D. Hill. *Scientific American* (January, 1963).

(George J. Flynn)

André-Marie Ampère

Areas of Achievement: Chemistry, mathematics, and physics

Contribution: Ampère established the science of electrodynamics, the relationship between electrical and magnetic phenomena, on a firm experimental and mathematical basis.

Jan. 22, 1775	Born in Lyons, France
1802	Appointed a professor of physics and chemistry at the école centrale of Bourg-en-Bresse
1803	Appointed a professor of mathematics at the Lycée in Lyons
1808	Begins investigations into chemical phenomena
1809	Appointed to the faculty of the École Polytechnique in Paris
1809	Appointed inspector general of the French university system
1814	Awarded the Cross of the French Legion of Honor
1816	Publishes *Essai d'une classification naturelle pour les corps simples*
1820	Presents a paper on electromagnetism to the Académie des Sciences
1820	Authorized to offer a course in philosophy at the University of Paris
1824	Elected to the chair of experimental physics at the Collège de France
1827	Publishes a full-length work on electrodynamics
1834	Publishes *Essai sur la philosophie des sciences*
June 10, 1836	Dies in Marseilles, France

Early Life

André-Marie Ampère (pronounced "ahm-PEHR") was born in Lyons, France, in 1775, to Jean-Jacques Ampère, a wealthy silk merchant, and his wife, the former Jeanne Searcy. He was quickly recognized as a prodigy by his father, who, following the ideas of the French philosopher Jean-Jacques Rousseau, chose to allow his son to follow his own intellectual inclinations. The young Ampère spent much of his time reading in his father's extensive library. He taught himself Latin so as to read the works of the mathematicians Leonhard Euler and Daniel Bernoulli, and later in life he could recite entire articles that he had read as a child in the twenty-eight volume French encyclopedia published in 1772.

Tragedy entered Ampère's life in 1793 as a result of the French Revolution. Lyons had sided with the moderate Girondist faction. Ampère's father, who had been elected to a minor judicial post, had authorized the arrest of a man named Chalier, a member of the extremist Jacobin Party who was later executed. When the Jacobins came to power in Lyons, Jean-Jacques Ampère was tried and executed in retaliation, and most of the Ampère fortune was confiscated.

(Library of Congress)

Electromagnetism

Ampère discovered the basic law of force between current-carrying wires and the connection between electromagnetism and the behavior of permanent magnets. He is considered the founder of electrodynamics, the science of electricity and magnetism.

Although both electrical and magnetic phenomena were known to the ancient Greeks, little was understood about them and nothing at all about the relationship between them until the nineteenth century. It was known that for electrical charges, like charges attracted and unlike charges repelled each other. The behavior of magnetized objects was more complex. While it was clear that the north and south poles of a magnet behaved something like positive and negative charges, in that like poles repelled and unlike attracted each other, magnetic poles differed from electric charges because it was impossible to separate them. Breaking a magnet in two yielded two magnets, each with its own north and south poles.

A fundamental understanding of the magnetic force became possible only with the discovery by the Danish physicist Hans Christian Ørsted in 1920 that an electric current flowing in a wire could generate a magnetic field. At a meeting of the Académie des Sciences that same year, Ampère presented his discovery that two wires carrying parallel currents attract each other. His first published paper on the subject explained how the direction of the magnetic field at a point depended on the direction of the current flow and the location of the point with respect to the current. In doing so, he introduced the earliest form of what has come to be known as the right-hand rule, in which the first three fingers of the right hand indicate how the direction of the force produced by a magnetic field is related to the directions of the field and of the electric current experiencing the force.

Between 1820 and 1825, through a painstaking series of experiments, Ampère elucidated the fundamental equation of force between elements of wires carrying electrical current. Since in the laboratory currents can be generated only around complete circuits, breaking down the overall behavior into its simplest components required a master mathematician. Ampère also discovered the basic principle of the electromagnet and provided an explanation for the properties of permanent magnets as resulting from the sum of individual atomic currents.

The early decades of the nineteenth century were a period of intense exploration of electromagnetic phenomena. The work of Ampère, followed by that of British physicists Michael Faraday and James Clerk Maxwell, led to practical applications of electromagnetism in the telegraph, telephone, electric motor, generator, and transformer and in radio and television transmission. From this technology came the ability to transmit electrical energy as well as information safely over large distances, with an impact on every aspect of modern life and social organization.

Bibliography

College Physics. R.A. Serway and J. S. Faughn. 3d ed. Fort Worth, Tex.: W. B. Saunders, 1992.

Electricity and Magnetism. B. Kurrelmeyer and W. H. Mais. Princeton, N.J.: Van Nostrand, 1967.

The Feynman Lectures in Physics. Richard P. Feynman, R. B. Leighton, and M. L. Sands. Reading, Mass.: Addison-Wesley, 1963.

Ampère's marital life also involved much personal tragedy. His happy first marriage to Julie Carron in 1799 produced a son, Jean-Jacques, but ended with her death four years later. A second marriage, to Jeanne Potot, in 1806, quickly resulted in divorce, but not before a second child, Albine, was born. After the divorce, Ampère's mother and sister provided housekeeping for him and both children.

Mathematical Work

Lacking university credentials, Ampère began work as a private tutor of mathematics. With the assistance of friends, he was soon able to secure a teaching position at the école centrale at Bourg-en-Bresse. During this time, he wrote his first mathematical paper, *Des considérations sur la théorie mathématique de jeu* (1802), on the theory of probability, in which he demonstrated that a gambler could not possibly win in a game of chance against opponents with unlimited resources. As a result, he obtained a professorship in mathematics at the Lycée in Lyons, an outstanding residential college. In 1809, he was appointed to the faculty of the École Polytechnique in Paris and shortly thereafter appointed inspector general of the university system of France.

Ampère continued to focus on mathematics until about 1814, the year in which he published his longest mathematical work, *Mémoire sur l'integration des équations aux différences partielles*, on the solution to partial differential equations. Ampère's strong background in mathematics proved an indispensable foundation for his later work on electromagnetic phenomena.

Philosophy and Chemistry

Ampère's early environment included both traditional Catholic religious instruction and exposure to the skepticism of the French *philosphes*. Early on, he rejected the contemporary philosophy which held that only sensations were real. Driven by a conviction that both God and the external universe were realities, after much reading he developed his own unique blend of philosophy. From the great German philosopher Immanuel Kant, Ampère accepted the distinction between phenomena, received through the senses, and noumena, underlying objects. Unlike Kant, he believed that true knowledge of the noumena could be achieved by the mind.

It was within this framework that Ampère approached the remarkable chemical discoveries of the early nineteenth century, for to him atoms and molecules were the noumena underlying chemical phenomena. In 1808, the French chemist Joseph-Louis Gay-Lussac reported his discovery that gases, when they react chemically, combine in simple ratios of volumes, a discovery explained in 1811 by the Italian physicist Amadeo Avogadro's bold postulate that equal volumes of all gases under identical conditions contain the same number of molecules.

In "Lettre de M. Ampère à M. le comte Berthollet" (1814), Ampère combined these observations with the fact that even solid materials are often transparent to conclude that the forces between molecules hold them at separations large compared to their own sizes. He further proposed, based on the geometrical form of crystals, that molecules must contain atoms arranged at the vertices of polyhedrons and that chemical reactions could only occur if they resulted in such polyhedral molecules. Such chemical interests brought Ampère into contact with the English chemist Sir Humphry Davy, the discoverer of many new chemical elements.

Although quaint and somewhat misinformed by modern standards, Ampère's chemical work did lead him to an essentially correct interpretation of the magnetic properties of matter as resulting from atomic-level electrical currents. He died in 1836 at the age of sixty-one.

Bibliography

By Ampère
Des considérations sur la théorie mathématique du jeu, 1802
"Lettre de M. Ampère à M. le comte Berthollet sur la détermination des proportions dans lesquelles les corps se combinent d'après le nombre et la disposition respective des molécules dont leurs particules intégrantes sont composées," *Annales de chimie*, 1814
Mémoire sur l'integration des équations aux différences partielles, 1814
Essai d'une classification naturelle pour les corps simples, 1816
Mémoire sur l'action naturalle de deux courants électriques . . . , 1820
Mémoire sur la théorie mathématique des phénomènes électrodynamiques, uniquement déduite de l'éxperience, 1827
Essai sur la philosophie des sciences, 1834

About Ampère
"Ampère." L. Pierce Williams. In *Dictionary of Scientific Biography*, edited by Charles Coulston Gillispie. Vol. 1. New York: Charles Scribner's Sons, 1970.
"Ampère's Electrodynamic Molecular Model." L. Pierce Williams. *Contemporary Physics* 4 (1962).
Giants of Electricity. Percy Dunsheath. New York: Thomas Y. Crowell, 1967.

(Donald R. Franceschetti)

Anaximander

Areas of Achievement: Astronomy, physics, and science (general)
Contribution: Anaximander was the first Greek to make a world map and a star map.

c. 610 B.C.E.	Born in Miletus, western Asia Minor (now Turkey)
c. 547 B.C.E.	Dies, probably in Miletus

Life

Anaximander (pronounced "a-NAK-sih-man-dur") was born of Greek heritage in or about the year 610 B.C.E. in a place now known as Turkey. Although he is called the first Greek scientist, he is more accurately categorized as a philosopher of nature. His theories on the workings of nature classify him as the second of the philosophers whose ideas propelled and established the culture of Western civilization.

His teacher was a man named Thales, who is universally considered to be the first Greek philosopher of nature.

Only Known Work

The only book that is known to have been written by Anaximander has been given the title *On the Nature of Things*. Throughout this work, he describes the origin and functioning of the natural world, which includes all the celestial spheres as well as the planet Earth.

Anaximander confirms the concept of geocentrism, the almost universally held theory of the ancient world. This theory stipulates that Earth is the center of the universe and that the stars, the sun and moon, and the planets revolve around Earth in circular patterns. Anaximander also proposed that Earth is shaped like a cylinder with dimensions in a ratio of 3:1, with the width three times the height.

Mapping the Universe

Mapmaking was an important and daunting task in the ancient world, and Anaximander excelled in this area. In addition to creating a map of the then-known world, he made an

The Origin of the Universe

The most distinctive feature of Anaximander's worldview is his theory of Apeiron, which is a Greek word that is variously translated as "Boundless," "Limitless," or "Infinite." He maintained that the Boundless is the material source out of which is derived all material, as well as immaterial, reality.

The *Apeiron* is the originating principle that itself is unlimited, yet it is solely responsible for the creation of the universe. Anaximander explains that the *Apeiron* surrounds and directs all things that exist. It is that substratum from which all things begin, both nonliving and living. It is that which sustains all things in their existence, and it is that which endures forever even though all things change and corrupt.

This boundless mass is eternal, in that it never had a beginning, and it is ageless, meaning that it will last forever. Although all other things come to be and pass away, the *Apeiron* itself remains imperishable and ungenerated. It alone is the underived, material source that provides the vital energy to account for the movement and regularity of nature. It accomplishes this task by a process of separating from itself the forces of hot and cold, dry and moist, from which are derived such qualities as hardness, softness, liquid, and vapor.

Anaximander's theory of *Apeiron* anticipates the modern scientific notions of energy and space. Many modern thinkers have marveled at the insight and wisdom of this great pioneer.

Bibliography

A History of Philosophy. Frederick Copleston. Vol. 1. New York: Image Books, 1960.
The Metaphysical Foundations of Modern Physical Science. E. A. Burtt. New York: Harcourt, Brace, 1925.
Origins of Modern Science. H. Butterfield. New York: Collier Books, 1962.

even greater contribution to science by devising a star map of the celestial spheres.

As a result, Anaximander is credited with being the originator of the first geometrical model of the universe. He introduced a visual schematic of the universe that featured mathematical proportionality and symmetry which, to this point, had been lacking in all previous attempts at this task.

Drawing on his resourcefulness as a skilled mapmaker, Anaximander adapted his mathematical proportions toward determining the hours of the day. He accomplished this by aligning the annual movement of the sun with the pointer on the already established sundial.

Insight into Evolution

Anaximander proposed that the origin of living beings was derived from the sea, arguing that both animal and human life were first contained in moisture.

He postulated a process of separation to explain the existence of distinct entities in their individual structures. From the original, chaotic moisture came the sea, and from the sea came aquatic life, which separated and branched off into life on dry land.

In fact, Anaximander speculated that the first human beings could not have survived as infants by their own power. Rather, he thought that they must have been nurtured from living beings of another kind that were already complete and established.

Bibliography

By Anaximander
On the Nature of Things, c. 6th century B.C.E. (not an extant text)

About Anaximander
Anaximander and the Origins of Greek Cosmology. Charles H. Kahn. New York: Columbia University Press, 1960.
The "Apeiron" of Anaximander. Paul Seligman. Westport, Conn.: Grenwood Press, 1974
A History of Greek Philosophy. W. K. C. Guthrie. Vol. 1. Cambridge, England: Cambridge University Press, 1962.

(Joseph R. Lafaro)

Anaximenes of Miletus

Areas of Achievement: Earth science, physics, and science (general)
Contribution: Anaximenes offered an explanation to account for the movement and causality present in the universe.

c. 585 B.C.E.	Born, probably in Miletus, western Asia Minor (now Turkey)
c. 528 B.C.E.	Dies, place unknown

Life

Very little is known about the life and background of Anaximenes of Miletus (pronounced "AN-ak-SIHM-ih-neeze"). Although it is known that he wrote specifically on nature and the forces that propel its activity, there is no surviving text or even a title attributed to him. Most of what is known of Anaximenes has been furnished by ancient writers, such as Theophrastus and Aristotle.

Anaximenes was probably born in or about the year 585 B.C.E. in a place called Miletus, which is situated on the western shore of what is now Turkey. The entire western coastline of Turkey was a region called Ionia in the ancient world, and Anaximenes was the third and last of an influential group of thinkers called the early Ionians. Thales, Anaximander, and Anaximenes formed this trilogy of Greek scientists, who are more appropriately referred to as philosophers of nature. Anaximenes was the younger associate and student of Anaximander.

The Structure of Nature

The key question that drove the theories of these earliest scientists was to determine the ultimate nature, order, and activity of reality. Prior to all other considerations in this quest was the question of "the one" and "the many." Was material reality composed of many different elements, such as fire, water, rocks, and flesh, or were these different elements simply derivatives of one ultimate and basic element?

According to Anaximenes' most notable theory, all the seemingly different structures of

Causality in Nature

Anaximenes described condensation and rarefaction as the mechanisms accounting for the causal connections that prevail throughout the universe.

The process of condensation is one of air thickening, whereas rarefaction is the opposite procedure of thinning. Air itself in its pure state is invisible. When it condenses or thickens, however, it becomes perceptible in the form of wind and clouds. As clouds become increasingly condensed, they form rain, and, when this water is squeezed tightly together under the influence of coldness, ice is formed. Ice is a hard substance from which all other solids such as wood and rocks are derived. Consequently, according to Anaximenes, all of these are simply attributes of air produced by condensation.

On the opposite scale, when air is rarefied or thinned, it becomes fire. Under the action of fire, material objects are thinned to the extent that they are broken down into their smaller constituent parts.

This action of thickening and thinning, causing cold and heat, can be illustrated by breathing with one's mouth wide open or closed. When one breathes with the mouth open, the air is warm because it is thin. When one breathes with the mouth nearly closed, the air is cool because it is condensed.

The most notable influence of Anaximenes on future scientific thought was the idea that variations in quality result entirely from degrees and conditions of quantity and, furthermore, that the intricate processes in nature are the result of a self-moving and mechanized universe.

Bibliography

A History of Greek Philosophy. W. K. C. Guthrie. Cambridge, England: Cambridge University Press, 1962.

A History of Philosophy. Frederick Copleston. Vol. 1. New York: Image Books, 1960.

The Presocratic Philosophers. G. S. Kirk, J. E. Raven, and M. Schofield. 2d ed. Cambridge, England: Cambridge University Press, 1983.

matter are attributes of one ultimate and universal element. Anaximenes designated air as the primary substance that fills every corner of the universe and, furthermore, as the force propelling all the activity that occurs in the cosmos.

The Source of Life

When Anaximenes states that air is the universal element, he includes within its domain all reality, both inorganic and organic. Just as fire needs air to burn and be sustained, metal oxidizes and rusts in the atmosphere, and water can flow because of pressure provided by the air, so also life can only survive by the inhalation of air.

He observed that plants, animals, and humans are alive only when immersed in air and, conversely, that they die when bereft of air, such as by drowning or suffocation. In effect, all reality is a living, breathing animal in which air provides the underlying, dynamic unity amid the apparent multiplicity. In fact, Anaximenes is characterized as a hylozoist, which means that he believed that all matter is self-propelling and alive.

Consequently, air is equivalent to the spark of life, or soul, that animates living beings. Anaximenes explains that all of nature is an organically, self-regulative, and autonomous entity that exhibits intelligence.

Bibliography

By Anaximenes
No works have been attributed to him.

About Anaximenes
"Anaximenes." A. H. Coxon. In *The Oxford Classical Dictionary*, edited by M. Cary et al. London: Clarendon Press, 1949.

"The Date of Anaximenes." G. B. Kerford. *Museum Helveticum* (1954).

Early Greek Philosophy. John Burnet. 4th ed. New York: Meridian Books, 1957.

(Joseph R. Lafaro)

Carl David Anderson

Area of Achievement: Physics
Contribution: By careful study of cosmic rays, Anderson discovered the first antiparticle, called the positron, as well as the mu-meson, or muon.

Sept. 3, 1905	Born in New York, New York
1923	Graduated from Los Angeles Polytechnic High School in California
1927	Receives B.S. degrees in physics and engineering from the California Institute of Technology (Caltech)
1930	Earns a Ph.D. in physics from Caltech
1930-1933	Serves as a Research Fellow under Robert A. Millikan at Caltech
1932	Discovers the positron
1933	Appointed assistant professor of physics at Caltech
1935	Sets up a cloud chamber on Pike's Peak near Colorado Springs, Colorado, and discovers the mu-meson, or muon
1936	Awarded the Nobel Prize in Physics for his discovery of the positron
1939	Named professor of physics at Caltech
1941-1945	Serves with the Office of Scientific Research and Development during World War II
1962	Selected as chair of the physics division at Caltech
1976	Retires and is named emeritus professor
Jan. 11, 1991	Dies in San Marino, California

Early Life

Carl David Anderson was born on September 3, 1905, in New York City to Swedish immigrants. Shortly after his birth, the family moved to California, where he was graduated from Los Angeles Polytechnic High School in 1923.

Anderson attended the California Institute of Technology (Caltech), where he earned bachelor of science degrees in physics and engineering in 1927 and a Ph.D. in physics in 1930. His doctoral research involved the investigation of the electrons emitted by gases when they are bombarded by X rays.

Anderson became a research fellow at Caltech in 1930, working on the research team of Robert A. Millikan, a distinguished scientist who was awarded the 1923 Nobel Prize in Physics for his measurement of the negative charge of the electron.

The Discovery of the Positron

At the time that Anderson joined his group, Millikan had become interested in cosmic rays, the high-energy particles from space that continually bombard the earth. Anderson perfected the technique of photographing the tracks of cosmic rays passing through a cloud chamber, a device in which droplets of liquid condense along the paths of subatomic particles and make them visible.

In August, 1932, after examining thousands of photographs, Anderson identified a particle that was otherwise identical to the electron, except that it had a positive charge. He had discovered the positron, the first antiparticle, which had been predicted by Paul A. M. Dirac when he developed the quantum theory of the electron. Anderson barely edged out Patrick M. S. Blackett, who confirmed the existence of the positron later in 1932.

Anderson followed up on his discovery of the positron by demonstrating, in an experiment with Seth Neddermeyer, that positrons are also produced by the irradiation of metals by gamma rays. He was awarded the Nobel Prize in Physics in 1936 for his discovery of the positron.

The Discovery of the Mu-Meson

Anderson continued his cosmic-ray research after his discovery of the positron. In 1935, he

The Positron, the First Antiparticle

Using a special cloud chamber to record the paths of subatomic particles, Anderson discovered a particle with the same properties as an electron but a positive charge, dubbing it the positron.

In 1928, Paul A. M. Dirac developed a new theory of the electron, which combined the principles of quantum mechanics and relativity. Dirac's model was remarkably successful in predicting the fine structure of the atom. His theory, however, was predicated on the existence of an antiparticle, one having all the same properties as the electron but a positive electric charge. Antiparticles have the unusual property that when they interact with their corresponding particle,

the passage of a subatomic particle through the chamber serve as condensation nuclei, and a trail of liquid droplets forms along the path of the particle.

Anderson improved the techniques used to illuminate these droplet trails, thus allowing many photographs to be taken and producing a record of all the particles passing through the chamber. He also placed his cloud chamber between two strong magnets, so that charged particles would travel in circular paths once they entered the chamber. He could then determine the energy of each particle by measuring the radius of its circular path. If he could establish in which direction the particle was moving, he could also determine its charge, since positively charged particles will bend in one direction and negatively charged ones in the opposite direction in a magnetic field.

The cloud chamber photograph, however, records only a single image of the entire path of the particle. In order to determine the direction of motion of each particle, Anderson divided his chamber in half with a thick lead plate. When a particle passed through the plate, it lost energy, and the spiral in the magnetic field became tighter. Thus, Anderson could tell which way the particle had traveled through the lead plate by observing which part of the spiral

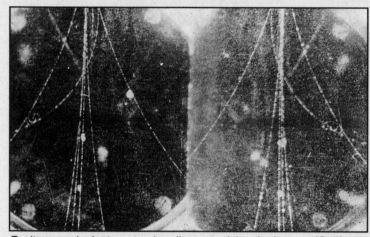

Positron and electron tracks discovered by Anderson. (California Institute of Technology)

they annihilate—that is, both particles disappear, being replaced by electromagnetic radiation.

Anderson developed a special cloud chamber, a device in which droplets of vapor condense along the paths traveled by charged subatomic particles, in order to determine the charge and energy of particles in cosmic rays. The original cloud chamber, developed by C. T. R. Wilson in 1912, saturates vapor in a chamber and then, by moving a piston, increases the volume and reduces the pressure of the gas so that it becomes overly saturated. Under these conditions, the presence of a nucleus for condensation, such as a dust particle, results in the condensation of small droplets of liquid. The charged ions produced by

was tighter. By the direction of the curvature, he could determine if the particle was positively or negatively charged.

Anderson examined thousands of photographs of particle trails in his cloud chamber before he found one that curved in the wrong direction. He called this new particle, the first antiparticle ever seen, a positron, short for "positive electron."

Bibliography

"The Positive Electron." Carl D. Anderson. *Physical Review* (March, 1933).

The World of Elementary Particles. Kenneth W. Ford. New York: Blaisdell, 1963.

set up a cloud chamber on Pike's Peak near Colorado Springs, Colorado, and identified another new particle. Anderson observed a track that was less curved than the track of an electron but more curved than that of a proton, indicating that it had a mass that was intermediate between the two.

Such a particle had been predicted earlier that year by Hideki Yukawa, who proposed that neutrons and protons are held together in the nuclei of atoms by the exchange of particles each having a mass between those of a proton and an electron. Anderson's new particle, which he called a mesotron but which other scientists quickly dubbed a meson, had a mass 130 times that of an electron but only one-quarter that of a proton.

Anderson quickly determined, however, that the meson—now called the mu-meson (or muon)—did not interact easily with the nuclei of atoms and thus could not be the particle predicted by Yukawa. Yukawa's particle, now called the pi-meson (pion), was not discovered until 1947.

Later Years

World War II interrupted Anderson's cosmic-ray research, and he served with the Office of Scientific Research and Development from 1941 until 1945. Following the war, he resumed his investigation of cosmic rays, flying a 5,000-pound cloud chamber up into the stratosphere on a B-29 aircraft. Particle physics changed after the war, however, with large particle accelerators replacing the cosmic rays as the source of high-energy particles for scientific research.

Anderson remained at Caltech for his entire career. He retired in 1976 and was named an emeritus professor. He died in San Marino, California, on January 11, 1991, at the age of eighty-five.

Bibliography

By Anderson

"Energies of Cosmic-Ray Particles," *Physical Review*, 1932

"The Positive Electron," *Physical Review*, 1933

(The Nobel Foundation)

"Cosmic-Ray Positive and Negative Electrons," *Physical Review*, 1933

"Mechanism of Cosmic-Ray Counter Action," *Physical Review*, 1934

"The Positron," *Nature*, 1934

About Anderson

"Carl David Anderson." In *The Nobel Prize Winners: Physics*, edited by Frank N. Magill. Pasadena, Calif.: Salem Press, 1989.

Understanding Physics: The Electron, Proton, and Neutron. Isaac Asimov. New York: Signet Science Library, 1966.

The World of Elementary Particles. Kenneth W. Ford. New York: Blaisdell, 1963.

(George J. Flynn)

Philip W. Anderson

Areas of Achievement: Mathematics and physics

Contribution: Anderson, a theoretical scientist, contributed to the understanding of the electron movements in materials called superconductors and semiconductors.

Dec. 13, 1923	Born in Indianapolis, Indiana
1943	Earns a bachelor of science degree from Harvard University
1943-1945	Serves in the U.S. Navy, working as a radio engineer during World War II and rising to the rank of chief petty officer
1949-1984	Conducts research at Bell Telephone Laboratories
1949	Earns a doctorate at Harvard
1964	Receives the Oliver E. Buckley Award
1967-1975	Serves as a professor at Cambridge University in England
1975-1984	Appointed a professor at Princeton University
1975	Awarded the Dannie Heineman Prize
1977	Awarded the Nobel Prize in Physics jointly with John Van Vleck and Sir Nevill Mott
1978	Given the Guthrie Medal
1978	Earns a master of arts degree from Cambridge
1982	Awarded the National Medal of Science

Early Life

Philip Warren Anderson was born in Indianapolis, Indiana, in 1923. His school work was outstanding, and he was admitted to Harvard University at the age of sixteen. There, he was known as a quiet and scholarly student, qualities that continued after his graduation and throughout his graduate work.

Anderson was graduated from Harvard in 1943, while the United States was fighting in World War II. He had intended to study for a doctoral degree, but that plan was interrupted while he served for three years in the U.S. Navy. By the end of his Navy duty, he had become a chief petty officer.

At Harvard once more after his military service, Anderson became a student of physicist John Van Vleck, whose major interest was to discover why various materials are affected differently by electricity and magnetism. Anderson followed in his instructor's footsteps, building mathematical models to explain how electrons, the negatively charged parts of atoms, behave in conductors of electricity such as copper and silver.

Superconductors and Atom Smashers

A strange behavior of helium had been discovered by Dutch scientists. They had cooled he-

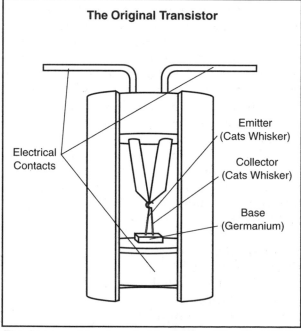

The first transistor, invented by William Shockley, Walter Brattain, and John Bardeen, which Anderson helped to modernize and make more practical. (from Ross R. Olney and Ross D. Olney's The Amazing Transistor, *1986)*

Semiconductors and Transistors

Anderson developed mathematical theories to guide the experiments that resulted in modern transistors.

Early radios were called "crystal sets" because crystals of germanium, silicon, or carborundum were needed to make them. These crystals, which allowed the flow of electricity in one direction only as was needed to carry sounds, are known as rectifiers. The crystal rectifiers offer poor passageways for electricity—better than glass, but not as good as copper. Thus, they are called semiconductors.

Natural rectifiers are not always predictable because they are impure; atoms of other elements are mixed with the silicon, carborundum, or germanium. Nevertheless, they promised to operate without a great loss of energy as heat and light.

Directors of the Bell Laboratories decided to search for a better way to make rectifiers. Anderson was a theoretical physicist assigned to this task. He created mathematical equations and models to predict what might happen with certain crystals and their impurities. Those impurities, Anderson thought, could be useful. He devised theories to explain how the impurities might control the electric flow in crystalline rectifiers.

The impurities sometimes supplied additional electrons and improved the flow of electricity and sometimes formed pools where electrons could be collected. He was then able to predict what impurities could be added to pure semiconductors and in what amounts they should be added to gain the conductivity needed.

In the early 1950's, experimental physicists William Shockley, Walter Brattain, and John Bardeen demonstrated an arrangement they had discovered that both rectified electric current and made it stronger (amplified the current). Their tool consisted of a set of wires connected to pieces of gold foil that sent a signal through a block of germanium. It was very delicate and not much smaller than a radio tube, but it was much cooler and made the electric signal that emerged forty times stronger than the one going in. The scientists at Bell Laboratories had made the first transistor.

Anderson's theoretical work helped direct other experiments that soon produced very pure slices of germanium or silicon that could be made either to encourage more electrons to flow or to discourage them by adding precise amounts of impurities to the slices.

A block of semiconductors could be made like a sandwich—for example, with two pieces of electron "encouragers" separated by a piece of electron "discourager." Electric flow could be started in one of the two similar pieces. Electrons would tend to gather at the edge of the other kind of material, until a very small electric flow through the second material acted as guards at a gate. When the small electric flow began, the gate would open and electrons would rush through, creating a more excited electron flow on the other side.

Anderson's theoretical work pointed to inexpensive and readily available materials that could be used to make very small transistors. These devices could be placed in electric circuits to regulate electric flow or to act as switches, turning the flow off and on in television sets, automobiles, watches—almost any tool that needs a controlled flow of electricity.

Bibliography

The Amazing Transistor. Ross R. Olney and Ross D. Olney. New York: Atheneum, 1986.

The Breakthrough. Robert B. Hazen. New York: Summit, 1988.

Miracle Chip: The Microelectronic Revolution. Stanley L. Englebardt. New York: Lothrop, Lee and Shepard, 1979.

Superconductors: Conquering Technology's New Frontier. Randy Simon and Andrew Smith. New York: Plenum Press, 1988.

lium to –289 degrees Celsius. At that temperature, helium is a liquid that flows through even the smallest openings without any friction. When mercury is cooled by this very cold helium, it reaches a temperature at which the metal conducts electricity without a loss of energy as heat or light. The very cold helium allows a flow of atoms and molecules without

(AP/Wide World Photos)

temperatures of superfluids or superconductors, friction would cease and the magnets could be made to provide much more energy. Particles would move faster and take on more energy, and the impacts that caused atoms and parts of atoms to break up would be much greater. Cooling mercury with liquid helium at very low temperatures was impractical and expensive. Anderson studied the arrangement of atoms in superfluids and superconductors and suggested other materials to test.

Superconductors and superfluids have some qualities in common with lasers. Lasers concentrate light energy in a single direction, superfluids direct the flow of atoms and molecules in a single direction, and superconductors direct the flow of electrons in a single direction.

Anderson studied all three of these actions. With his mathematical models, he was able to predict the behaviors of superconductors—including the fact that superconductors, if cooled too much, develop the usual resistance to electric flow. His work led experimenters to discover superconductors that required less cooling and that could be used by particle physicists to build ever stronger tools for atom smashing.

Bell Laboratories

Anderson had joined the team of physicists at the Bell Laboratories immediately after he earned his doctorate in 1949. The year before he arrived, three scientists there—William Shockley, Walter Brattain, and John Bardeen—had invented the transistor. This device could both regulate the direction of the flow of electricity and amplify it (make the electric flow stronger). The Bell scientists, including Ander-

friction and is known as a superfluid. Materials that allow a free flow of electricity, such as the cooled mercury, are called superconductors.

Anderson used mathematics to determine the arrangements of atoms in superfluids and superconductors. The ideas that he developed were important to the scientists who were building new tools to break up atoms and discover smaller particles. These tools required great amounts of electromagnetic energy produced by very large magnets with large coils of conducting material such as copper or silver.

The more energy created by the magnet systems, however, the hotter the coils became—until they were no longer usable. If economical ways could be found to cool the coils to the son, then turned their attention to making the new transistors practical.

Awards
Anderson received many honors during his career, culminating in the Nobel Prize in Physics, which he shared with Van Vleck and Sir Nevill Mott in 1977. In 1982, he was awarded the National Medal of Science.

Bibliography
By Anderson
"New Approach to the Theory of Superexchange Interactions," *Physical Review*, 1959
Concepts in Solids: Lectures on the Theory of Solids, 1963
Basic Notions of Condensed Matter Physics, 1984

About Anderson
Biographical Encyclopedia of Science. New York: Facts on File, 1981.
"Philip W. Anderson." In *The Nobel Prize Winners: Physics*, edited by Frank N. Magill. Pasadena, Calif.: Salem Press, 1989.
Profiles of Science: Nobel Prize Winners in Physics. Robert L. Weber. London: Institute of Physics, 1980.

(George Wilson)

Christian B. Anfinsen

Areas of Achievement: Biology, chemistry, and immunology

Contribution: Anfinsen proved that the primary structure of a protein, the amino acid sequence, contains the information necessary to determine the three-dimensional sequence of the protein.

Mar. 26, 1916	Born in Monessen, Pennsylvania
1937	Earns a B.A. in chemistry from Swarthmore College
1939	Awarded an M.S. in organic chemistry by the University of Pennsylvania
1939	Wins a fellowship from the American Scandinavian Foundation to study at the Carlsberg Institute in Denmark
1943	Earns a Ph.D. in biochemistry from Harvard University
1947-1948	Serves as an American Cancer Society Senior Fellow at the Medical Nobel Institute in Sweden
1950-1962	Works at the National Heart Institute
1962-1963	Accepts an appointment as professor of biological chemistry at the Harvard Medical School
1963-1981	Serves as chief of the Laboratory of Biological Chemistry at the National Institute of Arthritis and Metabolic Diseases
1966	Delivers a Harvey Lecture
1972	Awarded the Nobel Prize in Chemistry
1982	Accepts an appointment as professor of biology at The Johns Hopkins University
May 14, 1995	Dies in Randallstown, Maryland

Early Life

Christian Boehmer Anfinsen (pronounced "AN-fehn-sehn"), the son of a Norwegian engineer, was born in Monessen, Pennsylvania, just north of Pittsburgh, on March 26, 1916. At Swarthmore College, he majored in chemistry and, in 1937, earned a B.A. degree. Anfinsen then studied at the University of Pennsylvania and earned a M.S. in organic chemistry in 1939.

At his point in his career, on a fellowship from the American Scandinavian Foundation, Anfinsen studied at the Carlsberg Institute in Denmark. In 1940, he returned to the United States and began studies in the department of biological chemistry at the Harvard School of Medicine, earning a Ph.D. there in 1943. His doctoral dissertation involved a study of the enzymes present in the retina of the eye.

The Thermodynamic Hypothesis of Protein Folding

Ribonuclease is a globular protein with four sulfur-to-sulfur (disulfide) bonds.

The telegram that Anfinsen received in 1972 announced that he had received the Nobel Prize in Chemistry for "studies on ribonuclease, in particular the relationship between the amino acid sequence and the biologically active conformation." Anfinsen used the accompanying diagram to explain his experiment.

Anfinsen used a solution of urea and 2-mercaptoethanol to break both the hydrogen bonds and the disulfide bonds of the protein; that is, he denatured it. In this uncoiled form, ribonuclease was no longer an active enzyme. Next, he removed the added chemicals, and the enzyme returned to its original shape and was again able to break down ribonucleic acid (RNA).

The remarkable feature of this reaction is that while the eight sulfhydryl groups in the uncoiled form could reform four disulfide bonds in 105 possible ways, they always reformed in the one correct way. It was evident that the sequence of amino acids had sufficient information to determine the proper three-dimensional shape. Anfinsen hypothesized that the protein in its normal environment (of pH, salt concentration, and temperature) was assuming the shape that corresponded to the lowest energy of the whole system; this was the thermodynamic hypothesis. Studies with other protein systems, including staphylococcal nuclease, supported this hypothesis.

Anfinsen's work established the relationship between the structure and function of proteins. It introduced the possibility that the shape of a protein or peptide sequence could be determined

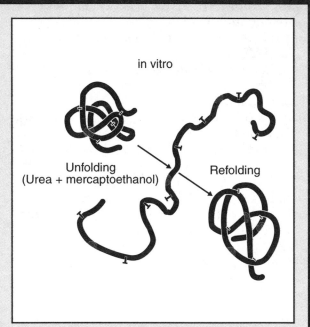

A schematic representation of the denaturation and renaturation of ribonuclease. (from "Principles That Govern the Folding of Protein Chains," by Christian B. Anfinsen)

from theoretical studies. The molecular modeling that scientists use today to design peptides on computers is directly dependent on Anfinsen's work.

Bibliography

Biochemistry. Lubert Stryer. San Francisco: W. H. Freeman, 1988.

"Genetic Control of Tertiary Protein Structure: Studies with Model Systems." Charles Epstein, Robert Goldberg, and Christian Anfinsen. *Cold Spring Harbor Symposia on Quantitative Biology* (1963).

Anfinsen taught at the Harvard School of Medicine until 1950. In addition, he served as an American Cancer Society Senior Fellow in the Medical Nobel Institute in Sweden during the 1947-1948 academic year. Although he was promoted to associate professor upon his return to Harvard, Anfinsen accepted a position as head of the National Heart Institute's Laboratory of Cellular Physiology.

Initial Studies with Ribonuclease

Anfinsen chose the enzyme ribonuclease as the focus of his research in the early 1950's. Armour, Inc., of Chicago had prepared rather large quantities of this enzyme, which breaks down ribonucleic acid (RNA), from the pancreatic tissue of cattle during World War II. Because this enzyme was available at low cost and with high purity, many scientists were studying it.

Anfinsen used paper chromatography to study the size and shape of the enzyme. Then, using methods developed by Frederick Sanger, Anfinsen determined the primary structure or amino acid sequence of parts of the ribonuclease chain. Stanford Moore and William Howard Stein at the Rockefeller Institute were also working on the structure of ribonuclease and used column chromatography methods to determine its complete primary structure.

A sabbatical year at the Carlsberg Laboratory in Copenhagen, under the direction of Kai Linderstrom-Lang, introduced Anfinsen to the techniques that he would use to study the denaturing of ribonuclease. He now had the tools that would lead to his Nobel Prize-winning determination that the primary structure of a protein dictates its tertiary, or three-dimensional, shape.

Explorations of Other Proteins

After winning the Nobel Prize in Chemistry in 1972, Anfinsen continued his research career at the National Institute of Arthritis and Metabolic Disease. In 1982, he accepted an academic position as professor of biology at The Johns Hopkins University.

Anfinsen remained a prolific researcher, studying several facets of protein chemistry. In the mid-1970's, interferon was of interest to Anfinsen. Interferon is a sugar-containing pro-

(The Nobel Foundation)

tein that shows antiviral and anticancer activities. Anfinsen isolated and determined the primary structure of the major interferon of the human lymphoblast.

In the 1980's, Anfinsen focused on the purification and characterization of enzymes from thermophilic, or heat-stable, organisms.

Bibliography

By Anfinsen

The Molecular Basis of Evolution, 1959

"Studies on the Principles That Govern the Folding of Protein Chains," *Science*, 1973

"Amino Terminal Sequence of the Major Component of Human Lymphoblastoid Interferon," *Science*, 1980 (with Kathryn C. Zoon, Mark E. Smith, Pamela J. Bridgen, Michael W. Hunkapiller, and Leroy E. Hood)

Advances in Protein Chemistry: Enzymes and Proteins from Hyperthermophilic Microorganisms, 1996 (as editor)

About Anfinsen
"Christian B. Anfinsen." In *The Nobel Prize Winners: Chemistry*, edited by Frank N. Magill. Pasadena, Calif.: Salem Press, 1990.
"The 1972 Nobel Prize for Chemistry." Frederic M. Richards. *Science* (1972).
Notable Twentieth-Century Scientists. Emily J. McMurray, ed. New York: Gale Research, 1995.

(Helen M. Burke)

Virginia Apgar

Area of Achievement: Medicine
Contribution: A pioneer in anesthesiology, Apgar developed a newborn scoring system to evaluate infants.

June 7, 1909	Born in Westfield, New Jersey
1933	Earns an M.D. at the College of Physicians and Surgeons of Columbia University
1937	Certified as an anesthesiologist
1938	Named director of the anesthesiology division at Columbia-Presbyterian Medical Center
1949	Made the first full professor of anesthesiology at Columbia
1952	Introduces her newborn scoring system
1959	Earns a master's degree in public health from The Johns Hopkins University
1959-1968	Appointed to several important positions within the National Foundation-March of Dimes
1972	Publishes *Is My Baby All Right?*
1973	Receives the Ralph M. Waters Award from the American Society of Anesthesiology
1973	Becomes the first woman to receive the Gold Medal for Distinguished Achievement in Medicine of the College of Physicians and Surgeons' Alumni Association
1973	Voted the *Ladies' Home Journal* Woman of the Year in Science and Research
Aug. 7, 1974	Dies in New York, New York

The Apgar Score

This scoring system is used to evaluate newborns and identify infants at risk.

Attending births as an anesthesiologist, Apgar became aware that delivery room personnel focused on the mothers and that infants were not immediately examined. As a result, some newborns died from treatable respiratory and circulatory problems.

In 1952, she created a scoring technique to detect urgent health concerns. She wrote an article entitled "A Proposal for a New Method of Evaluation of the Newborn Infant," published in *Anesthesia and Analgesia* in 1953. Officially known as the Newborn Scoring System but popularly called the Apgar score, this examination helps nurses and physicians to evaluate infants' physical condition.

Apgar's system requires an assessment at one minute after birth. Infants are evaluated for appearance (color), pulse (heart rate), grimace (reflex), activity (muscle tone), and respiration.

In each category, a 0 indicates poor health and a 2 reveals vigor. A perfect score of 10 is rare, and infants scoring 7 and above are considered healthy. Those identified with low scores receive immediate medical attention and emergency procedures to correct their condition.

The Apgar score has become a standard system to evaluate newborns. One physician wrote, "Every baby born in a modern hospital anywhere in the world is looked at first through the eyes of Virginia Apgar." Her system was later modified to examine the infant again at five minutes after birth.

Bibliography
"The Apgar Score: A Living, Working Memorial." H. Medovy. *Canadian Medical Association Journal* 111 (1974).

"Apgar Scores as an Indicator of Fetal Asphyxia." *American Family Physician* 38 (December, 1988).

"Statement on Use and Abuse of the Apgar Score." *American Family Physician* 54 (September 1, 1996).

Early Life

Virginia Apgar grew up in New Jersey, where her father, a businessman, experimented with wireless telegraphy and astronomy. Her teachers also encouraged her love of science and medicine. Apgar enrolled in Mount Holyoke College in 1925 and studied zoology and chemistry. She received her A.B. in 1929.

Apgar graduated fourth in her class at the College of Physicians and Surgeons of Columbia University in 1933. She earned a prestigious surgical internship at the Columbia-Presbyterian Medical Center; few female physicians pursued this specialty.

After two years, she decided to become an anesthesiologist, a medical professional who administers sensation- and pain-reducing drugs to patients, instead of a surgeon. She hoped to be a pioneer in this emerging scientific field.

Professional Development

Apgar studied with nurse-anesthetists at Columbia University, the University of Wisconsin, and Bellevue Hospital. By 1937, she was the fiftieth physician certified as an anesthesiologist by the American Board of Anesthesiology.

Appointed director of the division of anesthesiology at Columbia-Presbyterian Medical Center, Apgar established programs to train physician-anesthesiologists. In 1949, Columbia named her the first full professor of anesthesiology. She was the first woman to hold these positions.

Newborns

Concerned with maternal health, Apgar focused on childbirth anesthesia. She had attended approximately 17,000 births, observing both mothers and infants, and became aware that many newborns suffered complications that required immediate treatment.

By 1952, her scoring system, known as the Apgar score, was introduced. Within sixty seconds of birth, newborns are rated for heart rate, color, muscle tone, respiration, and reflexes. Soon, Apgar's newborn scoring system was

(Library of Congress)

adopted by hospitals worldwide. In her honor, the perinatal section of the American Academy of Pediatrics presents the annual Apgar Award to honor physicians who have contributed to the well-being of mothers and newborns.

National Foundation-March of Dimes
Seeking further education, Apgar earned a master's degree in public health from The Johns Hopkins University in 1959. She accepted an executive position with the National Foundation-March of Dimes and conducted research on birth defects.

Apgar raised funds and educated the public about the prevention, early detection, and treatment of birth defects. Her book *Is My Baby All Right?: A Guide to Birth Defects* (1972) informed parents about genetic and physiological concerns.

She was also a clinical professor of pediatrics at Cornell University Medical College and a lecturer in the medical genetics department at Johns Hopkins.

A humanitarian, Apgar promoted the practical use of medicine to help people and improve the quality of life. She wrote sixty scientific papers and received many awards. Apgar died in 1974 at the age of sixty-five.

Bibliography
By Apgar
"A Proposal for a New Method of Evaluation of the Newborn Infant," *Anesthesia and Analgesia*, 1953

Is My Baby All Right?: A Guide to Birth Defects, 1972 (with Joan Beck)

About Apgar
"Fond Memories of Virginia Apgar." L. Stanley James. *Pediatrics* 55 (January, 1975).

"In Memoriam: Dr. Virginia Apgar '29." Christianna Smith. *Mount Holyoke Alumnae Quarterly* 58 (Fall, 1974).

"Virginia Apgar: A Woman Physician's Career in a Developing Specialty." Selma Harrison Calmes. *Journal of the American Medical Women's Association* 39 (1984).

(Elizabeth D. Schafer)

Sir Edward Victor Appleton

Areas of Achievement: Earth science and physics

Contribution: Appleton determined the structure and made theoretical models of the ionosphere, giving a sound basis to the behavior of radio waves.

Sept. 6, 1892	Born in Bradford, Yorkshire, England
1914	Graduated from St. John's College, Cambridge University, with first-class honors
1914	Serves as a radio officer during World War I
1920	Works on vacuum tubes at Cambridge's Cavendish Laboratory
1924	Demonstrates the existence of the ionosphere
1924	Becomes a professor of physics at King's College, the University of London
1926	Named a member of the Radio Research Board
1927	Offers his initial theoretical treatment of the ionosphere
1936	Appointed Jacksonian Professor of Physics at Cambridge
1936	Serves as a member of the Tizard Committee to study scientific defense
1939	Acts as secretary of the Department of Scientific and Industrial Research
1941	Made Knight Commander, Order of Bath
1947	Awarded the Nobel Prize in Physics for his ionosphere studies
Apr. 21, 1965	Dies in Edinburgh, Scotland

Early Life

Edward Victor Appleton was born on September 6, 1892, in Bradford, Yorkshire, England, to a working-class family. His evident early abilities earned him scholarships that allowed his education to proceed through King's College at Cambridge University. Lectures there by Sir J. J. Thompson and Sir Joseph Larmor awakened Appleton's interest in all aspects of radio.

The outbreak of World War I immediately followed his graduation, and Appleton enlisted. He soon became recognized for his competence with radio communications in the Army Signal Service, developing skills that would be of great benefit when he returned to scientific research.

The Study of Radio Waves

One of the surprises of early radio was the propagation of some wavelengths beyond the horizon and the fading of other signals, especially at night. By 1920, it was generally thought that this behavior was the result, as suggested in 1902 by Oliver Heaviside, of a conducting layer of ionized gas at the top of

(The Nobel Foundation)

the atmosphere. Appleton began considering ways to verify the existence of this layer and learn its properties, which were puzzling because of the strange reception that radio receivers experienced.

His early observations showed that the conducting layer rose to higher altitudes at night, and he devised a method, with the cooperation of the British Broadcasting System (BBC), of observing the interference of the direct wave with the reflected wave by having the transmitter change the wavelength on a prearranged schedule. As expected, the path length and then the reflected wave changed with wavelength; the total signal received grew or fell, depending on whether the interference from the layer was constructive or destructive.

The Ionosphere

As a more straightforward method of studying the ionosphere, as this conducting layer had come to be called, Appleton adopted the pulsed reflection method invented by Gregory Breit and Merle Tuve and entered into a re-

search program extending over two decades. He was an especially capable teacher and attracted excellent students, whom he managed as a team to provide data about the complex phenomena.

A startling discovery came while Appleton was observing in northern Norway. One night, the ionosphere ceased to reflect signals on any wavelength. This event proved to be associated with time variations of the earth's magnetic field, called magnetic storms, and was an indication of the complicated structure in space and time of the earth's external field and the ions trapped in it.

Much long-distance communication in the 1930's was achieved using radio and was strongly dependent on the operator's knowledge of which wavelengths to use to reach a given station. Much credit is given to Appleton for systematizing this information and making it accessible to those who needed it. Appleton collaborated with many other scientists in his attempts to derive a mathematical equation to describe the ionosphere for various condi-

The Ionosphere

Appleton performed important experiments on the nature of the ionosphere, the conducting layer at the top of Earth's atmosphere.

Toward the end of the nineteenth century, laboratory experiments showed that, at low pressure, air becomes a conductor of electricity. Inasmuch as it was known that the atmospheric pressure drops with increasing altitude, eventually reaching the condition of an excellent vacuum, it was thought that the earth must be enveloped with an electrically conducting layer. The aurora borealis (northern lights) resembled discharges observed in low-pressure experiments and was thought to occur in the conducting layer.

Electron-ion pairs are produced by photoionization from the sun's radiation and introduced by the charged-particle flux from the sun (solar wind) that interacts with the earth's magnetic field. The free electrons in these regions reflect radio waves. During the day, photoionization produces enough electron-ion pairs to force the conducting layer below 100 kilometers. At night,

however, these pairs recombine, and those remaining are found much higher in the atmosphere.

The ionosphere reflects radio waves according to their wavelength, which gives the appearance of layers although the effect is continuous. The ionosphere becomes transparent for wavelengths shorter than a few meters, with this value depending on the electron density.

The general method of examining the ionosphere is by the use of short trains of waves from a transmitter for which the travel time to and from the reflecting layer is measured. In the first half of the twentieth century, stations were placed worldwide to determine the heights for various wavelength reflections as functions of time and place, but many aspects of ionospheric structure had to await the use of space probes.

Bibliography

"Atmosphere." In *Encyclopaedia Britannica*. 15th ed. Vol. 2. Chicago: University of Chicago Press, 1983.

tions, efforts that culminated in the Appleton-Hartree equation.

As World War II approached, Appleton served on the Committee for the Scientific Survey of Air Defence, called the Tizard Committee, which was responsible for Britain's radar development. In 1939, he took charge of the government's Department of Scientific and Industrial Research. Appleton was knighted in 1941, and, after the war, he became principal and vice chancellor of the University of Edinburgh.

In 1947, Appleton was honored with the Nobel Prize in Physics for his studies of the ionosphere. He died in 1965 in Edinburgh, Scotland, at the age of seventy-two.

Bibliography
By Appleton
"On the Nature of Atmospherics," *Proceedings of the Royal Society*, 1923 (with Robert Watson-Watt)
"Local Reflection of Wireless Waves from the Upper Atmosphere," *Nature*, 1925 (with Miles Barnett)
"The Existence of More than One Ionized Layer in the Upper Atmosphere," *Nature*, 1927
Thermionic Vacuum Tubes and Their Applications, 1931
"Ionospheric Investigations in High Latitudes," *Nature*, 1933 (with R. Naismith and G. Builder)
Scientific Progress, 1936
Science, Government, and Industry, 1947
The Practical Importance of Fundamental Research, 1948
Science and the Nation, 1957

About Appleton
Sir Edward Appleton. Ronald Clark. Oxford, England: Pergamon Press, 1971.
"Sir Edward Victor Appleton." In *The Nobel Prize Winners: Physics*, edited by Frank N. Magill. Pasadena, Calif.: Salem Press, 1989.
"Wilhelm Altar, Edward Appleton, and the Magneto-ionic Theory." C. Stewart Gillmore. *Proceedings of the American Philosophical Society* 126 (1982).

(Louis Brown)

François Arago

Areas of Achievement: Astronomy and physics

Contribution: Arago's greatest contribution to science came through his encouragement of others and his publication of the results of their experiments. On his own, he investigated the orbits of the planets and performed experiments with electricity and light.

Feb. 26, 1786	Born in Estagel, France
1803	Enters the École Polytechnique
1805	Appointed secretary of the French Bureau of Longitudes
1807	Joins Jean-Baptiste Biot on a team to measure a section of Earth's circumference
1808	Becomes a prisoner of war in Spain
1809	Elected to the Académie des Sciences and appointed professor of geometry and geodesy at the École Polytechnique
1811	Presents a paper to the academy on the polarization of light
1812	Begins a lecture series in Paris that popularizes astronomy
1816	Helps establish the journal *Annales de Chemie et Physique*
1818	Publishes an account of his observations in geodetics, astronomy, and physics
1825	Receives the Copley Medal of the Royal Society of London
1830	Becomes director of the Paris Observatory and secretary of the Académie des Sciences
1831	Named a member of the Chamber of Deputies
Oct. 2, 1853	Dies in Paris, France

Early Life

Dominique-François-Jean Arago (pronounced "a-ra-GOH") was born in Estagel, a small town in the Pyrenees near the French border with Spain. His mother, Marie Roig, and father, François Bonaventure Arago, were landowners, and his father was mayor of the town. Three years after Arago's birth, the family moved to nearby Perpignan, where his father became the cashier at the government mint.

Arago planned for a career in the military and attended the schools in Perpignan in preparation for entrance to France's École Polytechnique in Paris. At the age of seventeen, he passed the examinations with very high scores, then became the top student in his class.

Measuring the Earth

After only two years, in 1805, Arago was appointed secretary of the French Bureau of Longitudes and sent to Spain. He and Jean-Baptiste Biot were to complete the measurement of a section of a meridian, a circle around the earth that passes through both North and South Poles. The section to be measured lay between Barcelona and the Balearic Islands in the Mediterranean Sea east of Spain. The team's calculations would contribute to an improved standard of measure in the metric system.

Arago and Biot established a base on a peak above the Mediterranean on the coast of Spain. They were to cooperate with a Spanish team of scientists on the small island of Ibiza with whom they could communicate by signals.

In 1808, war broke out between Spain and France. The Spanish government became suspicious of Arago's signaling to Ibiza, and he was taken as a prisoner of war. A few months later, Arago was released on the condition that he take a long route back to France, traveling first to Algiers in Africa. Three attempts to sail from Algiers to France were thwarted by a second capture by a Spanish warship, a sudden storm that threw the escape ship from near the European coast all the way back to Africa, and a near-capture by a British gunboat. Arago finally managed to reach France again at the age of twenty-three.

Two years later, Arago married. The couple lived in an apartment at the Paris Observatory, where they reared three boys.

Popularizing Science

As a reward for his work in Spain, Arago was elected to the exclusive Paris Académie des Sciences and appointed professor of geometry and geodesy (a branch of science dealing with the size and shape of the earth) at the École Polytechnique.

Arago's first interest at that time, however, was astronomy. In 1812, he began a series of public lectures to explain that branch of science to Parisians. He was always warm and friendly but explosive and dramatic as well. The lectures brought the latest infor-

Lith. de Delpech.

(Library of Congress)

The Polariscope

Arago gained fame for developing tools for astronomers studying the nature of light and of objects in the universe.

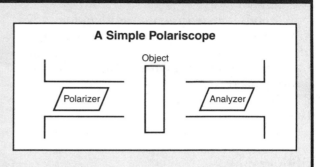

A century before Arago, Robert Hooke, secretary of the Royal Society of London, had gained fame as an inventor and builder of experimental equipment for the society. Arago followed this track as an inventor in his role as secretary of the French Académie des Sciences.

That reflected light sometimes changes so that all the light seems to travel in waves in one direction had been known for hundreds of years. Arago used this information to invent a polariscope to observe the amount of polarized light coming to the instrument from sources of light in the universe. Chemicals inserted between a polarizer crystal and analyzer presented different views of light reflected from molecules and larger masses in the universe.

As white light passed through this machine, it was affected by polarization that cause light waves of different lengths, now all traveling along the same path, to interfere with one another. Some colors that make up white light were blocked out so that materials in the universe presented different patterns of remaining colors of light.

Plates and screens that diverted parts of the reflected light were carefully placed and made adjustable so that Arago and other scientists could measure the wavelengths of some of the bands of light—information that helped determine how much of the light of the universe is reflected.

Arago was able to demonstrate how much of the light was reflected and whether that light came from the surface of a solid or a liquid. He also looked at the tails of comets using his polarimeter and was able to determine the contents of the tail.

Bibliography
Modern Optics. Earle B. Brown. New York: Reinhold, 1965.

Modern Optics. Robert D. Guenther. New York: John Wiley & Sons, 1990.

Polarimetry: Radar, Infrared, Visible, Ultraviolet, and X-Ray. Russell A. Chipman and John W. Morris, eds. Bellingham, Wash.: SPIE, 1990.

mation about the skies to his audiences and excited both scientists and nonscientists. It was the beginning of one of Arago's greatest contributions to science—supporting other scientists and writing and lecturing about their scientific discoveries.

Arago and His Contemporaries
Arago was interested in many areas of science. He was a good friend of Baron Alexander von Humboldt and studied ecology, geography, and climate around the world. Humboldt proposed that one way to understand world geography and climate was to try to construct a world map showing lines, called isotherms, along which the temperature ranges were similar. This idea was exciting to Arago, and he supported Humboldt in speeches and writing.

For two hundred years, scientists had worked to discover the true nature of light, whether light traveled as small pellets of energy or as waves. Arago joined with Augustin-Jean Fresnel in experiments that made the two Frenchmen champions of the wave theory of light.

In 1820, Arago was invited to Geneva, Switzerland, to see the experiments by Hans Christian Ørsted that demonstrated a relationship between electricity and magnetism. André-Marie Ampère also learned of these experiments. Ampère, supported by Arago, is credited with discovering the magnetic field of force around an electric wire. The work of these two colleagues resulted in the invention of the solenoid, a current-carrying coil that acts as a magnet.

In another experiment completed in 1825, Arago rotated a copper disk near a compass and found that the rotation exerted an electromagnetic influence on the compass. Michael Faraday used Arago's work to develop the idea of induction, the basis for electric motors and dynamos.

Arago died in 1853 at the age of sixty-seven.

Bibliography

By Arago
Astronomie populaire, 1854-1857 (4 vols.)
Oeuvres complètes de François Arago, 1854-1862 (17 vols.; J. A. Barral, ed.)
Portions of these publications translated into English:
Tract on Comets, 1832
Popular Lectures on Astronomy, 1841
Meteorological Essays, 1855
Popular Astronomy, 1855-1858 (2 vols.)

About Arago
History of My Youth. François Arago. Translated by Baden Powell. London: Longman, Green, Longman, and Roberts, 1862.
Light. R. W. Ditchburn. 2d ed. New York: John Wiley & Sons, 1969.

(George Wilson)

Archimedes

Areas of Achievement: Invention, mathematics, physics, and science (general)

Contribution: Archimedes discovered the law of buoyancy, determined the value of pi (π), and devised a way to transport water uphill.

287 B.C.E.	Born in Syracuse, a city located on the western tip of Sicily
212 B.C.E.	Dies in Syracuse, Sicily

Early Life

Archimedes was born in the year 287 B.C.E., of Greek lineage and culture, in a place called Syracuse, located in Sicily. At that time, Syracuse was ruled by a king named Hiero II, who knew of the genius of Archimedes. Archimedes became familiar with the royal family and in the king's service gained fame as a scholar.

The Circle

As a mathematician, Archimedes was the first person to calculate the ratio between the circumference of a circle and its diameter. He determined that this value is the ratio of 22:7 (approximately 3.14), which subsequently became known by the Greek letter pi (π), because it is the first letter in the word "perimeter."

He accomplished this task by the ingenious method of drawing two polygons of ninety-six sides each. He drew one of these polygons outside a circle, known as a circumscribed polygon, and he drew the other polygon inside the same circle, known as an inscribed polygon. He then proceeded to measure the perimeters of both polygons to determine that π equals approximately 3.14.

A Method for Lifting Water

One of the problems that Archimedes attempted to solve was the transportation of water uphill, for which he invented what has come to be known as Archimedes' screw. This device is useful in irrigation systems, in the obtaining of drinking water, and in drainage.

Archimedes' screw consists of a long cylinder, originally made of wood, inside of which is constructed a spiral that runs the length of the cylinder and resembles the threads of a screw. The end of the cylinder is angled down and submerged into a pool of water, with the opposite end of the cylinder raised to the location of the required effluence. The screw is operated by rotating it on its axis, which results in the water being lifted upward on the moving threads. The turning motion was originally accomplished by walking on the cylinder. Later, the rotating motion was produced by the use of a crank.

Weapons of War

During Archimedes' lifetime, Syracuse was involved in a war with the Roman army known as the Second Punic War. In anticipation of an invasion by the Romans, Archimedes invented weapons designed to hold off the enemy forces. Among his most notable inventions are the catapult, the compound pulley, and a burning glass sphere that was hurled at the enemy. So successful were these weapons that they kept the invading army at bay for three years

(Library of Congress)

Archimedes' Principle of Flotation

The law of flotation states that when immersed in a liquid, a body is buoyed by a force equal to the weight of the liquid that is displaced.

By means of observing his displacement of water in a bathtub, Archimedes reasoned that bodies of different densities would displace different amounts of water and that density is determined by a body's weight and volume. This realization provided the solution to a dilemma in which the king of Syracuse had ordered Archimedes to determine whether his new crown was made of pure gold or was an alloy. Since silver or any other metal is lighter or less dense than gold, an alloy equal in weight to a given amount of gold will necessarily be bulkier and will displace more water.

By experimentation, Archimedes observed that the crown displaced more water than a block of gold of the same weight. This proved

that the crown was bulkier and indeed contained not pure gold, but rather some gold alloyed with a lighter metal.

Both weight and volume (known as relative density), compared with the fluid in which a body is immersed, determine the buoyancy force that enables a body to float. By virtue of his discovery, Archimedes established the parameters used in determining the buoyancy and dimensions of ships in water, as well as the principles involved in balloons rising in air.

Bibliography

Archimedes: Works. Thomas L. Heath, ed. Mineola, N.Y.: Dover, 1897.

Science in Antiquity. Benjamin Farrington. 2d ed. London: Oxford University Press, 1969.

A Source Book in Greek Science. Morris R. Cohen and Israel E. Drabkin. Cambridge, Mass.: Harvard University Press, 1948.

before the Romans were able to overwhelm and capture Syracuse.

The conquering Roman forces were under the command of a brilliant general named Marcus Claudius Marcellus. He was so impressed by the effectiveness of these weapons that he gave specific orders to his army to spare the life of Archimedes. Nevertheless, during the siege of Syracuse, with its attendant chaos, Archimedes was killed.

His Most Notable Achievement

The preeminent contribution of this gifted individual to the development of science was his discovery of the natural laws of flotation and buoyancy, which came about because of his affiliation with King Hiero II. Hiero commissioned a goldsmith to make a crown of pure gold. Upon its completion, he wanted to make sure that the crown was not alloyed with any cheaper metal, such as silver. To determine this, he called on Archimedes to devise a method that could be used to certify whether the crown was made of pure gold.

According to tradition, Archimedes spent many long hours in an unsuccessful attempt to discover a solution to this dilemma. In those days, when the king gave an order to do something, one's entire reputation, standing in the community, and life itself were at stake. One day, when Archimedes went to a designated place to take a bath, he was struck with the solution. He entered the bathtub, which was filled to the brim with water, and realized that the placement of his body was causing water to spill over the sides. At that moment, the solution became apparent to him, and he leapt from the tub shouting "Eureka"—which means "I have found it"—as he ran naked through the streets of Syracuse. Gold and silver have different densities and therefore displace different amounts of water. When the crown was placed in water, it was found that it was not pure gold.

Bibliography

By Archimedes

Epipledon isorropion (2 books; *On the Equilibrium of Planes*, 1897)

Tetragonismos ten tou orthogonion konoy tomes (*On the Quadrature of the Parabola*, 1897)

Peri sphairas kai kylindron (*On the Sphere and Cylinder*, 1897)

Peri helikon (*On Spirals*, 1897)

Peri konoeideon kai sphairoeideon (*On Conoids and Spheroids*, 1897)

Peri ochoymenon (*On Floating Bodies*, 1897)

Kykloy metresis (*On the Measurement of the Circle*, 1897)

Psiammites (*The Arenarius of Archimedes*, 1784; also as *The Sand-Reckoner*, 1897)

Peri ton mechanikon theorematon pros Erathosthenen ephodos (*On the Method of Mechanical Theorems, Addressed to Eratosthenes*, 1912)

The above translations from 1897 are found in *The Works of Archimedes*, by L. Heath.

About Archimedes

Greek Science in Antiquity. M. Clagett. Salem, N.H.: Arno Press, 1955.

Fundamentals of Physics. David Halliday and Robert Reswick. 2d ed. New York: John Wiley & Sons, 1981.

The New Columbia Encyclopedia. William H. Harris and Judith S. Levy, eds. New York: Columbia University Press, 1975.

(Joseph R. Lafaro)

Aretaeus of Cappadocia

Areas of Achievement: Medicine, pharmacology, physiology, and psychiatry

Contribution: Aretaeus, an important early physician in Greece, described the nature of many diseases, such as diabetes mellitus and tetanus, on the basis of observation and rational interpretation.

probably 2d century	Born in Cappadocia, Roman Empire (now Turkey), practices medicine, writes many texts on diseases and treatments, and dies, place and date unknown
6th century	First mentioned by such Greco-Roman authors as Aëtius of Amida, Alexander of Tralles, and Paul of Aegina
1552	His works are rediscovered when a Latin translation is published by Junius Paulus Crassus
1554	The first Greek edition of his works is published by Jacobus Goupylus
1856	The first English translation of his works is published by Francis Adams on behalf of the Sydenham Society

Historical Background

Almost nothing is known about the life of Aretaeus (pronounced "ar-uh-TEE-us") the Cappadocian. His name indicates that he was born in Cappadocia, Asia Minor, currently a portion of Turkey about 200 miles south of Ankara.

In the centuries immediately before and after the beginning of the Christian era, Asia Minor was colonized and ruled by Greeks. The area had been under Persian rule from the time of Alexander of Macedon. It became a part of the eastern Roman Empire at the beginning of the Christian era, but the nature of the inhabitants and the culture remained essentially Greek through this time. Many of the famous Greek physicians were of this Asiatic stock.

A Contemporary of Galen

Indirect evidence suggests that Aretaeus flourished in the second century and could have been a contemporary of the celebrated Greek physician Galen. One eminent authority has stated that Aretaeus was active around the year 50.

Both Galen and Aretaeus were greatly influenced by Hippocratic teaching. They also show similarity in their knowledge of anatomy and in their preferred methods of treatment. They never mention each other in their writings, a curious phenomenon that has been explained as a rivalry.

Clues to His Life

The Roman Empire was in its days of glory at this time, while the Greek Ptolemies ruled over northern Egypt. Alexandria was a great center of learning, especially for medical and scientific studies. Although Romans held the political power, Greek teaching and practice had become the intellectual driving force. Many Greek physicians came to Rome, however, to establish their practice and seek their fortune.

Aretaeus probably studied in Alexandria and Egypt, as he mentions diseases seen in Egypt. He later practiced or spent some time in Rome, as he mentions Roman foods and wines. The actual place of his practice and the date of his death, however, remain unknown.

(Library of Congress)

Aretaeus wrote in Ionic Greek, a variety of the language that was not in much use at this late date. The Hippocratic Corpus, which probably predated Aretaeus' time by four or five hundred years, was written in Ionic Greek, but the language commonly employed during the second century was the more modern Attic Greek. Aretaeus' use of

The Description of Diseases

In his description of diseases, Aretaeus depicted the characteristics of the illness with precise observation and little theory.

The great physician Hippocrates depended on observation of the patient and rejected supernatural causes of disease. Aretaeus also used inspection, palpation, and percussion in his clinical examination of patients, and many of his descriptions of diseases are superior to those of Hippocrates.

Greek medicine was based on a theory of the four humors: blood, phlegm, yellow bile, and black bile. With these were interspersed, either in conjunction or separately, qualities such as hot, cold, moist, and dry. Aretaeus was the protagonist of a school that believed in *pneuma*, a vital force. His concepts of human physiology and anatomy were generally as erroneous as his contemporaries.

Thus, Aretaeus believed the heart to be the seat of the soul and animal heat, the source of respiration and life. He thought that it drew in *pneuma* through the lungs and distributed it throughout the body through the aorta and the arteries. The liver was thought to be the source of veins and to produce blood and bile from food brought to it by the stomach and intestines. The blood was then carried to the heart by the venae cavae.

Aretaeus' description of the kidneys, the urinary bladder, and the brain are largely correct, although he believed (as did his contemporaries) that the brain secreted phlegm. His characterization of the uterus is entirely fanciful: He portrays it as a mobile organ with a capricious tendency.

Aretaeus described many diseases with great clarity. He is probably best known for his description of a wasting disease associated with unquenchable thirst and frequent, massive urination. He called this disease *diabetos* (today known as diabetes mellitus) and noted that death is rapid once the disease is fully established.

He characterized tetanus masterfully. He noted the forward-bending (*Opisthotonos*) and backward-bending (*Emprosthotonos*) forms and recognized the relationship with punctured wounds and abortion in women (although he also mentioned a blow to the neck or severe cold as other possible causes). He described the severe spasm of the jaws that prevents opening of the mouth, the impossibility of a cure, and the quick, fatal course.

He discussed jaundice arising from obstruction of the bile passages going from the gallbladder to the intestines, which causes the gallbladder to dilate, the stool to become like clay, and the skin to turn a yellowish-green. His explanation of jaundice produced by obstruction is correct, but Aretaeus also wrongly believed that it could arise in connection with the spleen, colon, stomach, and kidneys.

Aretaeus recognized the stoppage of urine from bladder stones and recommended diuretics and other measures for relief. He mentioned the use of a catheter and possible operative removal of a bladder stone. He also offered excellent descriptions of lung diseases, epilepsy, and such psychiatric conditions as mania, melancholia, and hysteria.

His therapeutic measures were rational for his time, and he used many herbs and specific foods. However, he also recommended bloodletting, although he warned against excess.

Bibliography

"Aretaeus the Cappadocian on Mental Illness." S. Kotsopoulos. *Comprehensive Psychiatry* 27, no. 2 (March/April, 1986).

Greek Medicine in Rome. Sir Thomas Allbutt. New York: Macmillan, 1921.

An Introduction to the History of Medicine. Fielding H. Garrison. 4th ed. Reprint. Philadelphia: W. B. Saunders, 1929.

"On the Term Diabetes in the Works of Aretaeus and Galen." F. Henschen. *Medical History* 13, no. 2 (April, 1969).

Ionic Greek has been ascribed to his respect for Hippocrates.

Obscurity

After Hippocrates, Aretaeus can be considered the most observant and rational of the Greek medical authors. It is thus surprising that his work was not discussed in any extant texts of the following three hundred years. He is finally mentioned by such Greco-Roman authors as Aëtius of Amida and Alexander of Tralles in the sixth century, as well as by Paul of Aegina almost seventy years later.

He was also totally neglected by the Arabs, who had great respect for the Greco-Roman medical authors and translated many of their ancient texts into Syriac and later Arabic and Persian. The resurgence of medical knowledge in Europe started through the introduction of these Arab medical texts and, as the Arabs had ignored Aretaeus, so did the early European medical schools.

Rediscovery

The rediscovery of Aretaeus' opus was quite accidental. With the invention of printing and the rebirth of academic activity, large numbers of ancient Greek and Latin texts were printed. The first edition of the works of Aretaeus was a 1552 Latin translation of "an old and worm-eaten book written in Greek, which accidentally has fallen into my hands" by Junius Paulus Crassus, a professor in Pavia, Italy.

The first Greek edition of Aretaeus' works was published in 1554 from Paris by Jacobus Goupylus, who brought out a Latin edition the same year and a more complete, revised Latin edition in 1581. A number of Greek-Latin editions were subsequently published in Germany and England.

Evidence of the importance of Aretaeus' place in the Hippocratic tradition is an edition under the direction of Hermann Boerhaave, who had already edited the texts of Hippocrates and Galen. Boerhaave, the most fa-mous European physician and teacher of his time, was known as *Hippocrates redivivus* ("Hippocrates reborn"). His edition is noted for its excellent comments and detailed indexes.

The first Greek-English edition was published in 1856 by Francis Adams on behalf of the Sydenham Society. Unfortunately, the reprint of this edition by the Classics of Medicine Library in 1990 omits Adams' valuable introduction. In addition, an excellent Greek-German edition edited by Karl Hunde was published in 1923.

Books by Aretaeus on fever, surgery, gynecology, prophylaxis, and pharmacy have been mentioned in other texts but have never been found.

Bibliography

By Aretaeus

On the Causes and Symptoms of Acute Diseases: Books I and II

On the Causes and Symptoms of Chronic Diseases: Books I and II

On the Cure of Chronic Diseases: Book I

On the Therapeutics of Acute Diseases: Books I and II

On the Therapeutics of Chronic Diseases: Book II

These extant works were written in Greek. The English titles are taken from *The Extant Works of Aretaeus, the Cappadocian*. Francis Adams, ed. and trans. London: Sydenham Society, 1856. Reprint. Birmingham, Ala.: Classics of Medicine Library, 1990.

About Aretaeus

"Aretaeus of Cappadocia." Fridolf Kudlien. In *Dictionary of Scientific Biography*, edited by Charles Coulston Gillespie. Vol. 2. New York: Charles Scribner's Sons, 1970-   .

"Aretaeus the Cappadocian: His Contribution to Diabetes Mellitus." E. Leopold. *Annuals of Medical History* 2 (1930).

(Ranès C. Chakravorty)

Aristarchus of Samos

Areas of Achievement: Astronomy and mathematics

Contribution: Aristarchus was the first person to calculate the size of the sun and its distance from the earth and to propose a heliocentric theory of the universe.

c. 310 B.C.E.	Born on Samos
280 B.C.E.	According to Ptolemy, makes observations of the summer solstice
c. 250 B.C.E.	Completes the work known as *On the Sizes and Distances of the Sun and Moon*
c. 250 B.C.E.	Proposes the first heliocentric theory of the universe
c. 230 B.C.E.	Dies in Alexandria

Life

Very little is known about the life of Aristarchus (pronounced "ar-uh-STAHR-kus"). He was born about 310 B.C.E., and his native island, Samos, is in the Aegean Sea off the coast of Turkey. He studied with Strato of Lampsacos, probably in Alexandria before Strato went to Athens to head Aristotle's Lyceum.

Although he was known as "the mathematician," Aristarchus clearly had a practical bent. The Roman writer Vitruvius credited him with inventing a type of sundial, and Ptolemy refers to his observations of the summer solstice of 280 B.C.E. He died in Alexandria about 230 B.C.E.

Calculations Regarding the Sun and Moon

The only surviving work of Aristarchus is the manuscript commonly known as *On the Sizes and Distances of the Sun and Moon* (written c. 250 B.C.E.; English translation, 1913). Reminiscent of an exercise in Euclidean geometry, the work poses the problem of finding the size of and distance to the sun relative to the moon and the earth.

Aristarchus found that the sun is between eighteen and twenty times further than the moon and between 7.1666 and 6.333 times bigger than the earth. Although these results are much too low, they were the first hints of the immense size of the universe.

A Heliocentric Universe

Possibly impressed by the great size of the sun, Aristarchus entertained the possibility that the earth might circle the sun, rather than the other way around. It probably made sense to him to assume that the heavenly body that was thought to be the largest in the universe would dominate the motions of the other bodies. In all likelihood, Aristarchus assumed that all the planets circled the sun. The early Pythagoreans had believed in a similar scheme with ten bodies circling a "central fire" that was definitely

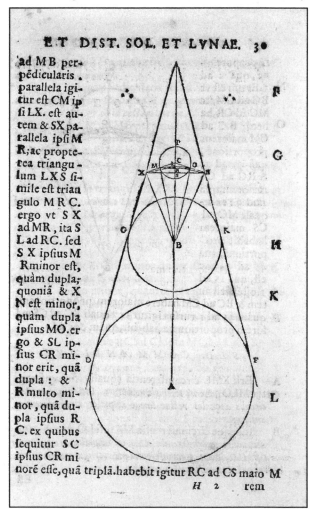

A geometric figure of the moon, earth, and sun calculated by Aristarchus. (Library of Congress)

The Size of and Distance to the Sun

Aristarchus observed that the sun is much further from the earth than the moon and, consequently, much bigger than the earth.

Aristarchus' *On the Sizes and Distances of the Sun and Moon* begins in accepted mathematical style, listing assumptions. He explicitly notes three assumptions: first, that the sun illuminates the moon; second, that the earth's shadow at the moon is twice the diameter of the moon; and, third, that the moon appears half full when the moon-earth-sun angle is 87 degrees. He also tacitly assumes, fourth, that the moon's orbit is a perfect circle around the earth and, fifth, that the sun's rays are parallel at the earth and moon.

From the third and fifth assumptions, Aristarchus calculated that the sun is 19 times further from the earth than the moon; the correct figure is more than 400 times. His third assumption is wrong: The angle is not 87 degrees but 89.87 degrees. With the correct value, his method provides reliable results.

Since the moon is the same visual (angular) size as the sun, using the second assumption Aristarchus then calculated that the sun is about 7 times bigger than the earth; the correct figure is about 109.

Despite the shortcomings of Aristarchus' results, his work led to important improvements. In the next century, his methods were used and improved by Hipparchus of Rhodes to obtain excellent values of the size and distance of the moon.

Bibliography

"Archimedes and Aristarchus." Otto Neugebauer. *Isis* 39 (1942).

A History of Planetary Systems from Thales to Kepler. John L. E. Dreyer. Cambridge, England: Cambridge University Press, 1953.

Theories of the World from Antiquity to the Copernican Revolution. Michael J. Crowe. New York: Dover, 1990.

not the sun. Thus, the Pythagorean system was not heliocentric (sun-centered).

The heliocentric idea brought ridicule to Aristarchus. The Stoic poet Cleathes charged him with impiety for daring to put in motion "the hearth of the heavens." From a scientific perspective, the daily motions of the sun and other heavenly bodies in a heliocentric system can only be explained by requiring the earth to rotate. At the time, there was no reason to believe in a rotating earth. Furthermore, any motion of the earth around the sun should produce an apparent change in the position of the stars (parallax), which was not observed.

Aristarchus explained this lack of parallax by assuming that the stars were very far away and, in so doing, he made the universe unacceptably large. As a result, heliocentric theory languished until it was revived by Nicolaus Copernicus in the sixteenth century and extended by Johannes Kepler and Sir Isaac Newton.

Bibliography

By Aristarchus

On the Sizes and Distances of the Sun and Moon, c. 250 B.C.E. (English translation, 1913)

About Aristarchus

"Aristarchus of Samos." In *The Dictionary of Scientific Biography*. New York: Charles Scribner's Sons, 1970.

Aristarchus of Samos. Sir Thomas Heath. Oxford, England: Oxford University Press, 1913.

"Copernicus' Relation to Aristarchus and Pythagoras." Thomas W. Africa. *Isis* 52 (1961).

(John A. Cramer)

Aristotle

Areas of Achievement: Astronomy, biology, physics, physiology, and zoology

Contribution: Aristotle founded the systematic study of logic and greatly influenced the methodology of science. His writings have been particularly important to astronomy, biology, physics, psychology, and theology.

384 B.C.E.	Born in Stagirus, Chalcidice, Greece
367 B.C.E.	Travels to Athens and begins studies at Plato's Academy
347 B.C.E.	Leaves the Academy upon the death of Plato
347-343 B.C.E.	Attends the court of Hermias at Assos in Asia Minor, marries Pythias, and moves to the island of Lesbos to continue his biological investigations
342 B.C.E.	Called to the court of Philip of Macedonia to tutor Philip's son, Alexander
335 B.C.E.	Returns to Athens, where he founds the Lyceum and begins teaching there
323 B.C.E.	Moves to Chalcis on the Aegean island of Euboea
322 B.C.E.	Dies in Chalcis, Euboea, Greece

(Library of Congress)

Early Life

Aristotle (pronounced "AHR-uh-stawt-ul") was born in the Ionian colony of Stagirus in northern Greece. His father, Nicomachus, was the personal physician to Amyntas II, king of Macedonia and grandfather of Alexander the Great. Both of Aristotle's parents died while he was young, so Aristotle was reared by Proxenus, a friend of the family.

When he reached seventeen years of age, Aristotle was sent to Athens to study at Plato's Academy. His studies continued for twenty years, but he left the Academy to study with others during the latter part of that time. Upon the death of Plato, Aristotle was passed over for leadership of the Academy, and with anti-Macedonian sentiment increasing, it seemed wise to leave Athens.

Life Abroad

Aristotle traveled with Xenocrates, a fellow student at the Academy, to the court of Hermias, the king of Atarneos and Assos in Ionia. Hermias had once been a student at the Academy and was gathering a group of scholars at his court. While there, Aristotle met and married his first wife, Pythias, and also found a new friend in the naturalist Theophrastus. Pythias eventually bore a daughter, also named Pythias, and a son, Nicomachus.

Aristotle moved his family to the nearby island of Lesbos, where he worked with Theophrastus and made many excellent zoological observations. In 343 B.C.E., Philip of Macedonia asked Aristotle to come to Mieza, near Pella in Macedonia, to tutor his thirteen-year-old son, Alexander, who was to become known as Alexander the Great. After three years of study with

Aristotle, affairs of state so occupied the young Alexander that his formal studies came to a halt. Aristotle was well paid and eventually became quite wealthy.

The Lyceum in Athens

Athens was now ruled by the Macedonians, and Aristotle returned there about 335 B.C.E. Aristotle began teaching at the Lyceum, one of three public centers of learning in Athens. The character of the Lyceum was so influenced by Aristotle that he is often considered its founder.

Whereas Plato and his Academy concentrated on abstract ideas, Aristotle promoted a hands-on study of the material world. To this end, Aristotle, along with his students and colleagues, collected specimens for a natural history museum and gathered maps and manuscripts for a library. Exhibits from the museum and the contents of the Lyceum library were later taken to Alexandria, Egypt, where they

Inductive Reasoning

Scientific reasoning is often based on induction, a rational method to go beyond the evidence at hand and reach a conclusion that is probably true.

The field of logic concerns the methods and principles used to distinguish between valid and invalid arguments. Aristotle not only created logic as a field of study but also produced an amazingly complete system of logic. No one since Aristotle has matched this feat.

Aristotle's writings on logic are grouped together under the title, *Organon*, meaning "instrument"; that is, logic is the instrument used to obtain abstract knowledge. What today is called "logical," Aristotle called "analytic" or "following from the premises." In a valid deductive argument, if the premises are true, the conclusion must of necessity be true. For example:

Premise A: All canaries are yellow.
Premise B: This bird is a canary.
Conclusion C: Therefore, this bird is yellow.

If the premises were correct, even a colorblind person could deduce that a particular bird is yellow, if this person could otherwise determine that it was a canary. Deductive arguments typically use general statements to establish knowledge about a particular individual or case.

A common form of scientific argument requires a general truth to be abstracted from the examination of many individual cases. This process is called inductive generalization. For example, if one drops keys and they fall, drops a book and it falls, and drops an apple and it falls, one may conclude by inductive generalization that if one drops a dinner plate, it will probably fall.

For inductive arguments, the conclusion is not tied as firmly to the premises as it is for deductive arguments. To reach the stronger conclusion that whenever something is dropped, it will necessarily fall, one would need to drop every possible object under every possible condition—clearly an unrealistic requirement.

In concluding that if one drops a dinner plate, it will probably fall, one has actually made the generalization that whenever one drops something, it will fall. While it is reasonable, this generalization is not strictly logical, in that it does not follow of necessity from the premise statements.

Can one be 100 percent certain of the result if all the known factors that might affect the outcome of dropping a plate are taken into account? (For example, the plate must not be held by someone else when one lets go, and there must not be a strong wind blowing upward.) Strictly speaking, the answer is no, since no guarantees exist that some currently unknown factor will not occur. The great success of science, however, has come by assuming that the same laws of physics that operate today will also operate tomorrow (itself an inductive generalization). If one drops a plate tomorrow, one expects it to fall.

Bibliography
Aristotle. John Ferguson. New York: Twayne, 1972.
A History of Formal Logic. I. M. Bochenski. Translated by Ivo Thomas. New York: Chelsea, 1970.
A History of Western Science. Anthony M. Alioto. Englewood Cliffs, N.J.: Prentice Hall, 1987.

became the core of the great research library and museum of Alexandria.

During this time period, Aristotle's wife died, and he took a second wife, Herpyllis. When Alexander the Great died in 323 B.C.E., Aristotle was threatened by the anti-Macedonian party of Athens. He fled to the safety of his mother's hometown, Chalcis, on the Aegean island of Euboea. Aristotle died from an illness a year later, at the age of sixty-two.

Legacy

Aristotle's writings comprise the greatest encyclopedia of the ancient world. For better, but sometimes for worse, his conclusions and philosophy have exerted enormous influence. For nearly two thousand years, most of the important advances in the Western world in philosophy, physical science, and biological science were made with inspiration from Aristotle's works. (Plato's works also had great influence, especially in philosophy.)

Sometime after Aristotle's death, his works were taken to the great library in Alexandria, Egypt. During the fourth and fifth centuries, they were translated into Syriac and Arabic

Mechanics of Motion

Aristotle's theories provided a coherent explanation for the commonly observed motions of objects.

Aristotle's theories of motion are an excellent example of his philosophy that the actions of nature should be not only observed and recorded but also explained, and that this explanation should be as general as possible. According to him, how an object moved depended on its composition, its location, and the forces acting on it.

Aristotle considered all the objects in the universe to be constructed from five fundamental elements: ether, fire, air, water, and earth. It was the nature of each element to strive to reach its proper place in the universe. Thus, if bodies composed of earth were scattered throughout the universe, they would naturally draw together at the center of the universe. Since each portion of the earth would strive equally to reach the center, the resulting shape would be a sphere. This explained the known spherical shape of the earth.

The place of water was above the earth element, and the place of air lay above that. The proper realm of fire extended from the upper reaches of the atmosphere out to the orbit of the moon. (Fire was the element of change, and, above the orbit of the moon, the heavens were thought to be unchangeable.)

Natural motion resulted when a body was displaced from its natural position and sought to return. Raindrops fall through the air to the earth. Water under the ground bubbles up in springs, just as fire strives upward toward its realm above the air. Most objects were thought to be mixtures of elements. For example, a wooden block, being a different mixture of air, water, and earth, might fall more slowly than a stone. The motion of an arrow through the air was considered to be a combination of natural motion and violent (forced) motion.

The heavenly bodies were supposedly made of ether. Their natural motion was to move in circles. Aristotle realized that the apparent motions of heavenly bodies across the sky would also be explained if the earth rotated daily on its axis and orbited the sun yearly.

Aristotle supposed that two stars should appear to move closer together as the earth moved away from them in its orbit. Since he did not see this effect (called stellar parallax), he concluded that the earth does not orbit the sun. Aristotle's mistake lay in assuming that the stars were not much further from the earth than the sun is. Although stars are too far away for stellar parallax to be observed with the naked eye, its measurement with modern instruments is the fundamental way used to determine distances to the stars.

Bibliography

Foresight and Understanding. Stephen Toulmin. Bloomington: Indiana University Press, 1961.

"Galileo and the Fall of Aristotle: A Case of Historical Injustice?" Barry M. Casper. *American Journal of Physics* (April, 1977).

Revolutions in Physics. Barry M. Casper and Richard J. Noer. New York: W. W. Norton, 1972.

Studies in Biology

Aristotle is considered to be one of the greatest biologists of all times. His extensive observations and his theories were often far ahead of his time.

Although Aristotle made contributions to anatomy, physiology, and botany, his major success was in zoology. Indeed, he is often regarded as the founder of this field. He named and described more than five hundred currently recognized species. Most of them belong to Greece and its surrounding seas.

Since the Greeks used honey, it was natural for Aristotle to study honey bees. He carefully described their birth, the roles of drones and workers, and details of the bee sting, although he did mistake the queen bee for a king.

Although most fish produce eggs that later hatch, Aristotle described placental dogfish, which give birth to live baby dogfish. In studying a particular species of catfish, he noted that it was the male that cared for the eggs after they were produced by the female. In both of these cases, Aristotle's claims seemed so contrary to nature that later scientists scoffed at them. It was not until the nineteenth century that they were confirmed by other zoologists.

As might be expected, in passing on travelers' tales of exotic animals that he had not personally observed, Aristotle made mistakes. He did reject the tale of the mythical manticore. He discussed the leg joints of the lion and deduced that it did not need to lean against a tree to sleep, as tradition claimed, since it could lie down. He passed on such nonsense, however, as that lion bones were so hard that they produced sparks when struck and that the crocodile's upper jaw was jointed in the lower jaw.

Observing the growth of chicken embryos, he noted the appearance of the beating heart before other organs were formed. This may have led to Aristotle's view that the heart was the seat of the soul and mind. (He supposed that the brain was simply a radiator to cool the blood.)

Aristotle attempted to form a complete theory of biology beginning with what it is that makes living creatures alive. He supposed that each living thing had a soul that governed its growth and dictated its shape. The soul of a plant impelled it to seek nourishment and governed reproduction. The soul of an animal did all of this and also allowed the animal to feel and move. The human soul added the capacity to reason.

Such ideas led Aristotle to construct a "ladder of nature" that began with inanimate matter at the bottom, went through plants and increasingly complex animals, and reached humans at the top. Two thousand years later, this ladder of nature became the stepping stone to the theory of evolution. Along with Aristotle's other classification schemes, it also led to the classification schemes used today.

Bibliography

Aristotle. John Ferguson. New York: Twayne, 1972.

The History of Biology. Erik Nordenskiöld. Translated by Leonard Bucknall Eyre. New York: Tudor, 1928.

The Science of Life. Gordon Rattray Taylor. New York: McGraw-Hill, 1963.

and circulated in the Muslim world. Because of this, many of his works escaped destruction when the Alexandrian library was sacked and burned. The Western world's recovery of Aristotle's writings during the thirteenth and fourteenth centuries was one of the important forces in sparking the Renaissance.

Writings

Aristotle's works are divided into three groups: popular writings, memoranda, and treatises. The popular writings are generally in the form of Plato's dialogues and are thought to have been written while Aristotle was at the Academy. They received high praise from his contemporaries, but unfortunately only fragments have survived.

The memoranda were mostly collections of research notes and historical materials. While some, such as *Athenaion politeia* (c. 380 B.C.E.; *The Athenian Constitution*, 1812) have survived, most have been lost. The scientific and philosophical treatises constitute most of the surviving writings. They appear to be a combination of lecture notes, student notes, and texts written for student use.

Bibliography

By Aristotle
All of the following works were written between 335 and 323 B.C.E.:

Aristotelous peri geneseos kai phthoras (*Meteoroligica*, 1812)

Athenaion politeia (*The Athenian Constitution*, 1812)

De anima (*On the Soul*, 1812)

De poetica (*Poetics*, 1705)

Ethica Nicomachea (*Nicomachean Ethics*, 1797)

Metaphysica (*Metaphysics*, 1801)

Organon, made up of *Categoriae*, *De Interpretatione*, *Analytica Priora*, *Analytica Posteriora*, *Topica*, and *De Sophisticis Elenchis* (English translation, 1812, made up of *Categories*, *On Interpretation*, *Prior Analytics*, *Posterior Analytics*, *Topics*, and *On Sophistical Refutations*)

Physica (*Physics*, 1812)

Politica (*Politics*, 1598)

Techne rhetorikes (*Rhetoric*, 1686)

These works, as well as many others and a volume of fragments, are available as *The Works of Aristotle Translated into English*. William David Ross and John Alexander Smith, eds. 12 vols. Oxford, England: Clarendon Press, 1908-1952.

About Aristotle
Aristotle. G. R. G. Mure. New York: Oxford University Press, 1964.

Aristotle for Everybody. Mortimer J. Adler. New York: Macmillan, 1978.

Introduction to Aristotle. Richard McKeon. 1947. Reprint. Chicago: University of Chicago Press, 1973.

(*Charles W. Rogers*)

Arnold of Villanova

Areas of Achievement: Medicine and pharmacology

Contribution: Arnold of Villanova, a physician and medical scholar, was instrumental in rationalizing and making medical science systematic. He attempted to apply mathematics to medieval medicine, which helped to transform medical theory.

c. 1239	Born, perhaps in Valencia, Aragon, or the Provence region, France
c. 1260	Studies medicine at the University of Montpellier
c. 1281	Serves as personal physician to Peter III, king of Aragon
c. 1285	Translates Avicenna's *De viribus cordis* and Galen's *De rigore*
1288	Begins work on *De adventu antichristi*
1291-1299	Becomes a master of medicine at Montpellier
c. 1295	Completes *De intentione medicorum*
c. 1299	Completes *Aphorismi de gradibus*
c. 1299	*De adventu antichristi* is condemned by the Parisian faculty
1299	Serves as the personal physician to Pope Boniface VIII
1304	Completes *De esu carnium*
1305	Becomes physician and adviser to Pope Clement V
1309	Loses the favor of James II of Aragon and Pope Clement V
Sept. 6, 1311	Dies at sea near Genoa

Early Life
Arnold of Villanova—also known as Arnau de Villanova, Arnaud de Villeneuve, or Arnaldus Villanovanus, among other names—was born

in about 1239, probably in the kingdom of Aragon. Almost nothing is known of his early life or adulthood. It is possible that his parents were of Jewish origin and that his place of birth was Valencia, a city that had been recently reconquered from the Muslims by James I.

Arnold studied medicine around 1260 at the University of Montpellier, which was developing into a center of medical research and education. After the completion of his professional training, he secured the position of personal physician to Peter III of Aragon. He also served as personal physician to the succeeding kings, Alfonso III and James II.

Arnold was instrumental in the enormous task of translating and absorbing the accumulated heritage of medical knowledge of the Greeks and Arabs. He was perfectly qualified, and he was in the perfect place for such a task. Aragon was a region of fruitful mixing of Christian, Muslim, and Jewish cultures. Arnold was fluent in Arabic and for a short time had even studied Hebrew at a Dominican house in Barcelona in the early 1280's. Around this time, he began translating authoritative medical treatises. Into Latin from Arabic, he translated Avicenna's *De viribus cordis* and Galen's *De rigore*. The work of translating was one that he continued throughout his career.

Master of Medicine

In 1291, Arnold took up residence in Montpellier at the newly created *studium generale* (a medieval term for university) as a master (in modern terms, a professor) of medical science. This was a relatively quiet period in Arnold's life but one of great productivity and significance. He became immersed in the classical and Arab medical works that were to become, in large part because of him, the bedrock of medical learning.

Arnold continued translating and offered detailed lectures on the works of Hippocrates and Galen. He also began the process of creating unusually extensive commentaries on the same authors, which was the way in which medieval scholars absorbed, understood, and modified the scientific theories of earlier scientists.

The tradition of Western medicine to which Arnold was heir had not emphasized earlier knowledge, nor had it been at all systematic.

During this era, Arnold began to change that situation and started a process of synthesis between Greek-Arabic medical theory and western European empirical understanding of disease and treatment. It was during this time that he argued that medicine was not simply an art to be practiced (although he certainly believed in and practiced medicine as an art as well) but also a science to be understood. Sometime during this scientifically productive period, he wrote *De intentione medicorum* which was an effective and convincing argument that medicine must be reduced to rational elements, instead of merely practiced artfully. While a master of medicine, Arnold probably came cross al-Kindi's *Quia primas*, which suggested that there could be a precise way to quantify the effect of a drug on the body. This idea propelled Arnold into the advocacy of "mathematical medicine."

From Medicine to Theology

Arnold was not interested only in medicine. As early as 1288, he began to be interested in theology and apocalyptic ideas. While he was at

(New York Academy of Medicine)

Montpellier, this interest blossomed. There, he met Peter John Olivi of the Spiritual Franciscans and became convinced of the eminent return of Christ.

While on a diplomatic mission to Paris for James II of Aragon, he presented his ideas contained in *De adventu antichristi* to the faculty of theology and was condemned for his ideas.

The threat of imprisonment was lifted by the intervention of Pope Boniface VIII, who, because of Arnold's expertise as a physician, employed the renowned doctor.

The pope preferred that his personal physician focus his attention entirely on medicine and leave theology to the clergy. Arnold, however, would not take such advice, and, when

Mathematical Medicine

Arnold of Villanova argued that medicine was not merely an art but must be reduced to the rational principles that created a coherent science. He proposed a mathematical relationship between the amount of an administered compound drug and its effect on the patient's body.

Arnold of Villanova suggested that medicine, and more particularly pharmacology, ought to be guided by systematic theory grounded in precise mathematical relationships. Although his idea of mathematizing the effect of drugs was not ultimately correct, it did provide a foundation on which medical science could build.

Arnold suggested, as a result of the inspiration of al-Kindi, that one could relate the effects of a drug on the body, depending on the components of the drug itself and the relative increase in the quantity of those components. Put in more mathematical language, the degree of intensity of a drug (consisting of two parts) grows arithmetically when the ratio of those opposing parts grows geometrically.

Arnold's idea is impossible to understand except in the context of medieval medicine, which was based (when it evolved into a model) on the Galenic system of four humors: blood, phlegm, yellow bile, and black bile. These humors were closely associated with the four elements: air, water, fire, and earth. Blood was analogous to air, phlegm to water, yellow bile to fire, and black bile to earth. The body was conceived as consisting of these four humors which, when balanced, made the body healthy and, when unbalanced, caused disease. The purpose of compound medicines was to restore the balance among the four humors.

In addition, the humors were based on Aristotelian qualities that were explained in terms of opposing pairs: hot-cold, wet-dry. Therefore, a compound medicine, according to the theory of the time, consisted of two opposing qualities. If physicians wished to prescribe such medicine, they could then predict its effect on the patient by Arnold's law, which in symbols may be represented as

$$I = D/W, \; 2I = (D/W)^2 \ldots, \; nI = (D/W)^n$$

where I represents the perceived intensity of the effect on the body and D and W represent the qualities dry and wet, which may be substituted with any required quality. Notice that the geometric increase in the qualities is supposed to result in an arithmetic increase in the effect.

Arnold's mathematical principle, explained in his work *Aphorismi de gradibus* (c. 1299), although not strictly correct, was significant to the development of medicine and pharmacology because it encouraged the attempt to relate precisely the effects of a drug to the drug itself. The law did hint at the medical truth that increasing the quantity of a drug certainly fails to produce an equally large increase in its effect. Arnold's medical ideas, presented in such mathematical terms, were a forceful way of transforming medical thought from a virtual folk art into an early science.

Bibliography

"Arnald of Villanova and Bradwardine's Law." Michael McVaugh. *Isis* 58 (1967).

"The *Experimenta* of Arnald of Villanova." Michael McVaugh. *Journal of Medieval and Renaissance Studies* 1 (1971).

"Quantified Theory and Practice of Fourteenth-Century Montpellier." Michael Mc Vaugh. *Bulletin of the History of Medicine* 43 (1969).

his friend Bertrand de Got rose to the papacy as Clement V in 1305, Arnold strongly advocated church reform. Clement V was not open to implementing these ideas on church reform, but he did endorse Arnold's views about employing more classical texts and commentaries at the University of Montpellier.

Arnold's position came to an end when he called into question James II's orthodoxy and advocated radical reform too strongly. He fell out of favor in 1309 and spent the last two years of his life protected by James's brother, Frederick II of Sicily. Arnold died in 1311 while at sea and was buried in Genoa.

Bibliography
By Arnold of Villanova
De conservatione juventutis et retardatione senectutis, 1290 (*The Conservation of Youth and Defense of Age*, 1544)
Allocutio super Tetragrammaton, 1292 (addresses on the word of four letters)
De intentione medicorum, c. 1295 (on the practice of medicine)
Aphorismi de gradibus, c. 1299 (aphorisms on degrees)
De adventu antichristi, 1299 (on the coming of the Antichrist)
De sigillis, c. 1300 (on signs)
De esu carnium, 1304 (on the consumption of flesh)
Regimen sanitatis, 1307 (management of health)
Opera, 1504
Opera medica omnia, 1975 (incomplete)

About Arnold of Villanova
"Arnald of Villanova." John F. Benton. In *Dictionary of the Middle Ages*, edited by Joseph R. Strayer. Vol. 1. New York: Charles Scribner's Sons, 1982.
"Arnald of Villanova." Michael McVaugh. In *Dictionary of Scientific Biography*, edited by Charles Coulston Gillispie. Vol. 1. New York: Charles Scribner's Sons, 1970.
Medicine Before the Plague: Practitioners and Their Patients in the Crown of Aragon, 1285-1345. Michael McVaugh. Cambridge, England: Cambridge University Press, 1993.

(Peter K. Benbow)

Svante A. Arrhenius

Areas of Achievement: Chemistry and physics

Contribution: Arrhenius developed an explanation for electrolysis from which he was able to define acids, bases, and salts. He also developed the Arrhenius equation, a mathematical expression that describes the effect on temperature on the speed of a chemical reaction.

Feb. 19, 1859	Born in Castle of Vik, near Uppsala, Sweden
1884	Defends his doctoral thesis on the theory on ionic dissociation
1886	Receives a traveling fellowship from the Swedish Academy of Sciences
1895	Serves as a professor of physics at the Royal Institute of Technology in Stockholm
1901	Elected to the Swedish Academy of Sciences
1902	Awarded the Davy Medal of the Royal Society of London
1903	Receives the Nobel Prize in Chemistry
1905	Serves as the director of the Nobel Institute for Physical Chemistry in Stockholm
1911	Visits the United States, where he gives the Sillman Lectures at Yale University and receives the Willard Gibbs Medal
1912	Publishes *Theories of Solutions*
1915	Publishes *Quantitative Laws in Biological Chemistry*
Oct. 2, 1927	Dies in Stockholm, Sweden

Early Life

Svante August Arrhenius (pronounced "ahr-RAY-nee-uhs") was born near Uppsala, Sweden, in 1859. He was a very bright child, and it is said that he taught himself to read at the age of three. He developed his interest in mathematics by watching his father add up columns of numbers. He pursued his interests in chemistry, mathematics, and physics at Uppsala University.

Arrhenius moved to Stockholm to work with Erik Edlund, a well-known chemist at that time. Arrhenius developed an explanation for why certain substances conduct electric currents in solutions. This area was a difficult one in which to conduct research because little was known about the structure of atoms at that time.

The significance of Arrhenius' work was not appreciated, however, and he received a low

Arrhenius' Ionic Hypothesis

Arrhenius proposed that electrolytes in solution conduct electricity as a result of molecules splitting into positive and negative ions.

Chemists used electrochemical cells to isolate and identify many elements more than fifty years before Arrhenius began his work in the 1880's. It was known that electrical currents were conducted by certain substances and had no impact on other substances. Arrhenius proposed that some substances, when dissolved in an appropriate solvent such as water, separate (disassociate) into positively and negatively charged particles called ions. This process occurs because of an interaction between the molecules of the dissolved material and the molecules of the solvent.

Arrhenius believed that the kinds of ions present in a solution determine whether the dissolved substance (the solute) should be classified as an acid, a base, or a salt. He defined acids as substances that produce hydrogen ions and bases as substances that produce hydroxide ions. The ions produced by salts are neither hydrogen ions nor hydroxide ions. Prior to this time, acids and bases were characterized as molecules with certain properties in common, such as whether they produce reactions with indicators, taste sour or bitter, feel slippery, or neutralize the expressed properties of another substance. Acids and bases were also defined as substances derived from reactions when metals or nonmetals react with oxygen. Such later scientists as Johannes Brønsted and Gilbert N. Lewis developed more comprehensive definitions of acids, bases, and salts.

Many chemists were skeptical about the ionic hypothesis. Problems resulted from attempts to extend the concept of the ionization of dissolved

materials to nearly every chemical reaction and assumptions that molecules do not react at all. J. W. Mellor, a famous inorganic chemist, noted that "in spite of the ionic hypothesis, chemical reactions do take place in non-conducting solutions, and these reactions are similar in result and speed to those which occur in conducting aqueous solutions." Chemists at the beginning of the twentieth century had little knowledge about the interactions that occur between solutes and solvents. These interactions cannot be fully appreciated unless the "polar" character of many molecules is understood. This information was not widely available for another thirty years.

The ionic hypothesis did help explain why some substances when dissolved in solution produce changes in the physical properties of the solution that are inconsistent with the number of molecules that are present. When a substance dissolves in water or some other solvent, the normal freezing point, boiling point, osmotic pressure, and some other properties of the liquid change. The magnitude of the change depends on the number of particles present. When molecules form ions, the number of particles increases, thus increasing the boiling point or lowering the freezing point of the solution more than would be anticipated from a substance that remains in molecular form.

Bibliography

Foundations of the Theory of Dilute Solutions. Svante Arrhenius. 1887. Reprint. Edinburgh, Scotland: Alembic Club, 1929.

Modern Inorganic Chemistry. J. W. Mellor. London: Longmans, Green, 1916.

Theories of Solutions. Svante Arrhenius. Cambridge, Mass.: Harvard University Press, 1912.

The Arrhenius Equation

Arrhenius developed the mathematical relationship between the temperature of a chemical reaction and the rate at which reactants are converted into products.

Each chemical reaction has a reaction rate constant that is determined by the chemical nature of the molecules and the numbers of molecules involved in the reaction. The rate constant, which is sensitive to temperature, is determined by the individual reaction step that requires the most time. The activation energy, which determines the stability of the reactants, is the energy needed for reacting molecules to undergo "molecular damage" in collisions with other molecules. The higher the temperature of a chemical reaction, the easier it is to supply reacting molecules with the required amount of activation energy.

The equation proposed by Arrhenius has the form $k = s\, e^{-Ea/RT}$, where k is the reaction rate constant, s is a numerical constant for the reaction, Ea is the activation energy of the reaction, R is the thermodynamic constant, and T is the absolute temperature of the reaction. The following is a more useful form of the equation:

$$\log \frac{k_2}{k_1} = \frac{E_a}{2.303R}\, \frac{(T_2 - T_1)}{(T_1 T_2)}$$

The significance of the Arrhenius equation is that it allows scientists to predict how the rate of a reaction will change with temperature if the activation energy is known. Reaction rates can be measured easily at various temperatures, and this information can be used to calculate the activation energy.

Bibliography
Physical Chemistry. Farrington Daniels and Robert Alberty. 2d ed. New York: John Wiley & Sons, 1961.

passing grade when he submitted his theory as the thesis for his doctoral degree. Chemists at that time were more interested in accurate experimental work than they were in theoretical explanations for why certain chemical reactions occurred. He was also working in an area that was not clearly defined as either chemistry or physics.

Professional Development
From 1886 to 1890, Arrhenius used his traveling fellowship from the Swedish Academy of Sciences to work with many of the prominent scientists in Germany and the Netherlands. During this time, he refined his theory of ionization and gradually gained a following. When he was offered a post at one of the prominent universities in Germany, he soon received a position at the Royal Institute of Technology in Sweden. He was well known and well respected outside Sweden, but there was significant opposition to his election to the Swedish Academy of Sciences in 1901.

The international fame for Arrhenius reached its high point in 1903 when he was awarded the Nobel Prize in Chemistry. He was the first person from Sweden to win a Nobel Prize. The offer of a position as chair at the University of Berlin in 1905, the most prominent post available to an academic chemist in Europe, promoted the creation of a position for him in Sweden as the director of the Nobel Institute for Physical Chemistry in Stockholm. This job gave him an opportunity to continue his research and his writing.

Arrhenius, the Scientist
Arrhenius was unusual in that he was able to look beyond data and identify mathematical relationships. This talent was appreciated by only the more imaginative scientists of his time. His theory of ionization and its application in defining acids, bases, and salts have been cornerstones of chemistry. Other chemists have used the Arrhenius definitions as starting points for developing more comprehensive descriptions of the chemical activities of acids, bases, and salts. Arrhenius was able to use the work of J. J. Hood to develop a more comprehensive explanation of the impact of temperature on the velocity of a wide range of chemical reactions. This work has practical ap-

(Library of Congress)

plications in nearly every aspect of chemical research today.

Arrhenius was awarded the Nobel Prize at the midpoint of his career, and, as the director of the Nobel Institute, he was able to spend time pursuing scientific interests in immunology, geology, and cosmology. He proposed an explanation for the propagation of the universe that is not supported by the theories of modern cosmology, although his ideas were new and interesting.

Bibliography
By Arrhenius
Lärobok i theoretisk elektrokemi, 1900 (*Text-book of Electrochemistry*, 1902)
Lehrbuch der kosmischen Physik, 1903
Theorien der Chemie, 1906 (*Theories of Chemistry*, 1907)
Världarnas utveckling, 1906 (*Worlds in the Making*, 1908)
Immunochemistry, 1907
Människan inför världsgåtan, 1907 (*The Life of the Universe*, 1909)
Theories of Solutions, 1912
Quantitative Laws in Biological Chemistry, 1915
Stjärnornas Öden, 1915 (*Destinies of the Stars*, 1918)
Kemien och der moderna livet, 1919 (*Chemistry in Modern Life*, 1925)
Erde und Weltall, 1926

About Arrhenius
Arrhenius: From Ionic Theory to the Greenhouse Effect. Elisabeth Crawford. Science History Publications/USA, 1996.
"Styles in Scientific Explanations: Paul Ehrlich and Svante Arrhenius on Immunochemistry." *Journal of the History of Medicine and Allied Sciences* 35 (1980).
"Svante August Arrhenius." In *The Nobel Prize Winners: Chemistry*, edited by Frank N. Magill. Pasadena, Calif.: Salem Press, 1990.

(Thomas E. Van Koevering)

John James Audubon

Areas of Achievement: Biology and zoology

Contribution: The preeminent bird artist of the nineteenth century, Audubon portrayed all the birds and mammals of North America and described their anatomy and behavior.

Apr. 26, 1785	Born in Les Cayes, Saint-Domingue (now Haiti), French West Indies
1788	Moves to Nantes, France
1803	Begins to study and draw American birds in Mill Grove, Pennsylvania
1808	Marries Lucy Bakewell and moves to Kentucky
1819	Files for bankruptcy
1820	Travels to Louisiana to pursue his dream of painting every bird in North America
1826-1828	Tours England and Scotland to find patrons for his venture
1829	Travels and paints in New Jersey
1830	Travels to England and starts writing *Ornithological Biography* (1831-1839)
1832-1836	Explores Florida and the Florida Keys, the Canadian coast, Labrador, and the Gulf of Mexico
1838	Completes the engraving of *The Birds of America* (1827-1838)
1840	Starts work on *The Viviparous Quadrupeds of North America* (1845-1853)
1842	Moves to Minniesland, his Hudson River property
1843	Makes his last expedition, up the Missouri and Yellowstone Rivers
Jan. 27, 1851	Dies in New York, New York

Early Life

John James Audubon (pronounced "AW-dew-bon") was born on a plantation in the West Indies as Fougère or Jean Rabin. He was the illegitimate child of a prosperous French trader and sea captain. His mother died when he was an infant; from the age of four, he was reared by his father's wife in Nantes, France.

Young Audubon had a gentleman's upbringing, with lessons in dancing, drawing, fencing, violin, and flute. Even as a young boy, he spent much of his time drawing birds and small mammals. He was given the freedom to wander in the woods around the family's country villa in Coueron, collecting plants, rocks, bird nests, and eggs.

The Making of an American Woodsman

When Audubon was eighteen, he was sent to the United States to avoid conscription into Napoleon's army. On the farm that his father had purchased in Mill Valley, Pennsylvania, Audubon hunted, fished, skated, socialized, and sketched birds in his attic studio.

It was there that he had the idea of inserting wires into freshly killed birds and arranging them in natural poses. This helped him to create paintings in which the birds truly looked alive. Past artists had pictured birds as flat silhouettes.

Over his father's objections, Audubon married Lucy Bakewell, a neighbor's daughter, in 1808. The newlyweds moved to Kentucky, where he helped run a store and then a sawmill. Audubon often let his partners mind the store, however, while he roamed the woods, observing and collecting birds.

All the Birds of North America

A visit from the pioneer ornithologist Alexander Wilson, who was painting birds for his book *American Ornithology* (1808-1814), may have given Audubon the idea of launching a similar project. In 1820, after his business ventures had failed, Audubon put all of his energies toward what he afterward called his "Great Idea": He resolved to draw a picture of every type of bird in North America.

Penniless, he traveled by flatboat down the Ohio and Mississippi Rivers to Louisiana. There, he supported himself by painting portraits and giving drawing lessons. In his free time, he traveled the woods and bayous, studying and shooting birds and adding to his portfolio.

Audubon planned to sell his works as a subscription series. By 1824, he thought that he had enough paintings to interest patrons and a publisher, but trips to New York and Philadelphia were not successful in attracting subscribers. In 1826, he went to Great Britain, where he was an exotic sensation in his rough frontier clothes of buckskin and wolfskin, telling tales of Daniel Boone. Soon, he had enough subscribers to start producing *The Birds of America* (1827-1838).

Ultimately, 435 original watercolors were reproduced by copper-plate engraving. Robert Havell, Jr., was the engraver for most of the

(Library of Congress)

plates. Artists colored the prints by hand, using Audubon's original paintings as guides. The monumental work depicted 1,065 birds of 497 different species—all of them shown life-sized.

Referred to as the double elephant folio, the 29½" x 39½" pages were the largest that had ever been attempted in the history of book publishing.

Words for "The Birds"—and Mammals, Too
In 1830, when the success of *The Birds of America* seemed certain, Audubon decided to work his extensive field notes into a companion book, *Ornithological Biography*. Containing 3,500 pages of Audubon's detailed observations, it was published in five volumes between 1831 and 1839. Scottish zoologist William MacGillivray served as editor.

In 1840, Audubon began work on *The Viviparous Quadrupeds of North America*, the first publication ever to depict American mammals. Audubon's son, John Woodhouse, painted some of the species, and naturalist John Bachman helped write the text. The engravings were issued between 1845 and 1848, and the accompanying text was published in three volumes between 1846 and 1853.

An Energetic Explorer
Between 1826 and 1839, Audubon made a number of trips between Europe and the United States. In England, he directed the publication *A Synopsis of the Birds of North America* (1939), prepared new illustrations, recruited subscribers, and wrote the *Ornithological Biography*. When he was in the United States, he traveled extensively, searching for new birds to paint. These trips took him to New Jersey, Pennsylvania, Florida, and Labrador.

After a final expedition up the Missouri River by steamboat in 1843, Audubon's health began to fail. He died in 1851, leaving an inspiring legacy for generations of ornithologists and American artists to come.

Artist, Ornithologist, and Inspiration to Conservationists

Audubon was not the first artist to portray North American birds—Mark Catesby and Alexander Wilson preceded him—but he was the first to depict all the known species of the continent.

Designed to attract wealthy buyers, Audubon's illustrations were particularly useful to scientists. They were anatomically correct. He showed females and immature birds, which in some species look quite different from the males. *The Birds of America* (1827-1838) also broke new ground by showing birds from many perspectives and in natural poses—feeding, courting, and caring for their young.

Audubon was the first bird artist to work directly from his own field observations. His notes have been a major contribution to the knowledge of bird behavior. Charles Darwin quoted Audubon as he formulated his hypotheses on the origin of species. Arthur Cleveland Bent, the author of a preeminent twentieth century work on bird life histories, drew heavily on Audubon's observations.

Over the course of his life, Audubon described thirty-nine new bird species, of which twenty-three are still considered valid. He may also have been the first scientific bird bander. While in Mill Grove, Pennsylvania, he tied silver threads on the legs of Eastern Phoebe nestlings to see if they would return the next spring; they did.

Although he killed thousands of birds for study specimens, Audubon felt concern for the future of wildlife in America. He condemned the wastefulness of seal hunting in Labrador and the slaughter of buffalo on the plains. The first Audubon Society was founded in 1886 by George Bird Grinnell, a former pupil of Lucy Audubon. Its goal was to discourage "plume hunting," the practice of killing birds for feathers to decorate ladies' hats. The National Audubon Society, an influential conservation organization, still bears his name.

Bibliography

The Audubon Ark: A History of the National Audubon Society. Frank Graham, Jr., with Carl W. Buchheister. New York: Alfred A. Knopf, 1990.

The Bird with the Silver Bracelet: An Essay on Bird-banding. Erma J. Fisk. New York: Coalition of Publishers for Employment, 1986.

Life Histories of North American Birds. Arthur Cleveland Bent. Edited and abridged by Henry Hill Collins, Jr. New York: Harper, 1960.

Masterpieces of Bird Art: Seven Hundred Years of Ornithological Illustration. Roger F. Pasquier and John Farrand, Jr. New York: Abbeville Press, 1991.

Bibliography

By Audubon

The Birds of America, from Original Drawings, 1827-1838 (4 vols.)

Ornithological Biography: Or, An Account of the Habits of the Birds of the United States of America, Accompanied by Descriptions of the Objects Represented in the Work Entitled "The Birds of America," and Interspersed with Delineations of American Scenery and Manners, 1831-1839 (5 vols.)

The Viviparous Quadrupeds of North America, 1845-1853 (5 vols.; with John Bachman and John Woodhouse Audubon)

Journal of John James Audubon, 1929 (2 vols.; Howard Corning, ed.)

Letters of John James Audubon 1826-1840, 1930 (2 vols.; Howard Corning. ed.)

The 1826 Journal of John James Audubon, 1967 (Alice Ford, ed.)

About Audubon

Audubon: Life and Art in the American Wilderness. Shirley Streshinsky. New York: Villard Books, 1993.

John James Audubon: Selected Journals and Other Writings. Ben Forkner, ed. New York: Penguin Books, 1996.

On the Road with John James Audubon. Mary Durant and Michael Harwood. New York: Dodd, Mead, 1980.

(Cynthia Berger)

Avicenna

Areas of Achievement: Mathematics, medicine, and science (general)

Contribution: A prolific genius of the medieval Islamic world, Avicenna synthesized Aristotle's treatises on sciences with Arabic sources and his own original observations to produce an encyclopedic book on healing that profoundly influenced European scholarship. His treatise on medicine was regarded as the most authoritative medical textbook and guide for practicing physicians until the mid-seventeenth century.

Aug. or Sept., 980	Born in Afshena, Transoxiana Province of Bukhara, Persian Empire (now Uzbekistan)
988-997	Studies under private tutors in Bukhara
997	Appointed the personal physician to the emir of Bukhara
c. 1010	Works as a scholar in the court of the princess of Raiy
c. 1010	Begins *Kitab al-Qanun fi al-tibb* (*A Treatise on the Canon of Medicine of Avicenna*, 1930)
c. 1015	Appointed vizier to the prince of Hamadhan
c. 1015	Begins *Kitab al-Shifa'* (book of healing)
c. 1020	Flees Hamadhan against the wishes of the prince's successor
c. 1020-1030	Serves as a scholar in the court of the prince of Isfahan and writes the bulk of *Kitab al-Shifa'*
1030	Flees with the deposed prince as Isfahan falls to the armies of Mahmud of Ghazni
1037	Dies in Hamadhan, Persia (now Iran)

Early Life

Abu 'Ali al-Husain ibn 'Abdallah ibn Sina, known in the West as Avicenna (pronounced "av-uh-SEHN-uh") was born in 980 in a small town near Bukhara in present-day Uzbekistan, then an outpost of the Persian Empire. His father was a Persian tax collector, a member of a heretical Islamic sect, and evidently well educated. When his son showed early evidence of his prodigious mental powers, he engaged a series of tutors to instruct him. Situated on the Silk Road, Bukhara was cosmopolitan and wealthy; it afforded some of the best opportunities available at the time for an inquiring mind.

By the age of eighteen, Avicenna had a sufficient reputation in medicine that he was called to treat the emir of Bukhara; when he succeeded, he was appointed the emir's personal physician. This gave him access to the emir's private library, a treasure trove of unique ancient Greek manuscripts and Arabic commentaries, which burned not long afterward. His subsequent digests and commentaries on these sources are often the only window on a lost body of knowledge from the ancient world.

Scientific Career

Around 1004, following the death of his father, Avicenna left Bukhara. The exact chronology of events between then and his death in 1037 is uncertain. His scientific career played out against a background of warfare between rival Persian princes, prominent among whom was Mahmut of Ghazni.

Of Turkish rather than Persian origin, Mahmut conducted campaigns in India and Persia, establishing a short-lived empire that invites Napoleonic comparisons. Like most Islamic rulers of the era, he valued scholarship and sought to attach the most noted scholars to his court, by force if necessary. Since Mahmut was an Islamic fundamentalist, however, and Avicenna was both intellectually and morally liberal, Avicenna wisely avoided him.

After brief stays in a number of Persian principalities, Avicenna came under the patronage of the princess and regent of Raiy, where he established the pattern of activity that was to characterize the remainder of his career—serving as a practicing physician to noble patrons, writing summaries of and commentaries on ancient philosophical and scientific treatises, and composing original treatises ranging from letters and advice to book-length manuals.

The ninety-one books, essays, and letters cited by Abu Ubayd al-Juzjani and other contemporary sources speak authoritatively on such diverse topics as logic, metaphysics, theology, Arabic and Persian language and literature, physics, astronomy, biology, medicine, pharmacology, arithmetic and geometry, military strategy, ethics, and psychology. Avicenna also wrote poetry. While in Raiy, he began the *Kitab al-Qanun fi al-tibb* (*A Treatise on the Canon of Medicine of Avicenna*, 1930).

A dynastic struggle forced him to relocate to Hamadhan, where he first served as physician to the prince, Shams el-Dowleh, and was later appointed vizier (chief minister), which obliged him to devote considerable time to governing. In Hamadhan, he completed the *Canon of Medicine* and began work on the *Kitab al-Shifa'* (book of healing), an encyclopedic

commentary on Aristotle. When he attempted to transfer his allegiance to the prince of Isfahan, el-Dowleh's son imprisoned him; released from prison after several months, he escaped to Isfahan in disguise.

In Isfahan, under the patronage of Alah el-Dowleh, Avicenna was able to devote himself entirely to scholarship, completing the *Kitab al-Shifa'*, and an abridged version of it, the *Kitab al-Najat* (book of deliverance). His *Danish Nama-i 'Ala'i*, (partially translated as *Avicenna's Treatise on Logic*, 1971) was the first post-Islamic philosophical work written in Persian. It was not original in its thought, but it handled brilliantly the notoriously difficult problem of translating religious and philosophical writings into a language not closely related linguistically to the original.

An episode from the Isfahan period illustrates the flamboyant, arrogant style that won for Avicenna both devoted followers and bitter enemies. When rival scholars criticized him for

The Integration of Ancient Greek and Medieval Arabic Scientific Knowledge

Although Avicenna made original contributions to all the many disciplines in which he worked, no single discovery was exceptionally significant; his importance to the history of science lies in the voluminous body of ancient Greek and medieval Arabic learning that he abstracted, systematized, and transmitted.

Avicenna's *Kitab al-Qanun fi al-tibb* (*Canon of Medicine*) and *Kitab al-Shifa'* (book of healing) circulated widely in the Islamic world, which included Spain in the tenth and eleventh centuries. When the city of Toledo fell to the Christians in the twelfth century, a remarkable community of Arab, Jewish, and Christian scholars collaborated to translate the most important works into Latin. These Arabic sources profoundly influenced European scholars of the Scholastic period (the twelfth through mid-fifteenth centuries), among them Albertus Magnus (in the natural sciences and medicine), Thomas Aquinas (in ethics and logic), and Roger Bacon (in the physical sciences).

The *Canon of Medicine* is based on the medical writings of ancient Greek physicians, notably Hippocrates and Galen, and earlier Arab and Persian physicians, among whom there was a tradition of combining clinical experience with the ancient texts. This clinical experience was acquired over a vast and diverse territory, which included western China and Sub-Saharan Africa, and included diseases unknown in the ancient world.

The pharmacological section of the work contains the most original material. Avicenna introduced a number of herbs into medical practice and seems to have recognized the antiseptic properties of alcohol, since he advocates washing wounds with wine. He also suggested experimenting with animals.

The *Kitab al-Shifa'* transmits the entire body of Aristotelian philosophy, including physical and natural sciences; its sections on geology and meteorology contain much material introduced by Avicenna.

Bibliography
Arabian Medicine. E. G. Browne. Cambridge, England: Cambridge University Press, 1971.
Aristotle and the Arabs. F. E. Peters, New York: New York University Press, 1968.

(Library of Congress)

Isfahan. His extensive library, including the only copies of many of his works, was burned. For at least part of the ensuing seven years, he served as a physician on the prince's military campaigns. In 1037, he fell ill with what was termed "colic" and, recognizing that the disease was beyond his skill to treat, freed his slaves and disbursed his remaining possessions to the poor. He died in June or July at the age of fifty-eight. His followers suggested that he had been poisoned; detractors attributed his death to a dissolute lifestyle.

Bibliography

By Avicenna

Ahkam al-Adwiy ʿal-Qalbiyya (*Avicenna's Tract on Cardiac Drugs and Essays on Arab Cardiotherapy*, 1983)

Danish Nami-i ʿAla'i (book of scientific knowledge; partially trans. as *Avicenna's Treatise on Logic*, 1971)

Kitab al-Najat (book of deliverance, partially trans. as *Avicenna's Psychology*, 1952)

Kitab al-Qanun fi al-tibb (*A Treatise on the Canon of Medicine of Avicenna*, 1930)

Kitab al-Shifa' (book of healing)

Sirat al-Shaykh al-Rais (with Abu-ʿUbaid al-Juzjani; (*Life of Ibn Sina: A Critical Edition and Annotated Bibliography*, 1974)

About Avicenna

Avicenna: His Life and Works. Soheil M. Afnan. London: Allen and Unwin, 1958.

Avicenna, Scientist and Philosopher: A Millenary Symposium. G. M. Wickjens, ed. London: 1952.

Three Muslim Sages: Avicenna, Suhrawadi, Ibn Arabi. Seyyed Hossin Nasr. Cambridge, Mass.: Harvard University Press, 1964.

(Martha A. Sherwood)

the clumsiness of his Arabic, he undertook a systematic study of Arabic literary language and then wrote an original literary work, making it resemble an old manuscript. He gave it to his rivals, asking them to determine its authorship. He derived great satisfaction when they accepted it as genuine.

Later Life

Avicenna's personal life was unconventional by any standards; he never married but had numerous love affairs, and he was a heavy drinker in contravention of Islamic law. He is said to have been strikingly handsome.

In 1030, Isfahan fell to Mahmud of Ghazni, and Avicenna fled with the deposed prince of

Julius Axelrod

Areas of Achievement: Chemistry and pharmacology

Contribution: Axelrod explored the function of neurotransmitters and hormones and showed the relationships between these substances and mental and cardiovascular problems.

May 30, 1912	Born in New York, New York
1933	Obtains a B.S. from the City College of New York
1935	Takes a job as a chemist at the Laboratory of Industrial Hygiene
1938	Marries Sally Taub
1941	Receives an M.S. from New York University
1946	Begins work with pharmacologist Bernard Brodie, first at Goldwater Memorial Hospital, New York University, and then at the National Heart Institute in Bethesda, Maryland
1955	Receives a Ph.D. in pharmacology from George Washington University
1967	Receives the Gairdner Foundation International Award
1970	Shares the Nobel Prize in Physiology or Medicine with Bernard Katz and Ulf von Euler
1973	Receives the Torald Sollman Award from the American Society for Pharmacology and Experimental Therapeutics
1984	Retires from the National Institute of Mental Health
1993	Saved from severe cardiovascular problems by a drug related to catecholamines

Early Life

Julius Axelrod was born in New York City to Polish immigrants Isadore and Molly (Leichtling) Axelrod in 1912. Julius attended public elementary and high schools on Manhattan's East Side. Axelrod credits much of his general education to the voracious reading of books borrowed from New York's public libraries.

Axelrod attended the City College of New York and received a B.S. in biology and chemistry in 1933. He soon found a job as a laboratory assistant in bacteriology at New York University (NYU) Medical School. In 1935, he began work as a chemist at the Laboratory of Industrial Hygiene (LIH) of the New York City Health department. In addition to this job, Axelrod carried out graduate studies. On August 30, 1938, he married Sally Taub, and they had two sons. Axelrod received an M.S. in chemistry from NYU in 1941.

While conducting research at LIH and doing graduate work, Axelrod met professor Bernard Brodie. In 1946, they began to collaborate at NYU's Goldwater Memorial Hospital. Brodie and Axelrod discovered acetaminophen (Tylenol), and, after three years, they moved to the National Heart Institute in Bethesda, Maryland.

By this time, Axelrod's work on stimulant amphetamines, which resemble the natural catecholamine hormones epinephrine and norepinephrine, was very promising. He lacked, however, the Ph.D. needed to succeed in research science. Paul Smith of the pharmacology department at George Washington University knew the high quality of Axelrod's work. He was instrumental in helping Axelrod obtain a Ph.D. in pharmacology there in 1955, just after Axelrod became section head of pharmacology at the Laboratory of Clinical Science of the new National Institute of Mental Health (NIMH). He held that position until his retirement in 1984.

Axelrod's Work Flowers at NIMH

In the late 1950's and 1960's, Axelrod's research shifted to catecholamine hormones. Others had shown them to be neurotransmitters that control nerve impulse transmission in various parts of the nervous system. Among his earliest significant endeavors was the isolation of catechol-O-methyltransferase (COMT), one of the most important enzymes that destroy body catecholamines.

Surprisingly, although COMT and other important catecholamine-metabolizing enzymes have long-term control of bodily catecholamine levels, Axelrod found that their inactivation did not end the nerve impulses attributable to catecholamines. Instead, his group learned that impulse turnoff was caused by neurotransmitter resorption by the nervous tis-

Amphetamines and Catecholamines

Axelrod and his colleagues studied metabolism, showing neurotransmitter action modes and how psychoactive drugs alter neurotransmitter actions.

In the late 1940's, Axelrod started work at the National Heart Institute and examined drugs called sympathomimetic amines (SAs). These substances—such as amphetamines, mescaline, and ephedrine—have legitimate uses as medicines to enable the body's sympathetic nervous system to prepare for strenuous exercise. They also have related properties that enable their widespread use as illegal recreational drugs.

Axelrod was interested in the basis for SA function in the first place. His research group identified several enzymes that allow SA bioalteration and excretion. Later, as head of the pharmacology section at the Laboratory of Clinical Science, Axelrod and his colleagues studied the neurotransmitter action of epinephrine and norepinephrine, two natural catecholamines with structures similar to SAs. The Axelrod group identified enzymes that inactivate catecholamines and discovered both catecholamine quantization and resorption by nerve cells.

Further exploration in Axelrod's laboratory led to the discovery that antidepressants, amphetamines, and cocaine act by altering the deactivation and/or resorption of enzymatic catecholamines, thus changing the extent and direction of catecholamine action. This work had a huge impact on the understanding of normal and pathologic neurobiology and the means to treat mental disease.

Much of this research used radioactively labeled hormones whose metabolic fate in the body could be traced. These studies, first carried out by drug injection into laboratory animals, were later extended to experiments that injected them directly into the ventricles (spaces) in the brain. This technique allowed their direct uptake into the brain and opened a window on the understanding of neurobiology.

Part of the importance of intraventricular administration is attributable to the inability of many drugs to enter the brain. This is the result of the blood-brain barrier, which selects only some substances for entry into the nervous system. Ventricular injection bypasses this barrier.

In all cases, Axelrod and his colleagues, by examining the radioactive substances (metabolites) that neurotransmitters become, were able to identify the effects of SAs and other psychoactive drugs on the metabolism of catecholamines. Counting how many neurotransmitter molecules were in the vesicles was made possible by measuring the amount of radioactivity that they held. These techniques were important in the advancement of neurobiology.

For example, one common treatment of Parkinson's disease uses a mixed injection of dopa and carbidopa. Dopa can cross the blood-brain barrier and become catecholamine neurotransmitters. Carbidopa prevents the conversion of dopa to neurotransmitters and catecholamine hormones outside the brain, preventing side effects, but it cannot cross the barrier. This therapy and many others underscore the tremendous value of Axelrod's work.

Bibliography

"A Reduction in the Accumulation of H3-Norepinephrine in Experimental Hypertension." Julius Axelrod, J. de Champlain, and L. R. Krakoff. *Life Science* (1966).

"Biochemical Pharmacology of Catecholamines and Its Clinical Implications." Julius Axelrod et al. *Transactions of the American Neurobiological Association* (1972).

"Nobel Prize: Three Share 1970 Award for Medical Research." Sidney Udenfriend. *Science* (1970).

sue. They also found that neurotransmitter release was quantized (that it occurred in fixed numbers per cell). It is now known that this quantization is the result of neurotransmitter packaging in fixed numbers in storage granules that are released as needed.

Even more important was discovery by Axelrod's group that mental drugs—from addictive cocaine to the antidepressant drugs that heal psychiatric disease—alter the amount of neurotransmitter in each nerve cell vesicle. They also found that these substances change the rates of vesicle breakdown during neurotransmitter release and/or the resorption of neurotransmitters by nerve cells.

Axelrod's studies involved injecting radioactively labeled catecholamines into animals or directly into the brain. These methods were later extended to work that yielded information on relationships between neurotransmitters and hormones that in many cases were found to be closely related chemicals. Axelrod and his colleagues also delineated the effects of neurotransmitter injection on hormone production by the pineal gland, as well as the effects of hormone administration on neurotransmitter release by the adrenal glands.

The Nobel Prize and Afterward
Axelrod shared the 1970 Nobel Prize in Physiology or Medicine with Bernard Katz and Ulf von Euler for their discoveries about humoral transmitters in nerve terminals and mechanisms for their storage, release, and inactivation. His Nobel Prize lecture noted that the drugs used to treat mental and cardiovascular disease influenced the formation, metabolism, uptake, and storage or release of catecholamines.

Axelrod received other awards in his career, such as the Gairdner Foundation Award in 1967, the Torald Sollman Award of the American Society for Pharmacology and Experimental Therapeutics in 1973, honors from George Washington University and the University of Montreal, and memberships in the British Royal Society of London and the U.S. National Academy of Science.

Ever an active researcher, Axelrod continued to work even after his official retirement in 1984. Fortuitously, his life was saved after a

(The Nobel Foundation)

1993 stroke via one his early endeavors. Cardiologists identified his need for coronary bypass surgery, but Axelrod's very low blood pressure made him a poor candidate for surviving this procedure. The solution to the dilemma was the injection of a synthetic cousin of epinephrine. Axelrod survived and was soon at work once again. His efforts studying epinephrine had paid off in a personal way.

Bibliography
By Axelrod
"A Reduction in the Accumulation of H3-Norepinephrine in Experimental Hypertension," *Life Science*, 1966 (with J. de Champlain and L. R. Krakoff).
The Pineal, 1968 (with R. Wurtman and D. Kelly)
Biochemical Actions of Hormones, 1970 (with others; G. Litwack, ed.)
"Biochemical Pharmacology of Catecholamines and Its Clinical Implications," *Transactions of the American Neurobiological Association*, 1971 (with others)

About Axelrod

Biographical Encyclopedia of Scientists. John Daintith, Sarah Mitchell, and Elizabeth Tootill. New York: Facts on File, 1981.

"The Man Who Saved Himself." Carol Stevens. *Washingtonian* (1970).

"Nobel Prize: Three Share 1970 Award for Medical Research." Sidney Udenfriend. *Science* (1970).

The Who's Who of Nobel Prize Winners, 1901-1995. 3d ed. Bernard S. and June H. Schlessinger. Phoenix, Ariz.: Oryx Press, 1996.

(Sanford S. Singer)

Hertha Marks Ayrton

Areas of Achievement: Earth science, invention, physics, and technology

Contribution: Ayrton achieved insight into the electric arc, explained sand ripples formed under ocean waves, invented drafting and architectural instruments, and designed a defensive device used during World War I.

Apr. 28, 1854	Born in Portsea, England
1863	Moves to London to live with her aunt
1876	Enters Girton College, Cambridge University
1884	Attends Finsbury Technical College
1884	Invents a line-divider and studies electricity
1885	Marries William Ayrton and becomes stepmother to his daughter
1886	Gives birth to a daughter, Barbara
1899	Reads a paper before and is elected to the Institution of Electrical Engineers
1901	Nominated for membership in the Royal Society of London but rejected the following year
1902	Publishes *The Electric Arc*
1904	Becomes the first woman to read her own paper before the Royal Society of London
1906	Receives the Hughes Medal of the Royal Society of London
1916	Her antigas fan is deployed at the front during World War I
Aug. 23, 1923	Dies in North Lancing, Sussex, England

Early Life

Hertha Marks was born in 1854 in modest circumstances near Portsmouth, England, to Levi and Alice Marks. Her original name was Phoebe Sarah Marks—"Hertha" was a name that she assumed as a young adult and was probably inspired by a poem by Charles Swinburne.

Her father, a clockmaker, died when she was seven years old. One of eight children, she was sent in 1863 to live with an aunt, Mrs. Alphonse Hartog, in London. The aunt's family was sophisticated and well-educated, and it is through their influence that Hertha entered Girton College at Cambridge University in 1876 to study mathematics. Her tuition was paid by a group of benefactors—among them the great novelist George Eliot, whom she had met through mutual friends. It is likely that Marks served as the model for a character in Eliot's novel *Daniel Deronda* (1876).

Upon her graduation from Cambridge, Marks returned to London and in 1884 produced a marketable invention—a device employed by architects and draftsmen to subdivide a line accurately.

Electricity

London in the 1880's was being wired for the distribution of electric power, stimulating interest in the applications of electricity. Marks, caught in this enthusiasm, enrolled in courses at Finsbury Technical College taught by the distinguished electrical engineer William Ayrton, a widower with a small daughter. He and Hertha were married in 1885, and they began a collaboration in electrical investigations that continued until his death in 1908.

Hertha Marks Ayrton is best known for her research on the nature of the electrical arc. Such arcs were used for street illumination and in searchlights and lighthouses, although their intensity and noise made them impractical for the home. Ayrton's book *The Electric Arc* (1902) was greeted with acclaim.

In 1899, she read her paper "The Hissing of the Electric Arc" before a meeting of the Institution of Electrical Engineers and became the first woman elected to that organization. Her article "The Mechanism of the Electric Arc" was read before the Royal Society of London in 1901 by one of its members, marking the first time that a paper authored by a woman was presented to that venerable male group. Subsequently, Ayrton was nominated to be a Fellow of the society. Women had never been admitted, however, and she was rejected on the advice of legal council.

(Library of Congress)

The Electric Arc

Ayrton investigated the circuit used in an arc lamp and found that reshaping the device improved its performance.

The most fundamental electric circuit consists of a battery, a resistor, and some wire arranged to form a closed path. The flow of current is governed by Ohm's law: $V = IR$, where R is the resistance of the resistor, V is the voltage of the battery, and I is the current, in amperes, passing through the circuit.

The circuit used in arc lamps replaces the resistor with two carbon rods. The rods are heated by the passage of current. Eventually, they can be separated slightly from each other, and the current will continue to pass through the carbon vapor in the resulting gap. The vapor glows with a strong intensity.

Ayrton found that the current and voltage for such a circuit are governed by a more complex equation related to the size of the rods, the dimensions of the gap, and the nature of the carbon. For an ordinary resistor, if the voltage is graphed as a function of the current, the expression $V = IR$ is used and a straight line passing through the origin is obtained. Ayrton's equation for the arc, however, results in a complicated curve containing a dip. The nonlinearity of the curve and its negative slope indicate that the current can oscillate and produce a musical tone.

In addition, her experimental observations concerning the shape of the tips of the carbon electrodes helped explain an often-noticed additional phenomenon—an unpleasant hissing and unsteady illumination. Reshaping of the tips led to the elimination of the noise and to a constant light.

Bibliography

The Electric Arc. Hertha Ayrton. London: Electrician, 1902.

Fundamental Processes of Electrical Discharges in Gases. Leonard Loeb. New York: John Wiley & Sons, 1939.

The Study of Fluids

Beginning in 1901, Ayrton became interested in explaining the ripple marks formed by the ocean in the sand at the beach. Experimenting with water and sand in a tank, she arrived at a satisfactory explanation of the mechanism involved. She presented her findings in a paper read to the Royal Society of London in 1904, becoming the first woman to present her research directly before that organization. In 1906, for her work on electricity and sand ripples, the society bestowed on her its Hughes Medal; she was the first woman to be so honored.

Ayrton's work with fluids found application during World War I. Her invention, the Ayrton fan, was used to blow poison gas away from British troops at the front in 1915. In her later years, she was allied with women's rights causes in England. She died on August 23, 1923.

Bibliography

By Ayrton

"The Drop of Potential at the Carbons of the Electric Arc" in *Report of the Sixty-eighth Meeting of the Bristol Association for the Advancement of Science, Held at Bristol in September, 1898*, 1899

"The Mechanism of the Electric Arc," *Philosophical Transactions of the Royal Society of London*, 1901-1902

The Electric Arc, 1902

"Local Differences of Pressure Near an Obstacle in Oscillating Water," *Proceedings of the Royal Society of London*, 1915

About Ayrton

"Ayrton, Hertha Marks." Marilyn Bailey Oglivie. In *Women in Science*. Cambridge, Mass.: MIT Press, 1986.

Hertha Ayrton: A Memoir, 1854-1923. Evelyn Sharp. London: Edward Arnold, 1926.

"Hertha Ayrton: A Persistent Experimenter." James J. Tattersall and Shawnee L. McMurran. *Journal of Women's History* 7, no. 2 (Summer, 1995).

(A. David Wunsch)

Walter Baade

Areas of Achievement: Astronomy and physics

Contribution: Baade revolutionized stellar astrophysics with his finding that there appear to be two major categories of stars. He was also influential in demonstrating that Earth is located in a spiral galaxy and in measuring the size of the universe.

Mar. 24, 1893	Born in Schröttinghausen, Westphalia, Germany
1919	Earns a Ph.D. from the University of Göttingen
1919	Joins the staff of the University of Hamburg's Bergedorf Observatory
1920	Discovers the asteroid designated 944 Hidalgo
1922	Discovers Comet 1922c (Comet Baade)
1926-1927	Travels to California on a Rockefeller Fellowship
1928	Journeys to the Philippines to witness a solar eclipse
1931	Accepts a staff position at Mount Wilson Observatory in California
1944	Presents his findings of two stellar populations
1948	Discovers the asteroid designated 1566 Icarus
1954	Awarded the Gold Medal of the Royal Astronomical Society
1958	Retires from Mount Wilson Observatory
1959	Returns to the University of Göttingen as Gauss Professor
June 25, 1960	Dies in Bad Salzuflen, Westphalia, Germany

Early Life

Wilhelm Heinrich Walter Baade (pronounced "BAH-duh") was born in 1893 to Konrad and Charlotte Baade in Schröttinghausen, Germany, where his father was the director of schools. Baade's parents planned a career in the clergy for their son, but his interests in school clearly leaned toward science and mathematics, especially astronomy.

In 1913, Baade began studies in science at the University of Göttingen, where he stayed until he received his Ph.D. in astronomy in 1919. He was able to continue his studies through World War I because he was exempted from military service as a result of a birth defect in his hip.

After receiving his Ph.D., Baade worked as an assistant at the Bergedorf Observatory, operated by the University of Hamburg.

(California Institute of Technology)

There, Baade began his exceptional career in astronomy.

Travels Abroad

Baade was awarded a Rockefeller Fellowship for the year 1926-1927, which allowed him to travel to California to use the new large telescopes there. His careful and meticulous work impressed the American astronomers. This trip taught Baade that he would need larger telescopes to conduct his research than were available to him in Germany.

Upon his return to Germany, he became good friends with astronomer and optician Bernhard Voldemar Schmidt. Together, they traveled to the Philippines to observe a solar eclipse in 1929. With Baade's encouragement, Schmidt later constructed a new type of telescope that has been an important tool for astronomers.

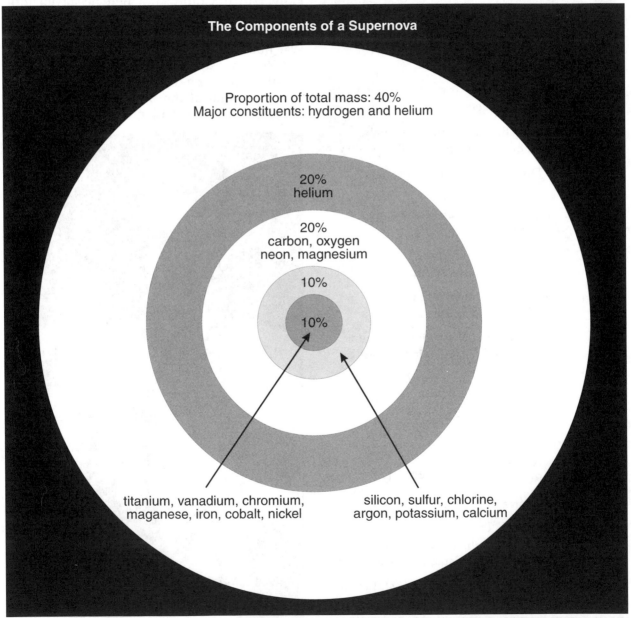

The Components of a Supernova

Proportion of total mass: 40%
Major constituents: hydrogen and helium

20%
helium

20%
carbon, oxygen
neon, magnesium

10%

10%

titanium, vanadium, chromium, maganese, iron, cobalt, nickel

silicon, sulfur, chlorine, argon, potassium, calcium

Baade coined the term "supernova" to describe the stage in a star's life when it suddenly releases large amounts of energy.

Stellar Populations

Stars can be classified based on their spectral characteristics into two different populations of stars.

During World War II, Los Angeles was under blackout conditions, which permitted Baade to use the equipment at the Mount Wilson Observatory to its fullest extent in order to study the heavens.

A long puzzle for astronomers had been why it was so difficult to photograph the central portions of the Andromeda galaxy and its two satellite galaxies, Messier 32 and NGC205. Ordinary photographic techniques at the time were more sensitive to blue light. Baade tried using a special photographic emulsion that was sensitive to red light, which resolved the images of the core of the Andromeda galaxy and its satellite galaxies.

Baade realized that this discovery meant that not all stars are alike. He called these two types of stars Population I and Population II. The sun is a Population I star. Further analysis indicated that Population II stars do not have as many metals in their spectra as do Population I stars. (To an astronomer, anything other than hydrogen or helium is called a metal.) Astronomers interpreted this information to mean that Population II stars formed at about the time that the galaxy formed and that Population I stars formed as a later generation.

Bibliography

The Discovery of Our Galaxy. Charles A. Whitney. New York: Alfred A. Knopf, 1971.
Exploration of the Universe. George O. Abell, David Morrison, and Sidney C. Wolff. 6th ed. Philadelphia: W. B. Saunders, 1993.

The California Years

In 1931, Baade accepted a position at the Mount Wilson Observatory in California. Collaborating on work with the Swiss astronomer Fritz Zwicky, Baade coined the term "supernova" to explain exploding stars. He was the first to suggest that neutron stars may be associated with supernovas, and he discovered the neutron star remnant of the supernova that formed the Crab nebula. Zwicky was unable accept Baade's German heritage after the rise of Nazism in Germany, and so their friendship ended with the advent of World War II.

When the United States entered World War II, Baade was classified as an enemy agent because he was a German citizen. He was required to remain in the immediate area of Mount Wilson for the duration of the war. During this time, Baade discovered that stars can be classified into two different populations.

After the war, Baade turned his attentions to galaxies. He was instrumental in showing that the Milky Way is a spiral galaxy. He also revised the scale whereby distances to other galaxies are measured. In 1952, Baade discovered a galaxy that was the optical counterpart to the strange celestial radio signal called Cygnus A.

Upon his retirement in 1958, Baade spent about a year traveling around the world and giving lectures. He then returned to Germany and died shortly thereafter.

Legacy

Baade had an extraordinary impact on astronomy. Most of his work was unpublished, but almost everything that was published had far-reaching consequences. Nevertheless, he was given few honors during his lifetime. He did receive awards from the Royal Astronomical Society and the Astronomical Society of the Pacific, both shortly before his retirement.

Bibliography
By Baade
"On Supernovae," *Proceedings of the National Academy of Sciences,* 1934 (with Fritz Zwicky)
"The New Stellar Systems in Sculptor and Fornax," *Publications of the Astronomical Society of the Pacific,* 1938 (with Edwin Powell Hubble)
"Photographic Light Curves of the Two Supernovae in IC4182 and NGC1003," *Astrophysical Journal,* 1938 (with Zwicky)
"The Crab Nebula," *Astrophysical Journal,* 1942
"Nova Ophiuchi of 1604 as a Supernova," *Astrophysical Journal,* 1943
"The Resolution of Messier 332, NGC 205, and the Central Region of the Andromeda Nebula," *Astrophysical Journal,* 1944

"A Program of Extragalactic Research for the 200-Inch Hale Telescope," *Publications of the Astronomical Society of the Pacific*, 1948

"Stellar Populations and Collisions of Galaxies," *Astrophysical Journal*, 1950 (with Lyman Spitzer, Jr.)

"A Revision of the Extra-Galactic Distance Scale," *Transactions of the International Astronomical Union*, 1952

"Identification of the Radio Sources in Cassiopeia, Cygnus A, and Puppis A," *Astrophysical Journal*, 1954 (with Rudolph Minkowski)

"On the Identification of Radio Sources," *Astrophysical Journal*, 1954 (with Minkowski)

"Polarization in the Jet of Messier 87," *Astrophysical Journal*, 1956

About Baade

The Great Copernicus Chase and Other Adventures in Astronomical History. Owen Gingerich. Cambridge, Mass.: Sky Publishing, 1992.

The Norton History of Astronomy and Cosmology. John North. New York: W. W. Norton, 1995.

The Star Lovers. Robert S. Richardson. New York: Macmillan, 1967.

(Raymond D. Benge, Jr.)

Francis Bacon

Area of Achievement: Science (general)
Contribution: Bacon influenced the aim of science from philosophy to a discipline in service of humankind that used observation and experiments to further its knowledge.

Jan. 22, 1561	Born in London, England
1573	Enters Trinity College, Cambridge University, at the age of twelve to study classical subjects
1575	Enters Gray's Inn to study law
1577	Travels to France with the English ambassador
1579	His father dies, leaving Bacon without an estate
1597	Publishes the first ten *Essayes*
1603	Receives knighthood from King James I
1605	Publishes *The Advancement of Learning*
1606	Marries Alice Barnham
1607	Appointed solicitor general under King James I
1617	Appointed Lord Keeper
1618	Appointed Lord Chancellor
1620	Publishes *Instauratio Magna* (the great instauration or restoration), which includes the *Novum Organum*
1622	Convicted on charges of corruption and banished from government service
1623	Publishes *De Augmentis Scientiarum*
Apr. 9, 1626	Dies of bronchitis in London, England

Early Life

Francis Bacon was born in London, England, on January 22, 1561. His father was Sir Nicholas Bacon, and his mother, Anne, was the daughter of Sir Anthony Cooke. As a boy, Francis was sickly, although very studious and thoughtful. As his father was lord keeper of the great seal to Queen Elizabeth I, the queen called the boy her "young lord keeper."

In 1573, at the age of twelve, Bacon entered Trinity College of Cambridge University, his age being typical for young men at the time to enter college. At Trinity, he studied the classical subjects, including the philosophy of Aristotle. He found Aristotle's philosophy and logical methods to be "unfruitful and barren," a theme that he would develop into his own philosophy of science.

Two years later, he entered Gray's Inn to study law. Just before completing his law studies, he traveled to France with the English ambassador, Sir Amias Paulet. In France, Bacon was influenced by the Scholasticism movement, which was spread through informal but regular discussion groups among those with legal training and experience in public affairs.

In February, 1579, Bacon's father died, and, as Bacon was the youngest son, he was left

(Library of Congress)

without an inheritance. He had to borrow money to finish his law degree, and he was never completely out of debt for the rest of his life.

Political Life

Bacon's only means of support was by ingratiating himself with the court of Queen Elizabeth I, and later that of King James I. He was not as successful with the queen as he was with her successor. In 1607, James appointed Bacon to the post of solicitor general, in 1613 to the post of attorney general, in 1617 to Lord Keeper, and finally, in 1618, to Lord Chancellor.

Unfortunately, Bacon was a rather lax administrator, and in 1620 he was accused of taking gifts from persons he would be prosecuting. Bacon admitted that he or his staff may have done so but claimed that there was no evidence that the gifts influenced any of his decisions. Nevertheless, he was convicted of corruption, fined £40,000 (which was later dropped), confined to the Tower of London for two or three days, and banished from any government position.

Contributions to the Philosophy of Science

Bacon was never himself a scientist, but he contributed substantially to the philosophy of science, historical science, and scientific method and logic. Bacon believed that three major inventions had revolutionized the course of humanity: the printing press, gunpowder, and the compass. Bacon's main theme was that science should have practical applications in the service of humanity, such as provided by those three inventions.

Bacon primarily disagreed with Aristotle's philosophical methods. Aristotle used statements or beliefs and reasoning to advance knowledge. Bacon stated that such methods did not provide truth as seen in nature, but rather were merely intellectual exercises. Science, according to Bacon, is not created by thinking only, but by thinking about what is revealed by acting. In other words, science should be judged by its contributions to the betterment of humanity.

Most of Bacon's publications dealt with his ideas about what knowledge currently existed, what "fruits" that knowledge bore, and what

Bacon vs. Aristotle: The New Logic and Scientific Method

Bacon was most critical of the logic of Aristotle and proposed an inductive method to expand human knowledge.

Aristotle developed deductive inference in the form of syllogisms, which are arguments of two premises and a conclusion. For example:

All persons are mortal. (a premise)

Socrates is a person. (a premise)

Therefore, Socrates is mortal. (the conclusion)

In a syllogism, the conclusion follows necessarily from the premises: If the premises are true, the conclusion is true also. Deductive inference can be criticized, however, on the grounds that the absolute truth of the premises can never be known. In essence, there can be no "facts," only observations and inferences about them. With this criticism, Bacon thus proposed an inductive method for science—that is, making generalizations from specifics, rather than deriving specifics from generalizations.

For example, a scientist might observe under what conditions metals rust. The scientist realizing that iron rusts quickly in humid environments might conduct an experiment such as putting iron into an environment of zero percent humidity, in which the iron would not rust. The observations and experimental results would lead the scientist to infer that rusting is a process involving iron and water. The scientist then could propose methods of keeping iron away from water or moisture in the air in order to prevent rusting.

Inductive inference introduces uncertainty because one must rely on observations. Humans are limited in their perceptions and cannot observe everything, or all instances, in order to draw an inference. Nevertheless, the inductive method does allow science to move forward, in that one does not have to discover the absolute truth about something before drawing conclusions.

For the inductive method to work, Bacon stated that science must proceed in an orderly and systematic way. His inductive method differs from Aristotle's version of induction, in that Aristotle paid little attention to experience and observations, preferring to spend time thinking.

Bacon was aware that there was no way to be certain in advance of the correct and systematic path to take while investigating the natural world. In other words, the rules for investigation or experimentation often evolve during the investigation itself. In the end, Bacon's aim was not to teach people how to argue correctly but how to invent new arts and works that benefit humanity.

Bibliography

Francis Bacon: Philosophy of Industrial Science. Benjamin Farrington. London: Lawrence and Wishart, 1951.

Introduction to Cognitive Science. Paul Thagard. Cambridge, Mass.: MIT Press, 1996.

Looking at Philosophy. Donald Palmer. Mountain View, Calif.: Mayfield, 1994.

needed to be done to obtain more knowledge. He chronicled much of the natural and physical knowledge known during his times. He also suggested many projects that his type of science should tackle, such as the creation of metal alloys and clearer, unbreakable glass and the development of methods for making fruits and vegetables ripen earlier in the summer and for preserving food.

Bacon argued that, in order to accomplish his goals, scientists should be skilled in observation and experimental methods. This type of science would offer penetrating insights into the nature of materials, as well as the causes for their natures. For example, if scientists learn not only how to make unbreakable glass but also why it is unbreakable, then anything can be made unbreakable.

After Bacon was forced from public service following his conviction, he devoted the last four years of his life to writing down his ideas. He also tried a scientific experiment himself, which ironically led to his death. After a snowfall, Bacon stuffed a hen with some of the snow to see if it would preserve the meat. He caught a chill that developed into bronchitis, from which he died on April 9, 1626. He was sixty-five years old.

Bibliography
By Bacon
Essayes, 1597, 1612, 1625
The Two Bookes of Francis Bacon of the Proficience and Advancement of Learning, Divine and Humane, 1605 (commonly known as *The Advancement of Learning*)
Instauratio Magna (the great instauration or restoration), 1620 (includes the *Novum Organum*)
De Dignitate and Augmentis Scientiarum, 1623 (commonly known as *De Augmentis Scientiarum*; translated as *Of the Advancement and Proficience of Learning: Or, The Partitions of Sciences, IX Bookes*, 1640)

About Bacon
Francis Bacon: Essays, Advancement of Learning, New Atlantis, and Other Pieces. Richard Foster Jones. New York: Odyssey Press, 1937.
Francis Bacon: Philosophy of Industrial Science. Benjamin Farrington. London: Lawrence and Wishart, 1951.

(Todd A. Shimoda)

Roger Bacon

Areas of Achievement: Mathematics and science (general)

Contribution: Bacon was an early promulgator of experimental science, especially optics, mathematics, and calendar reform.

c. 1220	Born in Ilchester, Somerset, England
c. 1237	Takes a B.A. degree at Oxford University
c. 1240	Awarded an M.A. degree from the University of Paris
c. 1241-1246	Serves on the arts faculty of the University of Paris
c. 1242	Publishes a recipe for gunpowder
c. 1251	Returns to Oxford University
c. 1263	Creates a revised calendar
1267	Publishes *Opus majus*, *Opus minus*, and *Opus tertium*
c. 1278-1288	Imprisoned on suspicion of heresy
c. 1292	Dies, probably in Oxford, England

Early Life

What little is known of Roger Bacon's early life comes from remarks in his works. His family's fortune and position were lost supporting King Henry III against the English barons, and his relatives were unable to assist his work financially. Bacon evidently took a B.A. degree at Oxford University around 1237 and a master's degree at the University of Paris around 1240.

As was customary, he taught at the University of Paris for several years after taking his degree. One of the earliest to lecture on the natural philosophy of Aristotle, he was apparently a popular teacher and was called *Doctor mirabilis*, "wonderful teacher." He entered the Franciscan order probably in the 1240's and by about 1251 had settled at Oxford University again.

(Library of Congress)

Life as a Scholar

An early indication of the direction that Bacon would take was his publication in 1242 of the recipe for gunpowder, which he evidently had learned from Arab sources. All of his academic life, Bacon assimilated and promulgated the new learning that was flooding into the West from Arab scholars. He was also interested in questions of calendar reform, calling attention to errors. A copy of his calendar of 1263 is in the library of University College, Oxford University.

Bacon's friendship with Robert Grosseteste, dating from 1247, made him especially interested in optics and the need for experimental science. He became a major promoter of mathematics and experiments as a means of detecting errors and advancing knowledge, although he himself performed few experiments.

His reputation for breadth of knowledge led to a request that he secretly prepare a book for Pope Clement IV expounding his views on the new learning. The result was his *Opus majus*, which Bacon extended with *Opus minus* and

An Improved Theory of Vision

Although Bacon was primarily a transmitter of ideas, he improved theories of vision, preparing the way for later advances.

Two main theories of vision were known in medieval Europe. In extramission theories, a visual stream from the eye mingles with light from objects. With only a well-defined beam of rays from the eye to analyze, these theories were quite precise mathematically. In intromission theories, light from objects is the sole cause of vision. The multiple light beams from all points on an object made these theories mathematically difficult.

In the newly translated works of the great Arab scientist Alhazen (Abu ʿAli al-Hasan ibn al-Haytham), Bacon found a mathematically successful intromission theory. Because authorities such as Plato, Euclid, and Ptolemy supported extramission, however, Bacon was unwilling to dismiss it. Consequently, he held that the emitted rays prepared the medium and the incident rays so that vision could occur.

Bacon was probably original in his discussion of the details of refraction, for which he gave eight rules for classifying the behavior of refracting surfaces with respect to vision. He was also the first to speak of "laws of reflection and refraction."

Bacon's views dominated the next several centuries of Western thought on vision, providing the foundation on which Johannes Kepler and others would build.

Bibliography

Robert Grosseteste and the Origins of Experimental Science. A. C. Crombie. Oxford, England: Oxford University Press, 1969.

Roger Bacon and His Search for a Universal Science. S. C. Easton. Oxford, England: Oxford University Press, 1952.

Roger Bacon: Essays Contributed by Various Writers. A. G. Little, ed. Oxford, England: Oxford University Press, 1914.

Opus tertium, publishing all three in 1267. Pope Clement died before he could evaluate the work, an encyclopedic effort to demonstrate the value of the new learning and to show how it did not conflict with theology. It secured Bacon's reputation and allowed him considerable freedom in explaining his views.

Later Life

Bacon's views, however, were not universally appreciated. In 1278, possibly as a result of unrest at the University of Paris, the general of the Franciscan order (soon to be Pope Nicholas IV) condemned Bacon's views, banned his writings, and imprisoned him for about a decade, probably in Paris. Returning to Oxford by 1290, Bacon continued to pursue his interests in alchemy, optics, and astronomy. He died after completing the *Compendium studii theologiae* in 1292.

Bibliography
By Bacon
Opus maius, 1267 (*The Opus Maius of Roger Bacon*, 1928)
Opus minus, 1267
Opus tertium, 1267
Compendium studii philosophie, 1272
Compendium studii theologiae, 1292 (*Compendium of the Study of Theology*, 1928)
Epistola Fratris Roger Baconis de secretis operibus artis et naturae, 1542
De retardandis senectutis accidentibus et de sensibus conservandis, 1590 (*The Cure of Old Age and the Preservation of Youth*, 1683)
The Mirror of Alchimy, 1597

About Bacon
A History of Western Science. Anthony M. Alioto. Englewood Cliffs, N.J.: Prentice Hall, 1987.
"Roger Bacon." In *The Dictionary of Scientific Biography*, edited by Charles Coulston Gillispie. New York: Charles Scribner's Sons, 1970.
Roger Bacon: The Problem of the Soul in His Philosophical Commentaries. Theodore Crowley. Louvain, France: Éditions de l'Institut Supérieure Philosophie, 1950.

(*John A. Cramer*)

Robert D. Ballard

Areas of Achievement: Earth science and technolcgy
Contribution: A developer and user of advanced deep-water technology, Ballard derived a better understanding of the ocean floor, especially the Mid-Atlantic Ridge, through exploration with a variety of submersibles.

June 30, 1942	Born in Wichita, Kansas
1965	Receives a B.S. in physical science from the University of California, Santa Barbara
1969	Takes a position at the Woods Hole Oceanographic Institution
1974	Earns a Ph.D. in marine geology from the University of Rhode Island
1976	Receives the Underwater Society of America Science Award
1977	Explores hydrothermal vents deep off the Galapagos Islands with the submersible *Alvin*
1979	Discovers new thermal springs on the East Pacific Rise off Mexico
1981	Awarded the Newcomb Cleveland Prize from the American Association for the Advancement of Science
1985	Discovers and photographs the wreck of the luxury liner *Titanic*
1986	Develops *J. J.*, a mini-submersible for exploring objects on the deep-sea floor
1987	Chosen as *Discover* magazine's Scientist of the Year
1988	Receives the National Geographic Society Centennial Award

Plate Tectonics and Continents Adrift

Ballard's explorations showed how magma oozing from the Mid-Atlantic Ridge forms new crust and moves the continents.

In 1912, German meteorologist Alfred Lothar Wegener proposed that the earth's continents float like gigantic rafts over the molten magma layer. His theory helped explain many geologic phenomena. Unfortunately, he had no proof of the force that moves the continents.

In 1970, Ballard began his research on plate tectonics, the study of the drifting of the earth's continents and the forces that move them. Aboard *Alvin*, Ballard was able to observe magma oozing from the Mid-Atlantic Ridge in the ocean floor. In addition, he collected seafloor rocks in situ and examined their magnetic polarity. Measurements of the differential depth of ocean bottom silt in a line perpendicular to the ridge gave further evidence of crustal movement. As new seafloor is formed, it moves away from the rift in the Mid-Atlantic Ridge at a rate of between 2 and 3 centimeters per year.

Ballard also examined the circulation of seawater through the earth's crust. When it encounters the molten magma, the water is heated to about 345 degrees Celsius, hot enough to melt lead. In the crust, the water dissolves minerals which, on return, add to oceanic salinity. The mineral-rich heated water, venting into the ocean, supports rich ecosystems of clams, worms, and crabs. The ecosystems, observed by Ballard from *Alvin*, are based on the process of chemosynthesis, which differs from the terrestrial process of photosynthesis.

Bibliography

"Our Restless Planet Earth." Robert Gore. *National Geographic* 168 (February, 1985).

The Sea Floor: An Introduction to Marine Geology. E. Seibold and W. H. Berger. New York: Springer-Verlag, 1982.

Water Baby: The Story of "Alvin." Victoria A. Kaharl. New York: Oxford University Press, 1990.

(Frank Capri/Archive Photos)

Early Life

Robert Duane Ballard's father was an aerospace engineer who helped develop the guidance system for the Minuteman missile. Growing up in the Los Angeles area, Ballard became fascinated with the ocean. He entered the University of California, Santa Barbara, where he enrolled as a dual major in chemistry and geology. Graduate work in marine geology and oceanography followed at the University of Hawaii and the University of Southern California (USC). In 1974, Ballard earned a Ph.D. in marine geology and geophysics at the University of Rhode Island.

He was employed briefly in private industry, working in deep-submersible engineering. In 1967, Ballard became a U.S. Navy officer in the Office of Naval Research deep submergence program at the Woods Hole Oceanographic Institution. In 1969, he was appointed a research associate in the ocean engineering department at Woods Hole.

The Mid-Atlantic Ridge

For his doctoral dissertation, Ballard explored the ocean floor off New England with the submersible *Alvin*, a vehicle designed for underwater research and the collection of rock samples. This experience led Ballard, with *Alvin*, to join a French research team, with its submersibles *Archimede* and *Cyana*, in Project FAMOUS (French-American Mid-Ocean Undersea Study) in the summers of 1973 and 1974. The object of their studies was the Mid-Atlantic Ridge, where the earth's crust is pulling apart and new seafloor is forming. Project FAMOUS confirmed Ballard's standing as a scientist and validated the earth science theory of continental drift.

Exploring Sunken Ships

Ballard probably is best known for locating the sunken luxury liner *Titanic*. This ship, once dubbed "unsinkable," plunged to the bottom of the ocean in nearly 13,000 feet of water on her maiden voyage after colliding with an iceberg on April 15, 1912, off Newfoundland. Nearly 1,500 people drowned in the disaster.

On September 1, 1985, Ballard and his crew found the *Titanic*. Ballard explored and photographed the wreckage with remotely operated submersibles and also personally toured the site aboard *Alvin*. The resulting film footage, magazine articles, and books about his venture made Ballard a household name around the world.

Ballard continued his geologic research on the ocean floor, and he discovered and photographed the sunken wrecks of a number of other vessels. Some had foundered in storms centuries ago, while others were sunk during World War II.

The JASON Foundation

Ballard established the JASON Foundation for Education to involve students in the excitement of marine science and discovery. Using a satellite communication network, schoolchil-

Tubeworms and crabs were found in the deep-sea vents explored by Ballard. (Robert R. Hessler)

dren can take part, via television, in exploring wrecks and other features of the ocean floor with Ballard. From his office in Woods Hole, or anywhere on the vast world ocean, Ballard seeks to share the excitement of undersea research with the public at large as well as with his colleagues.

Bibliography

By Ballard

"Manned Submersible Observations in the FAMOUS Area: Mid-Atlantic Ridge," *Science*, 1975

"Window on Earth's Interior," *National Geographic*, 1976

Exploring Our Living Planet, 1983

"ARGO-JASON," *Oceans*, 1983

"NR-1: The Navy's Inner-Space Shuttle," *National Geographic*, 1985

"How We Found *Titanic*," *National Geographic*, 1985 (with Jean-Louis Michel)

The Discovery of The "Titanic," 1987 (with Rick Archbold)

"The *Bismarck* Found," *National Geographic*, 1989

"The MEDEA/JASON Remotely Operated Vehicle System," *Deep-Sea Research*, 1993

"Riddle of the *Lusitania*," *National Geographic*, 1994

Explorations: My Quest for Adventure and Discovery Under the Sea, 1995 (with Malcolm McConnell)

About Ballard

"A Man with Titanic Vision." Frederic Golden. *Discover* (January, 1987).

"The Real Captain Nemo." Doug Garr. *Reader's Digest* (April, 1992).

"Selling the *Titanic*: It's Full Speed Ahead." A. Beam. *Business Week* (December 1, 1986).

(Albert C. Jensen)

David Baltimore

Areas of Achievement: Cell biology, immunology, and virology

Contribution: Baltimore shared the 1975 Nobel Prize in Physiology or Medicine for his discovery of the enzyme reverse transcriptase.

Mar. 7, 1938	Born in New York, New York
1964	Earns a Ph.D. in biology from Rockefeller University
1965	Becomes a research associate in virology at the Salk Institute of Biological Studies
1968	Appointed associate professor of microbiology at the Massachusetts Institute of Technology (MIT)
1972	Promoted to full professor
1974	Elected to the National Academy of Sciences and the American Academy of Arts and Sciences
1975	Awarded the Nobel Prize in Physiology or Medicine
1976	Helps found the Recombinant DNA Advisory Committee at the National Institutes of Health (NIH)
1979-1982	Serves on the NIH Recombinant DNA Advisory Committee
1982-1990	Appointed director of the Whitehead Institute
1990-1991	Serves as president of Rockefeller University
1994	Named Ivan R. Cottrell Professor of Molecular Biology and Immunology at MIT
1996	Appointed head of the AIDS Vaccine Research Committee
1997	Named president of the California Institute of Technology

Early Life

David Baltimore received his early education in the public schools of Great Neck, a suburb of New York City. He became interested in biology while still in high school when he attended a summer session at the Jackson Memorial Laboratory. He entered Swarthmore College in biology, but later switched to chemistry, earning a B.A. in 1960. He spent the summer before his senior year at the Cold Spring Harbor Laboratory.

Baltimore entered graduate school in biophysics at the Massachusetts Institute of Technology (MIT), but his decision to work on animal viruses led him to Albert Einstein Medical College, back to Cold Spring Harbor Laboratory, and then to the Rockefeller University, where he received his Ph.D. in biology.

After two stints as a postdoctoral fellow at MIT and Albert Einstein College, Baltimore garnered his first independent position, as a research associate in virology at the Salk Institute of Biological Sciences. There, he met virologist Alice S. Huang; they married in 1968. That year, they returned to MIT, where Baltimore became an associate professor of microbiology.

RNA Viruses

During his second summer at Cold Spring Harbor, Baltimore became interested in viruses that use ribonucleic acid (RNA) instead of deoxyribonucleic acid (DNA) as their genetic material. He wondered, "How does a virus hijack the chemical machinery of a cell and use it to make more virus particles?" One of his answers won for him the 1975 Nobel Prize in Physiology or Medicine, which he shared with Howard Temin and Renato Dulbecco.

Baltimore discovered that vesicular stomatitis virus particles contain an enzyme that copies viral RNA once the virus finds itself inside a cell, and he sought a similar enzyme in retroviruses.

Retroviruses were known to cause cancer in animals. This suggested to Temin in 1964 that these tumor viruses insert their genetic code into that cell's DNA, which required a DNA copy from the viral RNA. This "provirus" hypothesis contradicted the Central Dogma of molecular genetics and was not well received.

Baltimore had known Temin since they met

(The Nobel Foundation)

when Baltimore was a high-school student at Jackson Laboratory. Thinking that his old friend might be right, Baltimore searched for an enzyme that transcribed RNA into DNA and found it.

Temin performed a similar search, and, when the two friends realized they had made the same discovery independently, they decided to publish their results simultaneously. The enzyme that they discovered was later dubbed "reverse transcriptase."

A Cautious Scientist and Public Servant

Baltimore continued to study retroviruses, including the human immunodeficiency virus (HIV) that causes acquired immunodeficiency syndrome (AIDS). His research branched out into immunology.

When scientists developed techniques to cut strands of DNA from one organism and splice them into another, some feared that this might be dangerous. In 1974, Baltimore and ten like-minded members of the National Academy of Sciences called for a moratorium on experiments using this "recombinant DNA" tech-

Reverse Transcriptase

Baltimore showed that an enzyme in retroviruses can transcribe ribonucleic acid (RNA) into deoxyribonucleic acid (DNA).

The genetic material that makes up a cell's chromosomes is DNA, which determines the cell's proteins. Many of these proteins are enzymes, which control the chemical reactions in the cell.

A virus is a simple inert organism that invades a living cell and exploits the cell's metabolism to reproduce itself. The infected cell may die, live normally, or become "transformed." A virus, unlike a cell, may have either DNA or RNA as its genetic material.

Before Baltimore's studies, it was known that some RNA-containing viruses cause cancer in animals. Since cancer is uncontrolled cell reproduction, these viruses transform not only the infected cell but all of its descendants. How could a virus containing only RNA become part of the cell's DNA inheritance? It can do so if the viral RNA is transcribed into DNA and combined with the cell's DNA as a "provirus." Baltimore discovered the enzyme, reverse transcriptase, that performs this transcription.

Viruses that use reverse transcription are called retroviruses. This class of viruses includes the human immunodeficiency virus (HIV), which causes acquired immunodeficiency syndrome (AIDS). It is now recognized that reverse transcription occurs in normal cells and is the mechanism behind transposable genetic elements, or "jumping genes."

Reverse transcriptase has become an important reagent used in molecular biology and recombinant DNA techniques.

Bibliography
Molecular Design of Life. Lubert Stryer. New York: W. H. Freeman, 1989.
Reverse Transcriptase. Anna Marie Skalka and Stephen P. Goff, eds. Plainview, N.Y.: Cold Spring Harbor Laboratory Press, 1993.
"Reverse Transcription." Harold Varmus. *Scientific American* (September, 1987).
"RNA-Directed DNA Synthesis." Howard M. Temin. *Scientific American* (January, 1972).

nique. The moratorium lasted nearly two years while safety procedures were worked out.

Baltimore was instrumental in founding the Recombinant DNA Advisory Committee at the National Institutes of Health (NIH) to set further rules governing these genetic engineering experiments and was a member of the committee from 1979 to 1982. He served as one of the chairs of the Committee on a National Strategy for AIDS in 1986. In December, 1996, Baltimore was appointed by NIH director Harold Varmus to direct the effort to find an AIDS vaccine. The following year, he was named president of the California Institute of Technology (Caltech).

Bibliography
By Baltimore
"RNA-Dependent DNA Polymerase in Virions of RNA Tumour Viruses," *Nature*, 1970

Animal Virology, 1976 (as editor, with Alice S. Huang and C. Fred Fox)
Molecular Cell Biology, 1986 (with Harvey Lodish and James Darnell)

About Baltimore
"David Baltimore." In *The Nobel Prize Winners: Physiology or Medicine*, edited by Frank N. Magill. Pasadena, Calif.: Salem Press, 1991.
Nobel Laureates in Medicine or Physiology: A Biographical Dictionary. Daniel M. Fox, Marcia Meldrum, and Ira Rezak, eds. New York: Garland, 1990.
Nobel Prize Winners: An H. W. Wilson Biographical Dictionary. Tyler Wasson, ed. New York: H. W. Wilson, 1987.

(Randy Hudson)

Benjamin Banneker

Areas of Achievement: Astronomy, invention, and mathematics

Contribution: A free black man from colonial Maryland, Banneker achieved fame as a mathematician, an astronomer, a publisher of almanacs, and an inventor. He was a member of the commission that designed the layout of the District of Columbia.

Nov. 9, 1731	Born in Baltimore County, Maryland
1736-1740	Taught to read, write, and do simple arithmetic by his grandmother and a Quaker schoolmaster
1753	Creates the first striking clock made of wood in America
1759	Upon the death of his father, inherits the family tobacco farm
1771	Teaches himself trigonometry, calculus, and the fundamentals of astronomy from books loaned to him by a neighbor
1771	Serves as a technical assistant in designing and surveying the newly created District of Columbia
1791	Sends a letter to Secretary of State Thomas Jefferson challenging him to live up to the full meaning of his words "all men are created equal"
1792-1797	Publishes annual astronomical almanacs predicting the timing of such natural phenomena as tides, seasons, lengths of days, and eclipses
Oct. 9, 1806	Dies in Baltimore County, Maryland

Early Life

The son and grandson of former slaves, Benjamin Banneker was born near the Patapasco River in Baltimore County on November 9, 1731. Like many black children in colonial Maryland, he received little formal education. Fortunately, however, Banneker's natural intellectual abilities were cultivated—first by his maternal grandmother, Molly Walsh, who taught him how to read the Bible, and later by a Quaker schoolteacher, who introduced him to the world of mathematics.

During his youth, Banneker also learned from his father the tobacco farming skills that would provide him with the income that sustained him throughout most of his life.

From Tobacco Farmer to Astronomer

At the age of twenty-one, Banneker borrowed a watch from a well-to-do neighbor, Josef Levi. Fascinated by the watch, Banneker took the device apart to see how it worked. After sketching its components, he reassembled the watch and returned it to its owner. From the drawing, Banneker then began to construct out of wood an enlarged replica of each piece of the watch.

Constructing a wooden clock from scratch was no easy task. It required precise calculations of the proper number of teeth for each gear and the relationships between the gears. When Banneker's model was assembled, however, the wooden clock kept accurate time and even struck on the hour, as designed. His imaginative mind produced the first striking clock to be made entirely in America.

Around 1771, Banneker became close friends with George Ellicott, a Quaker formerly from Bucks County, Pennsylvania, who purchased with his four brothers the land adjoining Banneker's farm. Ellicott provided Banneker not only with friendship but also with a library of books on astronomy and mathematics and a collection of instruments for observing the stars.

Banneker taught himself trigonometry and calculus, constructed a work cabin with a skylight, and began to study the motion of stars. From this rudimentary observatory, he collected data that he used to predict the solar eclipse of 1789 and to produce a number of astronomical almanacs. Multiple editions of these almanacs sold throughout the mid-Atlantic states between 1792 and 1797.

Banneker had a key role in the planning of Washington, D.C. (The Associated Publishers, Inc.)

National Contributions

In 1791, Ellicott introduced Banneker to his cousin Major Andrew Ellicott, a man chosen to survey a ten-square-mile region known as the Federal Territory (now the District of Columbia). Major Ellicott hired Banneker as a technical assistant on the project, and together they worked with Pierre L'Enfant, the French architect in charge of planning the layout of the new national capital. When L'Enfant was suddenly dismissed from the project and took his designs with him, Banneker re-created the original plans from memory and thus played a prominent role in the completion of the project.

Banneker also is remembered for a literary exchange that he had with Thomas Jefferson. In August, 1791, Banneker sent a letter, along with a copy of his soon-to-be-published almanac, to Jefferson, who was then secretary of state. The letter reprimanded Jefferson for some unflattering remarks about Africans that appeared in Jefferson's *Notes on the State of Virginia* (1785) and politely challenged him to live up to the grand principles that Jefferson himself once elegantly conveyed in the preamble to the Declaration of Independence—that "all men are created equal." Jefferson responded with a kindly note that congratulated Ban-

Astronomical Almanacs

Banneker authored the first scientific book published by an African American, an astronomical almanac.

A popular literary genre of the late eighteenth century was the astronomical almanac. These almanacs typically contained a wide variety of practical and entertaining information: tide tables for those who lived near the ocean, sunrise tables and planting charts for those who lived on farms, medicinal suggestions for those with common illnesses, and predictions of future solar and lunar eclipses for sky watchers.

In 1792, Robert Thomas published the first edition of *The Farmer's Almanac*, a piece destined to become America's oldest continuously published periodical. In that same year, Banneker published a competing volume. Although Banneker's almanac would not have the longevity of *The Farmer's Almanac*, it would run through

twenty-nine editions and would be sold widely throughout the mid-Atlantic states. Moreover, as the first scientific book written by an African American, the book helped forge the reputation of a man affectionately remembered as the "sable astronomer," whose intellect demonstrated for many the absurdity of the myth of African intellectual inferiority.

Bibliography

Banneker: The Afro-American Astronomer. Will W. Allen. Freeport, N.Y.: Books for Libraries Press, 1971.

Benjamin Banneker, Scientist. Garnet Jackson. Cleveland: Modern Curriculum Press, 1993.

A Chronology of the Life of Benjamin Banneker, Son of Maryland, 1731-1806. African-American Bicentennial Center. Baltimore: Commission on Afro-American History and Culture, 1976.

neker on his scholarly publication and suggested that such works would help dispel erroneous notions about African intellectual inferiority.

Banneker died in 1806 at the age of seventy-four.

Bibliography

By Banneker

Benjamin Banneker's Pennsylvania, Delaware, Maryland, and Virginia Almanack, and Ephemeris for the Year of Our Lord 1792, 1791

Banneker's Almanack, and Ephemeris for the Year of Our Lord 1793, 1792

The Virginia Almanack, for the Year of Our Lord, 1794, 1793?

"The Banneker-Jefferson Correspondence" in *Constructing the American Past: A Source Book of a People's History*, Vol. 1, 1991 (Elliott Gorn et al., eds.)

About Banneker

Benjamin Banneker. Kevin Conley. New York: Chelsea House, 1989.

Benjamin Banneker: The Man Who Saved Washington. Claude Lewis. New York: McGraw-Hill, 1970.

The Life of Benjamin Banneker. Silvio A. Bedini. New York: Charles Scribner's Sons, 1972.

(Terry D. Bilhartz)

Sir Frederick Grant Banting

Areas of Achievement: Biology, medicine, and physiology

Contribution: Banting isolated the hormone insulin and implemented its use in the treatment of humans afflicted with diabetes.

Nov. 14, 1891	Born in Alliston, Ontario, Canada
1910	Abandons ministry studies for medicine at the University of Toronto
1916	Serves as a lieutenant in the Canadian Medical Corps during World War I
1918	Works as an orthopedic surgeon
1920	Teaches anatomy and physiology at the University of Western Ontario
1921	Resigns from teaching to begin pancreatic research at the University of Toronto
1922	Successfully isolates and administers insulin to treat diabetic dogs
1923	Receives the Nobel Prize in Physiology or Medicine with John J. R. Macleod
1930	The Banting Institute of the University of Toronto opens
1930	Appointed director of the Banting-Best Department of Medical Research
1939	Serves as a captain in the Canadian Army Medical Corps during World War II
Feb. 21, 1941	Dies near Musgrave Harbour, Newfoundland, Canada

Early Life

Sir Frederick Grant Banting was born in Ontario, Canada, in 1891. In 1909, after his education in local primary and secondary schools, he entered the University of Toronto for a ministry degree. After one year, he switched to a medical degree.

In 1918, Banting worked as an orthopedic surgeon. After two years, he taught anatomy and physiology at the University of Western Ontario. He also conducted medical research under the supervision of Frederick Robert Miller, a prominent neurophysiologist.

Interest in the Pancreas

Banting was dedicated to teaching. While researching the literature for an upcoming lecture on the pancreas, he became curious about previous work on diabetes and the pancreas. He read that if the pancreatic ducts were damaged but the islets of Langerhans remained intact, no diabetic symptoms developed.

Researchers theorized that the islets of

(National Institutes of Health)

Langerhans released a hormone preventing diabetes. Extracting this compound, however, was a problem. Investigators speculated that other pancreatic secretions outside the islets of Langerhans destroyed the mystery hormone during extraction procedures. Researchers discovered that, with blockage of the pancreatic ducts, all regions in the pancreas atrophied except for the islets of Langerhans.

Banting had a talent for synthesis. He read about many seemingly unrelated research discoveries about the pancreas and fit the pieces of the diabetes puzzle together. In October, 1920, he designed his famous experiment that increased the lifespan of diabetics.

Isolating Insulin

Banting planned to extract the mysterious diabetes-preventing hormone and use it to treat dogs with experimentally induced diabetes. He described his extraction idea to Miller, his research supervisor. Miller encouraged Banting to present his proposal to John J. R. Macleod of the University of Toronto, who was one of the foremost scientists studying carbohydrate metabolism.

Macleod had written in textbooks that the pancreas did not produce internal secretions and that the islets of Langerhans functioned as a detoxification center. Nevertheless, Macleod granted Banting laboratory space for eight weeks, ten dogs, and an assistant, Charles Best. Banting and Best surgically tied off the pancreatic ducts of some dogs, and surgically removed the pancreases of other dogs.

The depancreatized dogs developed diabetes. Banting removed the pancreases with tied off ducts and administered the pancreatic extract to the dogs with experimentally induced diabetes. Within two hours, the major diabetic symptoms vanished. This extract was identified as the hormone insulin.

Research to Help Diabetics

James Bertram Collip, a biochemist, helped Banting with the purification of insulin. In January, 1922, insulin was administered for the first time to a human diabetic. The results were positive, and soon insulin injections became the chief treatment for diabetes, along with diet monitoring.

The Function of Insulin

The hormone insulin helps maintain stable blood glucose levels. Immediately after eating, the pancreas releases insulin, which triggers the muscle and liver cells to remove any excess glucose in the blood.

Hormones are protein chemicals released by endocrine glands, ductless (tubeless) glands that release hormones directly into the blood. Examples of endocrine glands are the pancreas (which releases insulin and glucagon), the ovaries (which release estrogen and progesterone), and the pituitary (which releases thyroid-stimulating hormone and growth hormone). Because hormones from endocrine glands are carried through the bloodstream, they come into contact with the cells of all the different organs of the body.

Often, hormones have an impact on cells of only one or two organs. These cells have receptors on their cell membranes that fit perfectly the three- dimensional structure of the hormone. Immediately after meals, the pancreas releases insulin, to which the receptors of muscle and liver cells attach. This uptake triggers the muscle and liver cells to remove glucose from the bloodstream. The glucose is then converted to glycogen for temporary energy storage of about four hours. Thus, there is no drastic rise in blood glucose immediately after meals.

Four to six hours after a meal, the pancreas releases the hormone glucagon, which is also picked up by receptors on the muscle and liver cells. Glucagon stimulates the liver and muscle cells to convert glycogen back to glucose and release it into the bloodstream. Through this pancreatic release of insulin and glucagon, the body maintains stable blood glucose levels.

Individuals afflicted with diabetes have unstable blood glucose levels. After meals, they experience drastic rises in blood glucose levels, which cause many diabetes-related health problems. Two basic types of diabetes are insulin-dependent diabetes, also called juvenile-onset diabetes, and insulin-independent or adult-onset diabetes.

Insulin-independent diabetes generally occurs in obese individuals with a genetic predisposition for diabetes. The pancreas produces sufficient insulin, but the liver and muscle cells do not respond to the insulin circulating in the bloodstream. Therefore, the administration of insulin has no effect. The treatment for insulin-independent diabetes consists of exercise and dieting. With increasing exercise and weight loss, the liver and muscle cells become more sensitive to insulin.

Insulin-dependent diabetes occurs when the insulin-producing cells of the pancreas do not produce sufficient insulin, especially immediately after meals. Thus, the liver and muscle cells are not sufficiently stimulated to remove glucose from the blood, creating a drastic rise in blood glucose levels. Individuals with this type of diabetes can be treated with insulin injections administered a half hour before meals, which help to moderate blood glucose levels, as first established by Banting in 1922. Banting and his colleagues also recognized that diet, exercise activity, and emotional stress affect glucose blood levels, so that a diabetic's normal insulin dose may sometimes be too much. This is critical, since the injection of too much insulin results in diabetic shock or coma.

Diabetics continue to face radical fluctuations in blood glucose levels from artificial insulin administration, which causes health problems. Alterations in two amino acids of the protein insulin help to increase the rate of insulin absorption from the injection site to the bloodstream by thirty minutes. The increased absorption better mimics a healthy, functioning body in diabetics—a goal that was first realized because of Banting's research.

Bibliography

Diabetes Mellitus. John E. Fogarty. Washington, D.C.: National Institutes of Health, 1976.

Human Physiology. Stuart Ira Fox. Dubuque, Iowa: Wm. C. Brown, 1990.

Invisible Frontiers. Stephan S. Hall. New York: Atlantic Monthly Press, 1987.

In 1923, Macleod and Banting received the Nobel Prize in Physiology or Medicine for their research. Each of them divided their share of the prize money equally with Best and Collip.

Later Career

The Banting Institute of the University of Toronto opened in 1930, and Banting became the director of the Banting-Best Department of Medical Research that same year. Until the start of World War II, he primarily studied cancer and coronary thrombosis, and during the war he conducted research in aviation medicine.

On February 21, 1941, Banting died in a plane crash in Newfoundland en route to England to maintain a research liaison. Many hail Banting for significantly lengthening the lives of diabetics.

Bibliography

By Banting

"Internal Secretion of Pancreas," *Journal of Laboratory and Clinical Medicine*, 1922 (with C. H. Best)

"Pancreatic Extracts in Diabetics," *Journal of the Canadian Medical Association*, 1922 (with C. H. Best, J. B. Collip, W. R. Campbell, and A. A. Fletcher)

"Effect of Pancreatic Extract (Insulin) on Normal Rabbits," *American Journal of Physiology*, 1922

"Insulin in Treatment of Diabetes Mellitus," *Journal of Metabolic Research*, 1922 (with W. R. Campbell and A. A. Fletcher)

About Banting

Banting: A Biography. Michael Bliss. Toronto: McClelland and Stewart, 1984.

Banting's Miracle: The Story of the Discoverer of Insulin. Seale Harris. Philadelphia: J. B. Lippincott, 1946.

The Discoverer of Insulin: Dr. Frederick G. Banting. Israel E. Levine. New York: Julian Messner, 1959.

The Insulin Man: The Story of Sir Frederick Banting. John Rowland. London: Lutterworth Press, 1965.

Sir Frederick Banting. Lloyd G. Stevenson. Toronto: Ryerson Press, 1946.

(Jessica O. Ellison)

John Bardeen

Areas of Achievement: Invention and physics

Contribution: Bardeen was a pioneer in the development of modern solid-state physics and its application to electronics.

May 23, 1908	Born in Madison, Wisconsin
1928	Receives a B.S. in electrical engineering from the University of Wisconsin
1929	Receives an M.S. in electrical engineering from Wisconsin
1930	Joins the Gulf Research and Development Corporation
1935	Appointed a Junior Fellow at Harvard University
1936	Receives a Ph.D. in mathematics and physics from Princeton
1938	Appointed an assistant professor at the University of Minnesota
1941	Accepts a position as a physicist at the Naval Ordnance Laboratory
1945	Joins the technical staff of the Bell Telephone Laboratories
1951	Teaches electrical engineering at the University of Illinois
1954	Elected a member of the National Academy of Sciences
1956	Shares the Nobel Prize in Physics with William Shockley and Walter Brattain
1959	Appointed to the Center for Advanced Study at Illinois
1972	Shares the Nobel Prize in Physics with J. Robert Schrieffer and Leon N Cooper
Jan. 30, 1991	Dies in Boston, Massachusetts

Bardeen (second from left), standing between William Shockley (left) and Walter Brattain, is handed a gold medal to commemorate the twenty-fifth anniversary of their invention of the transistor. (Library of Congress)

Early Life

John Bardeen was born in 1908 in Madison, Wisconsin, the son of Charles Russell Bardeen, dean of the medical school at the University of Wisconsin, and Althea Harmer Bardeen. By the time that he was in the third grade in the Madison public schools, his exceptional academic ability had been recognized, and he was allowed to enter seventh grade at University High School the following year.

Having discovered a fondness for both science and mathematics, Bardeen decided to major in electrical engineering at the University of Wisconsin, with minors in mathematics and physics. He received bachelor's and master's degrees before beginning his first job at the Gulf Research and Development Corporation in Pittsburgh.

Bardeen resumed his formal studies in 1933 as a doctoral student at Princeton University under Professor Eugene P. Wigner, who, like Bardeen, would later win a Nobel Prize. Even before receiving his doctoral degree, Bardeen was appointed a Junior Fellow at Harvard University. This prestigious position, usually reserved for individuals who had completed their doctoral degree, would allow him to devote three years to research.

Bardeen began his academic career at the University of Minnesota, moving to the Naval Ordnance Laboratory at the start of World War II. In 1945, he joined the technical staff of the Bell Telephone Laboratories, where he worked with William Shockley and Walter Brattain in developing the first transistor. In 1951, he accepted a faculty position at the University of Illinois, where he soon turned his attention to the theory of superconductivity. Bardeen shared the Nobel Prize in Physics twice, in 1956 for the invention of the transistor and in 1972 for the theory of superconductivity.

Solid-State Physics

While Bardeen was a university undergraduate, several European physicists—including Werner Heisenberg of Germany, Niels Bohr of Denmark, Erwin Schrödinger of Austria, and Paul A. M. Dirac of England—were developing a mathematical theory called quantum mechanics that, in principle, made it possible to calculate all the properties of matter that resulted from the behavior of electrons in the

Transitors

The first miniature amplifier, the point contact transistor, was developed by Bardeen and Walter Brattain in 1948.

The inventions of the telegraph, the telephone, and radio transmission made real the possibility of nearly instant long-distance communication that is almost taken for granted today. Each of these technologies, however, required the ability to amplify electrical signals that had become extremely weak as a result of transmission over long distances.

The first satisfactory solution of this problem was the vacuum tube triode, patented by American inventor Lee De Forest in 1906. In this device, electrons were released from a heated metal cathode and attracted to a positively charged anode, traveling through the openings in a wire mesh grid. Through the application of a small signal voltage to the grid, large changes in the current from cathode to anode could be achieved, thus amplifying the signal.

De Forest's triode and subsequent refinements formed the basis of radio and television technology until the 1950's. Unfortunately, vacuum tubes were large and generated enough heat that special cooling arrangements were often needed. Furthermore, heating elements would burn out with some frequency. The first electronic computers, based on vacuum tube technology, occupied entire rooms and had to be tested after each calculation to ensure that no tubes had burned out, leading to a wrong answer.

By the close of World War II, it was apparent to many scientists that a miniature amplifier was badly needed and that the unusual electrical properties of semiconductors could provide the basis for one. The point contact transistor, unveiled by Bardeen and Brattain in 1948, was based on the change in the concentration of conducting electrons or holes that occurred in the region of a semiconductor near a metal point when current flowed through the metal into or out of the semiconductor.

Depending on the precise composition of the semiconductor, current flow into the semiconductor would result in an increase or decrease in conductivity, while current flow in the opposite direction would have the opposite effect. Placing two metal point contacts close to each other on the surface of a semiconductor and a third electrode on the other side made it possible for a small current flowing through one of the point contacts to regulate a much larger current passing through the other one, in much the same way that a small signal applied to the grid of a vacuum tube can control the much larger current flowing through the tube. This invention was followed by William Shockley's junction transistor, in which the localized introduction of impurities into the semiconductor material made it possible to use sturdier electrical contacts and yet have the same effect.

Unlike vacuum tubes, transistor technology has proven remarkably amenable to miniaturization. The semiconductor chips now found in all digital computers may contain a million or more transistors created in a single piece of semiconductor material.

Bibliography

Bell Laboratories. Arthur Gregor. New York: Charles Scribner's Sons, 1972.

Electrons and Holes in Semiconductors. William Shockley. Princeton, N.J.: Van Nostrand, 1950.

The Physical Basis of Electronics. D. J. Harris and P. N. Robson. New York: Pergamon Press, 1974.

component atoms. This new theory provided the first convincing explanation of why solid materials differ so greatly in their ability to conduct electricity and heat.

According to the quantum theory of solids, the allowed energy levels in a solid are grouped together in bands. Electrical conduction can only occur if some of the levels in a band are empty. Metals are characterized by a conduction band with many filled and many vacant energy levels. Semiconductors, intermediate in conductivity between metals and insulators, have a valence band nearly filled with electrons and a conduction band with only a few electrons. The vacant levels in the valence band give rise to the sort of behavior associated with moving positive charges, of electron "holes" rather than electrons. The vibrations of the atoms also correspond to well-defined energy levels, and it is useful to speak of quanta of vibrational energy called phonons that can interact with the electrons and one another.

Bardeen's initial scientific work involved calculating the work function, or the energy necessary to remove an electron from the surface of the two simplest metals, lithium and sodium. The new quantum mechanics provided a direct method to calculate such properties based solely on the arrangement of the atoms in the metal and the behavior of the inner-shell

Superconductivity

In the 1950's, Bardeen and his colleagues studied superconductivity and developed the BCS theory to explain this phenomenon involving the disappearance of electrical resistance at low temperatures.

One of the major triumphs of late nineteenth and early twentieth century science was the ability to achieve low temperatures, and the study of the properties of matter at low temperatures naturally drew the attention of many superb physicists. One of the greatest surprises in this field of research was the discovery in 1911 by Dutch physicist Heike Kamerlingh Onnes that the electrical resistance of certain metals disappears entirely below what is known as the superconducting transition temperature. Subsequent measurements revealed that about half of the elements in the periodic table and many compounds and alloys become superconducting at very low temperatures. It was also discovered that many superconductors completely expel any magnetic field as they become superconducting and that the superconducting transition temperature is related to the mass of the atoms composing the material.

Beginning with his appointment at the University of Illinois, Bardeen directed his attention to superconductivity. His partners in this research were Leon N Cooper, a young postdoctoral fellow, and J. Robert Schrieffer, a graduate student at the university. The key to the phenomenon turned out to be the interaction of the electrons and the phonons, or quantized lattice vibrations, suggested by the dependence of the transition temperature on the mass of the vibrating atoms.

In 1956, Cooper showed that it was possible for this interaction in effect to create a state in which two electrons form a pair that can travel together and that small disturbances do not pro-

vide enough energy to disrupt the pair. Proving that this effect could explain the complete disappearance of resistance, along with the exclusion of magnetic fields and the relationship between transition temperature and mass, involved very complex calculations in quantum mechanics, done mainly by Schrieffer under the guidance of Bardeen. The Bardeen, Cooper, and Schrieffer (or BCS) theory was quickly accepted as the explanation for superconductivity.

Applications of superconducting materials were being developed at about the same time, but the range of applications was limited by the cost of maintaining the materials at temperatures close to absolute zero, which as a practical matter required the use of liquid helium and very expensive refrigeration systems. The first major practical application of superconductors was in windings for powerful electromagnets; this made it possible to maintain strong magnetic fields without the continuous input of electrical energy.

New technological possibilities became apparent in 1987 when Paul Chu, a professor at the University of Alabama, discovered the first of many complex chemical compounds that would exhibit superconductivity above 77 degrees Celsius absolute temperature, the boiling point of liquid nitrogen, which is easily prepared from air at very low cost. These semiconductors have stimulated a new era of superconductivity research.

Bibliography
The Path of Least Resistance. Bruce Schecter. New York: Simon & Schuster, 1989.

The Solid State. H. M. Rosenberg. 3d ed. New York: Oxford University Press, 1988.

Superconductivity. J. R. Schrieffer. Reading, Mass.: W. A. Benjamin, 1964.

(The Nobel Foundation)

electrons. The equations involved, however, could be solved only by approximate numerical techniques, which, prior to the invention of the electronic computer, meant weeks of painstaking calculations using a hand calculator.

This research provided Bardeen with financial support to spend three years conducting basic research. During this period, he did some of the first work on the interaction of electrons and phonons. Bardeen retained his interest in electrical conductivity and its control throughout his career, turning first to the semiconductor, in his work on the transistor and superconductors.

Bardeen died in Boston in 1991; he was eighty-two years old.

Bibliography
By Bardeen
"An Improved Calculation of the Energies of Metallic Li and Na," *Journal of Chemical Physics*, 1938

"The Transistor, a Semi-Conductor Triode," *Physical Review*, 1948 (with Walter Brattain)

"Physical Principles Involved in Transistor Action," *Physical Review*, 1949 (with Brattain)

"Microscopic Theory of Superconductivity," *Physical Review*, 1957 (with Leon N Cooper and J. Robert Schreiffer)

"Reminiscences of Early Days in Solid State Physics," *Proceedings of the Royal Society of London* A, 1980

About Bardeen
"Consultant to Industry, Advisor to Government." George Pake. *Physics Today* (April, 1992).

"An Extraordinary Man: Reflections on John Bardeen." David Pines. *Physics Today* (April, 1992).

"Recollections from the Early Years of Solid State Physics." Conyers Herring. *Physics Today* (April, 1992).

(Donald R. Franceschetti)

Christiaan Barnard

Area of Achievement: Medicine

Contribution: Barnard pioneered surgical methods for kidney and heart transplantation essential to the evolution of organ transplantation in general.

Nov. 8, 1922	Born in Beaufort West, South Africa
1947	Becomes an intern at Capetown's Groote Schuur Hospital
1948	Marries Aletta Gertruda Luow
1950	Becomes senior resident at Capetown's City Hospital
1953	Receives an M.D. from the University of Capetown
1956	Begins work in cardiothoracic surgery at the University of Minnesota Medical School
1966	Learns kidney transplantation techniques at the Medical College of Virginia
1967	Performs the first kidney transplantation in South Africa
1967	Performs the first successful human heart transplantation
1970	Divorces his first wife and marries Barbara Zoeller
1974	Performs the first successful double heart transplantation
1983	Retires from his position as head of Cardiac Research and Surgery at Groote Schuur
1985	Becomes a senior consultant and scientist at the Oklahoma Heart Center, Baptist Memorial Hospital

Early Life

Christiaan Neethling Barnard was born in Beaufort West, South Africa, on November 8, 1922. He was one of the five sons of Adam Hendrik Barnard and Maria Elisabeth de Swart Barnard, Afrikaner missionaries. Christiaan's father was a minister of the Dutch Reformed Church, and his mother had been a teacher before her marriage.

Christiaan Barnard attended local elementary and high schools. In 1946, he earned a preliminary medical degree from the University of Capetown. In 1947, Barnard became an intern at Capetown's Groote Schuur Hospital and then spent two years in general practice in Ceres, South Africa. In 1948, he married Aletta Gertruda Luow; they had a son and a daughter.

In 1950, Barnard became Capetown City Hospital's senior resident. There, he began research, writing a thesis on treating children with tuberculosis. In 1953, the University of Capetown granted him an M.D.

Surgery on Hearts and Intestines

Upon his graduation, Barnard entered a surgery residency at Groote Schuur. There, he began work that would lead to his fame as a transplantation surgeon, carrying out experiments that perfected open-heart surgery in dogs. First, Barnard developed means to slow life processes, making the surgery safer, by using a cold water-filled balloon inserted into the stomach of the subject. This method was later used on humans.

At this time, Barnard also studied deadly intestine atresia, a birth defect in which newborns have holes in their intestines. Work on pregnant dogs showed that atresia is caused by inadequate blood supply to the fetus. Barnard then designed a means to repair the defect.

Surgical Methods in the United States

In 1956, Barnard obtained a Charles Adams Scholarship to work with Owen Wangensteen, a pioneer cardiothoracic surgery at the University of Minnesota Medical School in Minneapolis. There, Barnard helped in designing and implanting artificial heart valves and set the stage for his later work.

Thanks to this association, Barnard was able to bring a heart-lung machine back to South Africa. The machine, relatively rare at the time, oxygenates the blood of surgery patients and pumps it through the body during open-heart

Kidney and Heart Transplantation

Barnard's work pioneered the transplantation of kidneys and hearts, which are now common procedures.

Barnard's excellent background in cardiovascular surgery prepared him to pioneer heart transplantation in 1967 in Capetown, South Africa. Early in his career, Barnard perfected, in dogs, methods crucial to human open-heart surgery, especially slowing life processes via a coolant balloon in the stomach of the surgical subject. At the University of Minnesota, he learned state-of-the-art cardiothoracic surgery. As a result of his international interactions, Barnard was able to bring back to South Africa an essential heart-lung machine.

Back in his own country, Barnard developed methods for working with the main heart blood vessels, surgically replacing natural heart valves with artificial ones, and for transplanting the hearts of dogs. In addition, prior to surgery on humans, he surmounted the huge problem of preventing a patient's immune system from rejecting the transplanted organ. This was accomplished by using drugs and radiation to stop the rejection of transplanted kidneys. In 1967, Barnard then carried out the first human kidney transplantation in South Africa.

Therefore, later in 1967, Barnard was ready to transplant into Louis Washkansky the heart from deceased accident victim Denise Darvall. This surgical feat was both a success and a failure: Although Washkansky survived the operation, he died eighteen days later from pneumonia because of the failure of his immune system, which had been suppressed by antirejection treatments.

The surgery, carried out by Barnard and a twenty-person surgical team, used a method in which the bottom parts of donor and recipient hearts were removed and interchanged. The process simplified the surgical task and increased Washkansky's chance of prolonged survival. This procedure was possible because his heart's main blood vessels, as well as the nerve cells that regulate the heartbeat, were in good shape and could be conserved. It should be noted that although Barnard had tried the method in dogs, it was first developed in those animals by Norman Shumway of California's Stanford University. Barnard's transplant surgery occurred first because he was presented with the first viable human subject.

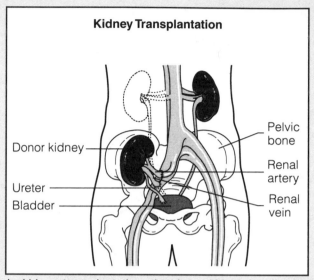

Kidney Transplantation

Donor kidney
Ureter
Bladder
Pelvic bone
Renal artery
Renal vein

In kidney transplantation, the donor kidney is often attached near the pelvic bone. The dotted lines indicate the former location of the damaged kidney that has been removed. (Hans & Cassady, Inc.)

Barnard's honor and his impeccable care for human patients is shown by his unwillingness to take the donor's heart until it had stopped beating. As stated in his 1969 autobiography, cowritten by Curtis Bill Pepper, Barnard did not want to touch the heart of the donor, a young woman, until she was truly a cadaver. Thus, no unseemly rushing to take the organ before the patient had died naturally, under excellent care, was carried out by Barnard. This kind of conduct continued in all of Barnard's other transplantation procedures over the next fifteen years as head of Cardiac Research and Surgery at South Africa's Groote Schuur Hospital.

Bibliography

Christiaan Barnard: One Life. Christiaan Barnard and Curtis Bill Pepper. New York: Macmillan, 1969.

The Transplanted Heart. Peter Hawthorne. Chicago: Rand McNally, 1968.

surgery. Without it, Barnard's famous work would have been impossible.

Back to South Africa, a Prelude to Fame

Back at Groote Schuur Hospital, Barnard developed techniques to correct heart defects, including methods for working on the main blood vessels and the use of artificial heart valves to replace malformed natural ones. Barnard also began to experiment with heart transplantation in dogs. A major problem with such procedures was stopping the patient's immune system from destroying the transplanted organ.

A stepping stone toward heart transplantation was kidney transplantation using drugs that stopped the immune system's rejection of the transplant. Barnard learned this method in 1966 at the Medical College of Virginia. In 1967, he carried out the first South African kidney transplantation.

The First Heart Transplantation

In November, 1967, the chance for Barnard's first heart transplantation procedure arose when fifty-five-year-old Louis Washkansky was hospitalized. The patient expected to die within weeks as a result of a failing heart and agreed to the surgery. The transplanted heart came from Denise Darvall, who was hospitalized in a vehicular accident and died on December 3. The organ was used immediately after her death.

Initially, the surgery was deemed a success, but eighteen days later, Washkansky died of pneumonia. His immune system had been turned off by the drugs and radiation used to minimize transplant rejection, and his body was unable to fight bacterial infection. Nevertheless, the operation led surgeons to carry out a hundred transplants, worldwide, in the ensuing year.

Barnard's groundbreaking surgery opened ethical questions, such as the possibility that the deaths of possible donors would be hastened in order to obtain organs. This concern did not stop transplantation from taking place. Instead, early enthusiasm waned as most subjects quickly died of infections. By the mid-1980's, however, survival rates had climbed, the methodologies had improved, and heart transplantation surgery had become common.

In 1970, Barnard divorced his first wife in order to marry steel heiress Barbara Zoeller, with whom he had two sons; they divorced in 1982. He served as head of Cardiac Research and Surgery at Groote Schuur until he retired in 1983. He wrote several books, including an autobiography and a text on surgery for congenital heart problems. In 1985, Barnard became senior consultant and scientist at the Oklahoma Heart Center at Oklahoma City's Baptist Memorial Hospital. Two years later, he married his third wife.

As a result of his many pioneering surgical endeavors, Barnard won numerous honorary doctorates and awards, including the Dag Hammarskjold International Prize, the Kennedy Foundation Award, and the Milan International Prize for Science.

(Library of Congress)

Bibliography
By Barnard
The Surgery of the Common Congenital Cardiac Malformations, 1968 (with Velva Schrire)
Christiaan Barnard: One Life, 1969 (with Curtis Bill Pepper)
Good Life/Good Death: A Doctor's Case for Euthanasia and Suicide, 1980

About Barnard
Christiaan Barnard: One Life. Christiaan Barnard and Curtis Bill Pepper. New York: Macmillian, 1969.
The Transplanted Heart. Peter Hawthorne. Chicago: Rand McNally, 1968.

(Sanford S. Singer)

Edward Emerson Barnard

Area of Achievement: Astronomy
Contribution: Barnard discovered numerous comets and the fifth satellite of Jupiter. His observations and photographs helped prove that space includes vast clouds of dust.

Dec. 16, 1857	Born in Nashville, Tennessee
1866	Becomes a photography assistant
1881	Discovers his first comet with a 5-inch telescope
1883-1887	Appointed an astronomer at Vanderbilt University
1888	Joins the staff at Lick Observatory in California
1889	Begins to photograph the Milky Way
1892	Wins the Gold Medal of the French Académie des Sciences
1892	Discovers Amalthea, the fifth satellite of Jupiter
1894	Makes detailed observations of the planet Mars
1895	Joins the staffs of the University of Chicago and Yerkes Observatory in Wisconsin
1897	Wins the Gold Medal of the Royal Astronomical Society
1898	Named vice president of the American Association for the Advancement of Science
1913-1916	Concludes that "dark nebulas" are interstellar clouds
1916	Discovers the star with the fastest known apparent motion
Feb. 6, 1923	Dies in Williams Bay, Wisconsin

Early Life

Edward Emerson Barnard was born in Nashville in 1857 after his father's death, and his impoverished mother struggled to support her two boys through the Civil War. Edward attended school for only two months, but he learned astronomy from a popular book. In 1866, he became a photographer's assistant, a job that acquainted him with film and lenses.

In 1877, young Barnard met the famed astronomer Simon Newcomb, who was visiting Nashville. Newcomb brusquely told the boy that he must learn mathematics to become an astronomer, unless he intended to discover comets.

Astronomical Discoveries

In 1881, using a 5-inch telescope, Barnard found a new comet and received a $200 award. In 1883, he was appointed astronomer at the Vanderbilt University observatory in Nashville, where he found seven more comets by 1887. During his entire life, he would discover at least sixteen comets.

Barnard joined the staff of the new Lick Observatory near San Jose, California, in 1888.

There, he discovered the fifth satellite of Jupiter, later named Amalthea. Barnard used a telescopic camera to photograph the rich details of the Milky Way, including its "dark nebulas." Initially, he suspected that these were "holes" or areas without stars.

The planet Mars was in the news at that time. The Boston astronomer Percival Lowell incorrectly claimed to see long, thin lines on its surface that he believed were canals built by Martians. In 1894, Barnard made detailed observations of Mars through the 36-inch Lick telescope and saw no such lines.

Yerkes Observatory

In 1895, Barnard accepted a post as an astronomer at the University of Chicago, which was erecting Yerkes Observatory in Wisconsin. He would spend the rest of his career at Yerkes.

Between 1913 and 1916, he gradually changed his mind about the dark nebulas. They were not holes after all, he decided. Rather, they were clouds of matter obscuring distant stars.

In 1916, Barnard discovered a star crossing the sky at ten seconds of arc per year, the fastest

Interstellar Matter

Barnard's observations and photographs of the Milky Way helped to persuade astronomers that the vast spaces between stars are not entirely empty and that huge clouds of diffuse matter exist between them.

When Barnard began his observations in the 1890's, astronomers were puzzled by nebulas, fuzzy patches of light in the sky. Some thought they were distant galaxies of stars. Others suggested that they were clouds of matter condensing into new planetary systems.

Barnard photographed the Milky Way in great detail and found it to be covered with dark blotches. At first, he assumed that the blotches were "holes" in space where stars were absent. In the summer of 1913, however, as he was photographing the southern Milky Way, small cumulus clouds passed over the galaxy. Against the brilliant band of stars, the clouds appeared ink-black. In fact, they resembled the dark markings that he had photographed previously. He concluded that

the galactic blotches are huge interstellar clouds that appear dark against the Milky Way.

It was subsequently determined that some nebulas are, indeed, independent galaxies of stars far from the Milky Way. Others, however, including the dark blotches on the Milky Way, are vast clouds of dust, as other astronomers established after Barnard's death. Later theorists would explain how these enormous dust clouds condense under gravitational pull into new stars and planetary systems.

Bibliography

The Birth of the Earth. David E. Fisher. New York: Columbia University Press, 1987.

In Darkness Born: The Story of Star Formation. Martin Cohen. Cambridge, England: Cambridge University Press, 1988.

Solar System Evolution: A New Perspective. Stuart Ross Taylor. Cambridge, England: Cambridge University Press, 1992.

(Library of Congress)

"proper motion" known at that time. It was later named Barnard's Star.

Honors
In 1897, Barnard won the Gold Medal of the Royal Astronomical Society. In 1898, he served as vice president of the American Association for the Advancement of Science. From 1900 to 1917, he received other major prizes from the French Académie des Sciences, the French Astronomical Society, and the Astronomical Society of the Pacific.

Barnard married Rhoda Calvert in 1881; they had no children. His wife died in 1921, and Barnard became ill the next year. A few weeks before his death in 1923, he was still making astronomical observations from his bed.

Bibliography
By Barnard
"Observations of Jupiter with a Five-Inch Refractor, During the Years 1879-1886," *Publications of the Astronomical Society of the Pacific*, 1889
"Visual Observations of Halley's Comet in 1910," *Astrophysical Journal*, 1914
"A Small Star with the Largest Known Proper Motion," *Astronomical Journal*, 1916
"On the Dark Markings of the Sky, with a Catalogue of 182 Such Objects," *Astrophysical Journal*, 1919

About Barnard
Biographical Memoir: Edward Emerson Barnard, 1857-1923. Edwin B. Frost. Washington, D.C.: National Academy of Sciences, 1924.
The Immortal Fire Within: The Life and Work of Edward Emerson Barnard. William Sheehan. Cambridge University Press, 1995.
Interstellar Matters: Essays on Curiosity and Astronomical Discovery. Gerrit L. Verschuur. New York: Springer-Verlag, 1989.

(Keay Davidson)

Sir Derek H. R. Barton

Area of Achievement: Chemistry
Contribution: Barton is best known for the studies of steroids and other complex molecules in nature. The chemical role played by the various geometric patterns that these molecules formed won for him the Nobel Prize in Chemistry in 1969.

Sept. 8, 1918	Born in Gravesend, Kent, England
1940	Granted a B.S. degree, with first-class honors, from Imperial College, University of London
1942	Earns a Ph.D. at the same school
1949	Acts as a visiting professor at Harvard University
1950-1954	Serves on the faculty of Imperial College
1950	Publishes "The Conformation of the Steroid Nucleus"
1955-1957	Serves as a professor at Glasgow University, Scotland
1956	Wins the Fitzche Medal from the American Chemical Society
1957-1977	Serves as a professor at Imperial College
1958-1960	Acts as a visiting professor at various U.S. universities
1961	Wins the Davy Medal from the Royal Society of London
1969	Awarded the Nobel Prize in Chemistry
1977-1985	Serves as director of research at the Centre Nationale de la Recherche Scientifique in Gif-sur-Yvette, France
1985	Becomes a Distinguished Professor at Texas A & M University

Early Life

Derek Harold Richard Barton was born in Kent, England, in 1918. He actually worked in his father's wood business for a few years. After this manual labor, Barton wrote in his autobiography, "I felt there must be something more interesting in life. I decided to go to the university." In spite of his good elementary education, there was little indication of Barton's future scientific career, much less a Nobel Prize.

After a year at Gillingham Technical College, where he obtained the background necessary to pass the entrance examinations, he selected Imperial College at the University of London. Barton's reasoning in this selection might suggest his general approach to problem solving: "Since the fees at Imperial College were 50 percent higher . . . I concluded that Imperial College was 50 percent better . . . This was, in fact, an underestimate."

A Wandering, Productive Scholar

The course of Barton's career is unusual. Most scientists spend a career in one setting; from

(The Nobel Foundation)

The Shape and Movement of Carbon Molecules

A successful physical model of molecules demands a specific geometry and consists of spherical beads that represent atoms; the pegs or springs holding them together are chemical bonds. These simple models are widely used for teaching and research.

The small molecule methane, natural heating gas, is represented as:

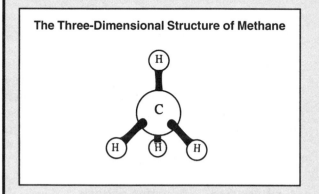

The Three-Dimensional Structure of Methane

The shaded bonds imply that the molecule has the three-dimensional structure of Plato's simplest regular solid, the tetrahedron.

Yet, however useful this model is for simple molecules and even for much larger molecules found in nature, it is deficient. The model appears to be static (that is, without motion), but appearances are sometimes deceiving. Scientific theory and experimentation show that all matter is in constant motion.

Bond movement creates an infinite number of possible structures, each one having its own potential energy. Each of these specific structures is called a conformer; the study of such structures, pioneered by Barton, is termed conformational analysis.

Understanding chemical reactions depends on this vibrant, three-dimensional model and its energy. The breaking and forming of chemical bonds is usually represented in terms of bond vibrations. Chemical changes that facilitate or retard the rate of a reaction are frequently understandable only on the basis of bonds in motion.

Bibliography

Advanced Organic Chemistry. Francis A. Carey and Richard J. Sundberg. 3d ed. New York: Plenum Press, 1990.

"Conformational Analysis in the Elementary Organic Course." Norman L. Allinger. *Journal of Chemical Education* (1964).

Fundamentals of General, Organic, and Biological Chemistry. John McMurry and Mary E. Castellion. 2d ed. Upper Saddle River, N.J.: Prentice Hall, 1992.

the beginning, Barton held positions at a variety of academic, industrial, and research laboratories. He took part in a large number of scientific meetings, colloquia, and conferences and also held posts as visiting professor at an impressive number of universities. Barton showed an unusual desire to communicate with his colleagues. He was amazingly productive despite the special demands imposed by adjustments to new surroundings and the time required to prepare talks. During his ten years in France, Barton published more than two hundred scientific articles. This accomplishment, he once noted, equaled his previous high decade.

The reasons for Barton's achievements extend beyond brilliance and hard work. His style of studying many different chemical problems—for example, steroids, alkaloids, terpenes, kinetics, energetics, and chemical physics—accounts for his seminal contributions to a wide range of chemical areas. In addition, his efforts to communicate the results and application of his studies to a broad spectrum of other chemists led him to forums where exciting new ideas were constantly being discussed.

A Chemist in Foreign Lands

One of Barton's remarkable traits is the ease with which he moved from culture to culture. It must be extraordinary for an Englishman to head an important French research establishment. Of some help, no doubt, was his own basic linguistic skills and the fact that his wife was French, but much more is required to direct a foreign laboratory. Surprising too is Barton's productivity after only a short time in another foreign culture—Texas, where he moved in 1985 to become a Distinguished Professor at Texas A & M University.

Throughout his career, Barton displayed both a talent for finding the most important idea in a new science problem and an amazing ability to discover the most promising aspects of stimulating colleagues in every new locale.

Bibliography
By Barton
"The Conformation of the Steroid Nucleus," *Experientia*, 1950
"The Stereochemistry of Cyclohexane Derivatives," *Journal of the Chemical Society*, 1953
"The Principles of Conformational Analysis" in *Les Prix Nobel en 1969*, 1970
"Some Approaches to the Synthesis of Tetracycline," *Proceedings of the Royal Society of London, A*, 1970
"Chemical Relationships Between Cephalosporins and Penicillins," *Proceedings of the Royal Society of London, B*, 1971
Some Recollections of Gap Jumping, 1991

About Barton
"Barton and Hassel Share the Nobel Prize for Determining the Three-Dimensional Shapes of Organic Compounds." K. T. Finley and P. J. Siegel. In *Great Events from History II: Science and Technology*, edited by Frank N. Magill. Pasadena, Calif.: Salem Press, 1991.
"Derek H. R. Barton." Massimo D. Bezoari. In *The Nobel Prize Winners: Chemistry*, edited by Frank N. Magill. Pasadena, Calif.: Salem Press, 1990.

(K. Thomas Finley)

Laura Bassi

Area of Achievement: Physics
Contribution: Bassi helped spread Newtonian and experimental philosophy during the eighteenth century. Her career proved that a woman could practice science in a university setting.

Oct. 20, 1711	Born in Bologna, Papal States (now Italy)
1730	Distinguishes herself at scientific meetings in her home
1732	Named a member of the Bologna Academy of Sciences
1732	Participates in a public disputation
1732	Defends forty-nine theses to earn her doctorate
1732	Gives her first public lecture by defending twelve theses
1732	Appointed to a lectureship at the University of Bologna
1734	Presents her first annual public anatomy lecture
1738	Marries Giovanni Giuseppe Veratti
1738	Gives birth to the first of twelve children
1745	Becomes a member of the Benedittina Academy
1746	Presents her first dissertation to the Academy of Sciences
1749	Begins to teach experimental physics from her home
1766	Named preceptor to experimental physics students at the Collegio Montalto
1776	Appointed professor of experimental physics at the Institute of Sciences
Feb. 20, 1778	Dies in Bologna, Papal States

Early Life

Laura Maria Caterina Bassi, the daughter of a moderately wealthy lawyer with aristocratic connections, began to learn Latin from her cousin at the age of five. Quickly revealing herself to be a remarkable student, she then studied mathematics, philosophy, anatomy, natural history, and languages with the family's doctor between the ages of thirteen and twenty.

As Bassi's talents became known to Bolognese intellectuals, philosophical discussions were held in her home. At the age of twenty, she was invited to a public debate before city leaders and received a doctorate from the University of Bologna. She asked for and was granted a lectureship in philosophy at the university.

An Exceptional Professor

As a member of the Bologna Academy of Sciences and a university lecturer, Bassi wrote scientific papers and was paid a stipend—ultimately one of the highest at the university. Because she was a woman, however, she was not allowed to teach regular classes. Instead, she lectured in public only at the annual carni-

(Library of Congress)

The Propagation of One-Fluid Electricity

Bassi's support of Benjamin Franklin's one-fluid theory included acceptance of his ideas about lightning rods.

According to Franklin's theory, electricity was composed of a single "subtle fluid," which had physical properties but no mass. A body with excess fluid was positively charged, while a body lacking fluid was negatively charged. In developing this theory and experimenting with lightning rods, Franklin concluded that pointed conductors drew off electricity.

This conclusion touched off a debate concerning the advantages of pointed over blunt objects, in which Bassi participated. For example, she used the conclusion that pointed objects had a greater capability for attraction to explain her results in a 1747 lecture on the causes of bubbles in various liquids and vessels. In those experiments, she found that air bubbles appeared most intensely in capillary tubes. That made sense to

her, since she assumed a greater attraction between the glass of the tube and the air and liquids in that shape of vessel, the most pointed type.

Franklin's system was successful in explaining most electrical phenomena. Fluid theories of electricity were then gradually replaced by quantification techniques in the nineteenth century. Physicists also later ascertained that the height of lightning rods was important, rather than their shape.

Bibliography

Electricity in the Eighteenth and Nineteenth Centuries. John L. Heilbron. Berkeley: University of California Press, 1979.

The History and Present State of Electricity. Joseph Priestley. 1769. Reprint. New York, 1966.

"Prejudice Against the Introduction of Lightning Rods." I. Bernard Cohen. *Journal of the Franklin Institute* 253 (1952).

val anatomy, a popular citywide ceremony.

Shortly after their marriage in 1738, Bassi's husband, Giovanni Giuseppe Veratti, began to teach natural philosophy at the university. By that time, Bassi had already begun to shift from Aristotelian to Newtonian physics in her own work. Her new role as her husband's assistant and collaborator further influenced her to study experimental physics and electricity.

Bassi began to hold private classes in her home in 1749. Allowed to design her own curriculum, she promoted Newtonian philosophy and Benjamin Franklin's ideas about electricity. She taught physical theory and performed experiments to demonstrate principles about light and fire.

Seeking Patronage

Rewards were showered on Bassi throughout her lifetime. For example, city leaders gave her a medal and ring when she earned her doctorate. She also had highly placed friends in Bologna and Rome who intervened on her behalf. One such sponsor was the archbishop of Bologna, who helped her to receive her degree and university appointment. This archbishop later became Pope Benedict XIV, creator of the elite Benedittina Academy.

Throughout her career, Bassi actively sought patronage for her academic life. She hoped that her exceptional public recognition would help her to become a regular practicing experimentalist. She also developed an impressive list of scientific correspondents, placing herself at the center of debates in eighteenth century physics.

An Academic and Scientific Equal

In 1773, Bassi began to seek a professorship at the Institute of Sciences. Its leaders eventually divided the chair of physics into two sections, naming Bassi professor of experimental physics with her husband as her assistant. After pursuing a professional career in science all of her life, she finally taught in public on a regular basis. Her professorship, however, was an extra position that was not filled again after her death in 1778. No women were immediately able to follow Bassi's model of official academic recognition.

Bibliography

By Bassi

De aqua corpore naturale elemento aliorum corporum, 1732 (on the natural relation of water to another element of the whole)

"De aeris compressione," *Commentarii*, 1745 (on the compression of air)

"De problemate quodam hydrometrico," *Commentarii*, 1757 (on a certain problem in measuring water)

"De problemate quodam mechanico," *Commentarii*, 1757 (on a certain problem in mechanics)

"De immixto fluidis aere," *Commentarii*, 1791 (on the bubbles observed in freely flowing fluids)

About Bassi

"The Desire to Contribute: An Eighteenth-Century Italian Woman of Science." Gabriella Berti Logan. *American Historical Review* 99 (June, 1994).

"'In Lode Della Filosofessa Di Bologna': An Introduction to Laura Bassi." Alberto Elena. *Isis* 82 (1991).

"Science as a Career in Enlightenment Italy: The Strategies of Laura Bassi." Paula Findlen. *Isis* 84 (1993).

(Amy Ackerberg-Hastings)

William Bateson

Areas of Achievement: Genetics and zoology

Contribution: Bateson introduced Gregor Mendel's work to Great Britain, and his breeding experiments established basic Mendelian phenomena for plants and animals.

Aug. 8, 1861	Born in Whitby, Yorkshire, England
1883	Receives a B.A. from Cambridge University
1885	Elected a Fellow of St. John's College, Cambridge University
1894	Publishes *Materials for the Study of Variation*
1894	Elected a Fellow of the Royal Society of London
1900	Reads Gregor Mendel's paper on crossing pea plants
1902	Publishes *Mendel's Principles of Heredity: A Defence*
1904	Awarded the Darwin Medal of the Royal Society
1904-1910	Conducts research with E. R. Saunders and Reginald Crundall Punnett
1908-1910	Serves as a professor of biology at Cambridge University
1909	Publishes *Mendel's Principles of Heredity*
1910	Becomes director of the John Innes Horticultural Institution, Merton
1910	Founds the *Journal of Genetics* with Punnett
Feb. 8, 1926	Dies in Merton, London, England

Early Life

Educated at Rugby and St. John's College, Cambridge University, William Bateson earned first-class honors in the natural science tripos. Excelling in embryology and zoology, he took a B.A. in 1883. During several research trips to America, Bateson studied marine biology and met W. H. Brooks at The Johns Hopkins University. In 1885, he became a Fellow of St. John's College.

Journeys to central Asia and Egypt sharpened his observational skills and his interest in evolutionary theory, particularly the origin of species. Returning to Cambridge, Bateson focused on the nature of variation as the key to evolutionary change. By surveying the existing literature and making direct observations, he amassed many examples of variation in plants and animals.

Mutations and Mendelism

Upon examining the evidence, Bateson determined that saltations, or discontinuous variations, drove evolutionary change. Attacking natural selection's focus on continuity, Bateson's *Materials for the Study of Variation Treated with Especial Regard to Discontinuity in the Origin of Species* (1894) rejected the idea that adaptive agents alone directed evolution. Saltations, he argued, arose from forces internal to the organism and new characters persisted regardless of adaptive value. He concluded that "the discontinuity of species results from the discontinuity of variation."

Bateson's emphasis on discontinuity led him to appreciate the mutation theory of Dutch botanist Hugo de Vries. De Vries' writings also led Bateson to read the 1865 paper on pea hybridization by Gregor Mendel. Between 1900 and 1902, Bateson became gradually convinced of the universal validity of Mendel's laws.

Controversy with the Biometricians

Opposing natural selection, Bateson drew harsh criticisms from the biometrical school led by Walter Weldon and Karl Pearson. Using a statistical approach to continuous variations, the biometricians endorsed natural selection. Personal animosities between Bateson and Weldon added fuel to the fire as Weldon's attacks on Mendel prompted Bateson's re-

Bateson (left) with R. A. Emerson. (California Institute of Technology)

Complementary Genes

In particular crosses of plants and animals, Bateson and Reginald Crundall Punnett proposed that two different genes act in consort.

One of the early studies of Bateson and Punnett clearly illustrated the notion that two genes can affect a single physical character, or phenotype. Crossing certain strains of white-flowered

---

A Punnett Square Showing Flower Pigmentation

	White CCpp	× ↓ Purple CcPp ↓	White ccPP

F_1

		CP	Cp	cP	cp
F_2	CP	CCPP purple	CCPp purple	CcPP purple	CcPp purple
	Cp	CCPp purple	CCpp white	CcPp purple	Ccpp white
	cP	CcPP purple	CcPp purple	ccPP white	ccPp white
	cp	CcPp purple	Ccpp white	ccPp white	ccpp white

When white-flowered sweet pea plants were crossed, the first-generation progeny (F_1) all had purple flowers. When these plants were self-fertilized, the second-generation progeny (F_2) revealed a ratio of nine purple to seven white. This result can be explained by the presence of two genes for flower pigmentation, P (dominant) or p (recessive) and C or c. Both dominant forms, P and C, must be present in order to produce purple flowers.

---

sweet pea plants resulted in all purple flowers in the first generation (F_1) progeny. When these purple-flowered plants self-fertilized, however, the second generation (F_2) gave colored flowers in a ratio of nine purple to seven white. In this case, called a dihybrid cross, F_2 usually resulted in phenotypic ratios of 9:3:3:1, meaning four kinds of offspring.

Bateson and Punnett's result was unexpected and seemingly inexplicable. To explain the appearance of only two phenotypic classes, they suggested that two different gene pairs contributed to the production of the purple pigment. Purple flowers, therefore, required the presence of both genes. Consequently, the two original white-flowered parents had to be genetically different.

Later researchers confirmed the presence of two dominant genes, designated C and P, needed for the development of purple flowers. The absence of one or both of these complementary genes results in white flowers.

Without contradicting Mendel's laws, Bateson and Punnett's hypothesis convincingly accounted for dihybrid ratios other than the familiar 9:3:3:1. While confirming Mendelian principles, the concept of complementary genes also extended the explanatory scope of Mendelism.

Bibliography
Elements of Genetics. Edward C. Colin. New York: McGraw-Hill, 1956.
Principle of Genetics. Eldon J. Gardner. 4th ed. New York: John Wiley & Sons, 1972.

---

sponse, *Mendel's Principles of Heredity: A Defence* (1902).

The controversy reached a turning point at the 1904 meeting of the British Association for the Advancement of Science. As president of the zoological section, Bateson challenged Weldon and apparently won the ensuing debate with forceful arguments in favor of Mendelism. Gathering supporters to confirm Mendel's laws experimentally, Bateson named the new science "genetics" in 1905.

Bateson's Achievement
Bateson's collaboration with L. Doncaster, E. R. Saunders, and Reginald Crundall Punnett confirmed that Mendel's laws applied to animals as well as to plants. Furthermore, breeding experiments with sweet peas and domestic fowl extended Mendelism to phenomena such as reversion, coupling, and complementary factors.

After persistent funding difficulties at Cambridge, Bateson left in 1910 to become director of the John Innes Horticultural Institution. The same year, he cofounded the *Journal of Genetics* with Punnett. Although rejecting new ideas in his later years, Bateson is commonly regarded as the founder of the first school of Mendelian genetics.

Bibliography

By Bateson
Materials for the Study of Variation Treated with Especial Regard to Discontinuity in the Origin of Species, 1894
Mendel's Principles of Heredity: A Defence, 1902
Mendel's Principles of Heredity, 1909
Problems of Genetics, 1913
Scientific Papers of William Bateson, 1928 (R. C. Punnett, ed.)

About Bateson
"Bateson, William." William Coleman. In *Dictionary of Scientific Biography*, edited by Charles Coulston Gillispie. Vol. 1. New York: Charles Scribner's Sons, 1970.
"William Bateson and the Promise of Mendelism." Lindley Darden. *Journal of the History of Biology* 10 (1977).
William Bateson, F. R. S. Naturalist. Beatrice Bateson. Cambridge, England: Cambridge University Press, 1928.

(Robinson M. Yost)

George Wells Beadle

Areas of Achievement: Cell biology, chemistry, and genetics

Contribution: Beadle, a pioneer in the study of the chemical action of genes within cells, helped to demonstrate that genes control specific chemical reactions.

Oct. 22, 1903	Born in Wahoo, Nebraska
1922-1927	Studies at the University of Nebraska
1927-1931	Works on a Ph.D. in biology at Cornell University
1931	Given a National Research Council Fellowship
1931-1937	Works as a research fellow at the California Institute of Technology (Caltech)
1937	Accepts a position at Stanford University
1946	Returns to Caltech as head of the division of biology
1950	Wins the Lasker Award
1953	Receives the Emil Christian Hansen Prize
1958	Shares the Nobel Prize in Physiology or Medicine with Edward L. Tatum and Joshua Lederberg
1959	Wins the National Award of the American Cancer Society
1960	Receives the Kimber Genetics Award of the National Academy of Science
1961-1968	Serves as president of the University of Chicago
1967	Wins the Edison Prize for Best Science Book for Youth
June 9, 1989	Dies in Pomona, California

Early Life

George Wells Beadle was born on a farm in Wahoo, Nebraska. His family took to calling him "Beets," a nickname that remained with him throughout his life. Growing up, Beadle planned to take over his father's farm. A teacher at his local high school, however, persuaded him to attend the University of Nebraska College of Agriculture.

Beadle completed his undergraduate degree at Nebraska and decided to stay for an extra year to earn a master's degree. This year of research convinced Beadle that he wanted to commit himself to science. He decided to continue his work at Cornell University, where he earned his Ph.D. in 1931.

Research at Caltech

After finishing his degree, Beadle went to the California Institute of Technology (Caltech) on a National Research Council Fellowship. He began to work on the genetics of the fruit fly *Drosophila melanogaster*. In collaboration with

(The Nobel Foundation)

Boris Ephrussi, Beadle made an important discovery about how genes in the flies' cells control the production of the chemical for brown eye pigment. Based on this research, he became convinced that the study of genetics needed to be approached through chemistry.

Scientific Breakthrough at Stanford

In 1937, Beadle left Caltech to become a professor of biology at Stanford University. He began a collaboration with a biochemist, Edward L. Tatum, to continue to explore the relationship between genes and cell chemistry. Working with a variety of bread mold called *Neurospora*, Beadle and Tatum proved that genes control specific chemical reactions. By doing so, they created a whole new area of research: biochemical genetics, or the study of gene action. Their discovery also helped to explain the similarity between parents and their offspring, since it demonstrated that their similar genes mean that children will be similar to their parents at the level of biochemistry.

From Scientist to Administrator

In 1946, Beadle was lured back to Caltech to become the head of the division of biology. This position made him the leader of one of the most prestigious biology programs in the country. Beadle focused on making Caltech into the premier research institution in molecular biology, while maintaining its strength in other areas of biology. His success in this venture brought him renown for his leadership ability.

Beadle's winning of the Nobel Prize in Physiology or Medicine in 1958 for his work while at Stanford confirmed his excellence as a scientist. This combination of skills made him an attractive choice to become president of one of the premier research universities in the world, the University of Chicago, in 1961. He served in this capacity until his retirement in 1968.

Back to Maize Research

After retiring as president of the University of Chicago, Beadle remained there as a researcher. He returned to his first research field, the genetics of maize (Indian corn). He continued to be an active researcher well into his

One Gene, One Enzyme

The genetic material within cells is used to produce enzymes. Each gene, or region of the genetic material that produces enzymes, produces a single enzyme.

Beadle helped to develop the understanding of how genes function within cells. Prior to his work, scientists had a general understanding that the genetic material of cells was carried on the chromosomes in the cell nucleus and that some regions of these chromosomes were significant sites controlling the expression of certain inherited characteristics. Scientists still did not know exactly how these important regions of the chromosomes, called genes, did their work.

While working with Boris Ephrussi at Caltech, Beadle conducted a series of experiments on the eye color of the fruit fly *Drosophilia melanogaster*. Beadle and Ephrussi proved that certain eye color mutations in the flies resulted from the turning off of certain genes that helped to produce the brown component of a fly's eye color. These experiments convinced Beadle that genes control the production of chemicals within cells.

At Stanford, Beadle continued to investigate this relationship with chemist Edward L. Tatum and graduate student Joshua Lederberg. Together, they proved more specifically how genes control these chemical reactions. They showed that each gene produces a unique enzyme. These enzymes are then used by cells to conduct chemical reactions that help to determine many characteristics of how the cell operates, which in turn helps to determine how the organism that the cells compose grows and functions. In this way, genes help to determine each individual's unique characteristics.

Bibliography
The Code of Life. Ernest Borek. New York: Columbia University Press, 1965.

Discovery: The Search for the DNA's Secrets. Mahlon B. Hoagland. Boston: Houghton Mifflin, 1981.

The Transforming Principle: Discovering That Genes Are Made of DNA. Maclyn McCarty. New York: W. W. Norton, 1985.

seventies. At the end of his life, he returned to Southern California, where he died on June 9, 1989.

Bibliography
By Beadle

An Introduction to Genetics, 1939 (with A. H. Sturtevant)

"Genetic Control of Biochemical Reactions in *Neurospora*," *Proceedings of the National Academy of Sciences*, 1941 (with Edward L. Tatum)

Genetics and Modern Biology, 1963

The Language of Life: An Introduction to the Science of Genetics, 1966 (with Muriel B. Beadle)

About Beadle

The Eighth Day of Creation: Makers of the Revolution in Biology. Horace Freeland Judson. New York: Simon & Schuster, 1979.

The Molecular Vision of Life: Caltech, the Rockefeller Foundation, and the Rise of the New Biology. Lily Kay. New York: Oxford University Press, 1993.

The Path to the Double Helix. Robert Olby. London: Macmillan, 1974.

(David A. Valone)

Antoine-Henri Becquerel

Areas of Achievement: Chemistry, earth science, physics, and science (general)

Contribution: Becquerel discovered radioactivity, for which he received the Nobel Prize in Physics in 1903, jointly with Marie and Pierre Curie.

Dec. 15, 1852	Born in Paris, France
1872-1874	Studies at the École Polytechnique
1874	Marries Lucie-Zoé-Marie Jamin
1874-1877	Studies at the École des Ponts et Chaussées
1879	His wife dies following the birth of their son
1879	Succeeds his father as *aide-naturaliste* at the Musée d'Histoire Naturelle
1886-1888	Studies the absorption of light in crystals
1888	Receives a doctorate from the Faculté des Sciences of Paris
1889	Elected to the Académie des Sciences
1894	Becomes engineer in chief at the École des Ponts et Chaussées
1896	Learns of the discovery of X rays
1899-1900	Identifies electrons in the radiation of radium
1901	Publishes the first evidence of a radioactive transformation
1903	Receives the Nobel Prize in Physics jointly with Marie and Pierre Curie
1906	Elected vice president of the Académie des Sciences
1908	Becomes president of the Académie des Sciences
Aug. 25, 1908	Dies in Le Croisic, Brittany, France

Early Life

Antoine-Henri Becquerel (pronounced "beh-KREHL") was born in Paris on December 15, 1852. Both his father, Alexandre-Edmond Becquerel, and his grandfather, Antoine-César Becquerel, were physicists. In addition, both his father and his grandfather were members of the Académie des Sciences and, in turn, professors of physics at the Musée d'Histoire Naturelle (museum of natural history) in Paris. Antoine-Henri Becquerel would represent the third generation in his family to become a physicist and to hold these positions.

Becquerel attended school at the Lycée Louis-le-Grand. From there, he went to the École Polytechnique from 1872 to 1874 and to the École des Ponts et Chaussées, the French department of bridges and highways, from 1874 to 1877, where he was trained in engineering. He then entered the École des Ponts et Chaussées as an engineer.

In 1874, Becquerel married Lucie-Zoé-Marie Jamin, the daughter of J.-C. Jamin, a professor of physics in the Faculté des Sciences in Paris. She died only a few years later, in March, 1879, following the birth of their son, Jean.

Early Research and Professional Life

Becquerel began his research career at the École Polytechnique in 1875 and began teaching there in 1876. In 1879, he succeeded his father as *aide-naturaliste* at the Musée d'Histoire Naturelle. Afterward, his professional life was shared between the museum, the École Polytechnique, and the École des Ponts et Chaussées.

Becquerel's early research was optical and dealt in part with the rotation of plane-polarized light by magnetic fields. He also studied infrared spectra by examining light emitted from phosphorescent crystals in infrared light and the absorption of light in crystals.

Becquerel earned his doctorate from the Faculté des Sciences in Paris in 1888, and in 1889 he was elected to the Académie des Sciences. After receiving his doctorate, Becquerel became largely inactive in research. In 1890, he married his second wife, the daughter of E. Lorieux, an inspector general of mines.

Becquerel's father died in 1891. The following year, he took over his father's two positions as chair of physics at the Conservatoire National des Arts et Métiers and at the Musée d'Histoire Naturelle. About the same time, he also took over the physics teaching duties of Alfred Potier at the École Polytechnique. In 1894, he became *ingénieur en chef* (engineer in chief) at the École des Ponts et Chaussées.

The Discovery of Radioactivity

X rays were discovered accidentally by the German physicist Wilhelm Röntgen in 1895 while he was studying cathode rays in a high-voltage gaseous-discharge tube. Becquerel

---

Radioactivity

Radioactivity is the spontaneous breakdown of the nucleus of an atom, which releases subatomic particles and radiation.

Radioactivity was discovered by Becquerel in 1896, shortly after the discovery of X rays by Wilhelm Röntgen in 1895. Becquerel learned that invisible radiation from a cathode-ray tube could penetrate through a black cardboard box and cause a nearby barium platinocyanide screen to fluoresce; these invisible rays were termed X rays. Becquerel began searching for a fluorescent crystal that could emit penetrating radiation, and he soon found that crystals of potassium uranyl sulfate would darken a photographic plate wrapped in black paper. Uranium was the source of the penetrating radiation. This radiation was initially called uranium rays or Becquerel rays, but it came to be known as radioactive radiation or radioactivity.

Elements that are unstable and spontaneously break down, or decay, to form other elements are referred to as radioactive elements. When the nucleus of a radioactive element decays, it releases subatomic particles, called alpha particles and beta particles, and radiation. An alpha particle (α) consists of two protons bound to two neutrons (a helium nucleus). A beta particle (β) is an electron that forms when a neutron splits into a proton and an electron. Gamma rays (γ) are high-energy photons, invisible electromagnetic radiation with a shorter wavelength than X rays.

A loss of subatomic particles from the nucleus changes the atomic number and produces a different element, called a daughter element. For example, carbon 14 decays to the daughter element nitrogen 14 through the release of a beta particle. Uranium 238 decays to lead 206 through a multistep process in which eight α particles and six β particles are released, forming more than a dozen intermediate radioactive daughter elements, such as thorium and radon, in the process. The stable daughter product of the radioactive decay of uranium is lead.

An isotope is a form of an element with a different number of neutrons. There are several isotopes of uranium, such as uranium 238 and uranium 235. The number following the name of an element is called the mass number; it is the sum of the number of protons and the number of neutrons. All uranium atoms have 92 protons, so uranium 238 has 146 neutrons and uranium 235 has 143 neutrons. Both of these isotopes of uranium are radioactive, and each has its own unique half-life (the time that it takes for half of a given quantity of radioactive element to decay). After one half-life, half of the original number of radioactive atoms remain; the others have decayed to daughter atoms.

Radioactivity has many useful applications in science, medicine, engineering, and industry. Radioactive tracers can be used to monitor the movement of biochemical components in the bloodstream, to measure flow rates through systems of pipes, and to clarify complex chemical reactions such as photosynthesis. A drawback is that radioactive materials are hazardous and must be handled using protective measures.

Bibliography

An Introduction to Radiation Chemistry. J. W. T. Spinks and R. I. Woods. 3d ed. New York: John Wiley & Sons, 1990.

An Introduction to Radiobiology. A. W. H. Nias. New York: John Wiley & Sons, 1990.

Principles of Isotope Geology. G. Faure. 2d ed. New York: John Wiley & Sons, 1986.

Radiochemistry and Nuclear Chemistry. G. Choppin, J. Rydberg, and J. O. Liljenzin. Oxford, England: Butterworth-Heinemann, 1995.

learned of this discovery on January 20, 1896, when two physicians, Paul Oudin and Toussaint Barthélemy, submitted an X-ray image of a hand to the Académie des Sciences.

Noting that visible light and invisible X rays were produced by the same mechanism, Becquerel wondered whether X rays might be associated with all types of light. Because he had studied phosphorescent crystals, he began to seek a crystal that could emit penetrating radiation. He soon found that fluorescent crystals of uranium salt would expose a photographic plate wrapped in black paper, and he reported his findings to the academy on February 24 and March 2, 1896.

Becquerel experimented with other luminescent crystals and found that only those containing uranium emit the penetrating radiation. Ultimately, he found that pure uranium metal produced penetrating radiation several times more intense than that produced by uranium salts. The significance of this finding, which was announced on May 18, 1896, was that penetrating radiation, or radioactivity, was a property of uranium.

This discovery opened the field of nuclear physics and set the stage for the research that Marie and Pierre Curie would perform, resulting in the discovery of radium. Becquerel later identified electrons in the radiation of radium and published the first evidence of a radioactive transformation in 1901.

It was soon found that radioactivity causes biological damage. When Becquerel went to London to make a presentation to the Royal Society, he carried a small amount of radium in a tube in his vest pocket and received a nasty burn on the skin of his stomach.

The Nobel Prize
In 1903, the Nobel Prize in Physics was shared by Becquerel and the Curies for their work with radioactive materials. In 1906, Becquerel was elected vice president of the Académie des Sciences, and he became its president in 1908. He was elected as one of two permanent secre-

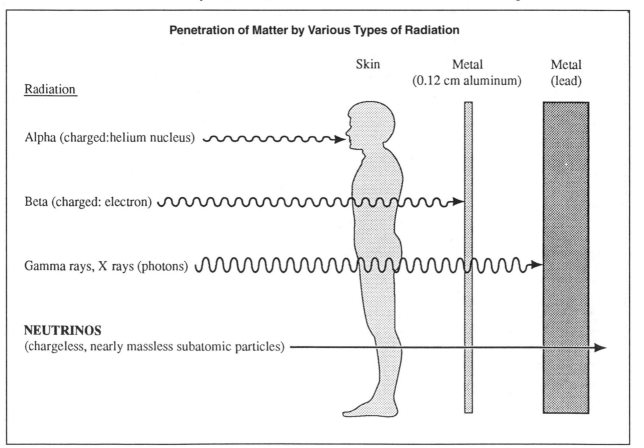

Penetration of Matter by Various Types of Radiation

taries of the academy later that year. He died soon afterward at the age of fifty-five on August 25, 1908, at the home of his wife's family in Le Croisic, Brittany, France.

Bibliography
By Becquerel

"Émission de radiations nouvelles par l'uranium métallique," *Comptes rendus de l'Académie des Sciences, Paris*, 1896

"Sur quelques propriétés nouvelles des radiations invisibles émises par divers corps phosphorescents," *Comptes rendus de l'Académie des Sciences, Paris*, 1896

"Sur les radiations émises par phosphorescence," *Comptes rendus de l'Académie des Sciences, Paris*, 1896

"Sur les radiations invisibles émises par les corps phosphorescents," *Comptes rendus de l'Académie des Sciences, Paris*, 1896

"Sur les radiations invisibles émises par les sels d'uranium," *Comptes rendus de l'Académie des Sciences, Paris*, 1896

"Sur diverses propriétés des rayons uraniques," *Comptes rendus de l'Académie des Sciences, Paris*, 1896

"Sur la loi de décharge dans l'air de l'uranium électrisé," *Comptes rendus de l'Académie des Sciences, Paris*, 1897

"Recherches sur les rayons uraniques," *Comptes rendus de l'Académie des Sciences, Paris*, 1897

"Influence d'un champ magnétique sur le rayonnement des corps radio-actifs," *Comptes rendus de l'Académie des Sciences, Paris*, 1899

"Sur le rayonnement des corps radio-actifs," *Comptes rendus de l'Académie des Sciences, Paris*, 1899

"Contribution à l'étude du rayonnement du radium," *Comptes rendus de l'Académie des Sciences, Paris*, 1900

"Déviation du rayonnement du radium dans un champ électrique," *Comptes rendus de l'Académie des Sciences, Paris*, 1900

"Sur la dispersion du rayonnement du radium dans un champ magnétique," *Comptes rendus de l'Académie des Sciences, Paris*, 1900

"Note sur le rayonnement de l'uranium,"

(The Nobel Foundation)

Comptes rendus de l'Académie des Sciences, Paris, 1900

"Sur la radioactivité de l'uranium," *Comptes rendus de l'Académie des Sciences, Paris*, 1901

"Recherches sur une propriété nouvelle de la matière: Activité radiante spontanée ou radioactivité de la matière," *Mémoires de l'Académie des Sciences, Paris*, 1903

About Becquerel

"Antoine-Henri Becquerel." In *The Nobel Prize Winners: Physics*, edited by Frank N. Magill. Pasadena, Calif.: Salem Press, 1989.

Crucibles: The Story of Chemistry. Bernard Jaffe. New York: Dover, 1976.

(Pamela J. W. Gore)

Emil Adolf von Behring

Areas of Achievement: Bacteriology, immunology, and medicine

Contribution: Behring's development of antitoxins to combat diphtheria and tetanus helped eliminate the threat of two dread diseases and opened the way for the medical application of immunology.

Mar. 15, 1854	Born in Hansdorf, Prussia (now Germany)
1866	Enters the gymnasium at Hohenstein, East Prussia
1874	Enters army medical school, the Friedrich-Wilhelm Institute, in Berlin
1878	Graduated and is posted to Royal Charite Hospital in Berlin
1887	Assigned to the Pharmacology Institute, the University of Bonn
1889	Joins Robert Koch at the University of Berlin
1891	Moves to Koch's Institute for Infectious Disease
1891	His antitoxin successfully treats a child with diphtheria
1894	Results of his antitoxin trials are presented at the International Congress of Hygiene, in Budapest
1894	Appointed Professor of Hygiene at the University of Halle
1895	Named chair of the department of hygiene at the University of Marburg
1901	Awarded the first Nobel Prize in Physiology or Medicine
1913	Announces a preventive serum for diphtheria
Mar. 31, 1917	Dies in Marburg, Germany

Early Life

Emil Adolf von Behring (pronounced "BAY-rihng") was born in 1854 in Hansdorf, Prussia, one of thirteen children of August Behring, a local schoolteacher. Emil proved an outstanding student, quickly surpassing his father's ability to serve as his teacher. A local pastor continued his education until Behring entered the gymnasium at Hohenstein in 1866.

Upon his graduation, Behring wished to study medicine, but his options were limited. He initially decided on a career in the ministry, but a friend recommended Behring to the army medical school in Berlin. In 1874, Behring entered the Friedrich-Wilhelm Institute.

Behring's training was rigorous, but the medical core was well noted for its enlightened training by a brilliant faculty. The curriculum included numerous laboratory courses, in addition to training in languages and the humanities. Behring was graduated in 1878, completing a doctoral thesis on eye disease.

Army Duty and Early Research

Following two years of internship, Behring began his formal military duties. Unmarried, he enjoyed his life as a young officer, once even changing posts because of gambling debts.

Behring also began developing an interest in medical research. He conducted his first formal experiments when assigned to Posen, testing the effectiveness of iodoform (triiodomethane) for treatment of wounds. He also enrolled in a course on bacteriological techniques taught by an associate of Robert Koch.

In 1886, Behring was assigned by the Army Medical Corps to the University of Bonn. It was there that he began his work on bacteriocidal agents, using anthrax as an experimental model. Behring was aware of the extensive work carried out by Koch in the area of germ theory; it was Koch who firmly demonstrated the role of the anthrax bacillus as the etiological agent of the disease. Behring requested an assignment with Koch and, in 1889, joined his laboratory at the University of Berlin.

A Diphtheria Antitoxin

Behring had previously demonstrated that chemical treatment of bacterial wounds could neutralize certain toxins. As a member of

The Development of a Diphtheria Antitoxin

Behring's development of an antitoxin against diphtheria provided a means to protect or cure children stricken with an often-fatal disease.

In the late nineteenth century, diphtheria was among the most dreaded of childhood diseases. In Germany alone, some 100,000 children were stricken each year, with a mortality rate of approximately 50 percent. Equivalent numbers could be found in other countries. From 1883 until well into the twentieth century, more than half of all deaths among children were the result of this disease.

In 1884, Robert Koch's associate Friedrich Löffler isolated the diphtheria bacillus; in 1889, Émile Roux and Alexandre Yersin demonstrated that the disease results from a toxin produced by the bacillus.

Having recently joined Koch's laboratory, Behring became interested in humoral (soluble) mechanisms by which the body responds to disease. He noted that therapeutic chemicals such as iodine trichloride or sodium chloroaurate, when applied directly to the sites on rabbits that had been infected with either diphtheria or tetanus bacilli, prevented the diseases from developing. The blood from these animals would then neutralize the toxins, rendering them harmless.

Behring continued to test various blood components to determine which fraction provided the best immunity. He found that while whole blood provided some immunity, the liquid portion present after the blood clotted, called serum, contained the highest level of protective power.

Behring and Shibasaburo Kitasato then tested whether the transfer of this immune serum to susceptible rabbits could also protect these animals. The tests were successful, and Behring concluded that a humoral agent in the blood of immunized animals could neutralize the toxin; the agent could also be passively transferred to other animals, thereby providing them with protection. The sooner the serum was provided after infection, the greater was its protective ability. Behring and Kitasato introduced the term "antitoxic" to characterize the substance.

Once Behring worked out the procedures that provided serum with the greatest potency, he decided to test the therapy in humans. At first, he was hesitant, because he was unsure whether large quantities of animal serum could be injected into children safely. Fortunately, Behring found that the necessary quantities were smaller than initially thought. He began the trials in 1892, using serum from immunized animals to treat children at the Charite Hospital who were seriously ill with diphtheria. Among eleven children treated with the serum, nine survived. This contrasted with a death rate of 65 percent among children at the hospital not previously treated.

Similar treatment proved equally successful among hundreds of children treated over the next two years. Indeed, in later trials carried out in London, the death rate from diphtheria between 1895 and 1910 dropped from 62 to 10 percent.

The results of Behring's trials, and similar ones carried out by Roux in France, were presented at the International Congress of Hygiene held in Budapest in 1894. Behring's discovery brought him international fame.

Bibliography

A History of Immunology. Arthur Silverstein. San Diego: Academic Press, 1989.

Microbe Hunters. Paul De Kruif. New York: Harcourt, Brace and World, 1953.

Three Centuries of Microbiology. Hubert Lechevalier and Morris Solotorovsky. New York: Dover, 1974.

Koch's laboratory, he decided to continue this line of research. He was joined in this quest by Shibasaburo Kitasato, the Japanese scientist who had already isolated the agent for tetanus.

Moving with Koch to the newly established Institute for Infectious Disease in 1891, Behring and Kitasato began their work on the treatment of both tetanus and diphtheria. It had already been established that both diseases are caused by toxins secreted by their respective etiological agents. Behring reasoned that if the body could survive exposure to these toxins, a lifelong immunity could be established.

Behring and Kitasato found that when rab-

(The Nobel Foundation)

bits or guinea pigs had been infected with the bacilli, and the site was then treated with certain toxic chemicals, the animal would usually survive the disease. Serum from these animals could then be used to protect, or cure, other animals exposed to the same bacilli.

On December 25, 1891, Behring successfully carried out the first treatment of a child with diphtheria, using serum obtained from a previously immunized animal. Large-scale trials proved equally successful.

International Acclaim

Behring and Koch, his work sidetracked by an ill-fated venture in attempting to develop a tuberculosis vaccine, soon developed an animosity that quickly escalated into a feud. In 1894, Behring requested a position in a university and was appointed acting Professor of Hygiene at the University of Halle.

Behring found teaching difficult and, requesting another change, was appointed chair of the department of hygiene at the University of Marburg in 1895. That same year, he was also admitted to the nobility, as Emil von Behring. Further honors raised him to the position of *Exzellenz* (excellency) von Behring.

In 1901, Behring was awarded the first Nobel Prize in Physiology or Medicine. He was honored even by the hereditary enemies of his country, receiving the French Legion of Honor.

Later Years

Despite international acclaim, Behring's last years were often spent in controversy. Like Koch, with whom he continued his feud, he was bogged down in the problem of tuberculosis. Convinced that this disease was also caused by a toxin, Behring continued his attempts to develop a therapeutic agent. By 1912, he finally gave up.

Despite poor health, however, Behring continued his success in the treatment of diphtheria. In 1913, he reported the development of a mixture of diphtheria toxin and antitoxin that proved particularly useful in immunization against the disease.

In 1914, Behring suffered a broken femur that never properly healed. A severe abscess compounded the problem. Bedridden, he developed pneumonia and died on March 31, 1917.

Bibliography
By Behring
"Über Iodoform und Iodoformwirkung" (iodoform and the use of iodoform), *Deutsche medizinische Wochenschrift*, 1882
"Über das Zustandekommen der Diphtherie-Immunität und der Tetanus-Immunität bei Thieren" (mechanism of immunity to diphtheria and tetanus in animals), *Deutsche medizinische Wochenschrift*, 1890 (with S. Kitasato)
"Untersuchungen über das Zustandekommen der Diphtherie-Immunität bei Thieren" (studies on the mechanism of immunity to diphtheria in animals), *Deutsche medizinische Wochenschrift*, 1890
Die Geschichte der Diphtherie: Mit besonderer ber Ucksichtigung der Immunit Atslehre, 1893

Allgemeine Therapie der Infectionskrankheiten, 1899

The Suppression of Tuberculosis, 1904 (Charles Bolduan, ed.)

"Über ein neues Diphtherieschutzmittel" (a new method for diphtheria treatment), *Deutsche medizinische Wochenschrift*, 1913

E. v. Behring's Gesammelte Abhandlungen, 1915

About Behring

"Emil Adolf von Behring." In *The Nobel Prize Winners: Physiology or Medicine*, edited by Frank N. Magill. Pasadena, Calif.: Salem Press, 1991.

(Richard Adler)

Georg von Békésy

Areas of Achievement: Medicine, physics, and physiology

Contribution: Békésy applied principles of physics to clarify the mechanisms by which sound waves are transmitted to the inner ear and converted into electrical nerve impulses going to the brain.

June 3, 1899	Born in Budapest, Austro-Hungarian Empire (now Hungary)
1916	Enters the University of Bern, Switzerland
1918	Returns to Hungary after the end of World War I
1923	Receives a Ph.D. in physics from the University of Budapest
1924	Begins research to improve the unreliable Hungarian telephone system
1930's	Studies ear anatomy by examining animals and cadavers
1939	Appointed a professor of physics at Budapest
1946	Moves to the Karolinska Institute in Sweden
1947	Invents an audiometer to measure hearing loss
1947	Conducts research at Harvard University's Psycho-Acoustics Laboratory
1961	Receives the Nobel Prize in Physiology or Medicine
1966	Retires from Harvard
1966	Joins the University of Hawaii as professor of sensory sciences
June 13, 1972	Dies in Honolulu, Hawaii

Early Life

Georg von Békésy (pronounced "BAY-kay-shee") was born in Budapest, the capital city of Hungary. His father was in the diplomatic service, so his family life included considerable travel. As a youth, he was a promising pianist, but he decided to pursue science as a career.

At the age of seventeen, he entered the University of Bern in Switzerland, planning to major in physics. After two years, however, he returned to Budapest because of the disruptions caused by World War I. He obtained a Ph.D. in physics at the University of Budapest in 1923.

Telephone Research

Békésy's first professional job was with the Hungarian telephone research laboratory. In the 1920's, the telephone system lacked reliability, and the quality of voice reproduction was poor. Békésy determined that the main source of voice distortion was not caused by the telephone mouthpiece or the transmission lines but came from the earphone in the receiver.

In the course of studying the mechanical vibrations of earphones, Békésy became interested in the remarkable sensitivity of the human ear. He focused his attention on the inner ear, where the fluid-filled cochlea converts sound vibrations into electrical impulses.

The inner ear is difficult to study because of its small size and inaccessibility inside the skull. Békésy developed miniature tools for microsurgery on the ears of human cadavers and laboratory animals. On one occasion when an elephant at the zoo had died, he obtained its ears for dissection.

Harvard University

After the end of World War II, Békésy immigrated to the United States in order to take a research position at the Psycho-Acoustics Laboratory of Harvard University. Based on

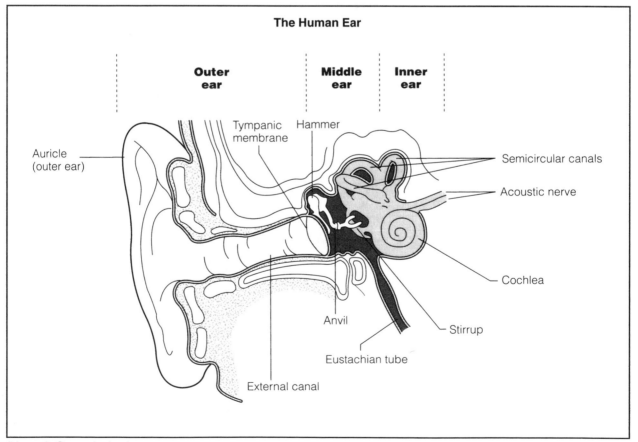

The Human Ear

Outer ear   Middle ear   Inner ear

Tympanic membrane   Hammer

Auricle (outer ear)

Semicircular canals

Acoustic nerve

Cochlea

Anvil

Stirrup

Eustachian tube

External canal

(Hans & Cassady, Inc.)

The Anatomy of the Human Ear

The ear consists of three interconnected regions: the outer, middle, and inner ear. Békésy's studies of the inner ear led to greater understanding of hearing loss.

Sound enters the outer ear and travels along a canal to the eardrum, whose thickness is only about 0.1 millimeter.

The middle ear has three tiny bones named the hammer, anvil, and stirrup. These bones form a system of mechanical levers that transmit vibrations from the eardrum to a small, oval window leading into the inner ear. The Eustachian tube internally connects the middle ear cavity to the throat for pressure equalization.

The section of the inner ear that deals with hearing is called the cochlea. It is shaped like a tiny snail, no larger than a pea, and is filled with fluid.

Békésy built an enlarged mechanical model of the cochlea in order to study how it functions. His model consisted of a tapered plastic tube filled with water, having a piston at one end that could vibrate at different frequencies. Békésy found that traveling waves in the water produced vibration peaks at different places along the tube as the input frequency was changed. He concluded that high and low frequencies stimulate the cochlea at different points along its length.

Several thousand hair cells are attached to a membrane that extends throughout the length of the cochlea. Nerve fibers at the base of these hair cells generate electrical signals that travel to the brain.

Bibliography

The Incredible Machine. Robert M. Poole, ed. Washington, D.C.: National Geographic Society, 1986.

Medical Physics. John R. Camerson and James G. Skofronick. New York: John Wiley & Sons, 1978.

The Physics of the Ear. T. S. Littler. New York: Macmillan, 1965.

his earlier anatomical research, he constructed a large mechanical model of a cochlea to analyze how it functions.

As a practical application of his research, Békésy invented an audiometer to test for hearing loss. The person being tested hears a tone that gradually gets softer until it becomes inaudible. After several trials, the threshold of hearing (minimum detectable intensity) is established for each ear. The procedure is repeated at various frequencies in order to detect deviations from normal hearing.

The Nobel Prize

Békésy received the 1961 Nobel Prize in Physiology or Medicine "for his discoveries of the physical mechanism of stimulation within the cochlea." He also contributed to an understanding of the transformation of sound waves into electrical nerve impulses.

Békésy's research led to improvements in the treatment of hearing disorders. For example, surgeons have learned how to bypass a defective middle ear by implanting wires directly into the cochlea.

(The Nobel Foundation)

The University of Hawaii

After retiring from Harvard University in 1966, Békésy went to the University of Hawaii as a professor of sensory sciences. He studied the receptors for other sensory organs, especially taste and touch. He died in 1972.

Bibliography
By Békésy
"Über die neuen Audiometer," *Archiv der elecktrischen Übertragung*, 1947 ("A New Audiometer," *Acta Oto-laryngolica*, 1947)
"The Mechanical Properties of the Ear" (with W. A. Rosenblith) in *Handbook of Experimental Psychology*, 1951 (S. S. Stevens, ed.)
Experiments in Hearing, 1960 (E. G. Wever, ed.)
Sensory Inhibition, 1967

About Békésy
"Georg von Békésy." In *The Nobel Prize Winners: Physiology or Medicine*, edited by Frank N. Magill. Pasadena, Calif.: Salem Press, 1991.
Nobel Prize Winners: An H. W. Wilson Biographical Dictionary. Tyler Wasson, ed. New York: H. W. Wilson, 1987.
Sound and Hearing. S. S. Stevens and Fred Warshofsky. New York: Time, 1967.

(Hans G. Graetzer)

Alexander Graham Bell

Areas of Achievement: Invention, physics, and technology

Contribution: Bell is known primarily for his invention of the telephone, which converts the human voice into an electrical signal for transmission along a wire, then reconverts it back into audible sound at the receiver.

Mar. 3, 1847	Born in Edinburgh, Scotland
1862	Begins teaching music and speech to children
1870	His family moves to Canada for health reasons
1871	Begins teaching at the Boston School for the Deaf
1875	Receives a patent for a multiple telegraph
1876	Receives a patent for the telephone
1876	Wins first prize at the Philadelphia Centennial Exhibition
1877	Demonstrates the telephone to Queen Victoria
1880	Receives the $10,000 Volta Prize from France
1882	Invents the Graphophone to record sound on wax cylinders
1883	Founds the journal *Science*
1892	Makes the first telephone call from New York to Chicago
1898	Becomes president of the National Geographic Society
1908	Experiments with giant kites for human flight
1919	Invents a hydrofoil boat, setting a speed record on water
Aug. 2, 1922	Dies at Baddeck, Cape Breton Island, Nova Scotia

Early Life

Alexander Graham Bell was born in Scotland in 1847. Both his father and his grandfather were well-known teachers of speech correction, called "elocution" in England. In the Broadway musical *My Fair Lady*, Professor Higgins uses the Bell system of elocution to teach Eliza Doolittle how to talk like a lady.

Bell received most of his early education through home schooling. He attended Edinburgh's Royal High School and graduated at the age of fourteen. His first job was teaching music and speech to young children. His two brothers both died of tuberculosis, so in 1870 the family moved to Canada to seek a healthier climate.

In 1871, Bell moved to Boston to teach deaf children. His father, Alexander Melville Bell, had written a book called *Visible Speech: The Science of Universal Alphabetics* (1867), which showed the proper lip and tongue positions to create the sounds for all the letters in the alphabet. Even people who could not hear their own voice made remarkable progress in learning to speak.

The Multiple Telegraph

The telegraph had been invented by Samuel F. B. Morse in the 1830's. Dots and dashes (the Morse code) were transmitted through a wire as short and long bursts of electric current. By 1862, a cross-country system of telegraph transmission lines had been built.

The Western Union Company offered a prize to any inventor who could send several simultaneous messages over a single wire, which would allow more telegrams to be sent without extra lines. Alexander Graham Bell had an ingenious idea for such a multiple telegraph.

Thin metal reeds of different lengths, like those in a music box, vibrate at different frequencies. Bell's idea was to create an electric current that vibrated with the same frequency as the musical note produced by a reed. At the receiver, only that reed which matched the sending frequency would start to vibrate. By using multiple reeds at the sending and receiving ends, this "musical telegraph" could sort out many simultaneous messages. Bell built a working model and obtained a patent in 1875.

The Telephone

The invention of the telephone was a direct outgrowth from the multiple telegraph. Bell found that a flexible membrane, called a diaphragm, worked better for the human voice than a metal reed. In the summer of 1876, Bell entered his invention at the Philadelphia Centennial Exhibition, which celebrated the hundredth anniversary of the United States. The exhibition judges were amazed to hear Bell's voice in the receiver at a distance of 300 feet. They awarded him first prize.

The Bell Telephone Company was started in 1877. The company manufactured telephones and put up individual lines for subscribers. A typical customer might be a businessperson who wanted a private telephone connection between office and home. Newspaper articles

(Library of Congress)

Bell's Telephone of 1876

The basic idea of Bell's telephone was to convert sound waves into a fluctuating electrical current and then to convert the signal back into sound at the receiver.

In a telegraph system, the electric current along a transmission line is in the form of intermittent pulses to represent dots and dashes. By contrast, a telephone system has a continuous current that fluctuates according to the voice frequencies. Bell's first telephone patent application, submitted in March, 1876, applied one of the basic principles of electromagnetism for converting the vibration of sound waves into electric current fluctuations. An iron magnet, when moved in and out of a coil of wire, will create an electric current in the coil. Michael Faraday, a British scientist, first observed this effect with a sensitive current detector in 1831. If the magnet is stationary, no current will be induced.

Bell's telephone transmitter had a funnel-shaped horn to concentrate sound waves against a small, flexible membrane (similar to the eardrum). The vibration of this diaphragm caused an attached magnet to move back and forth inside a coil of wire. In accordance with Faraday's observation, the vibrating magnet induced an electric current in the coil. The fluctuating current then traveled along a wire from the transmitter to the receiver.

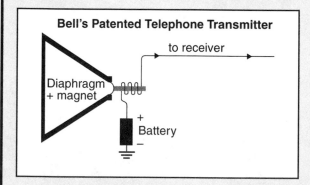

Bell's Patented Telephone Transmitter

At the telephone receiver, the fluctuating current had to be reconverted back to a mechanical vibration. Bell's telephone receiver used an electromagnet. Hans Christian Ørsted, a Danish physics teacher, had discovered the principle of the electromagnet in 1821 when he observed that an electric current creates a magnetic field that can attract or repel a compass needle. Evidently, a coil of wire in which a current flows is equivalent to a magnet.

In Bell's receiver, fluctuating electric current coming through the wire caused the coil to produce a varying magnetic field. An iron rod was alternately attracted and repelled, causing the attached flexible diaphragm to vibrate back and forth. The resulting sound waves were concentrated against the listener's ear.

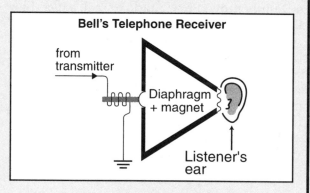

Bell's Telephone Receiver

Bell's transmitter and receiver were like symmetrical mirror images. In the transmitter, a vibrating iron magnet induces a fluctuating current in a coil. At the receiver, a varying current in a coil causes a magnet to vibrate.

The telephone patent awarded to Bell in 1876 was the most valuable patent ever issued by the government. The Western Union Company tried to set up a rival telephone system, but Bell Telephone sued it and other competing companies for infringement of patent rights. More than six hundred lawsuits were fought in court, but the priority of the Bell patent was consistently upheld.

Bibliography

American Science and Invention: A Pictorial History. Mitchell Wilson. New York: Bonanza Books, 1954.

Great Inventors and Discoveries. Donald Clarke, ed. London: Marshall Cavendish, 1978.

Physics: The Pioneer Science. Lloyd W. Taylor. New York: Houghton Mifflin, 1941.

provided increasing publicity about the telephone, and Bell was invited to give public demonstrations. The audience was particularly fascinated to hear four singers, standing at different locations, blend together into a quartet at the receiver.

In 1877, Bell married Mabel Hubbard, a deaf student, and he and his bride made a wedding trip to England. They received an invitation to give a demonstration of the telephone to Queen Victoria and the royal family. The European press gave wide coverage to this visit.

In 1880, France awarded the Volta Prize to Bell for his invention. Combining this monetary award with royalties from his patents, Bell founded the Volta Bureau for teaching speech to the deaf in Washington, D.C. Helen Keller, a deaf-mute prodigy who learned to speak, participated in the groundbreaking for the Volta building.

Telephone Networks

As the demand for telephone service increased, the concept of individual lines became obsolete. A central switchboard was set up in each town. Subscribers called the switchboard, where operators would make individual cable connections for each call.

By 1910, nearly ten million telephones were in operation in the United States. Telephone service became a financial success because people wanted long-distance voice communication.

Other Inventions

Bell had a wide range of interests. He invented a photophone to transmit sound waves over a light beam. In 1881, he invented a metal detector to locate the assassin's bullet that had entered President James Garfield's body.

The Bell Telephone Company gave him the wealth to pursue other endeavors. He became the president of the National Geographic Society and promoted the use of photography in its journal. Bell died at his summer home in Canada at the age of seventy-five.

Bibliography

By Bell

Visible Speech as a Means of Communicating Articulation to Deaf Mutes, 1872

Upon the Production of Sound by Radiant Energy, 1881

Upon the Electrical Experiments to Determine the Location of the Bullet in the Body of the Late President Garfield and upon a Successful Form of Induction Balance for the Painless Detection of Metallic Masses in the Human Body, 1882

The Bell Telephone: The Deposition of Alexander Graham Bell, in the Suit Brought by the United States to Annul the Bell Patents, 1908

About Bell

Alexander Graham Bell and the Conquest of Solitude. R. V. Bruce. Reprint. Ithaca, N.Y.: Cornell University Press, 1990.

Alexander Graham Bell: The Man Who Contracted Space. Catherine D. MacKenzie. New York: Houghton & Mifflin, 1928.

Hello, Alexander Graham Bell Speaking: A Biography. Cynthia L. Lewis. Minneapolis: Dillon Press, 1991.

The One Hundred: A Ranking of the Most Influential Persons in History. Michael H. Hart. New York: Hart, 1978.

(Hans G. Graetzer)

Jocelyn Bell Burnell

Area of Achievement: Astronomy
Contribution: Bell Burnell was the first astronomer to note the anomaly that resulted in the discovery of pulsars. She also worked in X-ray, infrared, and optical astronomy.

July 15, 1943	Born in Belfast, Northern Ireland
1956-1961	Attends Mount School in York, England
1965	Receives a bachelor of science degree from the University of Glasgow
1965	Begins work for a doctorate at Cambridge University under the supervision of Anthony Hewish
1967	Discovers pulsars using a powerful radio telescope
1968	Completes her doctorate
1968	Marries Martin Burnell
1968	Studies X-ray astronomy at the University of Southampton
1974	Hewish shares the Nobel Prize in Physics with Martin Ryle for discovering pulsars
1974-1982	Works at the Mullard Space Science Laboratory in X-ray astronomy
1982	Named a senior research fellow at the Royal Observatory in Edinburgh studying infrared and optical astronomy
1989	Divorces Martin Burnell
1991	Appointed a professor of physics at Open University in Milton Keynes, England

(The Open University)

Early Life

Susan Jocelyn Bell was born in Belfast, Northern Ireland, on July 15, 1943. From her teenage years, Bell wanted to become an astronomer. She became interested in the subject through reading the books of her father, the architect of Armagh Observatory in Northern Ireland.

Bell attended a Quaker girls' boarding school in England. Between the ages of fifteen and eighteen, she had a good physics teacher, an elderly man who had come out of retirement for a second time to teach. There was little equipment in the school, but Bell recalled that her teacher showed her "how easy physics was."

After completing secondary school, she went to Scotland to study science at the University of Glasgow. Upon receiving her baccalaureate in science from Glasgow in 1965, Bell began studies for a doctorate at the University of Cambridge in England.

Discovering Pulsars

Bell spent her first two years at Cambridge building a large radio telescope—a high-resolution dipole array—that her supervisor, Anthony Hewish, had designed. It was nearly 2 hectares (4.5 acres) in area and hence was very sensitive. It was able to record rapid variations in signals. When construction was completed and the telescope was operational in July, 1967, a sky survey began.

Bell was given the task of analyzing the signals received, which involved inspecting 400 feet of chart paper from a chart recorder every four days. In October, Bell noticed "a bit of scruff" occupying about half an inch of chart. She brought the anomaly to Hewish's attention, but he initially regarded it as insignificant. This reading could be caused by an equipment problem, interference, or satellites in orbit. All these possibilities had to be checked out.

Further observations indicated that the position of the strange signals stayed fixed with respect to the stars, which implied that the source was neither terrestrial nor solar in origin. In late December, Bell found another such source. Bell, under the direction of Hewish, had discovered pulsars, but their discovery was merely an appendix to her dissertation on twinkling quasars.

In 1974, Hewish shared the Nobel Prize in Physics with Martin Ryle, a radio astrophysicist. Hewish's award was given "for his pioneering research in radio astrophysics, particularly the discovery of pulsars." Bell's contribution was not mentioned in the Nobel citation.

Career

On finishing her Ph.D. thesis, Bell moved from Cambridge to the south coast of England to be near her fiancé, and she began to study gamma-ray astronomy at the University of Southampton. She married Martin Burnell in 1968 and thereafter was known as Jocelyn Bell Burnell. When her husband moved, she did as

Pulsars

A pulsar is a spinning neutron star of very small diameter and incredibly dense.

Pulsars are so named because the radio radiation that is received from them is pulsed. An ordinary star shines in every direction. Pulsars are more like lighthouses, as only a small part of the pulsar radiates and the radiation is strongly beamed into a cone of diameter between 5 and 50 degrees in size. As the pulsar rotates, if the beam points in the direction of the earth, a pulse is received. Information about the pulsar and its environment must be extracted by analyzing this pulse.

Pulsars are strongly magnetized neutron stars that contain huge amounts of energy. They have a shell, analogous to that of an egg, but pulsars are the most perfectly round thing ever found, made up of iron that is ten times more dense than iron found on Earth. Inside this shell is a super-fluid, a liquid state of matter characterized by apparently frictionless flow.

These power sources emit radio waves that have periods of milliseconds to several seconds. Pulsars spin incredibly fast—so fast in fact that the energy produced from this revolution can produce a thousand million volts. They are so dense that a teaspoonful of material from a neutron star would weigh 100 million tons. It is now evident that these objects must be very compact because they pulse rapidly. They also must be very massive because they are such good time-keepers. They have large reserves of energy and can send out signal after signal after signal, with no sign of diminution. Since the initial discovery, pulsars that pulse several hundred times a second have been found, as have planets around pulsars, even though there are theoretical reasons why such a thing should not be possible.

Bibliography

Pulsar Astronomy. A. G. Lyne and F. Graham-Smith. Cambridge, England: Cambridge University Press, 1990.

well and worked in X-ray astronomy at University College, London. She worked part-time for eighteen years running a satellite called Ariel V.

Working part-time, when carrying the load of domestic responsibilities and child rearing, meant less time for research. Following her husband around the country did not help Bell Burnell receive promotions. Only after they divorced in 1989 was she able to apply for a job solely on the basis of what it was, rather than where it was. In 1991, she was named a professor of physics at Open University, and she began work on neutron stars.

Bibliography
By Bell Burnell
"Little Green Men, White Dwarfs, or What?," *Sky & Telescope*, 1978

About Bell Burnell
Betrayers of the Truth: Fraud and Deceit in the Halls of Science. William Broad and Nicholas Wade. New York: Simon & Schuster, 1982.
The Biographical Dictionary of Scientists. Roy Porter, ed. 2d ed. New York: Oxford University Press, 1994.
"Discovery of Pulsars: A Graduate Student's Story." Nicholas Wade. *Science* 189 (1975).
Nobel Prize Women in Science: Their Lives, Struggles, and Momentous Discoveries. Sharon Bertsch McGrayne. New York: Carol, 1993.

(Maureen H. O'Rafferty)

Paul Berg

Areas of Achievement: Biology, cell biology, genetics, and virology

Contribution: Berg developed a technique to splice deoxyribonucleic acid (DNA) from different organisms. Splicing produces a tool for the study of chromosome structure and the biochemical basis of genetic disease via recombinant DNA technology.

June 30, 1926	Born in Brooklyn, New York
1944	Enters the U.S. Navy during World War II
1948	Graduates from Penn State University with a B.S. in biochemistry
1952	Receives a Ph.D. in biochemistry from Case Western Reserve University
1956	Becomes assistant professor of microbiology at Washington University Medical School
1959	Moves to Stanford University as an associate professor
1959	Receives the American Chemical Society's Eli Lilly Prize
1969-1973	Serves as chair of the biochemistry department at Stanford
1970	Named Wilson Professor of Biochemistry
1980	Receives the Nobel Prize in Chemistry
1983	Awarded National Medal of Science
1990	Becomes a trustee of Rockefeller University
1990	Becomes chair of the advisory board of the Human Genome Project

Early Life

Paul Berg was born in Brooklyn to a clothing manufacturer, Harry Berg, and his wife Sarah. He attended city public schools including Abraham Lincoln High School, from which he was graduated in 1943. There, Berg developed a strong interest in microbiology and biochemistry research. He credited much of this to Mrs. Wolf, who ran the school's science club.

Berg next entered Penn State University. His career plan, a degree in biochemistry, was interrupted by U.S. Navy service from 1944 to 1946. Afterward, Berg returned to Penn State. He married Mildred Levy in 1947 and had one son, John Alexander. In 1948, Berg was graduated from Penn State with a B.S. in biochemistry.

Berg entered graduate school at Case Western Reserve University in Cleveland, Ohio. There, he was a National Institutes of Health (NIH) Fellow from 1950 to 1952. After receiving a biochemistry Ph.D. in 1952, Berg did postdoctoral work with Herman Kalckar at Denmark's Institute of Cytophysiology in Copenhagen and then with Arthur Kornberg at Washington University in St. Louis, Missouri. He stayed at Washington as a scholar in cancer research until 1957.

Splicing Genes

By 1956, Berg was an assistant professor of microbiology at Washington University. He left in 1959 to become an associate professor at Stanford University in California. During the 1950's, Berg explored how amino acids, the building blocks (monomers) of proteins, become protein polymers via messenger ribonucleic acid (mRNA) and transfer ribonucleic acid (tRNA), members of a biomolecule class called nucleic acids.

Contemporary nucleic acid research had shown that mRNA and tRNA arise from the hereditary material deoxyribonucleic acid (DNA). DNA and RNA are huge polymers made of nucleotide subunits joined into long chains. Nucleotides contain components called bases in a genetic code. Base order (sequence) in DNA and RNA determines what each gene does.

Knowing this, Berg sought to combine genes from different species artificially, making "re-combinant DNA." He reasoned that he could then study a gene from one species without interference encountered in original organisms, amid many neighboring genes. He began this work in the 1960's with simian virus 40 (SV40) viruses that infect monkeys and cause cancer.

By the 1970's, Berg had a gene map that showed where genes from SV40 were found in host cell DNA, their sequences, and what each did. His work mixed SV40 genes with genes from monkeys, a virus called lambda, and the bacterium *Escherichia coli* (*E. coli*). Berg performed this "cut and paste" by a method using restriction endonucleases and DNA ligation (splicing).

For example, SV40 DNA and other DNAs are cut up into defined pieces with endonucleases. The pieces are then spliced to make recombinant DNAs, each of which contain one or several SV40 genes. Recombinant DNAs are next put into *E. coli* in order to make recombinant bacteria. Finally, the microbes are grown

(The Nobel Foundation)

DNA, SV40, and Splicing

Genes from different organisms can be cojoined (spliced) in order to study chromosome structure and the biochemical basis of disease.

The flow of hereditary information can be simplistically stated as from deoxyribonucleic acid (DNA) to ribonucleic acid (RNA) to proteins. This Central Dogma of molecular biology, stated by Francis Crick, indicates that DNA is used to make messenger RNAs (mRNAs), each of which encode the production of a specific protein. Berg's Nobel Prize in Chemistry was given for two accomplishments. First was artificially combining (splicing) genes from different species to make recombinant DNA. The other was sequencing and using the recombinant DNA to enable the study of individual genes from one species without interference found in the original organisms because of the presence of neighboring genes. This fundamental endeavor was based on the structure of DNA and on the availability of the enzymes (biological catalysts) that enabled Berg to cut and paste DNA into artificial constructs.

A DNA molecule, or chromosome, is composed of two DNA polymer strands, each made of cojoined subunits called nucleotides. Every nucleotide holds a sugar (deoxyribose), a phosphate, and one of four nitrogen-containing bases: adenine (A), cytosine (C), guanine (G), and thymine (T). The strands are actually two very long, intertwined polymer chains made up of chemically attached deoxyribose phosphate units. They are held together in ladderlike double helixes by interactions between bases that are found in pairs (such as AT), like ladder rungs.

The base order (sequence) in some portions of a DNA strand determines the readout of the genetic code that is ultimately used to determine the sequence of amino acids present in a given protein (amino acid polymer) made by the cell. As bases match up in a fixed way—(A binds only to T, and G binds only to C)—the base sequence of a strand determines the sequence of the other strand, termed complementary, in the duplex.

Berg's experiments used as a probe DNA from simian virus 40 (SV40), which causes tumors in monkeys. He began by utilizing enzymes called restriction endonucleases (REs). An RE cuts a DNA duplex into fragments with defined single-stranded ends (see figure). These single-stranded ends can bind to other fragments that have complementary base sequences (for example, TATA can bind to ATAT), so they are called "sticky ends."

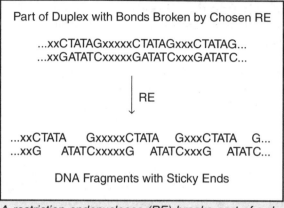

Part of Duplex with Bonds Broken by Chosen RE

...xxCTATAGxxxxxCTATAGxxxCTATAG...
...xxGATATCxxxxxGATATCxxxGATATC...

RE

...xxCTATA   GxxxxxCTATA   GxxxCTATA   G...
...xxG   ATATCxxxxxG   ATATCxxxG   ATATC...

DNA Fragments with Sticky Ends

A restriction endonuclease (RE) breaks part of a duplex into fragments with "sticky ends." Each x denotes an unspecified base in a nucleotide unit.

Berg worked most with SV40 DNA and the DNA of the bacterial virus (phage) lambda, which attacks the bacterium *Escherichia coli* (*E. coli*). After he prepared SV40 and lambda fragments having sticky ends, Berg caused them to rejoin to produce lambda phage chromosomes, each containing one or a few SV40 genes. He then put the new recombinant chromosomes into *E. coli* by infecting these bacteria with the phage and studied new proteins produced by the bacteria that could only have come from SV40 genes. The production of SV40 proteins was caused by the use of SV40 DNA to make mRNAs producing specific proteins. Berg also sequenced the DNA fragments with which he worked.

Bibliography

Biotechnology: Strategies for Life. Elizabeth Antebi and David Fishlock. Cambridge, Mass.: MIT Press, 1986.
"Construction of Hybrid Viruses Containing SV40 and Lambda Phage DNA Segments and Their Propagation in Cultured Monkey Cells." Paul Berg and S. P. Goff. *Cell 9* (1976).
The Ultimate Experiment. Nick Wade. New York: W. H. Freeman, 1977.

and the proteins made via SV40 genes are identified.

This work led to an understanding of what each portion of SV40 DNA does and enabled work with genes from other organisms. Refined by himself and others, Berg's research produced recombinant DNA technology. This technology has such lofty goals as making new organisms to suit societal needs; identifying the exact DNA sequence of all human genes, called the Human Genome Project; and curing human disease by inserting genes in molecules. Berg served as chair of the Human Genome Project in 1990. He also chaired the Stanford University biochemistry department from 1969 to 1974 and became its Wilson Professor of Biochemistry in 1970.

Altruism and the Nobel Prize

Berg recognized the danger of putting cancer genes in *E. coli*, which ubiquitously exist in sewage and the human body. Should recombinant bacteria escape laboratories, they could lead to huge rises in the incidence of cancer. Other laboratories, he feared, might also create dangerous recombinant organisms.

Consequently, Berg temporarily stopped his work and called together many other eminent scientists to discuss safeguards. Their dialogue, climaxing in a 1975 international meeting in Pacific Grove, California, outlined safeguards for federal regulations. Today, many such regulations, deemed unnecessary, have been relaxed. They might not, however, have existed without Berg's altruistic actions.

In 1980, Berg received the Nobel Prize in Chemistry for the fundamental study of nucleic acids and recombinant DNA. He also won other awards, such as an American Chemical Society's Eli Lilly Prize in 1959, the Lasker Medical Research Award in 1980, and the National Medal of Science in 1983. Berg was elected a member of the U.S. Academy of Arts and Sciences, France's Académie des Sciences, and Japan's Biochemistry Society. He was a trustee of Rockefeller University from 1990 to 1992. Throughout his career, Berg worked on recombinant DNA, including efforts to unravel the secrets of acquired immunodeficiency syndrome (AIDS).

Bibliography

By Berg

"An Enzymatic Mechanism for Linking Amino Acids to RNA," *Proceedings of the National Academy of Sciences*, 1958 (with E. J. Ofengand)

"Specificity in Protein Synthesis," *Annual Review of Biochemistry*, 1961

"Biochemical Method for Inserting New Genetic Information into DNA of Simian Virus 40," *Proceedings of the National Academy of Sciences*, 1972 (with David A. Jackson and Robert H. Symons)

"Construction of Hybrid Viruses Containing SV40 and Lambda Phage DNA Segments and Their Propagation in Cultured Monkey Cells," *Cell*, 1976 (with Stephen P. Goff)

Genes and Genomes: A Changing Perspective, 1991 (with Maxine Singer)

Dealing with Genes: The Language of Heredity, 1992 (with Maxine Singer)

About Berg

Biotechnology: Strategies for Life. Elizabeth Antebi and David Fishlock. Cambridge, Mass.: MIT Press, 1986.

"Paul Berg." In *The Nobel Prize Winners: Chemistry*, edited by Frank N. Magill. Pasadena, Calif.: Salem Press, 1990.

The Ultimate Experiment. Nick Wade. New York: W. H. Freeman, 1977.

(Sanford S. Singer)

Claude Bernard

Areas of Achievement: Biology, chemistry, medicine, and physiology

Contribution: Bernard actively explored the roles of nerves, the liver, the pancreas, and toxic substances. He helped establish the principles of experimental medicine.

July 12, 1813	Born in Saint Julien, France
1841	Hired by François Magendie as a research assistant
1843	Receives an M.D. from the University of Paris
1844	Fails the examination required to teach in the Faculty of Medicine
1845	Marries Marie François (Fanny) Martin
1846	Explores the mechanism of carbon monoxide poisoning
1847	Becomes Magendie's teaching alternate at the Collège de France
1848	Shows that sugar in the blood is not always a sign of diabetes
1849	Demonstrates the role of the pancreas in fat digestion
1853	His dissertation earns a doctorate in science
1855	Discovers glycogen (animal starch)
1858	Reports on the nerves controlling blood vessel size
1859	Studies the ability of placenta to make glycogen
1867	Elected president of the French Society of Biology
1868	Named the chair of general physiology at the Museum of Natural History
Feb. 10, 1878	Dies in Paris, France

Early Life

Claude Bernard (pronounced "behr-NAHR") was born in Saint Julien, France, to Pierre and Jeanne Bernard. His family was poor, and Claude was first schooled by parish priests; his secondary schooling was at Villefranche and Thoissey. Science was not taught at either school, but Bernard learned much from his first job, an apothecary apprenticeship.

His first actual career choice, carried out when not running errands for the apothecary, was writing. Bernard's local success with *La Rose du Rhône* (rose of the Rhone) led to a drama called *Arthur de Bretagne* (1887; *Arthur of Brittainy*). He took it to Paris, hoping to make his fortune in the theater. On the advice, however, of critic Saint-Marc Girardin—who thought Bernard's talent inadequate—he entered medicine.

From Medicine to Basic Science

At first, a weak scientific background placed Bernard twenty-sixth out of twenty-nine internship candidates. Nevertheless, passing the entry examination gave him a medical career, beginning with work for François Magendie, a physician-experimenter who became Bernard's mentor. Hired in 1841 as assistant in nerve physiology studies, he soon saw that his interest was physiology, not medicine.

Hence, although he was graduated in December, 1843, Bernard never practiced medicine, although his graduation dissertation, *Du suc pancréatique, et de son rôle dans les phénomènes de la digestion* (1848; on pancreatic juice and its role in digestion), was very important to medicine. It has long been cited as essential groundwork for understanding digestion.

In 1844, Bernard failed an examination needed to teach in the medical faculty and planned to return home, to practice medicine. He was saved from leaving Paris by an 1845 marriage of convenience to Marie Françoise (Fanny) Martin, a physician's daughter with a dowry. The marriage produced daughters Jean-Henriette and Marie-Claude but was unhappy and ended in divorce.

Fame Comes Quickly

Bernard made many physiological discoveries in the decade after his work on gastric diges-

The Study of Pancreatic Action

The role of pancreatic juice in fat digestion was identified through observation, hypothesis, and experimentation with pancreatic fistulas.

Among Bernard's most important discoveries was the function of the animal pancreas, especially the role of the pancreatic juice, secreted into the small intestine, in fat digestion and absorption. It is now known that this role is attributable to an enzyme, a biological catalyst, made by the pancreas and released into the intestine. Before Bernard's work, however, there was no information on the subject.

Reportedly, two observations led Bernard to the conclusions that he made. First, he saw that the urine of herbivores is alkaline and that the urine of carnivores is acidic. He thought that this might be the result of their vegetable and meat diets, respectively. Therefore, he tested the urine of fasting herbivores (they live on body fat under those conditions) and found that it becomes acidic. In contrast, Bernard soon discovered that the urine of carnivores, when they are fed only vegetables, becomes alkaline. Hence, he presumed that it is fat metabolism (or its lack) that causes urine acidity (or alkalinity).

Bernard then explored the uptake of fat by dogs (carnivores) and rabbits (herbivores), anatomically. He discovered that fat absorption occurs much further along the small intestine in the rabbit than it does in the dog. Noting that the location of fat absorption coincides with the point at which the pancreas discharges its secretions into the intestine, he hypothesized a role for that organ in fat metabolism.

Bernard then began to study pancreatic juice. To do so, he invented a pancreatic fistula, a surgically placed artificial duct between the pancreas and the surface of the body. Such fistulas enabled him to collect pancreatic juice from dogs and rabbits under various test conditions. Initially, Bernard found that pancreatic juice acts on fats by carrying out the process of saponification, which breaks them down into glycerol and fatty acids (see figure).

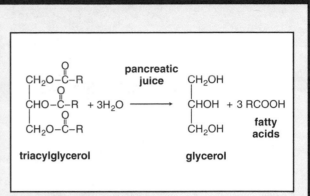

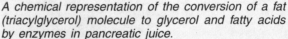

A chemical representation of the conversion of a fat (triacylglycerol) molecule to glycerol and fatty acids by enzymes in pancreatic juice.

Bernard's activities in this work demonstrate his careful research work and his experimental rationalism in scientific study. The latter is a planned agenda of using three stages of experimental procedure. The first is observation, in which he noticed that fat digestion occurs near the juncture of the pancreas and intestine. The next phase, hypothesis, was his proposition that the pancreas is involved in fat digestion and uptake. Finally, he tested his hypothesis by examining pancreatic juice collected from fistulas under various conditions and proved, by experimentation, that it can carry out fat digestion.

This study paved the way for others to examine the pancreas as biochemistry matured. Among the discoveries was pancreatic lipase, the enzyme that carries out the reaction shown in the figure.

Bibliography

Claude Bernard and His Experimental Method in Medicine. J. M. D. and E. H. Olmsted. New York: Henry Schuman, 1952.

Claude Bernard and His Place in the History of Ideas. Rieno Virtanen. Lincoln: University of Nebraska Press, 1960.

Claude Bernard: Father of Experimental Medicine. Jerome Tarshis. New York: Dial Press, 1976.

"Claude Bernard in the Light of Modern Science." *Bulletin of the History of Medicine* 14 (1943).

(Library of Congress)

and turned over to Bernard both the laboratory and the science chair.

Bernard was very active in the laboratory up to 1860. His other major endeavors include glycogen isolation in 1857, the discovery of nerves that control blood vessel dilation in 1858, and the study of the placental ability to make glycogen in 1859. Such research won for him a chair in general physiology and a professorship of medicine at the Faculté des Sciences and the Collège de France, respectively. He also achieved membership in the Académie des Sciences and the Académie du Médecine.

A Generalist and Philosopher

Bernard next began to generalize, creating concepts to aid in the development of experimental medicine. Prime was the *milieu intérieur* (internal environment) and its secretions. The term attempted to differentiate control processes in which secretions enter blood, rather than passing through ducts (like bile or urine). It led to endocrinology, the science of hormones.

Bernard later elucidated the action of poisonous curare and showed its therapeutic potential. He also studied heat production from food, tested anesthetic action, and compared the basic physiology of plants and animals. These efforts led to his presidency of the French Society of Biology in 1867.

Serious illness and a long convalescence from 1865 to 1867 caused Bernard slowly to give up laboratory research between 1860 and 1867. During that period, he published the famous *Introduction à l'étude de la médecine expérimentale* (1865; *Introduction to the Study of Experimental Medicine*, 1927), the preface to a much longer, never completed text. It stated that medical progress was based on experimental physiology. Also, it proposed that physical and chemical sciences are the foundation of physiology research, that the theory of vitalism does not explain life, that animal vivisection is essential to physiology, and that biology depends on the scientific determinism (the idea that identical conditions produce identical life phenomena). Bernard also proposed—as the recipe for medical research—observation, hypothesis, and experimentation.

In 1867, he was chosen by Napoleon III to

tion. These endeavors helped him skyrocket to fame by revealing principles of experimental medicine. One example was his explanation of innervation of vocal cords and the action of the cranial nerves. In 1846, Bernard first explored carbon monoxide poisoning. At that time, he also found that herbivore urine was alkaline and carnivore urine was acidic.

In 1847, Bernard became Magendie's teaching alternate and also produced additional important research data. He showed that sugar in blood need not be a sign of diabetes. Then, in 1849, Bernard identified a role for the pancreas in digesting fat. This effort led him to study the liver and to discover its sugar and glycogen (animal starch). His resultant dissertation, *Recherches sur une nouvelle fonction du foie* (1853; research on a new function of the liver) won a science doctorate a year after Magendie retired prepare *Rapports sur les progrès et la marche de la physiologie génerale en France* (1867; report on general physiology in France). At that time, he became a commander in the French Legion of Honor. From 1868 on, Bernard had a chair and laboratory at the Paris Museum of Natural History. On February 10, 1878, he died of kidney disease. Bernard was so important that he was given a national funeral, an honor previously reserved for important military and political leaders.

Bibliography
By Bernard
Précis iconographique de médecine opératoire et d'anatomie chirurgicale, 1854 (with C. Huette; *Illustrated Manual of Operative Surgery and Surgical Anatomy*, 1855)

Leçons de physiologie expérimentale appliquées à la médecine, 1855-1856 (2 vols.)

Leçons sur les effets des substances toxiques et médicamenteuses, 1857

Introduction à l'étude de la médecine expérimentale, 1865 (*Introduction to the Study of Experimental Medicine*, 1927)

Lectures on the Physiology of the Heart and Its Connections to the Brain, Delivered at the Sorbonne, the 27th March, 1865, 1867

Rapports sur les progrès et la marche de la physiologie générale en France, 1867 (also as *De la physiologie générale*, 1872)

Leçons sur les anesthésiques et sur l'asphyxie, 1875 (*Lectures on Anesthetics and on Asphyxia*, 1989)

Leçons sur le diabète et la glycogenèse animale, 1877

About Bernard
Claude Bernard and His Experimental Method in Medicine. J. M. D. and E. H. Olmsted. New York: Henry Schuman, 1952.

Claude Bernard and His Place in the History of Ideas. Rieno Virtanen. Lincoln: University of Nebraska Press, 1960.

Claude Bernard: Father of Experimental Medicine. Jerome Tarshis. New York: Dial Press, 1976.

"Claude Bernard in the Light of Modern Science." *Bulletin of the History of Medicine* 14, (1943).

(Sanford S. Singer)

Claude Louis Berthollet

Area of Achievement: Chemistry
Contribution: Berthollet showed that the simple laws of affinity between acidic and basic radicals were not enough to explain all compound formation, and factors like quantity of material and temperature must be considered.

Dec. 9, 1748	Born in Talloire, Savoy, Italy
1768	Graduated as a physician from the University of Turin, Italy
1772	Studies chemistry with P. J. Macquer and J.-B.-M. Bucquet in Paris
1778	Earns a D.Med. at the University of Paris
1779	Marries Marguerite Baur
1780	Elected a member of the Académie des Sciences
1792-1796	Serves in many positions, scientific and otherwise, under several governments and sovereigns
1798	Travels to Egypt with Gaspard Monge, at Napoleon's request, to look into natural resources
1801	Publishes *Recherches sur les lois de l'affinité* (*Researches into the Laws of Chemical Affinity*, 1804)
1803	Publishes *Essai de statique chemique* (*An Essay on Chemical Statics*, 1804), his definitive statement on the laws of affinity
1805	Partially retires to Arceuil, a suburb of Paris
1807	With Pierre Laplace, founds Société d'Arceuil to discuss scientific matters
Nov. 6, 1822	Dies in Arceuil, France

Early Life

Claude Louis Berthollet (pronounced "behr-toh-LAY") was born to a family from the minor aristocracy that had fallen on hard times. His connections opened doors, however, and he became the physician to Mme de Montesson in Paris, which gave him access to a private laboratory. His work brought him to the attention of the new chemists surrounding Antoine-Laurent Lavoisier and to the Académie des Sciences, where he presented seventeen memoirs between 1778 and 1780. In the latter year, he became a member of the academy.

Investigations in Chemical Theory

Berthollet began his career as an adherent to the "phlogiston" theory of chemistry, which held that combustible materials contained an element of fire, called phlogiston, that was released when burning took place. The "calx" that remains (for example, a metal oxide) was seen as having lost its phlogiston, but the metal could be reclaimed by transferring phlogiston from soot, oils, resins, sulfur, and the like, through heating.

(Library of Congress)

Chemical Affinity

Compound formation by simple affinity of one chemical fragment for another is affected by physical and chemical circumstances.

The theory of compound formation at the beginning of Berthollet's career rested on the doctrine of "chemical affinity." This theory stated that in any mixture of chemical fragments (now called ions or small molecules), those with the greatest affinity for each other would form a compound, leaving all others behind. Thus—to use the example that changed Berthollet's thinking in this matter—in a mixture of sodium chloride and calcium carbonate, the calcium and carbonate ions would seek out each other to form calcium carbonate, regardless of any interfering circumstances.

During his Egyptian expedition, Berthollet observed the formation of sodium carbonate from such a combination of reactants (salt, or sodium chloride, from surface evaporation, and limestone, or calcium carbonate, in rock formations) at the shores of Lake Natron. He reasoned that the tremendous amount of carbonate leached out of the limestone, together with the large quantity of sodium from the salt, must tip the scales to favor the formation of sodium carbonate rather than the calcium carbonate predicted by simple affinity theory.

Back in Paris, he tested his ideas on this and other chemical systems and found that quantity of reactants did indeed alter product formation, as did temperature. Berthollet stopped short of the actual cause, the solution concentration of reactants, but he opened the way for a broader and more subtle theory of compound formation that lasted for half a century.

Bibliography

"Berthollet, Claude-Louis." Satish C. Kapoor. In *Dictionary of Scientific Biography*. Vol. 2. New York: Charles Scribner's Sons, 1970.

"Claude-Louis Berthollet's *Essai de statique chimique* and Acidity." H. E. LeGrand. *Isis* 67 (1976).

This doctrine was radically opposed by Lavoisier, who showed that the calx was actually heavier than the metal, contrary to what the phlogiston theory would predict. Lavoisier correctly attributed this result to reaction with atmospheric oxygen and the recovery of the metal to the removal of oxygen. Berthollet became associated with Lavoisier's school because he thought that both sides of the argument could be modified to produce a unified chemistry. Later, he abandoned the phlogiston theory altogether.

Nomenclature

The point on which all the new chemists agreed was nomenclature, which in the 1780's was a hodgepodge of uninformative terms such as "oil of vitriol" (sulfuric acid) and "liver of sulfur" (potassium sulfide). This was replaced with a system that foreshadowed that of today, clearly identifying the elements or groups of atoms making up the compound named. The first textbook on nomenclature appeared in 1797.

Later Chemistry and Government Positions

By the turn of the nineteenth century, Berthollet had begun to study the laws of chemical affinity, an investigation that occupied his later years and produced his most important publication, *Essai de statique chimique* (1803; *An Essay on Chemical Statics*, 1804). In it, he introduced a broader view of chemical combination that served for nearly half a century before it was replaced with a theory that led to the current understanding of the subject.

Berthollet held influential positions under four separate regimes, before and after the French Revolution. He was at various times a member of commissions on monetary reform, munitions, agriculture, and the arts. With Gaspard Monge and Louis B. Guyton de Morveau, he founded and taught at the École Polytechnique. He was commissioned to bring back Italian paintings to Paris and restore them, as well as Egyptian natural resources in a 1798 expedition requested by Napoleon, who made Berthollet a count, a senator from Montpellier, administrator of the mint, and a grand officer of the Legion of Honor. Berthollet died in 1822.

Bibliography

By Berthollet

Éléments de l'art de la teinture, 1791 (2 vols.; *Elements of the Art of Dyeing*, 1791)
Recherches sur le lois de l'affinité, 1801 (*Researches into the Laws of Chemical Affinity*, 1804)
Essai de statique chimique, 1803 (2 vols.; *An Essay on Chemical Statics*, 1804)
Mémoires de physique et de chimie de la Société d'Arceuil, 1807-1817 (3 vols.)

About Berthollet

"Berthollet and the Antiphlogistic Theory." J. R. Partington. *Chymia* 5 (1959).
"Berthollet, Proust, and Proportions." S. C. Kapoor. *Chymia* 10 (1965).
"The 'Conversion' of C.-L. Berthollet to Lavoisier's Chemistry." H. E. LeGrand. *Ambix* 22 (1975).
"From Elective Affinities to Chemical Equilibria: Berthollet's Law of Mass Action." Frederic L. Holmes. *Chymia* 8 (1962).

(Robert M. Hawthorne, Jr.)

Jöns Jacob Berzelius

Area of Achievement: Chemistry
Contribution: Berzelius was preeminent in many areas of the new chemistry of the nineteenth century: analysis, atomic and equivalent weights and combining proportions, nomenclature, and the discovery of new minerals and elements.

Aug. 20, 1779	Born in Väversunda, Östergötland, Sweden
1796-1798	Begins medical studies at Uppsala
1798-1800	Analyzes the mineral content at Medevi mineral springs
1800	Builds a voltaic pile, using its electric current to treat patients
1802	Receives an M.D. from Uppsala
1803	Discovers the element cerium
1805	Practices as a physician to the poor in Stockholm
1807	Becomes a professor of medicine and pharmacy at the Medical College, Stockholm
1808	Made a member of Swedish Academy of Science
1810	Becomes the president of the academy
1812	Travels abroad, meets many major chemists of the day
1817	Isolates the element selenium
1817	Elevated to the nobility
1819	Elected secretary of the Academy of Science, a paid position
1829	Discovers the element thorium
1835	Marries Elizabeth Poppius
1835	Made a baron
Aug. 7, 1848	Dies in Stockholm, Sweden

Early Life

The forebears of Jöns Jacob Berzelius (pronounced "bur-ZEE-lee-us") on both sides of his family were clergymen for three generations. His father died when he was four years old, and Jöns lived with various relatives thereafter. Although he was expected to study for the ministry, Berzelius was an indifferent student, preferring to collect and classify birds, flowers, and insects.

His choice of medicine was almost the only one available to a science-minded student of the day; the sciences as they are now known were not offered as degree studies in the universities. Fortunately, Berzelius was introduced to chemistry by a cousin, and he worked for a time in a pharmacy where he learned glassblowing, a necessary art for chemists of the time.

Early Research and Academia

Berzelius' work in mineral water analysis and voltaic current caused the physician Sven Hedin to recommend him in 1802 as an unpaid assistant to the professor of medicine and

(Library of Congress)

Notation and Compound Formation

As Berzelius published the compositions of many chemical compounds, he realized that the symbols representing the elements and their proportions in the compounds could no longer be the geometrical and alchemical icons of the past; instead, an easy-to-remember, rational set of symbols was required.

By 1818, Berzelius and his students analyzed and produced the chemical formulas of nearly two thousand chemical compounds, and they also published accurate atomic weights of forty-five of the forty-nine known elements. Concurrently with this activity, Berzelius developed his system of element and compound notation.

Although Antoine-Laurent Lavoisier and others had developed a logical nomenclature based on the elements actually contained in the compound, notation was still at the stage of alchemical symbols—circles with dots, lines, and letters—of an earlier system. Numbers of elements or radicals were shown by drawing the symbol more than once, in cluster fashion.

Berzelius' notation was the kind of innovation that seems almost foolishly obvious after it is adopted but that requires rethinking the problem before it is arrived at. He suggested that they simply represent each element by the first letter of its Latin name, or the first two letters if necessary, and the numbers of atoms by superscript numbers following the symbol: Ag_2O or SnO_2, for example. Today's subscript numbers quickly came into use in all countries but France, but the system was established and spread immediately.

Thereafter, all the carefully determined compounds, expressed in dualistic, acid-base nomenclature (Berzelius' other major contribution), had rational names and formulas and could be readily listed in alphabetical order along with their molecular weights and appropriate physical data.

Bibliography

"Berzelius, Jöns Jacob." Henry M. Leicester. In *Dictionary of Scientific Biography*. Vol. 2. New York: Charles Scribner's Sons, 1970.

Enlightenment Science in the Romantic Era: The Chemistry of Berzelius and Its Cultural Setting. Evan N. Melhado and Tore Frangsmyr. Cambridge, England: Cambridge University Press, 1992.

pharmacy at the Medical College in Stockholm. At this time, he also met Wilhelm Hisinger, a mine owner who had the money and was himself enough of a scientist to support investigations in electrochemistry and mineralogy for many years, laying the groundwork for Berzelius' later discoveries.

The appointments in the Medical College finally gave Berzelius a secure position in the world of chemistry, although he spent many years repaying debts contracted through no fault of his own. The secretaryship of the Swedish Academy of Science, which in addition to a salary provided excellent laboratory facilities, consolidated his position both academically and financially. By about 1820, he began to take his place as an authority among the chemists of England and the Continent.

Later Research

Although Swedish chemistry had for about a generation excelled in the discovery of elements and minerals at the time that Berzelius began his career, it was unequally developed and lacked broad grounding in both theory and laboratory practice. Berzelius, virtually uneducated in the science, changed all that during his lifetime, becoming for a time the European authority in chemistry.

After he summed up his voltaic chemistry in an 1802 volume and finished his research in the area a decade later, Berzelius turned to a determination of combining weights in compounds, to atomic and equivalent weights, and to elemental analysis of chemical substances. He began by reviewing and tightening up existing analytical procedures, and even inventing new ones.

From sample selection and analytical reagents (which he had to produce for himself), through balance techniques, to the handling of solutions and precipitates—all were subjected to his relentless self-criticism. The results that he obtained on atomic weights and percent elemental composition of compounds are usually within a few hundredths of a percent of values accepted today.

Effect on Chemistry

The new information thus obtained about compounds required an improved notation and theory of compound formation. The notation that Berzelius devised is substantially that used today: elements represented by one-letter or two-letter symbols and proportions by numbers in the compound formula, the only difference being that Berzelius' numbers were superscripts rather than subscripts (for example, SO^3 rather than SO_3).

His new theory of compound formation was dualistic, with all compounds formed by the addition of a base to an acid (for example, the base K^2O and the acid SO^3 to make the compound K^2SO^4). This is a clear forerunner of the modern notation of inorganic salts, although it fell down, sometimes badly, when applied to organic compounds. Nevertheless, he recognized and named isomerism in organic compounds, allotropy in elements, and the effect of catalysts in reaction.

Influence

Chemists young and old made the pilgrimage to Stockholm during Berzelius' heyday, roughly 1820 to 1840. His findings were published in a series of enormously influential textbooks that were translated into all the languages of the scientifically developed countries.

Unfortunately, Berzelius became less and less able to absorb new ideas in his later years, particularly in organic chemistry, where molecular fragments that he knew clearly to be bases seemed to substitute freely for acids—chlorine for hydrogen, for example. He became engaged in polemics with other major chemists and produced ever-smaller investigations with often unsatisfying results.

His marriage at the age of fifty-six to twenty-four-year-old Elizabeth Poppius provided comfort and intellectual companionship in his declining years. Honors came his way, such as twelve royal orders and membership in ninety-four learned societies. He was made a baron in 1835. He died in 1848, just short of his sixty-ninth birthday.

Bibliography

By Berzelius

His works in Swedish have been compiled as *Bibliografi över Berzelius*, 1933-1953 (Arne Holmberg, ed.) English translations of the most important works are found in *A History of Chemistry*, vol. 4, 1964 (J. R. Partington, ed.)

About Berzelius

Jacob Berzelius, His Life and Work. J. Erik Jorpes. Translated by Barbara Steele. Berkeley: University of California Press, 1970.

Jacob Berzelius: The Emergence of His Chemical System. Evan N. Melhado. Madison: University of Wisconsin Press, 1981.

Jöns Jacob Berzelius: Autobiographical Notes. Jöns Jacob Berzelius. Translated by Olof Larsell. Baltimore: Williams & Wilkins, 1934.

(Robert M. Hawthorne, Jr.)

Friedrich Wilhelm Bessel

Areas of Achievement: Astronomy, earth science, mathematics, and technology

Contribution: Bessel founded modern precision astronomy. He measured the first stellar parallax that made possible the calculation of the distance between Earth and a star.

July 22, 1784	Born in Minden, Brandenburg (now Germany)
1799	Leaves the Gymnasium to become a bookkeeper for a trading company in Bremen
1805	Works as an assistant at the observatory in Lilienthal
1810	Supervises the construction of a new observatory at Königsberg for King Frederick William III of Prussia
1818	Publishes a catalog of 3,222 stars commonly known as *Fundamenta Astronomiae*
1823	Develops the method of the personal equation
1826	Determines the length of the seconds pendulum
1838	Makes the first definite parallax measurement of a fixed star, using the constellation known as the Swan
1841	Deduces a value of 1/299 for the ellipticity (deviation from a circle) of the earth
1844	Discovers the binary (double) character of the stars Sirius and Procyon from their disturbed proper motion
Mar. 17, 1846	Dies in Königsberg, Prussia (now Kaliningrad, Russia)

Early Life

Friedrich Wilhelm Bessel was born in 1784 in Minden, near Hannover. At the age of fifteen, he left the Gymnasium (high school) and became an apprentice to a merchant in Bremen. He would later put the skills that he acquired there as a calculator and bookkeeper to good use in astronomy.

Bessel was self-taught in the sciences. In his spare time, he studied how to determine the position of a ship at sea using planetary observations. This led him to study mathematics, astronomy, and the principles of astronomical instruments and to practice observing astronomical events.

His recalculation of the orbit of Halley's comet attracted the attention of Wilhelm Olbers, a Bremen astronomer who recommended Bessel for an assistant position at a nearby observatory in 1806.

Star Catalog

In 1810, Bessel became director of the new Prussian observatory in Königsberg. While the observatory was being built, he worked on the reductions of stellar observations made in the mid-eighteenth century by the English as-

(Library of Congress)

tronomer James Bradley. This work, published in 1818, brought him international recognition and honors. It provided a reference system for the measurement of the positions of the sun, the moon, the planets, and the stars and established him as the founder of modern precision astronomy. The Prussian king ordered Bessel to make a triangulation of East Prussia.

Bessel's careful comparison of astronomical observations led to the discovery of unavoidable systematic differences among trained observers. This discovery kindled interest in the nature of vision itself. The random variation between observations led Bessel to apply the probabilistic theory of errors in his work.

Parallax

The accomplishment that spoke most to the imagination of Bessel's contemporaries was the first accurate determination of the distance to a star. In his time, the radius of the earth's orbit was known, but astronomers had not been able to measure stellar distances. In principle, stellar distances can be derived from the change in angular direction from which the star is viewed as the earth circles the sun. This change is extremely small, however, and thus hard to detect.

The annual parallax of a star is the difference in position of the star as seen from Earth and from the sun. Bessel calculated the parallax of 61 Cygni as 0.314 inches, with a mean error of +/−0.020 inches. This measurement placed the star at a distance of about 10.4 light-years from Earth.

Instrumental Rigor

In order to determine the parallax, Bessel used a heliometer, a telescope in which the objective glass is cut along the diameter. As in his other projects, he subjected this instrument, and his entire measuring procedure, to a painstaking analysis in order to estimate systematic errors. He took account of these errors in his calculations. Such precise habits were soon adopted by German physicists and are now common throughout scientific studies.

Bessel died in 1846 at the age of sixty-one.

The Distance to 61 Cygni

As the earth revolves around the sun, the angle at which one sees a star varies slightly. Using this phenomenon, in 1838 Bessel made the first trustworthy estimate of an interstellar distance.

Bessel realized that the angular distance between two stars can be determined accurately. If one of these stars is close to the earth and the other is much farther away, the variation of angular distance is a sound basis for a determination of the distance to the nearby star.

In order to measure the angle between target star 61 Cygni and a comparison star, Bessel used a heliometer, a telescope in which the objective lens is cut along the diameter. Directed at a star, both parts will contribute to the image formed of the star. When the two parts are shifted along the cutting line, however, two images appear.

Pointing the heliometer at two stars, Bessel shifted the two parts along the cutting line until the image of one star formed by half of the lens coincided with the image of the other star produced by the second half. He measured this displacement and calculated the angle between the two stars, correcting for temperature fluctuations in his instrument.

In order to calculate the distance, Bessel had to eliminate many other factors, such as the relative aberration of 61 Cygni in relation to the comparison star.

Bibliography

Exploring the Distant Stars: Thrilling Adventures in Our Galaxy and Beyond. Clyde B. Clason. New York: G. P. Putnam's Sons, 1958.

The Norton History of Astronomy and Cosmology. John North. New York: W. W. Norton, 1995.

"Stellar Parallax." John Herschel. In *Essays in Astronomy*, edited by Edward Singleton Holden. New York: D. Appleton, 1990.

The Story of Astronomy. Lloyd Motz and Jefferson Hane Weaver. New York: Plenum Press, 1995.

Watchers of the Skies: An Informal History of Astronomy from Babylon to the Space Age. Willy Ley. New York: Viking Press, 1963.

Bibliography

By Bessel

Fundamenta astronomiae pro anno MDCCLV deducta ex observationibus viri incomparabilis James Bradley in Specula Astronomica Grenovicensi per annos 1750-1762 institutis, 1818

"Persönliche Gleichung bei Durchgangsbeobachtungen," *Königsberger Beobachtungen,* 1823

"Bestimmung der Entfernung des 61. Sterns des Schwans," *Astronomische Nachrichten,* 1838

Gradmessung in Ostpreussen und ihre Verbindung mit Preussischen und Russischen Dreieckketten, 1838 (with J. J. Baeyer)

"Untersuchungen über die Wahrscheinlichkeit der Beobachtungsfehler," *Astronomische Nachrichten, 1838*

About Bessel

"Bessel, Friedrich Wilhelm." Walter Fricke. In *Dictionary of Scientific Biography,* edited by Charles Coulston Gillispie. Vol. 2. New York: Charles Scribner's Sons, 1970.

A History of Astronomy. Anton Pannekoek. London: G. Allen & Unwin, 1961.

Physics as a Calling. Katryn M. Olesko. Ithaca, N.Y.: Cornell University Press, 1991.

(Zeno G. Swijtink)

Sir Henry Bessemer

Areas of Achievement: Chemistry, earth science, invention, and technology

Contribution: Bessemer, a British engineer and inventor, developed a process that made possible the widespread production and use of steel.

Jan. 19, 1813	Born in Charlton, Hertfordshire, England
1830-1840	Works as a precious metallurgist in his father's business
1833	Marries Anne Allen
1833	Invents a machine for dating government documents
1856	Presents the Bessemer process to the British Association for the Advancement of Science
1856	Publishes "On the Manufacture of Malleable Iron and Steel Without Fuel"
late 1850's	Grants licenses for his process to ironmakers
1859	Sets up his own steelworks in Sheffield, England
late 1860's	The "open hearth" process, which will eventually replace the Bessemer process, is developed
1871-1873	Serves as president of the Iron and Steel Institute
1878	A vital modification to the Bessemer process is presented by Sidney Gilchrist Thomas
1879	Bessemer is elected a Fellow of the Royal Society of London
1879	Knighted by the British government as payment for his date-stamping device of 1833
Mar. 15, 1898	Dies in London, England

(Library of Congress)

Early Life

Henry Bessemer was the son of an engineer and typefounder (maker of movable type) who fled France to England during the French Revolution. Although he lacked formal education, Henry demonstrated great creativity and inventiveness from an early age. While still a teenager, working as a metallurgist with his father, he designed a device for stamping dates onto government documents. The British government made use of the device but never paid the young Bessemer, who had not patented it.

In his thirties, he developed a special "gold" paint, using brass in a secret process. Wise by then to the patent system, he grew wealthy from the popularity of the paint, which was much in demand for the gilded artwork and decoration of the times.

French Artillery and the Crimean War

Bessemer's interest in precious metals turned to steel, which in the mid-nineteenth century was so costly and difficult to produce that it was considered a precious metal. The Crimean War was fought in the early 1850's by British and French armies against Russia. Bessemer turned his mind toward aiding in the war effort, and he devised a cannon that would be more accurate. One aspect of the new design involved using more force in the barrel of the cannon. More experienced metallurgists discarded the idea, believing that the cannons themselves would explode from the added force. The British government was uninterested in Bessemer's idea, but Napoleon III of France, ally of Britain in the war, decided to support Bessemer in his experiments.

Improvements to Cast Iron

Bessemer believed in his goal, and, rather that changing his design, he set about improving the strength of the cast iron used to make cannons. While cast iron was known to be brittle, wrought iron would be too soft. Cast iron contains about 4 percent carbon as an impurity. Wrought iron has almost none. Steel, the most difficult to make of the three alloys of iron and carbon, has between 0.1 percent and 1.5 percent carbon. Bessemer believed that steel would be the best suited to making his cannon, but it was too difficult to prepare for mass production.

Without having an extensive background in iron and steel forging, Bessemer tried several ideas that more knowledgeable ironmasters told him would never work. In spite of this, Bessemer developed a way of mass-producing steel quickly and at a fraction of the cost believed possible. In the end, Bessemer credited his ability to think freely and creatively about the steel problem to his lack of formal knowledge in that area.

Over the next twenty years, the process was improved. Other steelmakers developed related processes during the same time, and together these evolving technologies permitted industrial growth and the development of the railroads, shipping lines, skyscrapers, and automobiles that characterized the twentieth century.

Honors

Bessemer was rewarded for his ingenuity by election to the presidency of the Iron and Steel Institute from 1871 to 1873 and by membership in the Royal Society of London in 1879. Also in 1879, the British government knighted him as payment for the date-stamping device that he had invented forty-six years earlier.

Sir Henry Bessemer died in 1898 in London at the age of eighty-five.

Bibliography
By Bessemer
"On the Manufacture of Malleable Iron and Steel Without Fuel," *The (London) Times*, 1856
An Autobiography, 1905

About Bessemer
"Bessemer, Sir Henry." In *Encyclopaedia Britannica*. Vol. 2. Chicago: University of Chicago Press, 1992.
"Sir Henry Bessemer." Isaac Asimov. In *Asimov's Biographical Encyclopedia of Science and Technology*, Garden City, N.Y.: Doubleday, 1972.

(Wendy Halpin Hallows)

Steel Made Affordable

Although he did not originate the process for making steel, Bessemer invented a process that made possible its widespread production and use.

The blast furnace has been used for centuries for refining metals. Ore is heated in the presence of air, and additives such as limestone react with impurities and remove them as "slag." Coke is used to help eliminate excess oxygen. The molten metal sinks to the bottom of the furnace and is drawn off into ingot molds.

Cast (refined) iron contains impurities that make it brittle. Most important is the 3 to 4 percent carbon content that remains in the iron. Complete removal of the carbon yields wrought iron, which is soft and easily worked. Steel consists of 0.1 percent to 1.5 percent carbon and combines the best of wrought and cast iron. Early steel production involved first the formation of wrought iron, followed by the addition of precise amounts of carbon. This process was too slow for mass production.

Bessemer's contribution was to rush the molten cast iron from the blast furnace into a cauldron, where a blast of air bubbled through it, removing more impurities very quickly and without the expense of additional fuel. By timing the exposure to the air, any desired amount of carbon could be left in the steel.

Bibliography
Descriptive Chemistry. Donald A. McQuarrie and Peter A. Rock. New York: W. H. Freeman, 1985.
Kirk-Othmer Encyclopedia of Chemical Technology. Vol. 13. 3d ed. New York: Wiley-Interscience, 1981.

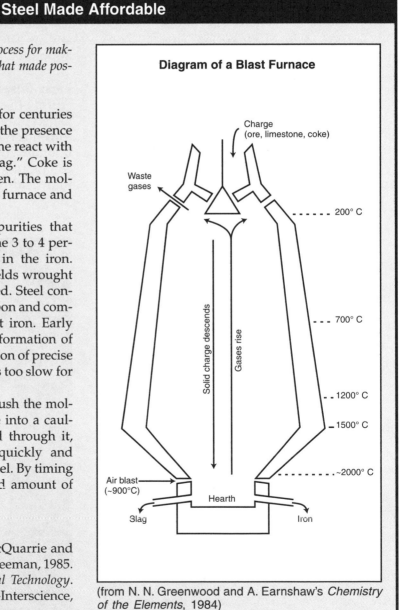

Diagram of a Blast Furnace

Charge (ore, limestone, coke)

Waste gases

200° C

700° C

1200° C

1500° C

~2000° C

Solid charge descends

Gases rise

Air blast (~900°C)

Hearth

Slag

Iron

(from N. N. Greenwood and A. Earnshaw's *Chemistry of the Elements*, 1984)

Hans Albrecht Bethe

Areas of Achievement: Astronomy and physics

Contribution: Bethe discovered the first detailed mechanisms for the sun's generation of energy through nuclear reaction. He also conducted significant research in nuclear and atomic physics and quantum electrodynamics.

July 2, 1906	Born in Strassburg, Germany (now Strasbourg, France)
1928	Receives a Ph.D. in physics from the University of Munich
1928	Hired as a physics instructor at the University of Frankfurt
1930	Appointed a lecturer at Munich
1933	Takes a position at the University of Manchester, England
1934	Appointed a Fellow at Bristol University, England
1935	Joins the faculty at Cornell University in New York
1936-1937	Publishes three important papers on nuclear physics
1938	Details the mechanism for energy production in stars
1943-1946	Heads the theoretical division at the Los Alamos Laboratory
1946	Awarded the American Medal of Merit
1947	Calculates the Lamb shift
1954	Elected president of the American Physical Society
1958	Serves as a delegate to the International Test Ban Conference
1967	Awarded the Nobel Prize in Physics
1976	Awarded the National Medal of Science

Early Life

Hans Albrecht Bethe (pronounced "BAY-tuh") was born in Strassburg, a city then in Germany but now in France, in 1906. The son of a physiology professor, he was reared in an academic environment. Bethe attended the University of Frankfurt from 1924 to 1926 and then moved to the University of Munich, where he worked under the direction of Arnold Sommerfeld, an early pioneer in the field of quantum mechanics.

In 1928, shortly after receiving his Ph.D. in physics, Bethe returned to Frankfurt as a physics instructor. In 1929, he moved to the University of Stuttgart and the following year was appointed to a lecturer position at Munich.

Early Research

During his three years in Munich, Bethe established himself as a leader in the field of quantum mechanics, based in part on the publication of two major research papers. The first, in collaboration with Enrico Fermi, applied quantum field theory to the interaction of charged

(The Nobel Foundation)

Energy Generation in the Sun

Energy is generated by the sun by the process of nuclear fusion. Two processes, the proton-proton cycle and the catalytic carbon cycle, are the most important reactions that occur.

The sun, like other main sequence stars, releases large quantities of energy to its surroundings. This energy release has taken place for the past five billion years and is expected to continue for the next five billion years, until the sun enters the next phase in its evolution.

The main source of energy for the sun and other stars is the transformation of hydrogen into helium by nuclear fusion. In this process, about 1 percent of the initial mass of hydrogen is converted into energy, as described by Albert Einstein's equation $E = mc^2$. The fusion reaction, which is approximately a million times more efficient at generating energy than chemical reaction, can occur only at high temperatures, such as that present in the sun's core.

The most important reaction sequence occurring in the sun's core is the proton-proton cycle. In the first step of the cycle, two protons combine to form a deuterium nucleus, with the release of a positron (positively charged electron) and an electron neutrino. The deuterium nucleus formed in this first step combines with a second proton to form a helium 3 nucleus and a high-energy photon of light. The final step in the reaction sequence occurs when two helium 3 nuclei collide to form a helium 4 nucleus and two protons. The net result of this set of reactions is conversion of four hydrogen nuclei into a helium 4 nucleus.

A second set of reactions, called the CNO or carbon cycle, converts hydrogen into helium catalytically. A carbon 12 nucleus is transformed into a nitrogen 15 nucleus by successive addition of three protons. In the last step of the cycle, the addition of a fourth proton reforms the initial carbon 12 nucleus along with a helium 4 nucleus. The net result of this reaction sequence again is the conversion of hydrogen into helium.

It is somewhat surprising that direct evidence for the occurrence of these cyclic processes can be obtained by Earth-based observations. Both reaction cycles contain steps involving the release of electron neutrinos. Since ordinary matter is almost completely transparent to neutrinos, most of these particles pass through the sun without being absorbed. Neutrinos created in the sun's core can be observed on Earth by detectors located deep underground.

Because of the enormous amounts of energy released by nuclear fusion reactions, there has been great interest in using nuclear fusion to meet the energy demands of modern society. The main difficulty in carrying out nuclear fusion is generating the high temperatures required for this process to occur. By the mid-1990's, however, prototype reactors had reached the point where the net production of energy by the fusion process was obtained for brief periods.

Bibliography

Blinded by the Light: The Secret Life of the Sun. John R. Gribbin. New York: Harmony, 1991.
Guide to the Sun. Kenneth J. H. Phillips. New York: Cambridge University Press, 1992.
Stars: Their Structure and Evolution. Roger J. Taylor. 2d ed. New York: Cambridge University Press, 1994.

particles, while the second, written with Sommerfeld, concerned the electron theory of metals. A third paper, a review of the quantum theory of the atom, helped expose quantum theory to a wider audience of physicists.

In 1933, following Adolf Hitler's rise to power in Germany, Bethe was fired from his academic position because of his Jewish ancestry. He moved to England, where he carried out extensive research in atomic and nuclear physics and on the properties of solids. In his most important work during this period, Bethe, in collaboration with Rudolph Peierls, carried out the first calculations on deuterium, demonstrating that quantum mechanics could be applied to atomic nuclei. In 1935, upon accepting a teaching position at Cornell University, he emigrated to the United States.

Nuclear Reactions in Stellar Interiors

Bethe soon entered his most productive period of research. In 1936 and 1937, he published a series of three papers in *Reviews of Modern Physics*: "Stationary States of Nuclei," "Nuclear Dynamics, Theoretical," and "Nuclear Dynamics, Experimental." These papers, informally called "Bethe's bible," summarized what was then known in nuclear physics and served as a basis for research in this area for more than a decade.

Bethe then applied his knowledge of nuclear physics to the processes by which energy is generated in the interior of stars. In 1938, he discovered a catalytic set of reactions involving the carbon 12 isotope that converted hydrogen into helium. This mechanism represented the first detailed process for the release of nuclear energy in stars. Bethe later found a second mechanism by which hydrogen was directly converted into helium 4, with deuterium and helium 3 as reaction intermediates. For this work, Bethe would be awarded the Nobel Prize in Physics in 1967.

Shortly after the start of World War II, Bethe temporarily halted his research in theoretical physics to concentrate on war-related activities. In 1942, he became a staff member at the Massachusetts Institute of Technology Radiation Laboratory, which was involved in the development of radar detection systems. From 1943 to 1946, Bethe was the head of the theoretical division at Los Alamos Laboratory, where he worked on the development of the atomic bomb and explored the possible use of fusion reactions in advanced nuclear weapons.

Postwar Work
Following the end of the war, Bethe, along with many other physicists, returned to academic research. In 1947, shortly after a conference of leading theoretical physicists at Shelter Island, New York, he carried out the first successful calculation of the Lamb shift, a small energy difference appearing in low-lying states of the hydrogen atom. This nonrelativistic calculation demonstrated that quantum electrodynamics (QED), the theory governing the interaction of atomic systems with electromagnetic fields, was consistent with experimental observation, and it served as the basis for further developments in relativistic quantum field theory.

While Bethe continued to carry out research in nuclear physics and astrophysics after 1950,

the focus of his attention gradually shifted to political issues. Beginning in the 1960's, he became a leading advocate for the abolition of nuclear weapons and the peaceful use of atomic energy. He later argued that space-based defensive missile systems are expensive, unworkable, and destabilizing. Bethe also wrote a number of articles and books discussing the development of physics in the twentieth century.

Bibliography
By Bethe
Nuclear Physics, 1936

"Nuclear Physics: Part I, Stationary States of Nuclei," *Reviews of Modern Physics*, 1936 (with R. F. Bacher)

"Nuclear Physics: Part II, Nuclear Dynamics, Theoretical," *Reviews of Modern Physics*, 1937

"Nuclear Physics: Part III, Nuclear Dynamics, Experimental," *Reviews of Modern Physics*, 1937 (with M. S. Livingston)

Elementary Nuclear Theory, 1947

"The Electromagnetic Shift of Energy Levels," *Physical Review*, 1947

Quantum Mechanics of One- and Two-Electron Atoms, 1957 (with Edward Salpeter)

Intermediate Quantum Mechanics, 1964 (with Roman W. Jackiw)

"Countermeasures to ABM Systems" in *ABM: An Evaluation of the Decision to Deploy an Antiballistic Missile System*, 1969 (Abram Chayes and Jerome B. Wiesner, eds.)

Reducing the Risk of Nuclear War, 1985 (with Robert McNamara)

From a Life of Physics, 1989

The Road from Los Alamos, 1991

About Bethe
Atomic Scientists: A Biographical History. Henry A. Boorse, Lloyd Motz, and Jefferson Hane Weaver. New York: John Wiley & Sons, 1989.

"Hans Albrecht Bethe." In *The Nobel Prize Winners: Physics*, edited by Frank N. Magill. Pasadena, Calif.: Salem Press, 1989.

Hans Bethe: Prophet of Energy. Jeremy Bernstein. New York: Basic Books, 1979.

The Making of the Atomic Bomb. Richard Rhodes. New York: Simon & Schuster, 1986.

(Jeffrey A. Joens)

Jean-Baptiste Biot

Areas of Achievement: Chemistry, earth science, mathematics, and physics

Contribution: Biot linked his training in mathematics and physics to develop sophisticated mathematical models of physical systems investigating the speed of sound, electromagnetism, and the polarization of light.

Apr. 21, 1774	Born in Paris, France
1792	Serves in a French artillery company
1794	Enters the École des Ponts et Chaussées but transfers later that year to the École Polytechnique
1797	Graduated from the École Polytechnique and appointed a mathematics professor at the École Centrale at Beauvais
1800	Named a professor of mathematics at the Collège de France
1803	Investigates the fall of a meteorite at l'Aigle
1804	Ascends in a balloon to demonstrate that the earth's magnetism does not decrease with altitude
1804	Conducts experiments on the conductivity of heat
1815	Demonstrates that organic substances rotate polarized light
1840	Awarded the Rumford Medal of the Royal Society of London for his work on polarized light
1840-1849	Serves as dean of the faculty at the Faculté des Sciences in Paris
1849	Retires
Feb. 3, 1862	Dies in Paris, France

Early Life

Jean-Baptiste Biot (pronounced "byoh") was born in Paris on April 21, 1774. His father, Joseph Biot, had been born a peasant in the Lorraine region of France but rose in stature to become an official in the treasury by the time of Jean-Baptiste's birth.

Biot studied at the Collège-le-Grand in Paris but left the school in 1791 and took private lessons in mathematics. In September, 1792, he enlisted in the army, where he served in the artillery, as a gunner, fighting the British. He entered the École des Ponts et Chaussées in January, 1794, but transferred to the École Polytechnique, where he studied mathematics, when it was founded later that year. Biot was graduated from the École Polytechnique in 1797 and was appointed a professor of mathematics at the École Centrale at Beauvais.

Developments in Mathematical Physics

Although his training was in mathematics, Biot's interests were in the discovery of mathematical formulations of the behavior of the natural world. He was appointed a professor

(Library of Congress)

of mathematical physics at the Collège de France in 1800.

In 1800, Alessandro Volta announced his invention of the voltaic pile, the first electrical battery. Biot began to study the chemistry of the voltaic pile and confirmed that it operated by absorbing oxygen.

Using a balloon left over from Napoleon's Egyptian campaign, Biot made an ascent to an altitude of 4 kilometers (about 2.5 miles) in August, 1804. He timed the oscillation of a magnetized needle at different altitudes and concluded that the earth's magnetic field is constant from the surface up to at least 4 kilometers of altitude.

In 1804, Biot conducted a series of experiments on the conductivity of heat through solid metal bars. By maintaining one end of the bar at a fixed temperature and placing thermometers in small holes down the length of the bar, he was able to show that the temperature of the bar decreased exponentially with the distance from the hot end.

The installation of an extensive system of water mains in Paris provided Biot with the opportunity to study the speed of sound waves. He located a section of cast-iron pipe that measured 951 meters (about 0.5 mile). Before it was filled with water, Biot sent sound waves down the pipe and the air filling the pipe and observed that sound traveled about 10.5 times faster through the iron than through the air.

Biot also developed a formula relating the intensity of solar radiation to the thickness of

The Polarization of Light

Biot investigated the colors produced when polarized light passes through thin layers of transparent material, and he pioneered the development of applications of this polarization in the fields of chemistry, medicine, and technology.

Light is an electromagnetic wave, having an electric field that oscillates in a plane perpendicular to the direction in which the wave is traveling. The orientation of the plane containing the electric field is called the direction of polarization of the light.

In August, 1811, Dominique-François Arago demonstrated that a beam of polarized light separates into beams of two different colors when it passes through thin layers of certain transparent materials. Biot repeated Arago's experiments and established the relationship between the color of the resulting light beam and the thickness of the material. This observation gave rise to a method for measuring the thickness of very thin films of material, far too thin to be measured by traditional mechanical devices.

Biot was most interested in optically active materials, substances that rotate the plane of polarization of the light passing through them. He demonstrated that for a given optically active material, the amount of rotation is proportional to the thickness of the material. He demonstrated that common types of the mineral mica are optically active, and, in 1847, J. F. L. Hausmann named a type of mica "biotite," after Biot.

Biot was the first person to observe that certain liquids, including dissolved sugars and turpentine, are optically active. While solid crystalline sugar is not an optically active substance, a solution containing this sugar is optically active. In 1833, he demonstrated that when cane sugar is heated with dilute sulfuric acid, the solution rotates the plane of polarization counterclockwise, rather than in the clockwise direction of the unheated cane sugar solution. The direction of rotation of the polarization was shown to depend on the direction in which the organic molecule is twisted around its central axis. This observation has evolved into the use of the direction of rotation of the polarization of light to infer the three-dimensional structure of organic molecules.

Bibliography

"Optical Rotary Dispersion: A Tribute to the Memory of Jean Baptiste Biot (1774-1862)." T. M. Lowery. *Nature* 27 (1926).

Seeing the Light: Optics in Nature, Photography, Color, Vision, and Holography. David Falk, Dieter Brill, and David Stork. New York: John Wiley & Sons, 1986.

Understanding Physics: Light, Magnetism, and Electricity. Isaac Asimov. New York: New American Library, 1966.

the atmosphere through which the sunlight had passed. He found that the intensity decreased exponentially with atmospheric thickness.

The Beginnings of Meteoritics

In the early nineteenth century, most scientists were skeptical of eyewitness accounts of rocks falling from the sky. Biot was sent by the minister of the interior to investigate a report that material had been observed falling near the town of l'Aigle on April 26, 1803.

Biot interviewed people from the region and obtained a sample of the l'Aigle stone. He compared its chemical composition with that of stones from the local area. Biot's investigation of the l'Aigle stone marked the beginning of the scientific study of meteorites in France, convincing the skeptics that these objects were authentic.

Investigations of the Polarization of Light

Although Biot made contributions to many areas of science, his most sustained effort was the study of polarized light. Although it had long been known that certain crystals, such as Iceland spar, could rotate the plane of polarization of light, it was not until 1808 that Étienne-Louis Malus demonstrated that light could be polarized by reflection. Biot spent much of the remainder of his career studying polarized light, investigating the materials that could alter the polarization of light, and developing applications for polarization as a measurement tool.

For his contributions to the understanding of polarized light, Biot was awarded the Rumford Medal by the Royal Society of London in 1840. He retired in 1849 and died in 1862 at the age of eighty-five.

Bibliography

By Biot

Analyse du Traité de mécanique céleste de P. S. Laplace, 1801

Traité analytique des courbes et des surfaces du second degré, 1802 (*An Elementary Treatise on Analytical Geometry*, 1840)

Traité élémentaire d'astronomie physique, 1802 (2 vols.; *Elementary Chapters in Astronomy*, 1850)

Essai sur l'histoire générale des sciences pendant la Révolution française, 1803

Recherches sur les réfractions extraordinaires qui ont lieu près de l'horizon, 1810

Précis élémentaire de physique expérimentale, 1817 (2 vols.)

Notions élémentaires de statique, 1828

Études sur l'astronomie indienne, 1859

About Biot

"Optical Rotary Dispersion: A Tribute to the Memory of Jean Baptiste Biot (1774-1862)." T. M. Lowery. *Nature* 27 (1926).

The Society of Arcueil: A View of French Science at the Time of Napoleon. I. M. P. Crossland. Cambridge, Mass.: MIT Press, 1967.

(George J. Flynn)

al-Biruni

Areas of Achievement: Astronomy, mathematics, and physics

Contribution: A versatile scholar and scientist, al-Biruni wrote a classic treatise of his travels in India, translated two Sanskrit books into Arabic, and derived or proved several theorems and properties related to trigonometry, astronomy, and medicine.

Sept., 973	Born in Khwarezm, Khorasan (now Uzbekistan)
983-1017	Studies languages, writes in Arabic, and corresponds with the physician and philosopher Ibn Sina (Avicenna)
1018-1038	Travels to India, translates Sanskrit books into Arabic, and studies Hindu numerals, astronomy, and Sanskrit philosophy
c. 1030	Writes *Tar'ikh al-Hind* (*Al-Beruni's India*, 1888)
1038-1047	Writes several classic scientific works, travelogues, and treatises on history and geography
c. 1050	Dies in Ghazna, Ghaznavid, Afghanistan

Early Life

The Persian scholar and scientist Abu al-Rayhan Muhammad ibn Ahmad al-Biruni (pronounced "al bee-REW-nee"), considered one of the most learned men of his age and an outstanding intellectual figure, was born in September, 973, in the city of Khwarezm, Khorasan, near the Ural mountains. He was a contemporary of the physician and philosopher Ibn Sina (also called Avicenna).

A versatile scholar and scientist, al-Biruni was proficient in physics, metaphysics, mathematics, geography, and history. He was known to have a profound and original mind of encyclopedic proportions. He was fluent in Turkish, Persian, Hebrew, and Sanskrit, in addition to the Arabic in which he wrote. In religion, he was a Shiite Muslim, but in general he had agnostic tendencies.

Travels in India and the Exchange of Ideas

When Sultan Mahmood Ghaznawi took al-Biruni along with him in his journeys to India beginning around 1017, al-Biruni used the opportunity to travel extensively there over the next twenty years. In the process, he learned Hindu philosophy, mathematics, geography, and religion from three pandits (Hindi for "learned men"). In return, he taught the pandits Greek and Arabic science and philosophy.

His well-known book *Tar'ikh al-Hind* (1030; *Al-Beruni's India*, 1888) gives a graphic account of the historical and social conditions of the subcontinent and its culture. Al-Biruni also translated Sanskrit books into Arabic. Of these, *Sakaya* deals with the creation of things and their types, and *Patanjal* deals with what happens when the spirit leaves the body. Indeed, al-Biruni's descriptions of India were so complete that six hundred years later, his book was used extensively as a resource by Emperor Akbar's historian Abu-l-Fazl Allami in his famous

(Library of Congress)

The Qanun al-Masudi and the Advent of Modern Science

Al-Biruni's most famous scientific work deals essentially with astronomy but also includes theorems of trigonometry, numerals, and measurements.

Al-Biruni discussed several theorems of astronomy, trigonometry, and solar, lunar, and planetary motions in *Kitab al-qanun al-Mas 'udi fi 'l-hay'a wa 'l-nujum* (c. 1030; *Canon Masudicus*, 1954-1956), popularly known as the *Qanun al-Mas 'udi*. In this and related books, he discussed the rotation of the earth and gave the correct values of the latitudes and longitudes of various places. He gave a clear account of Hindu numerals, elaborating the principle of position or decimal place. He developed a method for the trisection of an angle and other problems that cannot be solved with a ruler and a compass alone.

Al-Biruni's scientific methods, together with those of other Muslim scientists, contributed greatly to modern science. Centuries before scientists in the rest of the world, he discussed the question of whether the earth rotates around its axis. He ascertained that the speed of light is immense compared with that of sound. He also explained the working of natural springs and artesian wells using the hydrostatic principle of communicating vessels.

Bibliography
"Al-Beruni and His Contribution to Medieval Muslim Geography." M. M. Memon. *Islamic Culture* 13 (1939).
"The Semantic Distinction Between the Terms 'Astronomy' and 'Astrology' According to al-Biruni." S. Pines. *Isis* 55 (1964).

Ain-e Akbari. In his works on geography, al-Biruni claimed that the Indus Valley was an ancient sea basin eventually filled up with materials carried by river systems.

Return from India
Upon returning from India for the last time, around 1038, al-Biruni continued his scientific and sociocultural explorations, and he produced a prodigious number of books on a variety of scholarly subjects. He determined accurately the densities of eighteen different stones and wrote *Kitab al-Jawahir* (c. 1040), which deals with the properties of various precious stones. He wrote *Kitab as-Saydalah* (c. 1050; *A Book on Pharmacy and Materia Medica*, 1973), which combined the Arabic knowledge of medicine with that of India. He also developed a method for finding the sum of a geometrical progression.

Considered one of the greatest scientists of the Islamic world, al-Biruni combined a critical spirit, a love of truth, and a scientific approach with a sense of toleration. His enthusiasm for knowledge may be judged from his claim that the phrase "Allah is omniscient" does not justify ignorance. Al-Biruni died about 1050.

Bibliography
By al-Biruni
Al-Athar al-baqiyah 'an al-qurun al-khaliyah, c. 1000 (*The Chronology of Ancient Nations*, 1879)
Tar'ikh al-Hind, c. 1030 (*Al-Beruni's India*, 1888)
Kitab al-qanun al-Mas 'udi fi 'l-hay'a wa 'l-nujum, c. 1030 (*Canon Masudicus*, 1954-1956)
Kitab al-Jawahir, c. 1040 (a book on gemstones)
Kitab as-Saydalah, c. 1050 (*A Book on Pharmacy and Materia Medica*, 1973)

About al-Biruni
"Al-Biruni." Ahmad Ziauddin. *Islamic Culture* 5/6 (1931/1932).
"Al-Biruni." In *Great Lives from History: Ancient and Medieval*, edited by Frank N. Magill. Pasadena, Calif.: Salem Press, 1988.
Al-Biruni's India: An Account. Edward Sachau, ed. New Delhi: Oriental Reprint, 1983.

(Monish R. Chatterjee)

Vilhelm Bjerknes

Areas of Achievement: Earth science, mathematics, and physics

Contribution: Bjerknes is noted for his polar front theory, concerning the interactions of unlike air masses separated by fronts and the development of cyclones.

Mar. 14, 1862	Born in Christiania (now Oslo), Norway
1891-1894	Studies electrical resonance as an assistant to Heinrich Hertz
1892	Earns a Ph.D.
1893	Appointed a lecturer at Stockholm Högskola (school of engineering)
1895	Appointed a professor of applied mechanics and mathematical physics at the University of Stockholm
1897	Sets forth circulation theorems of hydrodynamics that explain the large-scale movement of air masses
1907	Appointed a professor of physics at the University of Kristiania (later renamed the University of Oslo)
1912-1917	As a professor of geophysics at the University of Leipsig, founds and directs the Leipzig Geophysical Institute
1917	Founds the Bergen Geophysical Institute
1917	Named a professor of geophysics at the Bergen Geophysical Institute
1920	Synthesizes ideas on hydrodynamics and thermodynamics into his polar front theory
1926	Appointed a professor of physics at the University of Oslo
Apr. 9, 1951	Dies in Oslo, Norway

Bjerknes (left) and Carl-Gustav Arvid Rossby discuss plans for meteorological investigations. (AP/Wide World Photos)

Early Life

Vilhelm Frimann Koren Bjerknes (pronounced "BYERK-nays") was born to Carl Anton Bjerknes, a scientist with no formal education in experimental physics, and Aletta Koren. His father's research in hydrodynamics greatly influenced the young Bjerknes' life.

Early on, he became interested in his father's ideas on the generation of forces between pulsating and rotating bodies in frictionless fluids. He collaborated with the senior Bjerknes even though he thought some of his father's ideas somewhat impractical. He even was able to give a critical evaluation of his father's work, which later in life he defended.

Research in Electrodynamics

While in Paris, Bjerknes attended lectures on electrodynamics by Henri Poincaré. There, he learned of Heinrich Hertz's work on the diffusion of electrical waves. Subsequently, Bjerknes joined Hertz as an assistant. Working with

Hertz, he published several documents on resonance in oscillatory circuits (continuous sounds in electrical circuits changing from maximum to minimum or changing direction). Also while assisting Hertz, Bjerknes discovered theoretical and experimental resonance curves important in the development of radio. They remained friends for the remainder of Hertz's life.

Hydrodynamic Research

After completing his Ph.D., Bjerknes turned to developing and simplifying his father's theories of hydrodynamics. He also generalized Lord Kelvin's and Hermann von Helmholtz's postulations of velocities of circulation and the dynamics of the circular vortex with applications to the atmosphere and oceans. His hydrodynamic models of the atmosphere and oceans contributed much to the acceptance of meteorology as a science.

Bjerknes saw fluids as thermodynamic systems, which led to his rejection of the concept of a unique relationship between pressure and the specific volume of a unit of mass. This position then led to his formulation of the theory of physical hydrodynamics. His goal was to use hydrodynamic and thermodynamic theories and current conditions in the atmosphere and oceans to predict the future conditions of these entities.

The Development of Dynamic Meteorology

Bjerknes' work at the University of Stockholm, University, along with several associates, led to the development of dynamic meteorology. During World War I, he and his son, Jacob, established a network of weather stations throughout Norway. Data collected at these stations gave rise to the polar front theory, which purported the existence of air masses with unlike temperature and moisture characteristics. Air masses are separated by zones of discontinuity, which he labeled fronts. Bjerknes likewise explained cyclogenesis as the formation of a cyclone at the junction of warm and

The Polar Front Theory of a Developing Wave Cyclone

The polar front theory was designed to explain the formation, life cycle, and ultimately the dissipation of a mid-latitude cyclone.

The formation of a wave cyclone begins along the polar front, which is a semicontinuous boundary separating cold polar air from warm subtropical air. In the initial stage, the polar front is stationary, with cold air flowing westward and warm air moving eastward along the boundary. Under proper conditions, a kink develops in the polar front with cold air pushing southward, creating a cold front, and warm air moving northward, overriding the colder air and forming a warm front.

In the open wave stage, a cold front extends southwesterly and a warm front stretches toward the east from the cyclone apex, with a warm sector separating the two fronts. Enclosed isobars encircle the storm's center, pressure drops at the apex, and wind velocities increase. Winds blow counterclockwise around and inward toward the storm center.

As the cyclone moves easterly, the cold front, traveling faster than the warm front, gradually shrinks the size of the warm sector. Eventually, the cold front overtakes the warm front and an occluded front results, in which the warm air is forced aloft above the cold air. This stage is usually the most violent in the storm's life cycle. With cold air lying on both sides of the occluded front and without the energy derived from air rising in the warm sector, the system then dissipates.

Bibliography

Atmospheric Circulation Systems and Climates. J. Chang. Honolulu: Oriental, 1972.
"The History of Polar Front and Air Mass Concepts in the United States: An Eyewitness Account." J. Namias. In *Bulletin of the American Meteorological Society*. Vol. 64. Boston: American Meteorological Society, 1983.
"An Introductory Review of Fronts: Part I—Theory and Observations." D. A. Bennetts, J. R. Grant, and E. McCollum. *Meteorology Magazine* 117 (1988): 357-370.

cold wedges of air over the Atlantic. He continued his work later at the Leipzig and Bergen geophysical institutes on the practical implementation of meteorological services on meteorological theory.

Bjerknes' theory of the cyclone, air masses, and fronts using mathematical models provided the basis for modern weather forecasting.

Bibliography

By Bjerknes
"Über die Dämpfung schneller electrischer Schwingungen," *Annalen der Physik*, 1891

"Über electrische Resonanz," *Annalen der Physik*, 1895

Über die Bildung von Cirkulationsbewegungen und Wirbeln in reibungslosen Flüssigkeiten, no. 5 in *Skrifter udgivet af Videnskabsselskabet i Christiania*, 1898

Vorlesungen über hydrodynamische Fernkräfte nach C. A. Bjerknes's Theorie, 1900-1902 (2 vols.)

Fields of Force, 1906

Die Kraftfelder, 1909

Dynamic Meteorology and Hydrography, 1910-1911 (2 vols.; vol. 1 with J. W. Sandström, vol. 2 with T. Hesselberg and O. Devik)

On the Dynamics of the Circular Vortex with Applications to the Atmosphere and to Atmospheric Vortex and Wave Motion, 1921

C. A. Bjerknes: Hans liv og arbejde, 1925

Teoretisk fysik, 1929

Physikalische Hydrodynamik mit Anwendung auf die dynamische Meteorologie, 1933 (with J. Bjerknes, H. Solberg, and T. Bergeron)

About Bjerknes
Dictionary of Scientific Biography. Charles Coulston Gillispie, ed. New York: Charles Scribner's Sons, 1970.

"Vilhelm Bjerknes." In *Great Lives from History: Twentieth Century Series*. Frank N. Magill, ed. Pasadena, Calif.: Salem Press, 1990.

(*Ralph D. Cross*)

Joseph Black

Areas of Achievement: Chemistry and physics

Contribution: Black has been called the founder of modern quantitative chemistry. He applied precise measurements to the study of chemical reactions and to the study of heat exchange between substances at different temperatures.

Apr. 16, 1728	Born in Bordeaux, France
1740	Sent to Ireland for schooling
1746	Enters the University of Glasgow, Scotland
1754	Earns an M.D. from the University of Edinburgh
1756	Publishes his classic dissertation *Experiments upon Magnesia Alba, Quicklime, and Some Other Alcaline Substances*
1756	Assumes the chair of anatomy and chemistry at the University of Glasgow
1757	Teaches a course in chemistry
1759	Begins his research on heat
1766	Assumes the chair of chemistry at Edinburgh
Nov. 10, 1799	Dies in Edinburgh, Scotland
1803	Black's chemistry lectures are published posthumously

Early Life
Joseph Black was born in 1728 in Bordeaux, France, where his father was a wine merchant. His father was a native of Belfast, so Joseph was sent to Ireland for schooling at the age of twelve. Six years later, he entered the University of Glasgow in Scotland, where he developed an interest in chemistry. Black earned an M.D. in 1754 from the University of Edinburgh.

The Nature of Heat

Black's greatest contributions as a scientist were the result of his studies on heat. Since he never published any of his results, the only record of his work can be found in his lecture notes, which were published posthumously.

When Black began his work on heat, the distinction between quantity of heat and intensity of heat as measured by a thermometer was not appreciated. Black clarified the difference by showing that different heating times were required to produce the same increase in temperature for different substances. This fact led to the development of the concept of specific heat. Specific heat is now defined as the quantity of heat required to change the temperature of a substance by 1 degree Celsius. It is an essential concept in calorimetry, the science of the measurement of heat changes in physical and chemical processes.

The other important contribution from Black's work on heat was the development of the concept of latent heat. His measurements indicated that when water froze, it gave up a certain quantity of heat. He then showed that the same quantity of heat had to be added to ice in order to melt it. Black surmised that the same had to be true for the vaporization and condensation of water. These observations were essential to an understanding of the processes involved in phase changes.

Black's development of techniques for the careful measurement of heat changes gained him the title of the founder of calorimetry.

Bibliography

The Early Development of the Concepts of Temperature and Heat: The Rise and Decline of the Caloric Theory. Duane E. Roller, ed. Cambridge, Mass.: Harvard University Press, 1950.

"Thermochemical Investigations for a First-Year College Chemistry Course." H. A. Neidig, H. Schneider, and T. G. Teates. *Journal of Chemical Education* 42, no. 1 (1965).

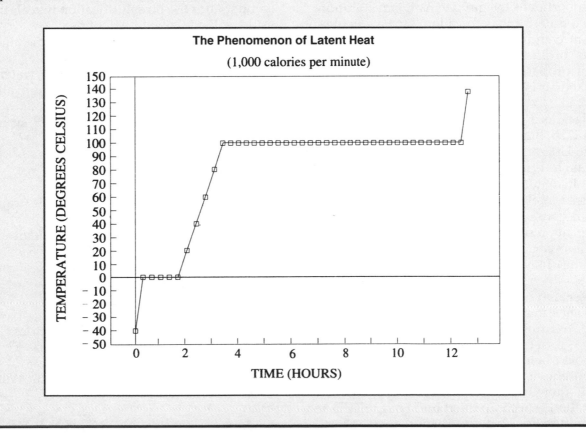

The Phenomenon of Latent Heat

(1,000 calories per minute)

Chemical Research at Edinburgh

Black did the chemical work for which he is most famous as part of his dissertation at Edinburgh, entitled *Experiments upon Magnesia Alba, Quicklime, and Some Other Alcaline Substances* (1756). In the course of his medical studies, he became interested in the chemistry of lime because of its properties as an antacid. A good deal of work had already been done with lime, so Black decided to work with magnesia alba ($MgCO_3$), which had similar properties.

He heated the $MgCO_3$, decomposing it to magnesium oxide, and then regenerated the $MgCO_3$ by reacting the oxide with potassium carbonate. By careful weighing, Black showed that the loss in weight in the first reaction was almost equal to the gain in the second. Black had demonstrated that the decomposition and regeneration of the magnesia alba had involved driving off and then replacing a gas that he called "fixed air."

Black collected some of the gas and determined that it would put out a flame, that it would not support life, and that it had the same properties as the gas given off in respiration. At that time, air was considered to be a single substance and the only gas. Black's demonstration that ordinary air and fixed air had much different properties showed that this was not true. Fixed air is now called carbon dioxide.

Black as a Teacher

In 1756, Black became professor of chemistry at the University of Glasgow. By all accounts, he was a brilliant teacher. Students from the United States and a number of European countries traveled to Scotland to attend his lectures.

Because Black had little interest in publishing his research, his lectures, published posthumously in 1803, contain the only record of some of his work.

Research on Heat

Black's major work in physics involved heat. For example, he was struck by an observation by Gabriel Daniel Fahrenheit that water can be cooled below its freezing point of 32 degrees Fahrenheit while remaining a liquid but then will quickly solidify when shaken. This solidification is accompanied by a sharp rise in temperature to 32 degrees Fahrenheit. The ther-

(Library of Congress)

mometer gives no indication of the presence of this heat in the supercooled water, and only the temperature rise on solidification reveals that it is there. Black called it latent heat.

Black also postulated that the same amount of heat should be given off in freezing as was required to melt a given weight of water. He had to wait until winter when ice was available to verify this theory.

Black died on November 10, 1799, in Edinburgh at the age of seventy-one.

Bibliography
By Black
Dissertatio medica inauguralis . . . , 1754 (trans. in *Journal of Chemical Education*, 1935)
Experiments upon Magnesia Alba, Quicklime, and Some Other Alcaline Substances, 1756
Lectures on the Elements of Chemistry Delivered in the University of Edinburgh, 1803

About Black
Dictionary of Scientific Biography. Charles Coulston Gillispie, ed. Vol. 2. New York: Charles Scribner's Sons, 1970.
Life and Letters of Joseph Black, M.D. Sir William Ramsay. London: Constable, 1918.

(Francis P. Mac Kay)

Patrick M. S. Blackett

Area of Achievement: Physics

Contribution: Blackett is recognized as one of the leaders in the development of modern experimental physics in the twentieth century. His work was in diverse fields, including elementary particle physics, geophysics, and the study of cosmic rays.

Nov. 18, 1897	Born in London, England
1910-1914	Studies at Osborne and Dartmouth Royal Naval Colleges
1914-1918	Serves in the Royal Navy during World War I
1921	Earns a B.A. in physics from Magdalene College, Cambridge University
1921	Begins research at the Cavendish Laboratory under Ernest Rutherford
1932	Begins pioneering studies of cosmic rays
1933	With Giuseppe Occhialini, confirms the existence of the positron
1933	Elected a Fellow of the Royal Society of London
1937	Appointed the head of physics at Manchester University
1948	Awarded the Nobel Prize in Physics
1953	Appointed the head of physics at Imperial College, London University
1965	Elected president of the Royal Society of London
1969	Made a life peer, Baron Blackett of Chelsea
July 13, 1974	Dies in London, England

Early Life

Patrick Maynard Stuart Blackett was born the son of a stockbroker in the borough of Kensington, London. His mother, whose own father had served in the British colonial army in India, was an important influence on her son's early interests in a naval career and on his lifelong devotion to Indian affairs.

The young Blackett loved model airplanes, home-built crystal radios, and bird watching. At the age of thirteen, he won admission to Osborne College (a boys' school for prenaval training), continued at Dartmouth Royal Naval College, and, upon the outbreak of World War I, began his naval service at sixteen.

Cavendish Laboratory and the Cloud Chamber

After four years at sea, Blackett decided to study science rather than continue his naval career. Under a program to facilitate the completion of a general education for those whose military studies had been interrupted by the war, he was sent to Magdalene College at Cambridge University. Its Cavendish Laboratory,

(Archive Photos/Express News)

the leading center for physics research, was headed at that time by Ernest Rutherford, who had discovered the nuclear atom and with whom Blackett would commence his research.

Blackett's first assignment brought him into contact with the cloud chamber techniques of Charles Thomson Wilson. Wilson's apparatus permitted photographs to be taken of the tracks of subnuclear particles and their collisions. Wilson had started his own career in science by exploring the formation of clouds in the atmosphere. Hence, his later invention of the cloud chamber, the forerunner of the bubble chamber, was a natural outcome of that work.

In 1922, Blackett's first paper described the cloud chamber photographs and showed the scattering of alpha particles (the positive nuclei of helium atoms). Within two years, his photographs would show direct evidence for the actual transformation of one atomic nucleus into another of higher mass—a transmutation of elements of the kind once sought by alchemists.

The Positron and Geomagnetism

The early years of the twentieth century saw a number of important advances on the theoretical side of physics, such as relativity and quantum mechanics. In 1930, the Cambridge theoretician P. A. M. Dirac, trying to reconcile certain aspects of these quite different theories, proposed the existence of a particle having the same mass as and opposite charge to an electron.

Much skepticism greeted this idea, since it was known that electrons are abundant in every atom and molecule and that they would surely have attracted and annihilated their positive counterparts had any existed. Nevertheless, American physicist Carl Anderson, who in 1932 was completely unaware of Dirac's theoretical prediction, found such particles, called positrons, while studying cosmic rays.

At about the same time, Blackett joined forces with the Italian physicist Giuseppe Occhialini to begin a series of experiments using a much-improved cloud chamber. Their joint

Cosmic Rays

Blackett's Nobel Prize was awarded for his improvements to the cloud chamber and its application to cosmic-ray physics.

The basic idea behind the cloud chamber is that, when a sample of air is saturated (that is, contains all the moisture possible at the given temperature and pressure), a small decrease in temperature causes the air to become supersaturated, and an immediate condensation of the excess moisture into the liquid phase occurs. Droplets form on particles such as dust, electric charges, ionized atoms, or molecules.

The base of the cylindrical cloud chamber is a piston that produces the sudden requisite drop in pressure and temperature when it is withdrawn rapidly from the chamber. The passage of a gamma ray or an X ray leaves a stream of gaseous ions along its track, on which moisture immediately condenses. These streams of condensed vapor are visible and can be photographed. Blackett's experiments also used a pair of Geiger counters, one above and one below the chamber, so that the device is triggered only by particles that pass through both counters.

Blackett and Occhialini, working with James Chadwick, found even more convincing evidence for the positron. Some photographs showed a pair of particles seemingly created from nothing and emanating from the same point within the chamber. They were identified as an electron-positron pair produced from high-energy gamma rays. For such pair production to occur, relativity theory requires that the gamma ray have a certain minimum energy. The value that they found provided strong confirmation for both relativity and quantum theories.

Bibliography

The Birth of Particle Physics. Laurie Brown and Lillian Hoddeson, eds. New York: Cambridge University Press, 1983.

The Discovery of Subatomic Particles. Steven Weinberg. New York: W. H. Freeman, 1990.

The Nature of Physics. Peter Brancazio. New York: Macmillan, 1975.

projects soon produced convincing evidence for the existence of the positron, the first "antiparticle" to be identified.

In 1937, Blackett moved to Manchester University, where his interest and skills in studying cosmic rays wrought dramatic changes in the research program of his department. His interests in astrophysics and the earth's magnetic field began to take shape. At Manchester, he built the world's most sensitive instrument for measuring rock magnetism and used it to trace the changes that had occurred over millions of years in the disposition of land masses in the British Isles.

Social Concerns and Atomic Weapons
As an eminent scientist, Blackett's views on political and social issues were sought both prior to and immediately following World War II. During the war, Blackett worked with the British Admiralty as an adviser on operational research. He also served on a committee that advised his government concerning the development of nuclear weapons, which he was reluctant to support.

Following the war, he served briefly on a government advisory committee on atomic policy, but his continuing critical attitude toward the developing policies of the United States and the United Kingdom finally led to his isolation from the centers of political power.

Nevertheless, the scientific community honored Blackett, with the Nobel Prize in Physics in 1948 and the presidency of the prestigious Royal Society of London in 1965. In 1969, he was made a life peer of the realm as Baron Blackett of Chelsea. Blackett died in 1974 at the age of seventy-six.

Bibliography
By Blackett
"Photographs of the Tracks of Penetrating Radiation," *Proceedings of the Royal Society*, 1933 (with G. Occhialini)

"The Craft of Experimental Physics" in *University Studies, Cambridge, 1933*, 1933 (Harold Wright, ed.)

Chapter 7 in *The Frustration of Science*, 1935

Military and Political Consequences of Atomic Energy, 1948

Atomic Weapons and East-West Relations, 1956

Lectures on Rock Magnetism, 1956

Studies of War, Nuclear and Conventional, 1962

Introduction to *A Symposium on Continental Drift*, 1965

Reflections on Science and Technology in Developing Countries, 1970

About Blackett
The Biographical Dictionary of Scientists. Roy Porter, ed. New York: Oxford University Press, 1994.

Nobel Prize Winners: An H. W. Wilson Biographical Dictionary. Tyler Wasson, ed. New York: H. W. Wilson, 1987.

P. M. S. Blackett: A Biographical Memoir. Sir Bernard Lovell. London: Royal Society, 1976.

"Patrick M. S. Blackett." In *The Nobel Prize Winners: Physics*, edited by Frank N. Magill. Pasadena, Calif.: Salem Press, 1989.

(David G. Fenton)

Elizabeth Blackwell

Area of Achievement: Medicine
Contribution: The first woman to be granted an M.D. degree from an American medical school, Blackwell continued her pioneering work in establishing the New York Infirmary for Poor Women and Children and in founding the first medical college for women.

Feb. 3, 1821	Born in Counterslip, near Bristol, England
1832	Immigrates to America
1838	After her father's death, her sisters open a boarding school for girls to support the family
1844-1847	Finds teaching jobs in Kentucky and North Carolina before being accepted at the Geneva Medical College in New York
1849	Graduated first in her class and interns at a Paris maternity hospital
1849	Contracts a severe eye infection that leads to the loss of her left eye
1850	Interns in London and meets Florence Nightingale
1853	Opens the New York Infirmary for Poor Women and Children, a clinic in Manhattan
1866	Establishes the first visiting nurse program
1868	Founds the Women's Medical College in New York City, the first such institution
1876	Cofounds the London School of Medicine for Women
1895	Publishes an autobiography, *Pioneer Work in Opening the Medical Profession to Women*
May 31, 1910	Dies in Hastings, Sussex, England

(Library of Congress)

Early Life

Elizabeth Blackwell was born into a large, prosperous English family of deeply religious and outspoken social reformers. By 1832, however, bankruptcy pushed the family to move to New York City. Another setback led them to Ohio by 1838, where Elizabeth's father died suddenly. In order to support the family, the eldest daughters opened a boarding school for girls that proved successful.

Several years later, Blackwell accepted teaching assignments in Kentucky and North Carolina, where she was first exposed to an excellent medical library. Her readings crystalized into her dream to study medicine.

Every medical school rejected her application because she was a woman. Finally, in 1847, the Geneva Medical College in Upstate New York decided to give her a chance. Two years later, Blackwell was graduated first in her class, the first woman to be granted an M.D. in the United States.

Paris and London

Unable to find a job in the United States because of her sex, Blackwell left for Paris. Again, extreme opposition to her status as a doctor led her to accept the only position that she could find: an assistant midwife at a local maternity hospital.

Toward the end of her stay there, she contracted a serious eye infection that led to the loss of her left eye, dashing her hopes of becoming a surgeon. After recuperating, Blackwell, undaunted, left for London, where she was offered only a student status at a general hospital.

The New York Infirmary

Returning to New York City and eager to begin practicing medicine, Blackwell faced more opposition: from landlords, hospitals, doctors, and patients. Unable to establish a private practice, she opened a clinic, the New York Infirmary for Poor Women and Children, in a building that she purchased in Lower Manhattan.

Staffed by women, the clinic was soon filled with poverty-stricken local immigrants. She was later joined by her sister Emily, who was a student at an Ohio medical school. In order to reach those at home, Elizabeth developed the first visiting nurse program in the United States.

The Women's Medical College

In 1868, after a long battle with government agencies and medical societies, Blackwell opened the Women's Medical College of the New York Infirmary. It was the first medical college of its kind in the world and paved the way for scores of young women to begin their medical studies.

Final Years

Believing that America was finally accepting women as doctors, Blackwell decided to return to England to see if she could help the women there. In 1869, through the influence of several prominent women, the London School of Medicine for Women was founded. She became a professor there, finally retiring at the age of seventy-three. Blackwell continued to crusade for women's health, the rights of the poor, and the need for women in medicine.

Opening the Doors of Medicine to Women

As the first female doctor in the United States, Blackwell continued her pioneering work by opening a clinic and a medical school.

By the mid-nineteenth century, women could still only practice on the fringes of medicine, as nurses and midwives. By 1910, however, the year of Blackwell's death, 7,399 female physicians were registered in the United States alone.

Having already broken a formidable barrier with her medical school, she responded to another rejection by opening a clinic in a house that she bought, which was soon filled with the community's poorest. Records indicate that within the first seven months, the infirmary handled 645 medical, 227 gynecological, 36 surgical, and 18 obstetrical cases.

Still, tremendous opposition led to several violent incidents. One recorded by Blackwell involved the death of a woman in childbirth. An angry mob descended on the clinic, assuming that the female doctors were to blame. Years of hard work finally proved their skill.

Blackwell fulfilled her next dream that bright, dedicated women deserved a supportive environment to learn and grow. The women's medical school that she founded broke even more ground: It was the most rigorous program in the United States. The first freshman class began with seventeen highly qualified medical students and a proud faculty of eleven professors.

Bibliography

Medicine in America: Historical Essays. Richard Harrison Shyrock. Baltimore: The Johns Hopkins University Press, 1966.

"Send Us a Lady Physician": Women Doctors in America, 1835-1920. Ruth Abram. New York: W. W. Norton, 1985.

Significant Sisters: The Grassroots of Active Feminism. Margaret Foster. New York: Oxford University Press, 1984.

She died peacefully in her English home in 1910, leaving behind an extraordinary autobiography, *Pioneer Work in Opening the Medical Profession to Women* (1895).

Bibliography
By Blackwell
The Laws of Life in Reference to the Physical Education of Girls, 1852
The Religion of Health, 1871
In Counsel to Parents on the Moral Education of Their Children, 1878
The Human Element in Sex, 1880
Pioneer Work in Opening the Medical Profession to Women: Autobiographical Sketches by Dr. Elizabeth Blackwell, 1895
Scientific Method in Biology, 1898

About Blackwell
Child of Destiny: The Story of the First Woman Doctor. Isabel Ross. New York: Harper & Row, 1949.
Elizabeth Blackwell. Jordan Brown. New York: Chelsea House, 1989.
The First Woman Doctor. Rachel Baker. New York: Scholastic, 1961.

(Connie Rizzo)

Felix Bloch

Area of Achievement: Physics
Contribution: Bloch won the Nobel Prize in Physics in 1952 for his development of nuclear induction, a technique for studying atomic nuclei.

Oct. 23, 1905	Born in Zurich, Switzerland
1924-1927	Attends the Federal Institute of Technology in Zurich
1927-1928	Studies at the University of Leipzig in Germany
1928	Earns a Ph.D. from Leipzig and works as a research assistant in Switzerland, Holland, and Denmark
1932	Returns to Leipzig as a lecturer
1933	Leaves Germany after Adolf Hitler takes power
1934	Begins teaching at Stanford University in California
1934-1942	Studies the behavior of neutrons
1942-1944	Joins the Manhattan Project, the government program to develop an atomic bomb
1944-1945	Conducts research on radar at Harvard University
1946	Performs a nuclear induction experiment on atomic nuclei
1952	Shares the Nobel Prize in Physics with Edward Mills Purcell for his nuclear induction experiment
1954	Named the first director of the Conseil Européen pour la Recherche Nucléaire (CERN)
1971	Retires from Stanford
Sept. 10, 1983	Dies in Zurich, Switzerland

(The Nobel Foundation)

Early Life

Felix Bloch was born on October 23, 1905, in Zurich, Switzerland, as the son of a wholesale grain dealer. As a teenager, Felix developed an interest in mathematics and astronomy, so his parents enrolled him in the Federal Institute of Technology in Zurich in 1924. While pursuing his studies at the institute, Bloch became interested in physics.

After his graduation in 1927, Bloch was admitted to the University of Leipzig in Germany, where he studied under Werner Heisenberg, a noted pioneer researcher in quantum physics. Then in his early twenties, Bloch was already beginning to contribute to the general knowledge of theoretical physics. In 1928, for example, he helped to develop the Bloch-Fouquet theorem, which describes certain electron wave functions in crystals and is used by physicists to study the nature of metals.

After receiving his Ph.D. degree in 1928, Bloch worked as a research assistant in Switzerland, Holland, and Denmark before returning to Leipzig as a lecturer in 1932.

Neutron Research

When Adolf Hitler came to power in 1933, Bloch left Germany. While working with noted physicist Niels Bohr at the University of Copenhagen, he received a cable informing him that Stanford University in Palo Alto, California, was offering him a position on its faculty. Bloch, who knew nothing about Stanford, accepted the offer on Bohr's recommendation. He arrived in Palo Alto in 1934.

At Stanford, Bloch became interested in neutrons, subatomic particles that had been discovered in 1932. He began an extensive study of these particles focusing on their magnetic "moment," or strength, that would last several years. In 1940, Bloch married Lore Misch, a German-born physicist.

The Atomic Bomb and Nuclear Induction

With the coming of World War II, Bloch temporarily left his research on neutrons to work on the Manhattan Project, the U.S. government's program to build an atomic bomb. He later conducted research on counter-radar techniques at the Harvard Radio Research Laboratory.

In September, 1945, Bloch returned to Stanford and resumed his research on neutrons. Soon, he was able to put the knowledge of radio techniques that he had acquired at Harvard to good use when he devised a method of using magnetic fields and radio waves to study atomic nuclei. In 1952, he would win a share of the Nobel Prize in Physics for developing this technique, which he called nuclear induction.

Later Years

Bloch continued to teach and conduct research at Stanford. In 1954, he took a leave of absence to serve as the first director of the Conseil Européen pour la Recherche Nucléaire (CERN), or European Organization for Nuclear Research, in Geneva, Switzerland. He returned to Stanford in 1955, where he remained until he retired in 1971.

Nuclear Magnetic Resonance

Bloch devised a method of studying atomic nuclei, which he called nuclear induction but which is now known as nuclear magnetic resonance, that turns them into tiny radio transmitters.

Bloch's technique involves placing a test tube containing a solution of iron nitrate and water between the poles of a powerful electromagnet. When the magnet is activated, the magnetic "moments" of the atoms within the sample align themselves according to the magnetic field.

Meanwhile, the sample is bombarded from right angles by radio waves, causing the atoms' magnetic moments to flip. In doing so, the atoms give off radio waves that can be picked up by the coil wrapped around the test tube. By monitoring these radio transmissions, scientists can learn much about the structure and behavior of the nuclei.

Bloch's technique, now known as nuclear magnetic resonance (NMR), has a variety of applications. Chemists have used it to identify unknown substances, and astronomers have used it to identify substances in space such as hydrogen clouds. NMR is employed extensively as an imaging technique for medical diagnosis. It is safer than X-ray analysis and can identify light atoms such as hydrogen. NMR imaging is often used to detect cancer.

Bibliography

Concise Encyclopedia of Nuclear Energy. D. E. Barnes et al., eds. New York: Interscience, 1962.

"The Principle of Nuclear Induction." Felix Bloch. *Science* 118 (October 16, 1953).

The World of Scientific Discovery. Bridget Travers, ed. Washington, D.C.: Gale Research, 1994.

Following his retirement, Bloch returned to his hometown of Zurich. He died there on September 10, 1983, at the age of seventy-seven.

Bibliography

By Bloch

Die Electronentheorie der Metalle, 1933

Les Électrons dans les métaux; Problèmes statistiques; Magnétisme, 1934

"The Magnetic Moment of the Neutron," *Annual of the Institut Henri Poincaré,* 1938

"Nuclear Induction," *Physical Review,* 1946

"The Nuclear Induction Experiment," *Physical Review,* 1946 (with W. W. Hansen and Martin Packard)

"The Principle of Nuclear Induction," *Science,* 1953

"Dynamical Theory of Nuclear Induction, II," *Physical Review,* 1956

Spectroscopic and Group Theoretical Models in Physics: Racah Memorial Volume, 1968 (as editor)

About Bloch

"Felix Bloch." In *The Nobel Prize Winners: Physics,* edited by Frank N. Magill. Pasadena, Calif.: Salem Press, 1989.

Illustrious Immigrants: The Intellectual Migration from Europe. Laura Fermi. Chicago: University of Chicago Press, 1968.

Notable Twentieth-Century Scientists. Emily J. McMurray, ed. Vol. 2. Detroit: Gale Research, 1995.

(Lawrence K. Orr)

Katharine Burr Blodgett

Areas of Achievement: Chemistry, physics, and technology

Contribution: Blodgett was a research scientist with the General Electric Company who was best known for her studies of thin films, including so-called Langmuir-Blodgett films.

Jan. 10, 1898	Born in Schenectady, New York
1917	Earns a B.A. in physics from Bryn Mawr College
1918	Earns an M.S. from the University of Chicago
1918-1924	Works as a scientist at the General Electric Research Laboratory
1926	Earns a Ph.D. in physics from Cambridge University
1926	Returns to General Electric
1933	Resumes monolayer work concerning Langmuir-Blodgett films
1938	General Electric announces her invention of nonreflecting glass
1939-1944	Receives honorary doctorates from Elmira College, Brown University, Western College, and Russell Sage College
1945	Receives the Achievement Award of the American Association of University Women
1951	Awarded the American Chemical Society's Francis P. Garvan Medal
1963	Retires from General Electric
1972	Becomes the first female recipient of the Progress Medal of the Photographic Society of America
Oct. 12, 1979	Dies in Schenectady, New York

Early Life

Katharine Burr Blodgett was born in Schenectady, New York, to George Reddington and Katharine Buchanan (Burr) Blodgett. George Blodgett, a patent attorney for the General Electric Company, died weeks before the birth of his daughter. Her mother moved Katharine and her older brother to New York City, from where they made extended visits to both France and Germany so that the children could learn foreign languages.

Blodgett attended public school for one year in Saranac Lake, New York. The remainder of her elementary and secondary education, however, was at Rayson School, a small private institution in New York City. She won a competitive matriculation scholarship from 1913 to 1914 to Bryn Mawr College, being graduated in 1917 with a B.A. in physics. The following year, Blodgett submitted a thesis on the chemistry of gas masks and acquired an M.S. degree from the University of Chicago.

(Library of Congress)

Irving Langmuir and General Electric

In 1918, Blodgett became the first female scientist employed by the General Electric Company at its research laboratory in Schenectady and began a close association with the physical chemist Irving Langmuir that lasted until his death in 1957. Her entire professional life was spent there, except for an absence of two years in England to attend the Newnham College of Cambridge University. There, she became the first woman awarded its newly established Ph.D. degree in physics for her work at the Cavendish Laboratory under Sir Ernest Rutherford.

A Practical Industrial Scientist

Blodgett is mostly remembered for her collaboration with Langmuir on thin films, first continuing his seminal work on monolayers (begun in 1916) and later pursuing more independent studies on Langmuir-Blodgett films (multilayers). This research provided new techniques for surface science and attracted public attention when Blodgett invented the first nonreflecting glass. Langmuir-Blodgett films have additional applications in microlithography, microelectronics, and integrated optics as a result of their controlled thickness and unique internal structure.

Blodgett assisted Langmuir in other fundamental projects concerning the space-charge limited currents of electrodes and improvements in the tungsten filaments of electric lightbulbs. During World War II, she studied aircraft wing de-icing and devised a better method to generate protective smoke screens that was credited with reducing Allied casualties. Later, Blodgett helped the Army Signal Corps invent a device for weather balloons to measure humidity, produced electrically conducting and semiconducting coatings for glass, and was working on the purification of inert gases in lightbulbs when she retired in 1963. She died in 1979 at the age of eighty-one.

Blodgett's career, during a time when science and industry tended to exclude women, is discussed by Alice Charlotte Goff in *Women Can Be Engineers* (1946), G. Kass-Simon and Pa-

Langmuir-Blodgett Films and Nonreflecting Glass

Langmuir-Blodgett films consist of single-molecule layers of organic molecules on a solid support that were successively deposited from an insoluble monolayer on an aqueous surface.

Certain organic molecules can be spread evenly on water to form a film that is one molecule thick called a monolayer, or Langmuir film. Blodgett developed a dipping technique that transfers the floating monolayer intact onto the flat surface of a glass or metal plate. Another monolayer adheres every time that the plate is lowered or withdrawn vertically through the aqueous surface, producing a built-up multilayer, or Langmuir-Blodgett film.

Blodgett discovered that transparency is increased and glare eliminated when light reflected from glass and a thin surface film cancel each other by destructive interference. Similar interference of light reflected from the film's upper and lower surfaces also creates iridescent colors that depend on its thickness. These color gradations are used to measure the thickness of extremely thin films and find the optimum value for nonreflection. Antireflection coatings are now common on picture frame glass and on optical equipment such as the lenses of cameras, projectors, binoculars, telescopes, and submarine periscopes.

Bibliography

"How the Amateur Can Experiment with Films Only One Molecule Thick." C. L. Strong. *Scientific American* 205 (September, 1961).

"Langmuir-Blodgett Films." J. A. Zasadzinski, R. Viswanathan, L. Madsen, J. Garnaes, and D. K. Schwartz. *Science* 263 (1994).

"Langmuir-Blodgett Films." Martin V. Stewart. In *Magill's Survey of Science: Applied Science Series*. Pasadena, Calif.: Salem Press, 1993.

Langmuir-Blodgett Films: An Introduction. Michael C. Petty. Cambridge, England: Cambridge University Press, 1996.

Order in Thin Organic Films. R. H. Tredgold. Cambridge, England: Cambridge University Press, 1994.

tricia Farnes in *Women of Science: Righting the Record* (1993), and Margaret W. Rossiter in *Women Scientists in America: Before Affirmative Action, 1940-1972* (1995).

Bibliography
By Blodgett
"Monomolecular Films of Fatty Acids on Glass," *Journal of the American Chemical Society*, 1934

"Interference Colors in Oil Films on Water," *Journal of the Optical Society of America*, 1934

"Films Built by Depositing Successive Monomolecular Layers on a Solid Surface," *Journal of the American Chemical Society*, 1935

"Built-up Films of Barium Stearate and Their Optical Properties," *Physical Review*, 1937 (with Irving Langmuir)

"Properties of Built-up Films of Barium Stearate," *Journal of Physical Chemistry*, 1937

"A Gauge That Measures Millionths of an Inch" in *Excursions in Science*, 1939 (Neil B. Reynolds and Ellis L. Manning, eds.)

"Use of Interference to Extinguish Reflection of Light from Glass," *Physical Review*, 1939

"Electrically Conducting Glasses," *Journal of the American Ceramic Society*, 1948 (with Robert L. Green)

"Surface Conductivity of Lead Silicate Glass After Hydrogen Treatment," *Journal of the American Ceramic Society*, 1951

"Birefringent Stepgauge," *Science*, 1952

About Blodgett
American Women of Science. Edna Yost. Rev. ed. Philadelphia: J. B. Lippincott, 1955.

"Katharine Blodgett and Thin Films." Kathleen A. Davis. *Journal of Chemical Education* 61 (1984).

"Obituary: Katharine Burr Blodgett (1898-1979)." Vincent J. Schaefer and George L. Gaines. *Journal of Colloid and Interface Science* 76 (1980).

"Woman of Science: Mistress of the Thin Films." Jo Chamberlin. *Science Illustrated 2* (December, 1947).

Women in the Scientific Search: An American Bio-Bibliography, 1724-1979. Patricia Joan Siegel and K. Thomas Finley. Metuchen, N.J.: Scarecrow Press, 1985.

(Martin V. Stewart)

David Bohm

Area of Achievement: Physics

Contribution: Bohm made major contributions to the understanding of quantum mechanical systems and the philosophy of quantum mechanics.

Dec. 20, 1917	Born in Wilkes-Barre, Pennsylvania
1943	Receives a Ph.D. from the University of California, Berkeley (UCB)
1943	Works at the Radiation Laboratory at UCB on the later phases of the Manhattan Project
1946	Takes a position as assistant professor at Princeton University
1948	Called before the House Committee on Un-American Activities to testify against colleagues and associates and, upon legal advice, takes the Fifth Amendment
1949	His plea to take the Fifth Amendment is rejected, and he is indicted for contempt of Congress
1951	Accepts a faculty position at the University of São Paulo, Brazil
1951	Publishes *Quantum Theory*, regarded as one of the best textbooks of its day
1952	Publishes the article "Hidden Variables and the Implicate Order"
1955	Takes a temporary position in Israel
1957	Holds a research fellowship at Bristol University, England
1961	Assumes a chair of theoretical physics at Birkbeck College, University of London
Oct. 27, 1992	Dies in London, England

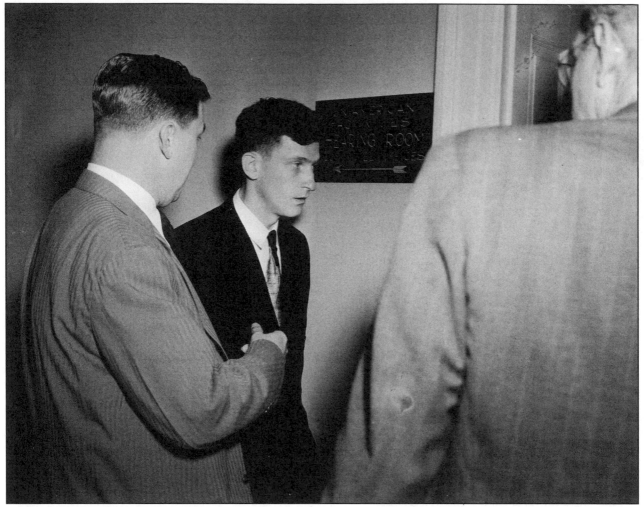

Bohm (center) arrives at a hearing of the House Committee on Un-American Activities in 1949, at which he refused to testify about possible communist ties. (AP/Wide World Photos)

Early Life

David Joseph Bohm was born in Wilkes-Barre, Pennsylvania, in 1917. His father ran a successful furniture business. Bohm became interested in science at an early age, despite the fact that no one else in his family had any background in science. He was fascinated by how things worked. His imagination was further fired by his early introduction to science fiction and by an astronomy book that impressed him with the order and regularity of the universe.

His father became concerned; he could not imagine anyone being able to make a living out of "scientism." To prove him wrong, Bohm decided to use his mechanical aptitude to make money from inventions. The process of trying to turn a profit, however, persuaded Bohm to become a theoretical physicist.

Bohm's interest in the fundamental questions of physics started in high school. As he began to study physics seriously, he was taken with the interconnectedness of phenomena that seemed superficially to be unrelated. He wondered how the theories of physics could enable one to build an understanding of reality. He was particularly fascinated by quantum mechanics and relativity.

Bohm went to graduate school at the University of California, Berkeley, where he worked under the supervision of J. Robert Oppenheimer on a theoretical study of neutron-proton scattering. He received his Ph.D. in 1943 and moved on to work on a theoretical study of the ionization of uranium hexafluoride in an electric arc, in an attempt to separate the isotopes uranium 235 and uranium 238. This began Bohm's interest in plasma physics.

Bohm and McCarthyism
In 1946, Bohm took a position as an assistant professor of physics at Princeton University. He began extending his earlier ideas of plasma to the behavior of electrons in metals, a purely quantum mechanical system. Bohm was recognized for his ability to express complicated theoretical ideas in a coherent manner. He

taught a course on quantum mechanics to undergraduates, which forced him to present a clear account of the subject. As a result, Bohm decided to write a definitive textbook on the subject, called *Quantum Theory* (1951).

While working on this book, he was called to appear before the House Committee on Un-American Activities. When asked to testify against colleagues and associates, Bohm took the Fifth Amendment. His plea was rejected, and he was indicted for contempt of Congress. While awaiting trial, the Supreme Court ruled

---

Hidden Variables and Quantum Mechanics

Classical physics is based on determinism: For every cause, there is an effect. At the beginning of the twentieth century, two experiments dramatically changed the picture.

A blackbody is a perfect emitter of radiation that produces a characteristic spectrum dependent on its temperature. With Thomas Young's double-slit experiment, light was proven to be a wave. Unfortunately, when wave theory was applied to a blackbody spectrum, the results failed drastically. Max Planck worked out an empirical formula to describe the spectrum. He explained that the atomic oscillators in the blackbody are quantized, a suggestion that was met with ridicule. In the photoelectric effect, light directed at a metal produces electrons; again, wave theory failed. Albert Einstein proposed that the light coming from the metal was being emitted in packets of energy, called photons. Was light a wave or a particle?

The explanation of this wave-particle duality led to a scientific revolution in the early twentieth century. Niels Bohr suggested complementarity, that light is something other than a wave or a particle that does not exist classically. The wave and particle properties complement each other, but neither one is the whole picture.

A group of theorists developed a formalism called quantum mechanics based on the idea that everything is represented by a wave function. These waves can be superposed on one another to form a wave packet that looks like a particle under certain circumstances. The details of this new theory were worked out and applied to at-

oms. They worked, but unfortunately the implications raised several difficulties. One characteristic of a wave is that its momentum and position cannot be determined simultaneously. The universe had become inherently probabilistic.

Several people found this idea disturbing. Einstein said that "God does not play dice with the universe." An alternative suggested by Bohm was that the reason the world seemed probabilistic was that one cannot see the whole picture. He developed a new formalism for quantum systems using hidden variable theory. Although this theory and its implications for order in the universe may be more aesthetically pleasing, experimental evidence at present points against it. New interest in this idea is arising, however, with attempts to develop a grand unified theory.

Bibliography
The Dancing Wu-Li Masters: An Overview of the New Physics. Gary Zukav. New York: Bantam, 1980.

Introductory Quantum Mechanics. Richard L. Liboff. Reading, Mass.: Addison-Wesley, 1992.

Quantum Reality: Behind the New Physics. Nick Herbert. New York: Anchor Press Doubleday, 1985.

Quantum Theory and the Schism in Physics. Karl Popper. Totowa, N.J.: Rowan and Littlefield, 1982.

Understanding Quantum Physics: A User's Manual. Michael A. Morrison. Englewood Cliffs, N.J.: Prentice Hall, 1990.

that no one should be forced to make a self-incriminating testimony, provided that no crime has been committed. The indictment was dropped.

Advised to stay away from Princeton, Bohm used the time to write his book. When his contract expired, he was unable to obtain a job in the United States. Oppenheimer advised him to leave the country before the full force of McCarthyism could take effect. He obtained a position at the University of São Paulo in Brazil in 1951.

Later Years

Bohm moved from Brazil to Israel to England, first taking a research fellowship at Bristol University and finally taking a chair of theoretical physics at Birkbeck College of the University of London, where he settled in 1961. Throughout this time, he continued to work diligently. Although he published papers in a variety of areas, his first interest and greatest contributions have come in the area of the interpretation of quantum mechanics, which are still quite controversial. His ideas have had an impact on artists and theologians as well as on physicists.

Bibliography
By Bohm
Quantum Theory, 1951
Causality and Chance in Modern Physics, 1957
"Classical and Non-Classical Concepts in the Quantum Theory," *British Journal for Philosophy of Science*, 1961-1962
"Quantum Theory as an Indication of a New Order in Physics: Part A, The Development of New Orders as Shown Through the History of Physics," *Foundations of Physics*, 1971
Wholeness and the Implicate Order, 1980
"An Ontological Basis for the Quantum Theory," *Physics Reports*, 1987 (with B. J. Hiley and P. N. Kaloyerou)
Science, Order, and Creativity, 1987 (with F. David Peat)

About Bohm
Quantum Implications: Essays in Honour of David Bohm. B. J. Hiley and F. David Peat, eds. London: Routledge & Kegan Paul, 1987.

(Linda L. McDonald)

Niels Bohr

Areas of Achievement: Chemistry and physics
Contribution: One of the founders of quantum mechanics, Bohr was awarded the Nobel Prize in Physics for his theory of atomic structure.

Oct. 7, 1885	Born in Copenhagen, Denmark
1903	Begins studying physics at the University of Copenhagen
1907	Awarded a gold medal by the Royal Danish Academy of Sciences and Letters for an essay on the surface tension of water
1911	Completes his doctoral dissertation on the electron theory of metals
1911-1912	Studies with Sir J. J. Thomson and Ernest Rutherford
1913	Publishes his theory of atomic structure
1916	Teaches theoretical physics at the University of Copenhagen
1917	Elected to the Royal Danish Academy of Sciences and Letters
1921	The Institute for Theoretical Physics is inaugurated
1922	Awarded the Nobel Prize in Physics
1936	Develops a model of the atomic nucleus
1939	Elected president of the Royal Danish Academy of Sciences and Letters
1943-1945	Becomes associated with the Anglo-American atomic energy project
1955	Named chair of the Danish Atomic Energy Commission
Nov. 18, 1962	Dies in Copenhagen, Denmark

Early Life

Niels Henrik David Bohr, who spent most of his early years in Copenhagen, Denmark, was the son of Christian Bohr, a distinguished professor of physiology at the University of Copenhagen. Professor Bohr often invited his friends philosopher Harald Hoffding, physicist Christian Christianson, and philologist Vilhelm Thomsen to his home for discussions of topics of mutual interest. Niels and his brother Harald, an accomplished mathematician, were permitted to listen to the discussions. In this way, Niels Bohr received his foundation in the collaborative methods that he would use throughout his life.

Bohr began the formal study of physics in 1903 at the University of Copenhagen. In 1907, he wrote an essay on the surface tension of water that was awarded a gold medal by the Royal Danish Academy of Sciences and Letters. Bohr decided to take his master's and doctor's degrees in physics, focusing on the electron theory of metals. By the time he finished his graduate studies, Bohr was so highly respected by the students and professors at Copenhagen that he defended his dissertation before an audience that overflowed the hall.

After completing his studies, Bohr went to England to work in the laboratories of first Sir J. J. Thomson and then Ernest Rutherford. Rutherford in particular recognized the potential of Bohr and gave him great support and encouragement, even though Rutherford generally did not regard theoreticians too highly.

The Trilogy

In 1912, Bohr married Margrethe Norlund and returned to the University of Copenhagen,

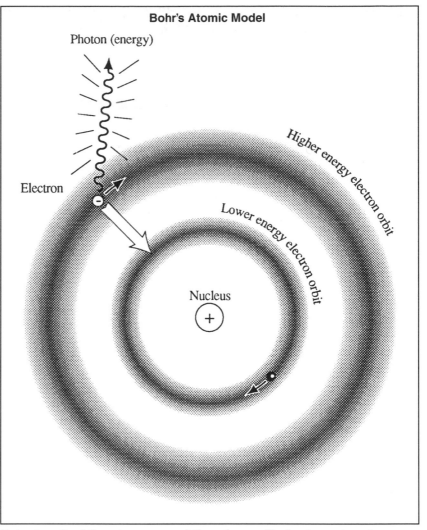

Bohr's Atomic Model

Photon (energy)

Electron

Higher energy electron orbit

Lower energy electron orbit

Nucleus
(+)

Bohr described the atom as consisting of a positively charged nucleus surrounded by negatively charged electrons traveling in stable orbits called stationary states. When an electron moves from a higher to a lower orbit, energy is released in the form of a photon.

where he received an assistant professorship. During this first year of teaching, Bohr completed three papers, published in the prestigious *Philosophical Magazine*, in which he laid out his theory of atomic structure. The theory represented a break from classical ideas and dramatically changed the fields of chemistry and physics. It was for this elegant theory that Bohr was awarded the Nobel Prize in Physics in 1922.

The Institute

In 1917, Bohr applied to the Faculty of Natural Sciences for funding to establish an institute.

The Bohr Model of the Atom

Bohr's model of the atom assumes that electrons move in orbits at fixed distances from the atomic nucleus and emit or absorb energy only when they move to different orbits.

At the beginning of the twentieth century, physicists were perplexed by the failure of classical physics to explain the phenomena of atomic spectra. Electrons were attracted to the nucleus by electrostatic forces. According to classical physics, a moving electron should radiate energy continuously and, because of this attraction, eventually spiral into the nucleus.

Gaseous samples of different elements subjected to electrical or thermal stimulation emitted light that, when dispersed by a grating or prism, showed a series of lines characteristic of the particular element. Johann Balmer showed in 1885 that the wavelengths of the lines in the visible spectrum of hydrogen could be calculated from the simple empirical equation "$(1/\lambda) = R\,[(1/2^2) - (1/n^2)]$," where λ is the wavelength of the line, n is some integer greater than 2, and R is known as the Rydberg constant. Other hydrogen spectra were found in the infrared and ultraviolet regions of the spectrum and obeyed the more general equation "$(1/\lambda) = R\,[(1/n_f^2) - (1/n_i^2)]$," where n_f must be greater than n_i for emission spectra.

Bohr's theory of atomic structure is a collection of some concepts from classical physics, the atomic model of Ernest Rutherford, the quantum hypothesis of Max Planck, and the photon theory of light of Albert Einstein.

Bohr's theory of the atom assumes that the electron moves in a circular orbit about the nucleus and is held in orbit by Coulombic forces (the force of interaction between two charged particles). The electron is restricted to very specific orbits in which the angular momentum of the electron is equal to some integral multiple of $h/2\pi$, where h is Planck's constant.

Contrary to the theories of classical physics, the electron does not radiate energy when it is in one of these allowed orbits; hence, it is stable. These stable orbits are called stationary states. The lines seen in atomic spectra arise when an electron jumps from one allowed stationary state to another. The frequency of the radiation absorbed or emitted obeys the formula "$h\upsilon = E_f - E_i$" where E_f and E_i are the energies of the final and initial states respectively and υ is the frequency of the radiation.

Calculation of the energies of the various stationary states of hydrogen allows determination of the frequencies of the spectral lines that are seen when the electrons jump among the states. The theoretical value of R obtained from these calculations is in excellent agreement with that obtained from experiment and is recognized as a major accomplishment of the Bohr theory.

Bibliography

"Atomic Structure and Spectral Lines." Abraham Pais. *Inward Bound: Of Matter and Forces in the Physical World*. New York: Oxford University Press, 1986.

"Early Discoveries About Quantized Matter and Radiation." Mendel Sachs. *Einstein Versus Bohr: The Continuing Controversies in Physics*. La Salle, Ill.: Open Court, 1988.

The Theory of Spectra and Atomic Constitution. Niels Bohr. London: Cambridge University Press, 1924

He envisioned it to be a place where scientists from many lands could gather for special studies, particularly in the newly emerging field of quantum mechanics.

The University of Copenhagen Institute for Theoretical Physics, built principally from funds from private donors and from the Carlsberg Foundation, was formally inaugurated on March 3, 1921. The name of the institute was changed to the Bohr Institute for Theoretical Physics in 1965 in commemoration of what would have been Bohr's eightieth birthday.

True to Bohr's vision, the institute has, since its foundation, welcomed the most famous physicists in the world to its laboratories and conference rooms. Among the famous visitors have been Albert Einstein, Wolfgang Pauli, Werner Heisenberg, and Arnold Sommerfeld.

During the 1920's, the institute was the site

of many discussions on the manner in which quantum mechanics describes physical reality. These discussions resulted in an entirely new philosophy of science. Among the important contributions to this new view of reality were the uncertainty principle of Heisenberg and Bohr's complementarity principle. Both were concerned with the impact that the process of measurement has on the system being observed.

Years of Unrest
During the 1930's, Bohr became involved in trying to explain some experimental evidence that seemed to indicate that the nuclei of atoms had a substructure and could be made to break

The Copenhagen Interpretation of Quantum Mechanics

A series of discussions in the 1920's on the way in which the mathematical formulations of quantum mechanics represented physical reality produced a philosophy of science that became known as the Copenhagen interpretation of quantum mechanics.

By the last decade of the nineteenth century, physicists were reasonably certain that the mathematical description known as classical physics could provide a satisfactory description of physical reality. In mechanics, the laws of Sir Isaac Newton were found to describe adequately the motions of objects of any size—from marbles to the planets in the solar system.

The long debate over whether light was a particle or a wave had been resolved in favor of the wave theory. The behavior of these waves could be explained and predicted by the laws of James Clerk Maxwell. Only a few unexplained observations such as the ultraviolet catastrophe, the photoelectric effect, and atomic spectra existed in the field of physics. These were explained by Max Planck, Albert Einstein, and Bohr, respectively. Their explanations ushered in the new age of quantum physics.

One of the central philosophical issues of quantum mechanics can be expressed in the question, "What is the 'it' that quantum mechanics describes?" The wave versus particle debate arose again, this time not only over the nature of light but also over matter itself, when Louis de Broglie introduced his theory of matter waves. Bohr's complementarity principle refers to the fact that the wave and particle descriptions of atomic systems are not in conflict but rather complement each other.

The debates of the 1920's which involved Bohr, Einstein, Werner Heisenberg, and other physicists of the day resulted in some startling new ways of looking at science. One of the first results was the loss of objectivity in the process of experimentation. It became clear that the way in which an experiment was devised interfered with and changed the atomic system that was being investigated. The uncertainty principle of Heisenberg stated this in terms of pairs of variables whose values could not each be simultaneously determined with unlimited accuracy.

A second loss was the one-to-one correspondence that existed in classical physics between the mathematical laws of behavior and each individual object to which they were applied. The equations of quantum mechanics cannot be applied to single atomic systems but are rather descriptions of the statistical behavior of large collections of systems. In this sense, quantum mechanics is probabilistic in nature. Einstein was never comfortable with this idea and worked for much of his life to find another solution.

Bohr and most of his contemporaries agreed that quantum mechanics formed a consistent mathematical description of physical reality. In other words, it does not really matter what the "it" is that quantum mechanics describes because it works.

Bibliography
Atoms, Metaphysics, and Paradoxes: Niels Bohr and the Construction of a New Physics. Sandro Petruccioli. New York: Cambridge University Press, 1993.
Paradigms and Paradoxes: The Philosophical Challenge of the Quantum Domain. Robert G. Colodny, ed. Pittsburgh: University of Pittsburgh Press, 1972.
Quantum Mechanics: Historical Contingency and the Copenhagen Hegemony. James T. Cushing. Chicago: University of Chicago Press, 1994.

(The Nobel Foundation)

Throughout this period, Bohr was at work assisting these scientists move to new positions in England, Sweden, and the United States. Bohr himself was eventually forced to leave Denmark. He spent the last few years of World War II in the United States working on the Manhattan Project to build an atomic bomb in the United States.

After the war, Bohr returned to Denmark, where he served for a number of years as chair of the Danish Atomic Energy Commission.

Bohr died of a heart attack on November 18, 1962, at the age of seventy-seven. On that day, the scientific community lost one of its greatest physicists and philosophers of science.

Bibliography

By Bohr
"On the Constitution of Atoms and Molecules," *Philosophical Magazine*, 1913 (3 parts)
On the Quantum Theory of Line Spectra I-III, 1918-1922
Atomic Theory and the Description of Nature, 1934
Essays, 1958-1962, on Atomic Physics and Human Knowledge, 1963

About Bohr
Harmony and Unity: The Life of Niels Bohr. Niels Blaedel. Madison, Wis.: Science Tech, 1988.
Niels Bohr: His Life and Work as Seen by His Friends and Colleagues. Stefan Rozental, ed. Amsterdam: North-Holland Physics Publishers, 1967.
Niels Bohr: Physics and the World. Herman Feshbach, Tetsuo Matsui, and Alexandra Oleson, eds. Switzerland: Harwood Academic Publishers, 1988.
Niels Bohr: The Man, His Science, and the World They Changed. Ruth Moore. New York: Alfred A. Knopf, 1966.

(Grace A. Banks)

down to smaller pieces with the release of large amounts of energy. The potential for both the peaceful production of energy and the creation of weapons of tremendous power was recognized almost immediately. Before either could be accomplished, however, many technical problems had to be overcome.

During the same period, the Nazi movement was sweeping through Germany, and many scientists of Jewish background found it necessary to leave their homelands as the German army moved into neighboring countries.

Ludwig Eduard Boltzmann

Areas of Achievement: Mathematics and physics

Contribution: Boltzmann applied the insights of thermodynamics to the molecular universe described by classical mechanics, developing the mathematical kinetic theory of gases in the process.

Feb. 20, 1844	Born in Vienna, Austria
1866	Earns a doctorate from the University of Vienna
1867	Becomes an assistant at the Institute of Physics at Vienna
1869	Takes a position as professor of mathematical physics at the University of Graz, Austria
1873	Becomes a professor of mathematics at Vienna
1876	Marries Henriette von Aigentler
1876	Appointed director of the Institute of Physics and professor of experimental physics at Graz
1890	Becomes a professor of theoretical physics at the University of Munich, Germany
1891-1893	Publishes *Vorlesungen über Maxwells Theorie der Elektricität und des Lichtes* (lectures on Maxwell's theory of electricity and light)
1893	Becomes a professor of theoretical physics at Vienna
1900	Becomes a professor of theoretical physics at the University of Leipzig
1902	Returns to Vienna as a professor of theoretical physics
Sept. 5, 1906	Dies in Duino, near Trieste, Italy

Early Life

Ludwig Eduard Boltzmann was the son of an Austrian state civil servant in the tax (internal revenue) department who died when Ludwig was fifteen years old. Ludwig studied at the Gymnasium in Linz, then moved to the University of Vienna, where he worked under Josef Stefan and Josef Loschmidt, receiving his doctorate when he was twenty-two years old.

He moved into a position at the university and remained in academia for his entire career, rising as one did in the German university of the time from fee-supported lecturer to full professor. He became world-renowned as both teacher and researcher.

Initial Research

Early in his career, Boltzmann produced experimental work in physics. In 1872, stimulated by James Clerk Maxwell's writings on electromagnetic theory, he studied dielectrics (insulators) with the intention of confirming Maxwell's technical prediction about the index of refraction of substances. He confirmed this prediction for both solids and gases. Boltzmann also confirmed that the speed of light varies in different directions in an anisotropic crystal (one with different symmetries on the x, y, and z axes).

Boltzmann also published work on diamagnetism (the property of some substances, placed in a magnetic field, to become polarized in a direction that causes them to be repelled by the field) and on electromagnetic radiation. Later, he would renew his interest in electromagnetic theory, but not in laboratory experimentation.

Later Research

Boltzmann's reputation rests not on his publications in experimental physics but on his deep and penetrating mathematical analyses of physical phenomena, particularly those of molecules in a gas. He began to publish these in his first days at Graz, and he continued more or less to the end of his life.

His first effort was built on Maxwell's equation for the distribution of molecular velocities in a gas. Using the methods and concepts of classical (Newtonian) mechanics, Maxwell had derived an exponential equation that described the distribution of velocities of molecules in a gas that consisted of moving particles of constant mass.

The resulting curve is roughly bell-shaped, peaking at the most probable molecular velocity, falling off in the directions of both high and low velocities. Boltzmann was able to generalize this function to any desired gas and even mixtures of gases, with and without external forces applied.

Thereafter, Boltzmann moved into considerations of probability of energy distributions in gases, with connections to thermodynamics and what is now called statistical mechanics. The essential connection is given in the equation on his gravestone in Vienna's central cemetery: "$S = k \log W$," where S is entropy as defined in the second law of thermodynamics, W is a number expressing the prob-

ability of the system, and k is the Boltzmann constant, a micro version of the universal gas constant R.

Last Years

Boltzmann also produced his so-called H-theorem, which states that nonequilibrium initial states in a gas proceed to equilibrium final states, a concept that links macroscopically irreversible processes with the microscopically reversible.

Toward the end of his life, Boltzmann found himself increasingly occupied with defending the reality of atoms and molecules against physicists and others who wished to find ultimate reality in energy or some even more tenuous entity. He sometimes felt himself the last defender of the atomist position and became deeply depressed from about 1902 onward. Whether his suicide by hanging in 1906 was

Reversibility and Irreversibility

It is difficult to single out any one of Boltzmann's findings in kinetic gas theory that is a landmark in his scientific career. A part of kinetic theory that is unique to Boltzmann, however, is the H-theorem, which resolves the problem of microscopic reversibility and macroscopic irreversibility.

Nothing in Newtonian mechanics implies a direction in physical processes, at least in systems at equilibrium. Set all the planets going in the opposite direction, and gravity will ensure that they follow the same orbits that they do now. Roll billiard balls backward from their final positions, and they will collide to return to their original positions.

How does this jibe with the thermodynamic experience that every system "runs down"—that is, irons out energy differences and becomes more disordered? Boltzmann stated that a nonequilibrium system tends toward equilibrium. In other words, a system in which all molecules have the same velocity will gradually become one in which the molecular velocities are those of the Maxwell-Boltzmann distribution. At this point, the system is in equilibrium, trading individual velocities as the molecules collide but not changing the overall distribution of velocities.

Moreover, the molecules have reached equilibrium through a series of microscopically reversible collisions and exchanges.

With the right setup, some work could be extracted as this system attains equilibrium. When equilibrium is reached, no further work is possible. Thus, one has a nonreversible macrosystem brought about by reversible microprocesses. The key to the relationship between them is statistical: The equilibrium is one of probability of velocity distribution, and the operation of probability produces an inevitable one-way march to equilibrium.

This was Boltzmann's unique contribution to the statistical understanding of reversibility and irreversibility.

Bibliography
The Conceptual Foundations of the Statistical Approach in Mechanics. P. and T. Ehrenfest. Translated by M. J. Moravcsik. Ithaca, N.Y.: 1959.

"Foundations of Statistical Mechanics, 1845-1915." Stephen G. Brush. *Archive for History of Exact Sciences* 4 (1967).

"Probability and Thermodynamics: The Reduction of the Second Law." Edward E. Daub. *Isis* 60 (1969).

the result of the atomist controversy is not known; it is bitterly ironic, however, that clear proof of the existence of atoms (through Brownian motion and the alpha decay of elements) came within a few years of his death.

Bibliography
By Boltzmann

Vorlesungen über Maxwells Theorie der Elektricität und des Lichtes, 1891-1893 (2 vols.)

Vorlesungen über Gastheorie, 1896-1898 (2 vols.; *Lectures on Gas Theory*, 1964)

Vorlesungen über die Principe der Mechanik, 1897-1904 (2 vols.)

Über die Prinzipien der Mechanik: Zwei akademische Antrittsreden, 1903

Populäre Schriften, 1905

Wissenschaftliche Abhandlungen, 1909 (3 vols.; scientific papers, F. Hasenöhrl, ed.)

Theoretical Physics and Philosophical Problems: Selected Writings, 1974 (Brian McGuinness, ed.)

About Boltzmann

"Boltzmann, Ludwig." Stephen G. Brush. In *Dictionary of Scientific Biography*, edited by Charles Coulstow Gillispie. Vol. 2. New York: Charles Scribner's Sons, 1970.

"Ludwig Boltzmann and His Influence in Science." D. Flamm. *Studies in the History and Philosophy of Science* 14 (1983).

Ludwig Boltzmann: His Later Life and Philosophy. John Blackmore, ed. 3 vols. Dordrecht/Boston: Kluwer, 1995.

Ludwig Boltzmann: Man, Physicist, Philosopher. Engelbert Broda. Translated by Larry Gay. Woodbridge, Conn.: Ox Bow Press, 1983.

(Library of Congress)

(Robert M. Hawthorne, Jr.)

Jules Bordet

Areas of Achievement: Bacteriology, immunology, and medicine

Contribution: Bordet's Nobel Prize-winning research into the basis of humoral immunity helped lay the groundwork for the science of immunology.

June 13, 1870	Born in Soignies, Belgium
1886-1892	Studies medicine at the University of Brussels
1892	Publishes his first scientific paper
1894-1900	Works at the Pasteur Institute in Paris
1901-1940	Serves as director of the Pasteur Institute in Brussels
1906	Isolates the bacterium responsible for whooping cough
1907-1935	Serves as a professor of bacteriology at the University of Brussels
1909	Describes the germ involved in bovine pleuropneumonia
1916	Inducted as a foreign member into the Royal Society of London
1920	Awarded the Nobel Prize in Physiology and Medicine
1920	Publishes *Traité de l'immunité dans les maladies infectieuses* (treatise on immunity in infectious diseases)
1930	Elected president of the First International Congress of Microbiology
1933	Serves as president of the scientific council for the Pasteur Institute, Paris
Apr. 6, 1961	Dies in Brussels, Belgium

Early Life

Jules-Jean-Baptiste-Vincent Bordet (pronounced "bawr-DAY") was born in Belgium in 1870 as the son of a schoolteacher. After demonstrating an early interest in chemistry, he enrolled in the University of Brussels at the age of sixteen and was graduated as a doctor of medicine in 1892.

During medical school, Bordet carried out experiments in bacteriology, and he won a government scholarship in 1894 to pursue further research. He traveled to Paris to begin studies with Élie Metchnikoff, one of the foremost scientists working in the new fields of bacteriology and immunology.

Immunological Studies in Paris

During his six years in Paris at the Pasteur Institute, Bordet made most of his fundamental discoveries in immunology. He showed that bacteria can be killed by serum (cell-free blood) and that this activity is controlled by two kinds of substances: a heat-sensitive component that Bordet named "alexin" (later called complement) and a heat-resistant component that he

(The Nobel Foundation)

named "sensibilizer" (later called antibody).

In several subsequent papers, Bordet elucidated many of the essential characteristics of this phenomenon, and he demonstrated its applicability in a range of experimental situations. His immunological experiments made his scientific reputation, and, in 1901, the Belgian government invited him to return to Brussels as director of a research institute.

Back to Brussels

Bordet continued his immunological work in Brussels at the new Pasteur Institute there. He developed the complement fixation test, one of the most widely applicable blood tests in diagnostic microbiology. By 1909, his work was recognized to be of such importance that an English edition of many of his scientific papers, most originally written in French, was pub-

The Complement System

The complement system is an important part of the body's defense against infection.

The complement system consists of more than thirty proteins found in the fluid part of the blood, called serum. This system, either on its own or in cooperation with antibodies also found in blood serum, functions to protect the body against infection. Because antibody and the complement proteins are found in the serum, they are part of the humoral (or noncellular) immune response. The name of the system derives from the fact that it "complements" antibodies, which are the most important part of the humoral immune response.

Because the body is not always engaged in fighting infections, the complement system is normally inactive. It can be activated by several mechanisms, including the presence of an antigen-antibody complex, such as an antibody bound to a bacterial cell (an antigen). Activated complement is associated with several important immune functions, particularly phagocytosis and immune lysis.

In phagocytosis, white blood cells (or phagocytes) neutralize microorganisms such as bacteria and viruses by ingesting and destroying them. Phagocytes only ingest those microorganisms that they recognize as a threat to the body. In order to assist phagocytes in this recognition process, the body "labels" microorganisms with specific substances; the principal "labels" are antibodies. Once an antibody binds to a bacterial cell, phagocytes readily ingest it. When complement components bind to an antibody-cell complex, the process of phagocytosis is further enhanced. This process of enhancing phagocytosis is called opsonization; complement thus func-

tions as an opsonin.

In immune lysis, activated complement proteins attach themselves to the bacteria-antibody complex and trigger what is termed the complement cascade. The terminal components of this cascade form the membrane attack complex (MAC), which causes the bacterial cell to break open (or lyse). In addition to enhancing phagocytosis and cell lysis, complement is also one of the substances that can initiate inflammation, and it may assist in the development of the immune response.

Bordet was the first person to show that blood contains the two components later identified as antibodies and complement. Although he did not realize that complement is not a single substance but is instead a group of proteins, his contemporaries immediately recognized the importance of his work, which laid the foundation for further studies of this component of the humoral immune system.

Bordet himself understood the practical implications of his discovery of complement, and he made it the foundation of the complement fixation test (CFT). This test was used by August Wassermann in 1906 to detect syphilis, thus making it the first blood test for an infectious disease. The CFT was subsequently applied in the diagnosis of a variety of infectious diseases.

Bibliography

Complement. S. K. A. Law and K. B. M. Reid. 2d ed. Oxford, England: Oxford University Press, 1995.

"The Complement System." Manfred M. Mayer. *Scientific American* 229 (November, 1973).

Immunology. Ivan Roitt, Jonathan Brostoff, and David Male. London: C. V. Mosby, 1996.

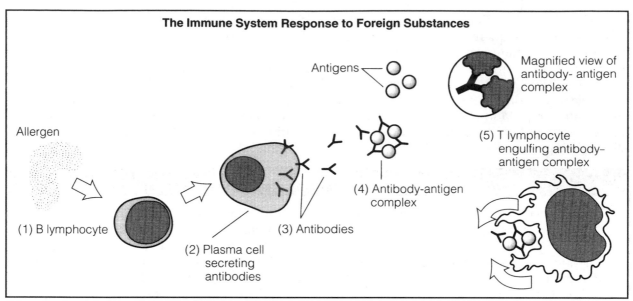

The Immune System Response to Foreign Substances

When the body is invaded by an allergen, a foreign substance (or antigen) that provokes an immune response, B lymphocytes release antibodies, which bind to the antigens to create antibody-antigen complexes. T lymphocytes (or phagocytes) then target these complexes and destroy them. (Hans & Cassady, Inc.)

lished. Bordet was also active in bacteriology, and, in 1906, he isolated the bacterium responsible for whooping cough (*Bordetella pertussis*) from his son, who was sick with the disease. Bordet was particularly gifted at designing media on which fastidious bacteria would grow, and he was the first to cultivate the organism responsible for bovine pleuropneumonia (*Mycoplasma mycoides*) on solid medium. In 1907, he was appointed professor of bacteriology at the University of Brussels.

A Statesman for Science

Bordet continued to perform original scientific studies after World War I, including work on the newly discovered bacteriophage. His direct involvement in research was diminished, however, by his heavy administrative and professional responsibilities. He held both the chair of bacteriology and the directorship of the Pasteur Institute in Brussels. In 1933, Bordet assumed the prestigious presidency of the scientific council of the Pasteur Institute in Paris, a post that he held until the outbreak of World War II. He also wrote several scientific textbooks at this time, as well as other popular scientific works.

Contemporary recognition of Bordet's scientific work followed quickly on the heels of his stay in Paris. He received numerous scientific awards and distinctions and was made a member of many academies, including the Royal Society of London and the National Academy of Sciences in the United States. In 1920, Bordet received the Nobel Prize in Physiology or Medicine for his work in immunology. He died in 1961 at the age of ninety.

Bibliography

By Bordet

La Vie et l'oeuvre de Pasteur, 1902
Studies in Immunity, 1909
Traité de l'immunité dans les maladies infectieuses, 1920
Brèves Considérations sur le mode de gouvernement, la liberté, et l'éducation morale, 1945
Infection et immunité, 1947
Éléments d'astronomie, destinés aux visiteurs du Planetarium, 1955?

About Bordet

"Jules Bordet, 1870-1961." J. Beumer. *Journal of General Microbiology* 29 (1962).
Men Against Death. Paul De Kruif. New York: Harcourt, Brace, 1932.

(James G. Hanley)

Max Born

Area of Achievement: Physics

Contribution: Born was one of the founders of quantum mechanics. His work in the dynamics of crystal lattices eventually became the foundation of modern solid-state physics.

Dec. 11, 1882	Born in Breslau, Germany (now Wroclaw, Poland)
1901	Enrolls in the University of Breslau, spending his summers studying at Heidelberg and Zürich
1907	Receives his Ph.D. in physics from the University of Göttingen
1908	Returns to Breslau and begins work in special relativity
1908	Returns to Göttingen
1909	Moves to Cambridge University to study with J. J. Thomson
1915	Offered a post at the University of Berlin and inducted into the army
1919	Moves to the University of Frankfurt-on-the-Main
1921	Becomes director of the Physical Institute at Göttingen
Apr. 25, 1933	Fired from his post as a result of Adolf Hitler's policies against Jews
June, 1933	Takes up the Stokes Lectureship at Cambridge
1939	Elected a member of the Royal Society of London
1948	Awarded the Max Planck Medal of the German Physics Society
1953	Retires and returns to Germany
1954	Shares the Nobel Prize in Physics with Hans Albrecht Bethe
Jan. 5, 1970	Dies in Göttingen, West Germany

Early Life

Max Born was born on December 11, 1882, in Breslau, Germany. His father, Gustav, was a professor of anatomy at the University of Breslau. His mother, Margarethe, died when Born was four years old. In 1890, his father married Bertha Lipstein. Her love of music probably accounted for Born's becoming an accomplished pianist.

Born entered the University of Breslau in 1901, spending his next two summers studying at Heidelberg and Zürich. He studied a wide range of subjects, but his greatest interest lay in the areas of mathematics and physics. In 1904, he entered the University of Göttingen, where he became David Hilbert's private assistant. He also studied special relativity under Hermann Minkowski.

Felix Klein was so impressed with Born's seminar paper on the stability of elastic wires

(The Nobel Foundation)

Quantum Mechanics

Quantum mechanics has provided explanations for observations in the areas of atomic, molecular, solid-state, and particle physics. It has also provided a whole new realm of philosophical questions about the basic nature of the universe.

With his explanation of photoelectric effect, Albert Einstein launched physics into a totally new realm. The nature of light had long been one of the fundamental problems facing physicists. Sir Isaac Newton and Robert Hooke had debated whether light was a particle or wave back in the late seventeenth century. At the time, the experimental evidence of geometrical optics was insufficient to settle the debate. Most scientists thought that light must be made of particles, since that was Newton's belief.

Finally, in 1801, Thomas Young performed an experiment in which he passed a coherent beam of light through two closely spaced apertures. The light produced an interference pattern on the screen beyond. Interference is a fundamental property of waves. Thus, light is a wave.

In the early twentieth century, it was found that when certain metals are irradiated with light, electrons are emitted. Unfortunately, the energy of the electrons is dependent on the frequency of the light, which did not agree with the basic assumption of light waves. Einstein explained this photoelectric effect by hypothesizing that light is made of small packets of energy called photons. The energy of each photon is directly proportional to its frequency. Again, the game was afoot. How could light be both a particle and a wave?

This wave-particle duality of light launched physics into a new realm: the quantum realm. When Louis de Broglie also proposed that matter must also exhibit this wave-particle duality, a whole new mechanics became necessary to explain phenomena on the quantum level. The Copenhagen interpretation of quantum mechanics proposes that everything, both light and matter, is described by a wave function that contains all the information about the particle at every point in space and time. The square of this wave function is the probability of finding the particle at some place at a specific time. Manipulation of the wave function through the application of various operators could then produce observable physical traits for the particle, such as its energy and momentum. The results, when applied to systems such as atoms and molecules, agree with experimental evidence. The problem with the theory, however, lies not in its application but rather in its implications.

Classical physics is based on determinism. The basic assumption is that the universe is predictable. Given the initial conditions and forces on a particle, its trajectory can be calculated for every subsequent point in time. For every cause, there must be an effect, an idea known as causality. In addition, it was assumed that the universe is objective, existing and functioning independent of the observer.

In quantum mechanics, objects can no longer be thought of as particles. The nature of microscopic entities is such that they behave like particles under certain circumstances and like waves in other experiments. Their properties are not well defined until they are measured. It cannot be said that an entity will be at a specific place at a specific time; rather, one can only find the probability of finding the particle. The universe is no longer deterministic but rather probabilistic.

Bibliography

The Dancing Wu-Li Masters: An Overview of the New Physics. Gary Zukav. New York: Bantam, 1980.

Introductory Quantum Mechanics. Richard L. Liboff. Reading, Mass.: Addison-Wesley, 1992.

Quantum Physics of Atoms, Molecules, Solids, Nuclei, and Particles, Robert Eisberg and Robert Resnick. New York: John Wiley & Sons, 1974.

Quantum Reality: Behind the New Physics. Nick Herbert. New York: Anchor Press/Doubleday, 1985.

Quantum Theory and the Schism in Physics. Karl Popper. Totowa, N.J.: Rowan and Littlefield, 1982.

The Strange Story of the Quantum. Banesh Hoffman. Magnolia, Mass.: Peter Smith, 1963.

Understanding Quantum Physics: A User's Manual. Michael A. Morrison. Englewood Cliffs, N.J.: Prentice Hall, 1990.

that he used it as the topic for a university competition. Born was more interested at the time in relativity and declined to enter a paper. Klein, who was very powerful at the university, obliged Born to submit a paper, which won the competition and became the dissertation that earned Born a Ph.D. in 1907.

Early Work

After graduate school, Born returned to Breslau, where he studied special relativity. Minkowski was impressed with his work and invited Born back to Göttingen as his associate. Unfortunately, this promising collaboration was cut short by Minkowski's untimely death. Born stayed on at Göttingen to put Minkowski's scientific papers in order.

In Göttingen, Born's attention turned to other areas. On August 2, 1912, he married Hedwig Ehrenberg. Professionally, Born became interested in the physics of crystals. In 1912, he and Theodore von Kármán published a paper on the heat capacity of solids, which became known as the Born-Kármán theory of specific heats. Born's work on crystals was eventually published in his book *Dynamik der Kristallgitter* (1915; *Dynamical Theory of Crystal Lattices*, 1954), which is a cornerstone of solid-state theory.

Quantum Mechanics

In 1915, Born was offered a post at the University of Berlin at the same time that he was inducted into the army. In what he called "an uncommon stroke of good luck," Born was assigned to Berlin in the office of ordnance testing. These years were some of the best of his life. He was able to work closely with Max Planck and formed a lifelong friendship with Albert Einstein.

After a brief time in Frankfurt doing experimental work, in 1921 Born returned to the University of Göttingen. Although originally intending to continue his study of crystal lattices, he became intrigued by Niels Bohr's correspondence principle, which held that some transition must exist between any quantum theory and classical physics. Born set out to establish a "quantum mechanics."

In 1925, Werner Heisenberg, one of Born's assistants, gave him a manuscript that proved to be fundamental to the development of this new quantum mechanics. It proposed a mathematical approach for dealing with observable quantities. Born recognized this approach as matrix algebra and set out to develop the fundamentals of matrix mechanics. Wolfgang Pauli applied this method to the hydrogen atom and was able to calculate the complete spectrum. The theory was refined with the help of Norbert Wiener, who suggested replacing the matrix with the more general concept of an operator.

In 1926, Erwin Schrödinger published his wave mechanics approach to quantum physics, which Born applied to atomic-scattering processes. The merger of the two approaches formed the basis of the Born approximation method, which is fundamental to the study of atomic and high-energy scattering. Although Schrödinger's wave mechanics worked, the interpretation of the wave function was still a problem. It was Born who solved the problem by suggesting that the square of the wave function can be understood as the probability of finding a particle at some point in space. It was this work that later earned for Born the Nobel Prize in Physics.

Later Years

Göttingen, under Born's leadership, was a center for theoretical physics. Young researchers flocked to work with Born and his colleagues. Unfortunately, in 1933, Born was placed on "leave of absence" in accordance with Adolf Hitler's removal of Jews from civil service. Born left Germany and took a position at Cambridge University, where he wrote several popular books. He later took a position at the University of Edinburgh where he was again able to establish a circle of students to continue his research. He taught extensively and published several books on the subjects he was teaching.

In 1953, Born retired and returned to Germany where he spent the rest of his life. He took on a new mission: To draw attention to the dangers of atomic weapons. In 1955, he was one of the signers of the Mainau Declaration, which condemned the development of atomic weapons. He continued to write and publish widely on the history of science and the social responsibilities of scientists until his death on January 5, 1970.

Bibliography
By Born
Dynamik der Kristallgitter, 1915 (*Dynamical Theory of Relativity*, 1922)

Die Aufbau der Materie, 1920 (*The Constitution of Matter*, 1923)

Die Relativitätstheorie Einsteins und ihre physikallischen grundlagen gemeinverstänlich dargestellt, 1920 (*Einstein's Theory of Relativity*, 1922)

Probleme der Atomdynamik, 1926 (*Problems of Atomic Dynamics*, 1926)

Atomic Physics, 1935

The Restless Universe, 1935

Principles of Optics, 1959 (with Emil Wolf)

Physik und Politik, 1960 (*Physics and Politics*, 1962)

About Born
The Born-Einstein Letters. Irene Born, trans. New York: Walker, 1971.

My Life and My Views. Max Born. New York: Charles Scribner's Sons, 1968.

Physics in My Generation. Max Born. New York: Pergamon Press, 1956.

"Recollections." Max Born. *Bulletin of the Atomic Scientist* 21, nos. 7-9 (September-November, 1965).

(Linda L. McDonald)

Walther Bothe

Areas of Achievement: Astronomy, invention, and physics

Contribution: Bothe was an important pioneer in very early nuclear and cosmic-ray physics, especially because of his experimental skills.

Jan. 8, 1891	Born in Oranienburg, Brandenburg, Germany
1914	Becomes a research assistant at the Physikalisch-Technische Reichsanstalt (PTR)
1914	Completes his Ph.D.
1914	Enters the Germany army and is taken prisoner by Russians
1920	Released from Siberia
1924	Demonstrates the collision nature of Compton scattering
1930	Invents an electronic coincidence circuit
1930	Becomes a professor at the University of Giessen
1932	Produces gamma rays by nuclear disintegration
1932	Named a professor at University of Heidelberg
1933	Forced to leave Heidelberg by the Nazis
1934	Appointed director of the Physics Institute, Kaiser-Wilhelm Gesellschaft (KWG)
1943	Completes the KWG cyclotron
1944	Reports the products of uranium fission
1955	Given the Nobel Prize in Physics for his coincidence method
Feb. 8, 1957	Dies in Heidelberg, West Germany

Early Life

Walther Bothe (pronounced "BOH-tuh") was born on January 8, 1891, in Oranienburg, Brandenburg, Germany, to a watchmaker. As a boy, he used the skills learned from his father to construct complicated apparatuses for physics experiments. When misfortune struck his parents, he supported himself and continued his education through scholarships and by tutoring other students.

After passing his *Staatsexamen* test, Bothe became a research assistant at the Physikalisch-Technische Reichsanstalt (PTR), the German bureau of standards. While employed there, he worked with Hans Geiger, who had just returned to Germany after working at Ernest Rutherford's laboratory in England, where he was introduced to the new field of nuclear physics. At the same time, Bothe wrote a dissertation under the supervision of noted physicist Max Planck in order to obtain a Ph.D. degree.

Bothe's research was broken off when he entered the army during World War I. While serving on the Russian front, he was taken prisoner and did not return until 1920. While a captive, he was able to remain scientifically active by making calculations in theoretical physics, teaching school, and giving lectures.

Experiments in Atomic and Nuclear Physics

On his return from war and prison, Bothe renewed his experimental work at the PTR with Geiger. In 1923, Arthur Holly Compton and Peter J. W. Debye independently observed that X rays were scattered in such a manner that the scattered photons lost energy. They postulated that a particle-like collision had occurred between the photons and the electrons, which was a startling explanation. Bothe devised an experiment that allowed him to establish that the scattered photons and the recoiling electrons entered two separate Geiger counters simultaneously, as predicted by Compton and Debye.

With the astronomer Werner Kolhörster, Bothe then applied the coincidence method to the study of cosmic rays. At that time, it was thought that cosmic rays were gamma rays, but Bothe demonstrated that many of them had to be particles and that they had enormous penetrating power, as Kolhörster had inferred from his balloon flights.

(The Nobel Foundation)

In 1927, Bothe began experiments with his students that used alpha particles from the natural radioactive isotope polonium 210 to induce nuclear transmutation reactions in the very light elements lithium, beryllium, and boron. Bombardment of beryllium showed that strong gamma rays resulted, the first instance in which gamma rays had been observed other than through natural decay.

This reaction also produced neutrons, and many books incorrectly state that Bothe missed observing this new particle. This is wrong, as his experiment had neither a detector capable of responding to neutrons nor a polonium source strong enough to yield enough neutrons for a reasonable chance of observing them.

These experiments used highly sensitive electrometers to respond to a discharge of the

Coincident Events as a Key to Three Kinds of Phenomena

Bothe conducted experiments with coincidence counters in order to study the Compton effect, cosmic rays, and nuclear transmutation.

Niels Bohr's quantum theory of the atom pictured electrons whirling about an atomic nucleus like a miniature planetary system. Unlike the later quantum theory of Erwin Schrödinger and Werner Heisenberg that replaced it, this theory accepted electrons as particles and photons as waves. In studying the scattering of X rays, Arthur Holly Compton measured a decrease in photon energy. He explained this so-called Compton effect as a collision of two particles—a photon and an electron. It was a direct challenge to Bohr's theory, and Bohr quickly offered another explanation.

The demonstration that the photon was scattered in coincidence with a recoiling electron took place at a time when other evidence was going against the old quantum theory. The experiment provided straightforward confirmation that the distinction between waves and particles, which had been fundamental to theory in physics, was no longer valid. The new quantum mechanics, often called wave mechanics, resolved the apparent contradiction.

Cosmic rays, radiation incident on the earth from external sources, were thought in 1929 to be composed of very-high-energy photons. Bothe set up his coincidence counting equipment so that two counters were separated by several centimeters. Generally, there was no correlation between the two detectors, but occasionally both counters responded together, implying that a cosmic ray had passed through both of them.

Bothe then introduced layers of lead between the two, which reduced the count rate and indicated that the energies of the quanta must be extremely high, because the rate at which charged particles lose energy in passing through matter was well understood by then. (This same energy-loss process also caused the counters to respond.) The simplest explanation of what had been observed was that cosmic rays were very-high-energy charged particles.

Ernest Rutherford had shown that alpha particles striking a nitrogen 14 nucleus transmuted the target nucleus into oxygen 17 plus a proton. This was the preliminary for decades of experiments in which particle accelerators were to bombard nuclei with beams of particles, protons and alpha particles being the most common. These early experiments were done with radioactive sources. When beryllium was bombarded with alpha particles, which are nuclei of helium, the result was the following:

helium 4 + beryllium 9 → neutron + carbon 12

In the experiment, the carbon 12 nuclei were left in excited states of 4.44 or 7.65 million electronvolts, which then decayed by emission of gamma rays detected in coincidence with a recoiling carbon 12. The gamma photons had far more energy than had ever been observed from natural radioactivity. This was an astonishing result, but one soon forgotten when James Chadwick found neutrons to be present.

Early experiments that determined the coincidence of two events observed with radiation counters applied the output of Geiger tubes to electrometers. Their coincident deflection was apparent, but electrometers responded slowly. In 1930, the radio industry manufactured electron tubes that could replace the slow electrometers.

Bibliography

"Atomic Structure." In *Encyclopaedia Britannica Macropaedia*. 15th ed. Chicago: University of Chicago Press, 1983.
"Cosmic Radiation." Peter Meyer. *Encyclopedia of Physical Science and Technology*. New York: Academic Press, 1987.
"Nuclear Physics." Lawrence Wilets. *Encyclopedia of Physical Science and Technology*. New York: Academic Press, 1987.

Geiger tubes. This method was very slow, as the electrometers required a substantial fraction of a second in order to recover. Bothe made use of a new electron tube to construct an electronic circuit capable of recording coincidence events at much higher count rates and much more conveniently. This was the introduction of electronic logic techniques into nuclear physics, something that grew beyond the imaginations of scientists in 1930.

Director of a Physics Institute

This chain of successful experiments led to Bothe's appointment as a professor at the University of Heidelberg in 1932, but he was forced from this post the following year because of his opposition to the Nazis. Max Planck, head of the autonomous Kaiser-Wilhelm-Gesellschaft, appointed him director of the society's Heidelberg laboratory.

Bothe kept his institute at the forefront of international scientific cooperation until the outbreak of World War II. He was involved in the unsuccessful German atomic bomb project but managed to publish ten papers in the open literature during the war describing much of this work, specifically on thermal neutrons and fission products. His efforts were instrumental in protecting the Paris laboratory of Frédéric Joliot-Curie, who was active in the Underground during the German occupation of France.

Bothe received the Nobel Prize in Physics in 1955 for his coincidence-counter studies. He died on February 8, 1957, in Heidelberg, West Germany.

Bibliography

By Bothe

"Über das Wesen des Comptoneffekts: Ein experimenteller Beitrag zur Theorie der Strahlung," *Zeitschrift für Physik*, 1925 (with Hans Geiger)

"The Nature of Penetrating Radiation," *Nature*, 1929 (with Werner Kolhörster)

"Das Wesen der Höhenstrahlung," *Zeitschrift für Physik*, 1929 (with Kolhörster)

"Zur Vereinfachung von Koinzidenzzählungen," *Zeitschrift für Physik*, 1930

"Die Gamma-Strahlung von Bor und Beryllium," *Die Naturwissenschaften*, 1932 (with Herbert Becker)

About Bothe

"Bothe, Walther Wilhelm Georg Franz." Isaac Asimov. In *Isaac Asimov's Biographical Encyclopedia of Science and Technology*. Rev. ed. New York: Avon Books, 1972.

"Walther Bothe." In *Encyclopaedia Britannica Macropaedia*. 15th ed. Chicago: University of Chicago Press, 1983.

"Walther Bothe." In *The Nobel Prize Winners: Physics*, edited by Frank N. Magill. Pasadena, Calif.: Salem Press, 1989.

(Louis Brown)

Robert Boyle

Areas of Achievement: Chemistry, invention, medicine, and physics

Contribution: Boyle is known for his development of the experimental method and for his careful recording and reporting of results. His work with air pressure and gases provided the basis for the kinetic theory of gases. His work in differentiating chemistry from alchemy earned for him the title of founder of chemistry.

Jan. 25, 1627	Born in Lismore, Waterford, Ireland
1635-1639	Studies at Eton College
1639-1644	Travels throughout continental Europe with tutors
1655	Moves to Oxford to work with leading scientists
1660	Becomes a founding member of the Royal Society of London
1660	Publishes *New Experiments Physio-Mechanicall, Touching the Spring of the Air and Its Effects*
1661	Publishes *The Sceptical Chymist*
1662	Publishes Boyle's law
1668	Moves to London
1679	French physicist Edme Mariotte publishes his version of what is commonly called Boyle's law
Dec. 31, 1691	Dies in London, England

Early Life

Robert Boyle was an Anglo-Irish chemist and natural philosopher born in Lismore, Ireland, in 1627. His father was Richard Boyle, one of the richest men in Great Britain and the lord treasurer of Ireland. Boyle was educated at Eton College from 1635 to 1639. He spent the next five years with private tutors touring the European continent, where he studied French, Latin, Italian, mathematics, history, theology, and philosophy.

In 1644, he returned to England, where he began his experimental scientific work and wrote moral essays. From 1656 to 1668, Boyle lived in Oxford. His father's fortune enabled Boyle to finance several scientific laboratories with trained associates to assist him in his experiments.

Experimental Methods

The seventeenth century was a time of rapid scientific advances. The century began with the studies of Galileo and ended with the monumental work of Sir Isaac Newton, who, along with many later scientists, was greatly influenced by Boyle.

Boyle is considered one of the founders of modern science and the chief founder of modern thinking in chemistry. He is noted for the development of the experimental method to test scientific theory. Boyle believed that ex-

(Library of Congress)

Boyle's Law

Boyle's law states that at a given temperature, the volume occupied by a gas is inversely proportional to the pressure.

At a constant temperature, the pressure (P) of a fixed amount of gas is inversely proportional to its volume (V). Mathematically, $P \times V = K$, where K is a constant. The law only applies to ideal gases, that is, gases in which molecules are considered to be mathematical points with totally elastic collisions. On the European continent, the relationship of pressure and volume is referred to as Mariotte's law, after the French scientist Edme Mariotte who published his results in 1679.

Boyle's law was first published in 1662. In his experiment, Boyle fashioned a J-shaped tube, with the short end of the J-tube sealed. He poured some mercury into the open end of the tube, waited until the mercury came to rest, and measured the volume of the gas trapped above the mercury in the enclosed end of the J-tube. Finally, Boyle measured the pressure in inches of mercury from the top of the mercury in the open end of J-tube to the top of the mercury in the shorter leg of the J-tube.

Boyle then added more mercury to the tube and measured the new pressure and volume. He added the atmospheric pressure in inches of mercury to the pressure readings that he had obtained. Boyle compared the products of pressure and volume in these two instances and found that they were the same within experimental error (plus or minus a few points). He added more mercury, made more measurements, and found the same value for the pressure-volume product.

As an example, if the volume of the gas in the J-tube is 50 cubic centimeters and the mercury in the open end of the tube is 10 inches with the barometer reading 30 inches of mercury, the total pressure on the gas is 40 inches of mercury. The product of the pressure and the volume is 200. If enough mercury is added to the tube to increase

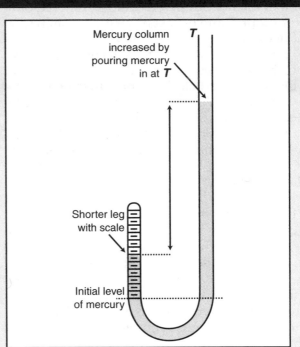

(from *Robert Boyle's Experiments in Pneumatics*, 1950, edited by James B. Conant)

the volume to 40 cubic centimeters, the mercury in the open end will be 20 inches above the mercury in the closed end. The total pressure will be 30 inches plus 20 inches, or 50 inches of mercury. The pressure-volume product again will be 200.

Boyle's law holds for real gases only over a small range of temperatures and pressures. The law makes poorer predictions at higher pressures and lower temperatures, where the gas molecules are closer together.

Bibliography

Robert Boyle's Experiments in Pneumatics. James B. Conant, ed. Cambridge, Mass.: Harvard University Press, 1950.
Statistical Physics and the Atomic Theory of Matter from Boyle and Newton to Landau and Onsager. Stephen G. Brush. Princeton, N.J.: Princeton University Press, 1983.

perimental demonstration, as opposed to simple observation and speculation, was the only path to knowledge. This methodology necessitated collecting facts as a foundation for theo-

ries. It was in contrast to the school of René Descartes, which attempted to deduce a comprehensive description of nature from principles, with the aid of mathematics. Boyle believed that such a description was an ultimate aim of science but that it could be derived only from a preliminary experimental examination of nature.

Boyle also was noted for recording and reporting his experiments in great detail so that others could repeat his work. In doing so, he established the scientific tradition of carefully documented research and the repeatability of experiments. Boyle's theoretical explanations followed the mechanical (clockwork) philosophy, which can be verified through laboratory demonstration.

The Classification of Chemical Properties

Considered by many philosophers of science as the founder of chemistry, Boyle succeeded in changing chemists' outlook in the whole field. It appears that he was the first to suggest that matter can be classified in terms of similar chemical properties and to distinguish between atoms and elements. Thinking about matter in this way separated chemistry from alchemy. Such classification replaced the obscure medieval theories based on Aristotle's view of the four elements (earth, air, fire, and water) and served as a forerunner of the modern theory of chemical elements and atomic theory.

The Study of Gases and the Vacuum Pump

One of Boyle's greatest accomplishments was in the field of pneumatics, or the study of gases. Indeed, he is probably best known for summarizing the properties of gases by the law that is given his name, Boyle's law. This law states that at a constant temperature, the pressure and volume of a gas are inversely related. He also showed that air had weight and that gases have elastic properties.

This view led Boyle to spend much time, money, and effort on the development of a vacuum pump for his investigations of gas properties. He developed an improved vacuum pump and developed air pressure gauges and compression pumps. Boyle conducted pioneering experiments in which he demonstrated the physical characteristics of air and the necessity of air for combustion and for the transmission of sound.

Other Experiments

Boyle's research threw light on such physiological processes as the digestion of food and the role of air in the respiratory mechanism. In his experiments, Boyle also studied the calcination of metals and proposed a means of distinguishing between acid and alkaline substances, which was the origination of the use of chemical indicators.

In 1660, Boyle became a founding Fellow of the Royal Society of London, in which he challenged the widely held view that the writings of the great classical philosophers were the only fountain of wisdom. In 1668, he moved to London and lived with his sister until his death on December 31, 1691.

Throughout his life, Boyle regarded himself as dedicated to God by the practice of charity and science in lay life. His inherited wealth provided money for religious and charitable endeavors, and in his will he endowed a yearly series of Boyle's Lectures, sermons to defend Christianity against atheism. The lectures continue to this day.

Bibliography

By Boyle
New Experiments Physio-Mechanicall, Touching the Spring of the Air and Its Effects, 1660
The Sceptical Chymist, 1661
The Works of the Honourable Robert Boyle, 1744 (5 vols.)
Selected Philosophical Papers of Robert Boyle, 1979 (M. A. Stewart, ed.)

About Boyle
Leviathan and the Air-Pump: Hobbes, Boyle, and the Experimental Life. Stephen Shapin and Simon Schaffer. Princeton, N.J.: Princeton University Press, 1985.
Robert Boyle's Experiments in Pneumatics. James B. Conant, ed. Cambridge, Mass.: Harvard University Press, 1950.
Statistical Physics and the Atomic Theory of Matter from Boyle and Newton to Landau and Onsager. Stephen G. Brush. Princeton, N.J.: Princeton University Press, 1983.

(Michael J. Wavering)

Sir Lawrence Bragg

Area of Achievement: Physics
Contribution: Bragg, who with his father helped found X-ray crystallography, used X-ray diffraction to determine the arrangements of atoms in many crystals.

Mar. 31, 1890	Born in Adelaide, South Australia, Australia
1901	Begins studies at St. Peter's College
1905	Enters Adelaide University
1909	Enters Trinity College, Cambridge University, England
1912	Shows how X-ray reflections from crystals reveal their structures
1913	Determines the crystal structures of diamond, iron pyrite, and calcite
1914	Commissioned as a second lieutenant in the Leicestershire Royal Horse Artillery
1915	Receives the Nobel Prize in Physics with his father
1919	Named Langworthy Professor of Physics, Manchester University
1921	Made a Fellow of the Royal Society of London
1925	Begins intensive research into the structures of silicate minerals
1931	Studies at Arnold Sommerfeld's institute in Munich, Germany
1937	Becomes Cavendish Professor of Experimental Physics at Cambridge
1954	Moves to the Royal Institution in London
1966	Retires from the Royal Institution
July 1, 1971	Dies in Ipswich, Suffolk, England

Early Life

William Lawrence Bragg was born in Adelaide, South Australia, in 1890. His father, William Henry Bragg, was a professor of mathematics and physics at the University of South Australia. Lawrence started school in 1895, and, when he shattered his left elbow in a childhood accident, an X-ray photograph was taken of his injured arm, the first medical use of X rays in Australia.

At eleven, he began attending St. Peter's College, and, when he was only fifteen, he entered Adelaide University, where he specialized in mathematics and chemistry and from which he was graduated at eighteen with first-class honors.

Within a short time of his graduation, his father accepted a position in physics at Leeds University, in England, and the family left Australia early in 1909. Following in his father's footsteps, Lawrence Bragg went to Trinity College, Cambridge University, where he studied mathematics and then switched to physics. He earned his degree with first-class honors in 1912.

X Rays and Crystals

In the summer after his graduation, Bragg heard from his father about the discovery of X-ray diffraction in Germany, and he soon developed an explanation for the pattern of spots on the photographic plate caused by the scattering of X rays from a crystal. He interpreted these spots as reflections of the X rays from the planes of atoms in the crystal.

The equation that Bragg derived to encapsulate this insight helped initiate the X-ray analysis of crystals. Using an X-ray spectrometer constructed by his father, together Lawrence and Henry Bragg determined the crystal structures of such basic substances as diamonds, zinc blende, fluorspar, iron pyrites, and calcite.

The outbreak of World War I in August, 1914, ended this period of Bragg's life. During the war, he became a technical adviser on sound ranging, a method of locating enemy guns from the sound of their firing. In 1915, he experienced both deep pain and exhilarating joy: His brother died at Gallipoli, and, jointly with his father, he was awarded the Nobel Prize in Physics for their prewar work in X-ray crystallography.

Sir Lawrence Bragg attends a ceremony in 1965 commemorating the fiftieth anniversary of the Nobel Prize in Physics that he shared with his father, Sir William Bragg. (AP/Wide World Photos)

Soon after the war's end, Bragg accepted a special Chair of Crystallography created for him at Manchester University and, succeeding Ernest Rutherford, the discoverer of the atomic nucleus, became Langworthy Professor of Physics. He continued his work in X-ray crystallography at Manchester and for his accomplishments in this field was made a Fellow of the Royal Society of London in 1921.

One of the letters of congratulation that he received was from Alice Hopkinson, a woman whom he had known earlier. She was then in her final year of history studies at Cambridge University. They were married in December, 1921. It was a happy and fruitful marriage, resulting in two boys and two girls.

In 1925, Bragg began an intensive program of research into the structures of silicate minerals. He first described the structure of olivine, a mineral silicate of iron and magnesium, and then turned to the analysis of beryl, a silicate containing aluminum and beryllium.

A crisis occurred in his life in 1930. His mother had died in 1929, and his relationship with his father had grown distant. Bragg recovered his equilibrium by taking a leave from Manchester and spending time at Arnold Sommerfeld's Institute for Theoretical Physics in Munich, Germany.

An Administrator of Science

After his return to England, Bragg drifted away from experimental work and became involved in administration. In 1937, he was named director of the National Physical Laboratory, but, after Rutherford's death in October, he was invited to Cambridge as Cavendish Professor of Experimental Physics.

Bragg's scientific interests and management style differed from those of Rutherford, and this was initially the source of problems, but he made some important appointments. For example, he hired Max Perutz, who introduced him to the analysis of protein structures, and Bragg thus became a worthy member of a distinguished lineage of Cavendish Professors that had begun with James Clerk Maxwell.

With the start of World War II in 1939, Bragg contributed what he could to Britain's effort to defeat Germany. As in World War I, he helped the sound-ranging section of the army, and he also contributed to the development of sonar for the navy. He made trips to Canada and Sweden in connection with his war service.

At the end of the war, Bragg played a pivotal role in organizing crystallographic research internationally and in founding a new journal, *Acta Crystallographica*. At Cambridge, he completed the break from the Rutherford tradition at the Cavendish Laboratory by decentralizing research, believing that it should no longer be dominated by one group under one powerful person.

Although Bragg played no direct part in the study of the structure of deoxyribonucleic acid (DNA), he did keep a close watch, as head of the laboratory, on the work of James D. Watson and Francis Crick. For example, he insisted that an expert in chemistry check their double-helix model for DNA.

In 1954, Bragg moved to the Royal Institution in London, where, for the third time in his life—Manchester and the Cavendish were the

The X-Ray Analysis of Crystal Structures

Bragg developed the theoretical basis for crystal-structure analysis and used it to determine the structures of several important crystals.

Before 1912, scientists had little knowledge of how atoms are actually arranged in crystals. Crystallographers applied geometric ideas in studying crystalline regularities, which, they believed, suggested that something in the crystals had to be systematically arranged in space. They did not know, however, whether the repetitive unit was an atom, a molecule, an ion (a charged atom or group of atoms), or several molecules or ions. X-ray crystallography provided scientists with the tool needed to discover atomic arrangements throughout the crystal.

Bragg was given this tool through a discovery made by Max von Laue, a German physicist, in 1912. Laue's idea was that if crystals have repetitive structures in three dimensions, they make up what is called a lattice, a periodic configuration of particles throughout a certain space. This lattice should diffract, or scatter, X rays in a patterned way. When Laue's idea was tested experimentally by transmitting X rays through a crystal of copper sulfate, the photograph revealed, besides the incident X rays, a circle of spots diffracted by the crystal lattice.

Bragg heard about Laue's discovery from his father, who recognized that this discovery challenged his view that X rays were made of particles. Lawrence Bragg became convinced of the correctness of Laue's wave interpretation of X rays, but he believed that Laue's explanation of X-ray diffraction, involving interfering wavelets in three-dimensional space, was needlessly complicated. His simpler explanation was that the X rays diffracted by the crystal are the result of reflections of the X rays by planes of atoms in the crystal. In other words, the waves are not merely diffracted in certain directions, as Laue had assumed, but reflected by certain layers of atoms, which behave like mirrors.

Atoms in a crystal are arranged regularly in space, so that if a plane is passed through one group of atoms—for example, those in a crystal face—then a parallel plane may be passed through the next group of atoms underlying the first layer. The waves reflected from the atoms in the lower plane may or may not be in phase with the waves reflected from the top layer. Whether they are depends on the perpendicular distance between the planes, the wavelength of the incoming X rays, and the angle of incidence between the rays and the surface of the plane. Lawrence Bragg derived a mathematical relationship among these variables, now known as Bragg's Law.

While his son was working on the theory of X-ray diffraction, William Henry Bragg was experimenting on an instrument for detecting and measuring the X rays diffracted from crystals. By March, 1913, he had made the first X-ray spectrometer, an instrument designed to measure the intensity of an X-ray beam reflected from a crystal face.

Using Henry Bragg's spectrometer and Lawrence Bragg's mathematical equation, father and son determined the structures of such important crystals as sodium chloride, which they proved contained no actual molecules but only sodium ions and chloride ions periodically arranged. Using their theoretical and experimental techniques, they were also able to establish that the carbon atoms in a diamond are tetrahedrally arranged.

By the end of 1913, the Braggs had standardized the X-ray analysis of crystals, and their techniques gave scientists the ability to visualize the detailed structures of matter well beyond the power of the best microscopes. Indeed, their discovery made possible the vast and influential field of modern structural analysis.

Bibliography

Crystals and X-Rays. Henry S. Lipson. London: Wykeham, 1970.

Fifty Years of X-Ray Diffraction. P. P. Ewald, ed. Utrecht, the Netherlands: N. V. A. Oosthoek Uitgeversmaatschappij, 1962.

From X-Rays to Quarks: Modern Physicists and Their Discoveries. Emilio Segrè. San Francisco: W. H. Freeman, 1980.

first two—he took on the task of reviving the fortunes of an institution experiencing financial and morale problems. He solved the Royal Institution's financial problems by generating support from corporate subscribers.

In the tradition of Sir Humphry Davy and Michael Faraday, he created public support by giving many lectures to large audiences. Through these lectures and a television series, he became an admired public figure. Even after his retirement from the Royal Institution in 1966, he continued to lecture and publish on various scientific topics.

Philosophy of Science

Lawrence Bragg approached the universe in the same way that he approached crystals: He believed that precisely structured, three-dimensional relationships undergird all natural phenomena and that these structures help to explain how matter behaves. This approach helped him to revolutionize mineralogy, metallurgy, chemistry, and molecular biology.

On the other hand, Bragg's work was, for the most part, untouched by the radical new ideas of quantum mechanics, and he remained throughout his career a classical physicist in the tradition of Rutherford, whose philosophy of science paralleled his own, emphasizing concrete physical instead of abstract mathematical models. This philosophy certainly created great successes for Bragg in X-ray crystallography, the celebrated story of which can never be told without including his contributions.

Bibliography

By Bragg

X Rays and Crystal Structure, 1915 (with William Henry Bragg)
The Structure of Silicates, 1930
The Crystalline State, 1933-1965
Electricity, 1936
Atomic Structure and Minerals, 1937
The Atomic Structure of Alloys, 1938
The History of X-Ray Analysis, 1943
Crystal Structure of Minerals, 1965 (with Gordon F. Claringbull)
The Start of X-Ray Analysis, 1967
Ideas and Discoveries in Physics, 1970
The Development of X-Ray Analysis, 1975

About Bragg

The Bragg Family in Adelaide: A Pictorial Celebration. John Jenkin. Adelaide, Australia: University of Adelaide Foundation, 1986.
The Legacy of Sir Lawrence Bragg: Selections and Reflections. Northwood, Middlesex, England: Science Reviews, 1990.
William Henry Bragg and William Lawrence Bragg: A Bibliography of Their Nontechnical Writings. Berkeley: Office for History of Science and Technology, University of California, 1978.
William Henry Bragg, 1862-1942: Man and Scientist. G. M. Caroe. Cambridge, England: Cambridge University Press, 1978.
"William Lawrence Bragg, 31 March 1890-1 July 1971." David Phillips. *Biographical Memoirs of Fellows of the Royal Society* 25 (1975).

(Robert J. Paradowski)

Robert Henry Bragg

Areas of Achievement: Physics and technology

Contribution: Bragg studied the structure and properties of different materials, especially various forms of carbon. Knowledge of these properties led to a better understanding of how these materials could be incorporated into manufactured goods.

Aug. 11, 1919	Born in Jacksonville, Florida
1947	Marries Violette McDonald
1949	Receives a B.S. degree from the Illinois Institute of Technology (IIT) in Chicago
1951	Earns an M.S. degree at IIT
1951-1956	Works as a physicist in the Research Laboratory of the Portland Cement Association in Skokie, Illinois
1956-1961	Serves as a physicist at the Research Institute of IIT
1960	Receives a Ph.D. degree in physics from IIT
1961-1969	Works as a research scientist at the Lockheed Missiles and Space Company in Palo Alto, California
1969-1987	Appointed a professor at the University of California, Berkeley (UCB)
1987	Named professor emeritus at UCB
1989	Serves as visiting professor at the Musashi Institute of Technology in Japan
1992-1993	Works as a visiting scientist at Obafemi Awolowo University, Nigeria

Early Life

African American physicist Robert Henry Bragg, Jr., was born on August 11, 1919, in Jacksonville, Florida, as the son of Robert Henry and Camelle (McFarland) Bragg. After his completion of high school and following World War II, he enrolled in the Illinois Institute of Technology (IIT) in Chicago, where he completed his bachelor of science degree in 1949. Two years later, in 1951, he received a master of science degree from the same institute.

Bragg accepted a position as a physicist at the Research Laboratory of the Portland Cement Association in Skokie, Illinois, a Chicago suburb. Upon leaving this organization in 1956, he returned to IIT as a scientist in their Research Institute.

During this time, he worked on various studies pertaining to the atomic and molecular structure of materials, particularly various forms of carbon, and on the improvement of measurement techniques using X rays and various radioactive sources. While active at the Research Institute, he also continued his studies at IIT, receiving his Ph.D. degree in physics in 1960.

Bragg then moved to California to accept a

(Lawrence Berkeley National Laboratory)

position as a research physicist at the Materials Science Laboratory of the Lockheed Missiles and Space Company in Palo Alto. There, he continued his studies on the effects and interactions of X rays on various materials and on the refinement of measurement techniques.

Studies of Crystalline Structure

Much of Bragg's early research dealt with an improved understanding of how matter is constructed—that is, the atomic and molecular arrangement of particles within a substance. One method for approaching this question is through the use of X rays, a highly energetic form of electromagnetic radiation.

The wavelengths of X rays are of the same dimensions as the spacings in crystalline solids. Therefore, when X rays strike a solid, they interact with its atoms and molecules, resulting in a unique X-ray pattern called a diffraction pattern. Bragg studied the X-ray diffraction of boron. He also studied imperfections in crystals, locations where atoms are misaligned and/or absent from the crystalline structure.

As part of his work with X-ray diffraction, Bragg studied the proper placement of the sample and the preferred size of the sample, as well as various other means to improve the interactions between X rays and crystalline solids.

The Study of Carbon

In 1969, Bragg accepted a position as professor in the Department of Materials Science and Mineral Engineering at the University of California, Berkeley (UCB), a position that he held until his retirement in 1987. He was chair of the department from 1978 to 1981. His position at UCB allowed him time to pursue more fully the research that he had started on the structure and properties of carbon in its various forms.

Bragg's study of pyrolytic and glassy carbon occupied much of his research interest. These two special forms of carbon are produced by carefully heating naturally occurring carbon and carbon-containing compounds. Bragg and his associates published many papers on the prepa-

The Various Forms of Carbon

Bragg studied naturally occurring and artificially produced forms of carbon for use in manufacturing.

Carbon occurs naturally as coal, an amorphous (unstructured) material, and as graphite, which contains ordered layers of carbon atoms. Diamond is a crystalline form of carbon. Other forms of carbon can be produced by heating carbon-containing materials at high temperatures under controlled conditions that allow only the carbon to remain intact while the other components in the compounds burn away.

One of the forms of carbon is vitreous or glassy carbon manufactured by the controlled heating of cellulose or other carbon-containing polymers to a temperature of around 2,500 degrees Celsius. The resulting material has the appearance of black glass and, like glass, is easily broken. Because of its hardness and resistance to chemical attack, glassy carbon is often used for laboratory vessels in which chemical reactions are heated to high temperatures.

Pyrolytic carbon can be made by the controlled decomposition of natural gas at temperatures approaching 2,000 degrees Celsius. The resulting material has different properties depending on the details of the manufacturing process. One form of pyrolytic carbon, because of its high heat resistance, is used for furnace linings and for the nose cones of rockets.

Strands of pyrolytic carbon were the first incandescent lamp filaments. Their high heat resistance and excellent electric conductivity made them ideal for this purpose. Because they are easily broken, however, they have been replaced by tungsten metal filaments.

Bibliography

Encyclopedia of Composite Materials and Components. Martin Grayson, ed. New York: John Wiley & Sons, 1983.

Encyclopedia of Materials Science and Engineering. Michael B. Bever, ed. Oxford, England: Pergamon Press, 1986.

Encyclopedia of Physical Science and Technology. Robert A. Meyers, ed. San Diego: Academic Press, 1992.

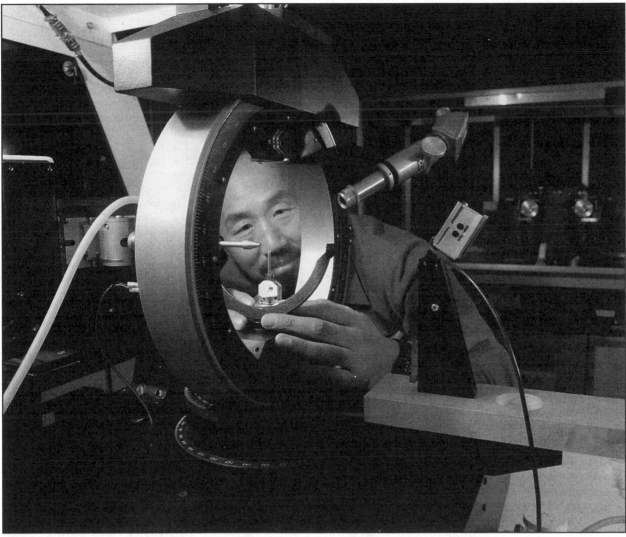

A scientist determines the structure of a protein crystal through X-ray diffraction. Bragg used such techniques to study how matter is constructed. (Lawrence Berkeley National Laboratory)

ration of these materials and on the properties that they exhibit. These properties include electrical conductivity, magnetic interactions, thermal stability, crystalline structure, imperfections, surface area, and mechanical strength.

Bibliography

By Bragg

"Multiple Foil Determination of the Effective Resolving Time of Geiger Counters Used with Diffractometers," *Review of Scientific Instruments*, 1957

"Orientation Dependence of Structure in Pyrolytic Graphite," *Nature*, 1962 (with Charles M. Packer)

"The Electrical Conductivity and Hall Effect of Glassy Carbon," *The Journal of Non-Crystalline Solids*, 1983 (with D. F. Baker)

"Nonkinetic Changes in Heat-Treated Glasslike Carbons," *Carbon*, 1987 (with J. Lachter, B. N. Mehrotra, and L. G. Henry)

About Bragg

American Men and Women of Science, 1995-96. Karen Hallard, ed. New Providence, N.J.: R. R. Bowker, 1996.

World Who's Who in Science. Allen G. Debus, ed. Chicago: Marquis Who's Who, 1968.

(Gordon A. Parker)

Tycho Brahe

Areas of Achievement: Astronomy and invention

Contribution: The accurate astronomical instruments that Tycho developed to measure the positions of stars and the motions of planets provided the data that enabled Johannes Kepler to deduce the laws of planetary orbits. Tycho's celestial measurements were the most accurate possible prior to the invention of the telescope.

Dec. 14, 1546	Born in Knudstrup Castle, Scania, Denmark (now in Sweden)
1559-1562	Studies law at the University of Copenhagen
1562-1565	Attends the University of Leipzig
Aug., 1563	Observes the conjunction of Jupiter and Saturn
1565-1570	Studied astronomy while constructing accurate instruments
1571	Constructs a small observatory in Denmark
1572	Precisely measures a supernova's position, proving that it was a star
1573	Publishes his first book, *De Nova Stella*
1576	Granted Hveen Island to construct a large observatory
1577	Proves that a comet in this year was well beyond the moon's orbit
1577-1597	Accurate measurements of star positions and planetary motions
1599-1601	Appointed Imperial Mathematicus to the Holy Roman emperor
1600	Appoints Kepler as his assistant
Oct. 24, 1601	Dies at Prague, Bohemia (now Czech Republic)

A monument to Tycho Brahe. (Library of Congress)

Early Life

Born to a wealthy Danish family, the infant Tyge Brahe Ottosøn—who is generally known by the name Tycho (pronounced "TI-koh)—was abducted, then reared as an heir, by his childless uncle. At the age of thirteen, Tycho was sent to the University of Copenhagen to study law. During his first year, an accurately predicted eclipse of the sun seemed so miraculous to the impressionable youth that he began to neglect his legal studies in order to learn astronomy.

After three years at Copenhagen, Tycho was sent to the University of Leipzig with a tutor instructed to cure him of his perverse preoccupation with astronomy. While his tutor slept, however, Tycho measured stellar positions. On August 17, 1563, he observed a conjunction (overlapping positions) of Saturn and Jupiter. Although the almanacs had predicted this event, they were grossly inaccurate, missing the event by as much as a month. Tycho, then and there, devoted his life to accumulating precise observations so that accurate tables could be published.

After Leipzig, Tycho spent five years traveling, studying, and designing bigger and better instruments for celestial measurements. In 1570, he returned to his family estate in Denmark, where he used his inheritance to build a small observatory.

On November 11, 1572, Tycho saw a very bright star where no star had been before. According to the established science, fixed stars never changed appearance or position. Only planets or comets moved through the fixed stars. Although many astronomers observed the new object, only Tycho was able to measure its position accurately.

Using his newly constructed instruments, he determined, unequivocally, that the new object (today called a supernova) was indeed a star. The following year, he published his observations, and descriptions of the instruments used, in his first book, *De Nova Stella* (the new star). Tycho's fame was thus established in a single stroke.

The Island Observatory

Having acquired some measure of renown, Tycho now wished to establish a large observatory. In 1576, Frederick II, king of Denmark, gave Tycho title to the Island of Hveen and generous financial support to realize this dream. For the next twenty years, Tycho collected observations and substantially corrected nearly every known astronomical record.

One of his first observations proved that the great comet of 1577 was not an atmospheric phenomenon of Earth, as had previously been believed, but located out among the planets. Under Tycho's direction, Hveen became the astronomical center of northern Europe; scholars and nobles flocked to see the impressive array of large and extremely accurate instruments.

After King Frederick's death in 1588, Tycho's income was greatly reduced. Nevertheless, he remained at Hveen, meticulously recording positions of stars and planets, until the one thousand brightest stars had been accurately pinpointed. Tycho left the island in 1597, traveling extensively until receiving an appointment by Emperor Rudolph II. In 1599, Tycho joined the emperor in Prague and began to construct another observatory.

Tycho and Kepler

On February 4, 1600, Johannes Kepler, a young mathematician searching for accurate data on planetary motions, joined Tycho's staff. Tycho had an impressive array of accurate data but

Precise Measurements in Astronomy

Tycho's sole discovery and greatest contribution was that, to be a science, astronomy requires precise and continuous observational data.

According to Ptolemy's Earth-centered theory of the universe, the stars, planets, sun, and moon all revolved around the earth in circular orbits. During the sixteenth century, Nicolaus Copernicus proposed a sun-centered model in which the earth and other planets revolved in circular orbits around the sun. Computations based on either model were used to predict planetary motions among the fixed stars. Tycho's extensive and extremely accurate data showed, however, that both theories were in error.

Before Tycho, the most accurate measurements were reliable to no more than ten minutes of arc (there are sixty minutes in a degree). Tycho's data were accurate to about one minute of arc. If a 12-foot pointer were used to sight a star, a shift of the end of the pointer by 1/25 of an inch would give an angular error of one minute of arc.

Previous observers were content to observe planetary positions at certain key points in their orbits. Tycho tracked them through their entire orbits by daily observation. His observations were made without benefit of the telescope (invented seven years after his death) but with various sighting tubes and pointers. Tycho, an unusually keen and meticulous observer, took great care to stabilize and calibrate his instruments carefully to ensure maximum accuracy.

Bibliography

"The Harmony of Worlds." Carl Sagan. In *Cosmos*. New York: Random House, 1980.

"The Sun Worshipers." T. Ferris. In *Coming of Age in the Milky Way*. New York: Anchor Books, 1988.

did not have the genius to use it to construct a coherent model of the universe. Kepler had the genius but lacked the precise data to check his models. Each needed the other, and each was afraid of being preempted.

Thus, a stalemate developed. Tycho tried to pick Kepler's brain while releasing the data in small dribbles, while Kepler, frustrated by this, did not share his insights. The situation was resolved on October 13, 1601, when Tycho became seriously ill, dying eleven days later. Kepler, appointed his successor, inherited the data, which he used to obtain the correct laws of planetary motion.

Bibliography

By Tycho

De nova et nullius aevi memoria prius visa stella, 1573 (commonly known as *De Nova Stella*; partially trans. in *A Source Book of Astronomy*, 1929)

Tychonis Brahe Dani Opera Omnia, 1913-1929 (commonly known as *Opera Omnia*; 15 vols.)

About Tycho

Tycho Brahe. J.L.E. Dreyer. Reprint. New York: Dover, 1963.

John Allyne Gade. *The Life and Times of Tycho Brahe*. 1947. Reprint. New York: Greenwood Press, 1969.

"Tycho de Brahe." A. Koestler. In *The Sleepwalkers*. Middlesex, England: Penguin Books, 1989.

(George R. Plitnik)

Sir David Brewster

Areas of Achievement: Physics and science (general)

Contribution: Best known for his work in physical optics, Brewster edited several scientific journals, wrote many books, and promoted the organization of Victorian science.

Dec. 11, 1781	Born in Jedburgh, Roxburghshire, Scotland
1794	Enters the University of Edinburgh
1800	Awarded an honorary master of arts degree from the University of Edinburgh
1807-1830	Serves as editor of the *Edinburgh Encyclopaedia*
1808	Elected a Fellow of the Royal Society of Edinburgh
1813	Publishes *A Treatise on New Philosophical Instruments*
1815	Elected a Fellow of the Royal Society of London
1815	Receives the Copley Medal of the Royal Society of London
1816	Invents the kaleidoscope
1819-1868	Edits various scientific journals
1831	Publishes *A Treatise on Optics*
1831	Helps found the British Association for the Advancement of Science (BAAS)
1851	Acts as president of the BAAS
1855	Publishes *Memoirs of the Life, Writings, and Discoveries of Sir Isaac Newton*
1864	Elected president of the Royal Society of Edinburgh
Feb. 10, 1868	Dies in Allerby, Melrose, Scotland

Early Life

As a boy, David Brewster studied the physical sciences and built telescopes, sundials, and microscopes. The son of a Scottish rector, he entered the University of Edinburgh in 1794 aspiring to a career in the clergy. A nervous disposition and an extreme fear of public speaking, however, led Brewster to pursue his love of science instead.

Working as a private tutor from 1799 to 1807, Brewster also began his long career in editing in 1802. He failed several times to gain university professorships in Scotland, and his primary income came from editing scientific journals such as the *Edinburgh Philosophical Journal*, the *Edinburgh Journal of Science*, and the *Philosophical Magazine*.

The Study of Optics

While still a student, Brewster began his extensive optical research. Of his thirty papers published in the *Philosophical Transactions of the Royal Society*, all involved optics. A tireless experimenter, Brewster investigated such phenomena as polarization, double refraction, and metallic reflection. He also invented the kaleidoscope, established Brewster's law, and helped create the fields of optical mineralogy and photoelasticity. He was highly regarded by his contemporaries, who called him the "Kepler of optics" and the founder of modern experimental optics.

Despite recognizing the usefulness and beauty of Thomas Young's law of interference, Brewster believed that the hypothesis regarding light as waves remained unproven. Yet, his rejection of the wave theory did not stem from scientific inability or incompetence. Rather, Brewster's religious, methodological, and epistemological views conflicted with those of the wave theorists.

In particular, he objected to the hypothetical luminiferous ether, the undetectable medium filling all space so that light would have something in which to create waves. Choosing to describe optical effects in terms of particles and forces, Brewster nevertheless did not blindly follow Sir Isaac Newton's corpuscular theory. While making significant theoretical alterations, he passionately defended the Newtonian emission theory until the end of his life.

(Library of Congress)

Contributions to Science

A prolific writer, Brewster published numerous popular books, encyclopedia articles, reviews, and papers. Totalling several hundred items, his publications encompass a wide variety of subjects, including astronomy, mechanics, magnetism, geology, color blindness, photography, and the philosophy of science. He also wrote several historical works, including the definitive nineteenth century biography of Newton entitled *Memoirs of the Life, Writings, and Discoveries of Sir Isaac Newton* (1855).

Also a key figure in scientific organization, Brewster helped found the Edinburgh School of Arts in 1821, the Royal Scottish Society of Arts in 1821, and the British Association for the Advancement of Science in 1831, the latter being the major disseminating force of science in

Brewster's Law

Brewster determined a simple relationship relating refraction, reflection, and polarization.

Refraction occurs when light rays change direction as a result of a change in the medium through which they are traveling. For example, light changes direction when it enters water or glass. When light enters certain substances, however, such as calcite, it is doubly refracted, emerging as two beams instead of one.

If a plate of polarizing material, such as tourmaline, is rotated in front of these emerging beams, one will be blocked while the other is not, depending on the plate's relative position. Analogously, a beam reflected off a glass plate causes the intensity of the reflected light to vary according to the angle of the plate. These examples illustrate the phenomenon of polarization by double refraction and reflection, respectively.

When the incident light hits the material at a certain angle, the refracted or reflected light is fully polarized. Brewster observed this special polarizing angle for numerous substances, including glass, water, and many minerals. In doing so, he discovered a simple law: The index of refraction of the substance equaled the tangent of the polarizing angle. This relationship, now called Brewster's law, means that when light falls on a substance at the polarizing angle, the refracted and reflected rays are at right angles.

Although Brewster advocated the emission theory of light, his many experimental results were reinterpreted by others to fit within the undulatory (wave) theory of light.

Bibliography
Development of Concepts of Physics. A. B. Arons. Reading, Mass.: Addison-Wesley, 1965.
Light: Principles and Experiments. George S. Monk. 2d ed. New York: Dover, 1963.
The Rise of the Wave Theory of Light. Jed Z. Buchwald. Chicago: University of Chicago Press, 1989.

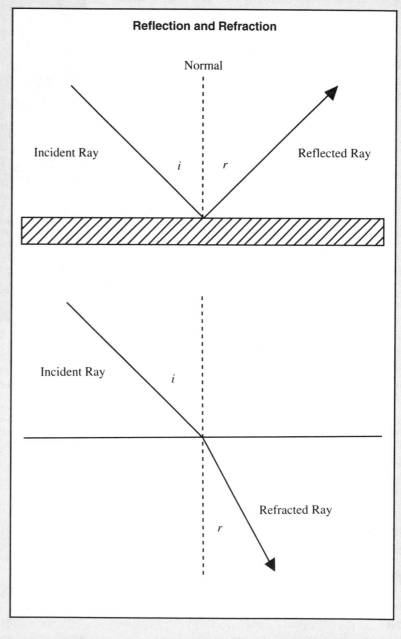

nineteenth century Britain. Despite his irascible and sometimes combative personality, Brewster contributed much to physical optics in particular and Victorian science in general.

Bibliography

By Brewster

A Treatise on New Philosophical Instruments, for Various Purposes in the Arts and Sciences, 1813

A Treatise on the Kaleidoscope, 1819

The Life of Sir Isaac Newton, 1831

A Treatise on Optics, 1831

A Treatise on Magnetism, 1837

The Martyrs of Science: Lives of Galileo, Tycho Brahe, and Kepler, 1841

Memoirs of the Life, Writings, and Discoveries of Sir Isaac Newton, 1855

The Stereoscope: Its History, Theory, and Construction, 1856

The History of the Invention of the Dioptric Lights and Their Introduction into Great Britain, 1862

About Brewster

"Brewster, David." Edgar W. Morse. In *Dictionary of Scientific Biography*, edited by Charles Coulston Gillispie. Vol. 2. New York: Charles Scribner's Sons, 1970.

"Martyr of Science": Sir David Brewster, 1781-1868. A. D. Morrison-Law and J. R. R. Christie, eds. Edinburgh: Royal Scottish Museum Studies, 1984.

"The Tenacity of Newtonian Optics in England: David Brewster, the Last Champion." Henry John Steffens. In *The Development of Newtonian Optics in England*. New York: Science History Publications, 1977.

(Robinson M. Yost)

Percy Williams Bridgman

Areas of Achievement: Physics and science (general)

Contribution: Bridgman investigated physical processes at high pressures, developing the laboratory apparatus used to subject materials to high pressures and investigating the behavior of those materials.

Apr. 21, 1882	Born in Cambridge, Massachusetts
1904	Receives a bachelor's degree in physics and mathematics from Harvard University, graduating summa cum laude
1908	Earns a Ph.D. in physics from Harvard
1910	Named an instructor at Harvard
1913	Named assistant professor of physics at Harvard
1927	Publishes *The Logic of Modern Physics*
1931	Publishes *The Physics of High Pressure*
1946	Awarded the Nobel Prize in Physics for his contributions to the physics of high-pressures
1954	Retires from the faculty of Harvard
1959	Publishes *The Way Things Are*
Aug. 20, 1961	Dies in Randolph, New Hampshire

Early Life

Percy Williams Bridgman was the only child of Raymond L. Bridgman and Ann Marie Williams Bridgman. He was born on April 21, 1882, in Cambridge, Massachusetts, but the family soon moved to Newton, Massachusetts, where he attended public schools. His father was a well-known newspaper reporter and the author of several books on public affairs.

Bridgman entered Harvard University in 1900, where he studied physics and mathematics and was graduated summa cum laude in 1904 and received a Ph.D. in physics in 1908. Upon his graduation, Bridgman was appointed a research fellow in the department of physics at Harvard. He became an instructor in 1910 and an assistant professor in 1913.

Research in High-Pressure Physics

In 1905, while Bridgman was working on his graduate education, the conventional apparatus that he was using to reach high pressures failed before reaching the pressure that he wanted to achieve. Bridgman, who had earned a reputation for having exceptional physical

(The Nobel Foundation)

intuition and dexterity in designing and manipulating equipment, set his attention to designing a high-pressure apparatus that would not fail.

He quickly developed an apparatus that could achieve a pressure of 128 tons per square inch. This pressure so far exceeded what could be attained with a conventional apparatus that Bridgman wrote: "The magnitude of the fluid pressure mentioned here requires brief comment, because without a word of explanation it may seem so large as to cast discredit on the accuracy of all the data." To reach these pressures, Bridgman developed a "massive support anvil" in which he replaced the conventional thin rod piston with a tapered cone, better distributing the forces over the structure.

Bridgman continued to improve his apparatus. By the 1940's, he had achieved pressures in excess of 2,000 tons per square inch. These pressures were so high that he had to develop new instruments to measure them. Since scientists had not previously performed experiments at such pressures, each experiment that Bridgman performed opened some new phenomenon for investigation. At these pressures, Bridgman was able to study the processes that occur deep in the interior of the earth.

The technology developed by Bridgman to reach high pressures resulted in the production of synthetic diamonds in the 1950's. Josiah Willard Gibbs had suggested, in the nineteenth century, that graphite could be converted into diamonds if it were compressed at high enough temperatures and pressures. When scientists at the General Electric Company produced the first synthetic diamonds, they used an adaptation of Bridgman's massive support anvil, and Bridgman himself served as a consultant on the project.

Bridgman was awarded the Nobel Prize in Physics in 1946 for his invention of an apparatus to produce high pressures and for the discoveries that he made in the field of high-pressure physics.

Research on the Philosophy of Science

Although many scientists begin to contemplate the meaning and philosophy of science late in their careers, Bridgman became convinced quite early that some basic scientific concepts

High-Pressure Physics

Over his fifty-four-year career, Bridgman investigated the behavior of materials at high pressures—developing the technology necessary to reach high pressures, performing experiments using his ingenious apparatus, and advancing the science of thermodynamics.

When Bridgman began his research, high pressures were achieved in the laboratory by placing a thin rod on the end of a large piston. The rod concentrated the force of the piston, resulting in a high pressure (force divided by the area over which the force is applied). The thin rod was the weak link in the system, however, frequently breaking when high pressures were achieved. Bridgman developed what he called a "massive support anvil" to reach higher pressures. He replaced the thin rod with a truncated cone having a very small flat surface, called the anvil, at one end, but tapering uniformly to the diameter of the larger piston. The truncated cone more evenly distributed the force, and Bridgman's device could sustain much higher pressures than the thin rod used previously.

By having two sets of pistons and anvils push against each other, Bridgman was able to achieve even higher pressures, but he needed a gasket to hold the sample between the two anvil surfaces. These gaskets had proven to be a weak point, limiting the pressure that could be achieved. Bridgman developed two solutions to the gasket problem. One, an ingenious solution, was to make the gasket from pyrophyllite, a volcanic rock. At high pressure, the pyrophyllite flows, conforming to the shape of the anvil surfaces. When it flows to a region of lesser pressure, however, the pyrophyllite solidifies immediately, preventing the escape of the sample from the high-pressure region.

Bridgman's second gasket design, which he called the "unsupported area seal," employed a geometrical solution. This design ensures that the pressure on the gasket always exceeds the pressure inside the chamber, so that the ultimate limit on the pressure vessel is the strength of the metal vessel, not the gasket.

Using his apparatus, Bridgman attained sustained pressures up to 400,000 atmospheres, or 2,500 tons per square inch. He was able to investigate how minerals behave near the center of the earth, and an adaptation of his apparatus was used in the first experiments that produced synthetic diamonds in 1955.

Bibliography

"High-Pressure Technology." Alexander Zeitlin. *Scientific American* (May, 1965).

The Physics of High Pressure. Percy Williams Bridgman. New York: G. Bell & Sons, 1931.

"Ultrahigh Pressures." H. Tracy Hall. *Scientific American* (November, 1959).

were misunderstood because of the use of ordinary language to describe science. He was impressed by Albert Einstein's demonstration that the ordinary concept of simultaneous events has no meaning for two events that occur at different places.

Bridgman began to think about how to define scientific problems. He developed an operational point of view, in which he suggested that for a specific question to be meaningful, "it must be possible to find (a series of) operations by which answers may be given to it." He presented his ideas in *The Logic of Modern Physics*, which was published in 1927. Coming at a time when quantum mechanics seemed to be robbing physics of its deterministic roots, Bridgman's operational approach garnered considerable interest.

In a series of lectures at Princeton University, published as *The Nature of Physical Theory* in 1936, Bridgman attempted to direct attention away from the apparent rigor of precise mathematical equations to the crude observations and the approximate verbal expressions that the equations symbolized.

Bridgman retired in 1954, but he continued his interest in the philosophy of science. In 1959, he published *The Way Things Are*, which offered his thinking on the philosophy of science more than thirty years after his original book. Bridgman died in 1961 in Randolph, New Hampshire, at the age of seventy-nine.

Bibliography
By Bridgman
Dimensional Analysis, 1922
A Condensed Collection of Thermodynamic Formulas, 1925
The Logic of Modern Physics, 1927
The Physics of High Pressure, 1931
The Thermodynamics of Electrical Phenomena in Metals, 1934
The Nature of Physical Theory, 1936
The Nature of Thermodynamics, 1941
The Nature of Some of Our Physical Concepts, 1952
Studies in Large Plastic Flow and Fracture, with Special Emphasis on the Effects of Hydrostatic Pressure, 1952
The Way Things Are, 1959
"Synthetic Diamonds," *Scientific American*, 1959
The Thermodynamics of Electrical Phenomena in Metals and a Condensed Collection of Thermodynamic Formulas, 1961 (revised)
A Sophisticate's Primer of Relativity, 1962

About Bridgman
"High-Pressure Technology." Alexander Zeitlin. *Scientific American* (May, 1965).
"Ultrahigh Pressures." H. Tracy Hall. *Scientific American* (November, 1959).
The Validation of Scientific Theories. Philipp G. Frank. New York: Macmillan, 1961.

(George J. Flynn)

Louis de Broglie

Area of Achievement: Physics
Contribution: De Broglie developed a wave-particle duality theory stating that matter has the properties of both particles and waves.

Aug. 15, 1892	Born in Dieppe, France
1909	Enters the Sorbonne as a student
1923	Publishes three papers on light quanta
1924	Defends his doctoral dissertation on the wave nature of matter
1928	Works at the Henri Poincaré Institute
1929	Awarded the Nobel Prize in Physics
1932-1962	Serves as a professor of theoretical physics at the Sorbonne
1933	Elected to the Académie des Sciences
1942	Made life secretary of the Académie des Sciences
1944	Elected to the Académie Française
1946	Becomes a senior adviser on the development of atomic energy in France
1952	Awarded the Kalinga Prize
1960	On the death of his elder brother Maurice, inherits the titles of duke and prince
Mar. 19, 1987	Dies in Paris, France

Early Life
Louis-Victor-Pierre-Raymond, the seventh duc de Broglie (pronounced "duh brohg-LEE") was the second son and the youngest of five children of a noble French family. In 1740, the de Broglie family had been given the hereditary title "duc" (duke), which was held only by

the head of the family. Subsequently, one of the de Broglies had been given the title "prinz" (prince) by the Austrians, and this title was borne by all male de Broglies. His father died when Louis was fourteen years old. Louis' secondary education was at the Lycée Janson de Sailly in Paris.

Interest in Physics

Louis' elder brother, Maurice, pioneered the study of X-ray spectra and in doing so pursued his scientific interests rather than those that family tradition suggested. The family had been noted since the seventeenth century for outstanding service in the army and in politics. His brother's lead helped de Broglie to avoid the military or diplomatic career that would normally have been expected of him and encouraged his interest in physics.

In 1909, he entered the Sorbonne in Paris to study history and, in 1910, at the age of eighteen, began to study physics. His studies were interrupted during a period of compulsory military service and by World War I. De Broglie served in the Radio-Télégraphique Militaire at a station at the Eiffel Tower. He had intended to enter the diplomatic service, but he became so interested in science that he took a physics topic for his doctoral dissertation at the Sorbonne.

A Dissertation of Great Significance

In 1923, de Broglie published three papers on the nature of light quanta. In November, 1924, he was examined on his doctoral dissertation by a committee chaired by noted physicist Paul Langevin. De Broglie proposed that matter might be thought of as having both particle and wave properties. He went further than the idea of a wave-particle duality, however, and mathematically described how matter waves should behave.

This theory was to be one of the most significant advances in physics made during the 1920's. Previously, particles such as electrons had been thought to behave consistently as particles and to display no properties associated with waves. The examiners of de Broglie's dissertation liked his mathematics but did not, in general, think that associating waves with particles had any physical meaning. De Broglie

The Wave Properties of Matter

As part of his dissertation, de Broglie proposed that since light could exhibit dualism—behaving sometimes as wave and sometimes as particle—matter might also be thought of as possessing both particle and wave properties.

Albert Einstein's explanation of the photoelectric effect was that under some conditions, light could behave as particles. It has long been known, however, that to explain some properties of light—diffraction and interference—it must be thought of as a wave. De Broglie later said that his brother Maurice had emphasized to him the reality of the dual properties of particle and wave. Thus, he suggested that the quantization proposed in an ad hoc manner in Niels Bohr's theory was attributable to wave property of matter. He further suggested that when an electron is confined in an atom, its wave properties are quantized and only a select few frequencies are observed. He arrived at an expression for the wavelength associated with a given particle by constructing an analog with photons. An expression for wavelength in terms of Planck's constant, mass, and velocity was obtained.

De Broglie's theoretical leap was in asserting that wave properties apply to particles and in working out the mathematics. Einstein assumed a wave-particle duality for light in order to explain the photoelectric effect. De Broglie's work extended wave-particle duality to all material particles. His theory was later used by Erwin Schrödinger as the basis for developing wave mechanics.

Bibliography

In Search of Schrödinger's Cat: Quantum Physics and Reality. John Gribbin. New York: Bantam Books, 1984.

The Wave-Particle Dualism: A Tribute to Louis de Broglie on His Ninetieth Birthday. S. Diner et al., eds. Dordrecht, the Netherlands: D. Reidel, 1984.

Wave-Particle Duality. Franco Selleri, ed. New York: Plenum Press, 1992.

(The Nobel Foundation)

suggested that it should be possible to diffract a beam of electrons using crystal. The great significance of this idea was realized by a number of scientists, including Albert Einstein, to whom Langevin sent a copy of the dissertation.

The association of wave properties with matter was demonstrated independently in 1927 by Clinton J. Davisson and Lester Germer, working in the United States, and Sir George P. Thomson, working in England. Both groups showed that wave properties are associated with electrons, providing great experimental support for de Broglie's theory. Particles had been shown to exhibit a property characteristic of waves. De Broglie received the Nobel Prize in Physics in 1929, only five years after he had presented his theory in his doctoral dissertation. Davisson and Thomson were themselves awarded the 1937 Nobel Prize in Physics "for their experimental discovery of the diffraction of electrons by crystals."

A Theoretical Physicist

In 1928, de Broglie became a professor in the Henri Poincaré Institute, and he became a professor of theoretical physics at the Sorbonne in 1932. He wrote forty-five books on physics, including *Matière et lumière* (1937; *Matter and Light: The New Physics*, 1939), *La Physique nouvelle et les quantas* (1937; *The Revolution in Physics*, 1953), and *Physique et microphysique* (1947; *Physics and Microphysics*, 1955). Many of his writings were popular works.

Throughout his lifetime, de Broglie was concerned with philosophical issues in physics. The probabilistic interpretation of quantum mechanics, advocated by Niels Bohr and his coworkers, was generally favored and wisely adopted by physicists after 1927. De Broglie was not wholly an adherent of the probabilistic interpretation of the Copenhagen School, although he taught this interpretation for more than thirty years. After 1952, he returned to the precise causal position that he had held prior to 1927. He died in 1987 at the age of ninety-four.

Bibliography
By de Broglie
Étude critique des bases de l'interprétation actuelle de la mécanique ondulatoire, 1963 (*The Current Interpretation of Wave Mechanics: A Critical Study*, 1964)
Introduction à l'étude de la mécanique ondulatoire, 1930 (*An Introduction to the Study of Wave Mechanics*, 1930)
Matière et lumière, 1937 (*Matter and Light: The New Physics*, 1939)
La Physique nouvelle et les quantas, 1937 (*The Revolution in Physics*, 1953)
Physique et microphysique, 1947 (*Physics and Microphysics*, 1955)
La Physique quantique restera-t-elle indeterministe?: Exposé du problème, 1953

About de Broglie
The Biographical Dictionary of Scientists. Roy Porter, ed. 2d ed. New York: Oxford University Press, 1994.
Biographical Dictionary of Scientists. Trevor Williams, ed. Glasgow, Scotland: HarperCollins, 1994.
"Last of the Quantum Pioneers." John Gribbin. *New Scientist* 114, no. 1554 (1987).
Notable Twentieth-Century Scientists. Emily J. McMurray, ed. Vol. 1. New York: Gale Research, 1995.

(*Maureen H. O'Rafferty*)

Giordano Bruno

Areas of Achievement: Astronomy and cosmology

Contribution: Bruno enlarged on the ideas of Nicolaus Copernicus. Directing attention away from the earth and planets, he was among the first to conceive of the universe as being a boundless expanse populated with stars and other worlds.

1548	Born in Nola, near Naples (now in Italy)
1563	Enters the Dominican Order at Naples
1576	Accused of heresy and leaves Italy for Switzerland
1582	Publishes *De umbris idearum* (on the shadows of ideas)
1583-1585	Stays at the court of Elizabeth I of England and teaches at Oxford University
1584	Publishes *De l'infinitio universo e mondi* (*On the Infinite Universe and Worlds*, 1950)
1584	Publishes *La Cena de le Ceneri* (*The Ash Wednesday Supper*, 1975)
1585-92	Delivers public lectures in France, Germany, Austria, and Switzerland
1592	Returns to Italy and is arrested by the Roman Inquisition
1598	Imprisoned in Rome
Feb. 17, 1600	Burned as a heretic in Rome

Early Life

Giordano Bruno was born in 1548 in the town of Nola, near the large cosmopolitan city of Naples (now in Italy). At the age of fifteen, he entered the Dominican Order of priests and received a comprehensive education. He began his scholarly career as a teacher of mnemonics, systems for developing and improving memory. By 1576, Bruno was openly challenging the fundamental Catholic Church tenets of transubstantiation and of the Immaculate Conception, and he fled Italy for Switzerland. Laypeople hoped that he would reveal the Dominican secrets of memory skills, and he did not disappoint them. His work *De umbris idearum* (1582; on the shadows of ideas) explained the methods and devices used in the art of memory.

By the time that Bruno left Italy, his religious and philosophical views had already been established. He had embraced the system of belief called Neoplatonism, which emphasized the ultimate nonmaterial nature of reality, the possibility of gaining real knowledge about the world and its basic laws, and the unity, goodness, and sacredness of the universe. Bruno saw Neoplatonism as a basis for reconciling Catholics and Protestants in an era of violent religious upheaval.

Bruno pictured nature in all of its diversity descending from divine unity to matter and darkness. He rejected the geocentric and an-

(Library of Congress)

Bruno's Idea of an Unbounded Universe

Bruno conceived of stars like the sun distributed throughout an infinite universe. He further speculated that orbiting these stars were planets that could be the abodes of intelligent beings.

Bruno's astronomical ideas were extensions of his philosophy of unity. He sought to bring together Protestants and Catholics by demonstrating the harmony and unity in nature, a theme sounded throughout his two major works, *De l'infinito universo e mondi* (1584; *On the Infinite Universe and Worlds*, 1950) and *La Cena de le Ceneri* (1584; *The Ash Wednesday Supper*, 1975).

In the Ptolemaic system, there was a fundamental distinction between the earth, which was considered stationary, and the planets and stars, which were supposed to move in concentric spheres about the earth. Once the Copernican view is accepted, the earth moves and the stars do not. If the earth moves and the stars do not, Bruno reasoned, then perhaps the stellar sphere does not even exist. Bruno populated an infinite universe with an infinite number of stars, all in motion and central to their surroundings in an equivalent way. In a like manner, he proposed a framework in which the Protestant and Catholic views on the Eucharist could be seen as essentially equivalent.

In Bruno's infinite universe of stars, he envisaged each star with its own retinue of planets. He believed that these planets might be populated and pointed out that the inhabitants would think that they were at the center of the universe. He was thus among the first to show that humanity's view of the universe is purely relative.

Bruno's ideas directly challenged the prevailing theology. Other worlds and other beings could not be fit into teachings of Original Sin and of humankind as redeemed by a savior.

Bibliography

Cosmology. Edward R. Harrison. Cambridge, England: Cambridge University Press, 1981.

The Cosmology of Giordano Bruno. Paul Henri Michel. Translated by R. E. W. Maddison. Ithaca, N.Y.: Cornell University Press, 1973.

Watchers of the Stars: The Scientific Revolution. Patrick Moore. New York: G. Putnam's Sons, 1974.

thropocentric universe, believing that the earth and human individuals are ultimately accidents of a single living world-substance.

Philosophy and Astronomy

In 1583, Bruno received a royal letter of recommendation to the court of Elizabeth I of England. He moved to London and remained there until 1585, occasionally teaching at Oxford University. During his English sojourn, Bruno wrote two of his most influential works, *De l'infinito universo e mondi* (1584; *On the Infinite Universe and Worlds*, 1950) and *La Cena de le Ceneri* (1584; *The Ash Wednesday Supper*, 1975).

The first tract published his speculations concerning the possibility that the universe might be infinite in extent; the second vigorously defended the Copernican system against its critics. These works were an amalgam of science and theology. They included exhortations that warring Catholic and Protestant factions in Europe could be brought together by a better appreciation of the new scientific view of Earth's and humanity's place in the universe.

Although Bruno was not an astronomer, he was well acquainted with the major work of Nicolaus Copernicus, *De revolutionibus orbium coelestium* (1543; *On the Revolutions of the Celestial Spheres*, 1939), and he became an avid proponent of the Copernican cosmology. Bruno violently attacked Andreas Osiander, who was the author of a preface to the work of Copernicus. Osiander attempted to excuse the daring new ideas, presenting them in the form of a modest hypothesis so as not to encounter the opposition of ecclesiastical authorities.

The Structure of the Universe

Bruno, however, enlarged and expanded on the Copernican cosmology. In the Copernican scheme, the stars were all equidistant from the central sun and set on a large celestial sphere beyond the orbit of Saturn. Bruno conceived of a universe infinite in extent and populated with stars. He speculated that the stars were all like the sun. He further conjectured that each might have many planets orbiting around them, offering abodes for other races of beings.

Bruno's thinking may have been influenced by Thomas Digge's treatise *A Perfit Description of the Caelestiall Orbes* (1576), which also depicted an unbounded universe of stars. That book had passed through two editions prior to Bruno's arrival in England. In contrast to Digge's approach, Bruno arrived at his notions entirely through metaphysical speculations. The Copernican theory was seized upon and incorporated into his philosophy merely because it could be made to seemingly support his ideas on religion.

Further Travels and Trial by the Inquisition

Bruno left England in 1585 and traveled extensively throughout much of Europe, lecturing on the theological implications of astronomy and science. His public lectures included remarkable imagery that was at once poetic and scientific. For example, he discussed optics using "light" both in the physical sense and in the theological sense as divine light. He also continually challenged the philosophical and theological view of humanity as the focal point of the universe.

Bruno's peculiar blend of astronomy and philosophy led to another clash with Church authorities. Bruno maintained that Jesus Christ was not God or divine, but "merely an unusually skilled magician" and that "the Devil will be saved." When he returned to Italy in 1592, he was denounced by a former friend and arrested by the Roman Inquisition for publicly proclaiming heresies. Refusing to abjure his heresies, Giordano Bruno was sentenced to death. He was burned alive on February 17, 1600, in Rome.

Bibliography
By Bruno
Cantus Circaeus, 1582

De umbris idearum, 1582 (on the shadows of ideas)

De la causa, principio'e uno, 1583 ("Concerning the Cause, Principle, and One" in *The Infinite in Giordano Bruno*, 1950)

De l'infinitio universo e mondi, 1584 (*On the Infinite Universe and Worlds*, 1950)

La Cena de le Ceneri, 1584 (*The Ash Wednesday Supper*, 1975)

Spaccio de la bestia trionfante, 1584 (*The Expulsion of the Triumphant Beast*, 1713)

About Bruno
The Ash Wednesday Supper. Giordano Bruno. Edited and translated by Edward A. Gosselin and Lawrence S. Lerner. Hamden, Conn.: Archon Books, 1977.

Giordano Bruno and the Hermetic Tradition. Frances Yates. Chicago: University of Chicago Press, 1964.

Giordano Bruno: His Life and Thought, with Annotated Translation of His Work, "On the Infinite Universe and Worlds." Dorothea Waley Singer. New York: Abelard-Schuman, 1950.

"Giordano Bruno in England." Oliver Elton. In *Modern Studies*. London: Folcroft, 1907.

The Renaissance Drama of Knowledge: Giordano Bruno in England. Hillary Gatti. London: Routledge, 1989.

(Anthony J. Nicastro)

Comte de Buffon (Georges-Louis Leclerc)

Areas of Achievement: Science (general) and zoology

Contribution: Buffon wrote *Histoire naturelle, générale et particulière* (1749-1789), a forty-four-volume encyclopedia that represented the first comprehensive attempt in modern science to describe everything known about the natural world.

Sept. 7, 1707	Born in Montbard, France
1723-1726	Studies law
1727	Moves to Angers to study medicine, botany, and mathematics
1728-1732	Travels extensively throughout Europe
1730	Elected a member of the British Royal Society of London
1732	Returns to France after his mother's death
1734	Elected to the Académie des Sciences
1735	Translates Stephen Hales's *Vegetable Staticks* (1727)
1739	Appointed keeper of the Jardin du Roi (king's garden)
1740	Translates Sir Isaac Newton's *De methodis serierum et fluxionum* (1671)
1749	Publishes the first of forty-four volumes of *Histoire naturelle, générale et particulière*
1752	Marries Marie de Saint-Berlin-Malain
1753	Elected to the Académie Française
1773	Made a count by Louis XV
Apr. 16, 1788	Dies in Paris, France

Early Life

Georges-Louis Leclerc, known as the Comte de Buffon (pronounced "byoo-FOHN"), was born on September 7, 1707, in Montbard, France, into an aristocratic family. His father, Benjamin Leclerc, who held a position as a state official, wanted his son to follow him into government service and so encouraged him to pursue an education in the law.

The young Leclerc began his education at the College of Codrans in Dijon, a Jesuit institute, and in 1723 began to study law. In 1727, he moved to Angers, where he pursued studies in medicine and botany as well as mathematics. Participation in a duel forced him to leave Angers for Nantes. Between 1728 and 1732, LeClerc appears to have traveled extensively, visiting both England and Italy, before his mother's death caused his return to France. It was at this time that he took the name "Buffon" from the family estate.

A bust of Buffon. (Library of Congress)

The Importance of the *Histoire Naturelle*

In Histoire naturelle, générale et particulière (1749-1789), Buffon not only attempted to describe everything that was known about the natural world in the eighteenth century but also formulated theories of organic change and the geological age of the earth.

The *Histoire Naturelle*, as it is commonly known, consists of forty-four volumes divided into several distinct sections. This massive undertaking consumed almost fifty years of Buffon's life, and even then the work had to be completed by his collaborators following his death.

The first fifteen volumes appeared between 1749 and 1767. They were followed by seven volumes, including Buffon's most influential work, *Époques de la nature* (1778). Nine volumes on birds followed, then five volumes on minerals. After Buffon's death in 1788, the remaining eight volumes on reptiles, fishes, and cetaceans were issued. To maintain reader interest, Buffon interspersed philosophical essays on a variety of topics between the descriptions of plants and animals.

Buffon speculated about two topics formerly not open to discussion: the age of the earth and changes in organic species over time. He questioned directly Christian doctrine that declared the earth to be only six thousand years old and all species to be unchanged since their creation.

Buffon theorized that the planet was in fact much older and suggested that species changed in response to their environment. He also discussed the similarities between humans and other primates and proposed that humans and apes might share a common ancestor. All these ideas preceded the work of nineteenth century scientists such as Baron Georges Cuvier, Charles Darwin, Sir Charles Lyell, and Jean-Baptiste Lamarck.

Although some of his contemporaries denigrated both Buffon and the *Histoire Naturelle*, the work enjoyed tremendous popularity with the general public. Buffon's writings were widely read in France and elsewhere, and his ideas formed the nucleus for the later development of scientific specialties such as paleontology.

Bibliography

Evolution: The History of an Idea. Peter J. Bowler. Berkeley: University of California Press, 1989.

The Forerunners of Darwin: 1745-1859. B. O. Glass and W. L. Strauss, Jr. Baltimore: The Johns Hopkins University Press, 1959.

A History of Biology. C. Singer. 3d ed. London: Abeland Schuster, 1959.

Investigations in Generation: 1651-1828. E. Gasking. London: Hutchinson, 1967.

After inheriting the estate, Buffon took over its management and continued to devote time to various studies in mathematics and botany. He had always had a strong interest in mathematics and soon began his first research into the calculus of probability. To strengthen his abilities with the English language, he undertook first a translation of Stephen Hales's *Vegetable Staticks* (1727), published in 1735, and then a translation of Sir Isaac Newton's *De methodis serierum et fluxionum* (1671) as *The Method of Fluxions and Infinite Series* in 1740.

Both publications included prefaces by Buffon in which he expressed his own ideas, the first on what constituted the scientific method and the latter a discussion on the differences between Newton and the German mathematician Gottfried Wilhelm von Leibniz over the discovery of the calculus.

An Encyclopedia of Natural History

In 1739, Buffon gained the patronage of Jean-Frédéric Phélypeaux de Maurepas, who recognized that Buffon's studies of the properties of timbers in the forests of Burgundy could prove important to the French shipbuilding industry. He secured Buffon's appointment as keeper of the Jardin du Roi (the king's garden), a forerunner of the modern natural history museum and included collections of botanical, zoological, and mineral specimens. The position of keeper of the Jardin du Roi was actually that of a curator and scientist—not, as the name implies, a gardener.

Buffon's new duties included compiling a catalog of the collections, a task that evolved into the writing of *Histoire naturelle, générale et particulière* (1749-1789; *The Natural History of Animals, Vegetables, and Minerals, with the The-*

ory of the Earth in General, 1775-1776, or *Natural History, General and Particuliar*, 1781-1812), commonly known as the *Histoire Naturelle*. Working with a number of assistants and collaborators, Buffon devoted the rest of his life to writing the forty-four volumes of the *Histoire Naturelle*, a task that was not completed until after his death in 1788.

Later Life

Buffon maintained an extensive correspondence with other scientists while he was in residence at his estate in Montbard, as well as participating actively in the literary and philosophical salons of Paris on his trips to that city. The Montbard estate included a menagerie, an aviary, and a large laboratory where Buffon was able to perform scientific experiments without neglecting his family obligations. His wife died in 1769, leaving Buffon with a five-year-old son to rear alone.

Buffon's health began to deteriorate in 1785. By 1788, recognizing that the end was near, he returned to Paris for his final days. Theologians had denounced him for questioning church doctrine with his speculations in the *Histoire Naturelle* regarding the age of the earth and for suggesting that humans might be related to other primates. Nevertheless, Buffon reportedly reaffirmed his faith in God on his deathbed. He died on April 16, 1788.

In addition to his interests in natural science, he enjoyed a reputation as a mathematician; in fact, by the late twentieth century, he was better remembered for his contributions to mathematics than for his life's most consuming work, the *Histoire Naturelle*.

Bibliography
By Buffon
Histoire naturelle, générale et particulière, 1749-1789 (44 vols.; commonly known as the *Histoire Naturelle* and trans. as *The Natural History of Animals, Vegetables, and Minerals, with the Theory of the Earth in General*, 1775-1776, 6 vols., and as *Natural History, General and Particuliar*, 1781-1812, 20 vols.)

Discours sur le style, 1753

Oeuvres complètes de Buffon, 1774 (many subsequent editions, including 12 vols., 1853-1855, and 14 vols., 1884-1885)

Époques de la nature, 1778 (from vol. 20 of the *Histoire Naturelle*)

Oeuvres philosophiques de Buffon, 1954 (Jean Piveteau, ed.)

About Buffon
Buffon. Otis E. Fellows and Stephen F. Milliken. Boston: Twayne, 1972.

Evolution: The History of an Idea. Peter J. Bowler. Berkeley: University of California Press, 1989.

Forerunners of Darwin: 1745-1859. B. Glass, O. Temkin, and W. L. Strauss, eds. Baltimore: The Johns Hopkins University Press, 1959.

"The Importance of French Transformist Ideas for the Second Volume of Lyell's *Principles of Geology*." Pietro Corsi. *The British Journal for the History of Science* 11 (1978).

"The Teaching of the Physical Sciences at the End of the Eighteenth Century." F. Sherwood Taylor. *The Philosophical Magazine: Natural Philosophy Through the Eighteenth Century and Allied Topics* (1948).

(Nancy Farm Mannikko)

Luther Burbank

Areas of Achievement: Botany and genetics
Contribution: Burbank, a largely self-taught botanist and plant breeder, developed several valuable vegetable and fruit varieties. His experiments in hybridization led the way for later researchers in plant genetics.

Mar. 7, 1849	Born in Lancaster, Massachusetts
1873	Develops the Burbank potato
1875	Sells the rights to the Burbank potato and moves to California
1877	Begins a nursery business in Santa Rosa, California
1885	Buys a farm to start plant breeding and experiments with raising Japanese plums
1891	Awarded the Wilder Medal from American Pomological Society for a superior quince
1893	Develops the "pomato," a cross between a potato and a tomato
1901	Develops the Shasta daisy and is awarded a gold medal at the Pan-American Exposition for a hybrid plum-apricot
1907-1908	Develops a thornless cactus for cattle food in deserts
1914-1915	Publishes the twelve-volume set *Luther Burbank: His Methods and Discoveries and Their Practical Application*
1921	Publishes the eight-volume set *How Plants Are Trained to Work for Man*
1926	Angers religious fundamentalists by publicly supporting Darwinism
Apr. 11, 1926	Dies in Santa Rosa, California

Early Life

Luther Burbank was born in Lancaster, Massachusetts, a small farming community, in 1849. His father, Samuel, was a farmer and a maker of brick and pottery. His mother Olive, the third wife of Samuel, loved nature and evidently passed on this love to Luther.

After completing the local district school, Luther attended the Lancaster Academy, a preparatory school for Yale and Harvard. He attended the academy only during the winter; in the summers, he worked locally to help support the family. Burbank had to leave the academy after four winters when his father died and he was forced to increase his support for the family.

There is no indication that Burbank received any intensive education in the biological sciences. Nevertheless, his work on the family farm, the influence of his mother, and a thirst for reading guided his future. He was especially impressed by the writings of Charles Darwin and his views on the evolution of plants.

In 1870, Burbank bought a small farm in nearby Lunenberg, where he tested some of his ideas for producing better varieties of plants. His first success came in 1873 when he grew a new variety of potato. Planting twenty seeds from one plant, he practiced Darwin's principle of selection and discarded all but the most superior seedlings. One produced an excellent tuber that was labeled the "Burbank potato." (It is best known as the Idaho russet potato.)

Some of Burbank's siblings had moved to California, and he soon followed. Selling the rights to the new potato, in 1875 he moved to Santa Rosa, California, where he established a small nursery on four acres with an additional eight acres a few miles away for large-scale growing of plants.

Other Horticultural Successes

California has long been the leading producer of commercially grown plums and their sun-dried form, the prune. When Burbank arrived on the scene, most of the growing stock was European varieties bought from nurseries in the eastern United States. Burbank learned of plums from Japanese stock and began to grow them in his nursery and offer them for sale to commercial growers. The fruits were larger

Burbank and the Science of Genetics

Although he had no formal technical training, Burbank was possessed of a keen mind and observant eye. Despite his lack of study in the science, he instinctively applied three principles of genetics in his work—heredity, environment, and natural selection.

The principles of genetics were formulated by the Austrian monk Gregor Mendel from 1857 to 1865, lost in an obscure journal, and then brought to light again in 1900. Burbank evidently was not aware of Mendel's work.

In the case of the Burbank potato, he recognized that the qualities of the vegetable were contained in elements in the seeds. These qualities were heritable traits—that is, they could be passed on from one generation to the next. When the planted seeds sprouted, Burbank practiced selection—artificial, not natural, selection—by discarding those plants that he deemed unfavorable.

Burbank manipulated heredity by crossbreeding certain plants, for example, the Shasta daisy project. He knew that the heritable factors were in the male pollen and the female eggs (or ova). Through application of the pollen from closely related plants with desirable traits to fertilize the ova of similar desirable plants, the resulting offspring often showed the characteristics for which Burbank was looking. Selection again was employed when he destroyed the crosses that he considered failures.

One of the basic principles of genetics is that the heritable traits interact with the environment to produce offspring with varying characteristics. Burbank utilized this principle when he planted Japanese plums in California in order to produce the very successful Santa Clara plum. (Conceivably, the cross could have worked in opposite fashion to result in a valueless fruit.)

Mendelian genetics also demonstrates that the desirable traits obtained by crossbreeding or hybridization often are not passed on beyond the second generation. Burbank was able to circumvent this rule by grafting twigs (scions) of favorable plants obtained by crossbreeding onto the stock of trees that had produced little fruit. The flourishing grafted material produced high-quality fruit regardless of the less-than-desirable stock.

Farmers had been utilizing the principles of heredity and selection from the origin of agriculture for ten thousand years ago. The development of new varieties of plants and animals did not have to await the discovery of the science of genetics. Burbank's creative powers were practical rather than theoretical. His work was carried out while the science was still in its infancy. He demonstrated that patience and a discerning eye could contribute to major technological advancements.

Bibliography

"Evolutionary Genetics of Plant-Pathogen Systems." *BioScience* 46 (February, 1996).

Genetics and Evolution: The Molecules of Inheritance. Jill Bailey. New York: Oxford University Press, 1995.

"Mendel's Laws." Ricki Lewis. In *Life.* Dubuque, Iowa: Wm C. Brown, 1992.

"130-Year-Old Pollination Mystery Solved." *Science News* 145 (February, 1984).

and red, rather than the blue or purple of European varieties.

Burbank again painstakingly selected only those trees that produced the very best fruits. His methodology was based more on ecology than biology—that is, he experimented with growing plants in new, perhaps more favorable environments. Those that succeeded, he kept; the others were discarded. Growers eagerly bought Burbank's superior plum trees. Later, he introduced a yellow-fleshed Japanese plum, which he marketed under his own name.

Burbank also was successful in the production of ornamental plants. His special pride was the Shasta daisy, which he developed following tried-and-true crossbreeding. He made multiple crossings between a common American daisy and a European daisy, using pollen from one plant to fertilize the flowers of another. The resulting hybrids were then crossed with a Japanese species. The outcome was a daisy with large, white, and exceptionally attractive blossoms.

In contrast to the painstaking work in producing the Shasta daisy, Burbank's discovery of the fragrant calla lily was the result of his powers of observation. The aromatic lily was a natural mutation, or "sport," which he noticed in a block of calla seedlings. He recognized the mutant's value, discarded the rest of the block, and carefully nurtured the new variety, which he named "Fragrance."

Not all of Burbank's creations were successes. He crossed the potato with a tomato (both are members of the same plant family). Customers, however, although marveling at the hybrid vegetable, quickly discovered that the "pomato" was neither a satisfactory potato nor a satisfactory tomato.

The Plant Wizard

Some people suspected Burbank of practicing wizardry and dabbling in the occult. All that he needed to do, they said, was wave his hand over a plant and it was transformed into a new and wonderful form. The truth is that Burbank was neither wizard nor scientist. He loved nature and working with plants. He also possessed the ability to recognize small details that could be used to advantage in plant breeding.

He sought out plants from foreign countries (exotics) that could be used for hybridization. He also established some exotics in new environments to determine if unique, improved strains might result. He was alert to mutations possibly resulting in higher yields, larger blossoms, improved flavor, or some other worthwhile characteristic. Above all, he was blessed with the patience that is required in working with plants and other living things.

Burbank died in Santa Rosa in 1926.

Bibliography
By Burbank
The Training of the Human Plant, 1906
Luther Burbank: His Methods and Discoveries and Their Practical Application, 1914-1915 (12 vols.)

(Library of Congress)

How Plants Are Trained to Work for Man, 1921 (8 vols.)
Harvest of the Years, 1927 (with Wilbur Hall)
Partner of Nature, 1939 (Wilbur Hall, ed.)

About Burbank
"Burbank's Legacy: Unfinished Experiments Languish on What's Left of Goldridge Farm." Jeff Cox and Robert Hornback. *Organic Gardening* 34 (September, 1987).
A Gardener Touched with Genius: The Life of Luther Burbank. Peter Dreyer. New York: Coward, McCann & Geoghegan, 1975.
Luther Burbank: Man, Methods, and Achievements, an Appreciation. E. J. Wickson. San Francisco: Southern Pacific, 1902.

(Albert C. Jensen)

Margaret Burbidge

Areas of Achievement: Astronomy and physics

Contribution: Burbidge increased astronomers' understanding of the synthesis of elements within stars, the rotation of galaxies, and the nature of quasars.

Aug. 12, 1919	Born in Davenport, England
1943	Earns a Ph.D. in astronomy from the University of London
1948-1951	Works at the University of London Observatory
1951-1953	Receives a fellowship to Yerkes Observatory
1955-1957	Receives a fellowship to the California Institute of Technology
1957-1959	Receives a Shirley Farr Fellowship to Yerkes Observatory
1959	Shares the Warner Prize with Geoffrey Burbidge
1959-1962	Works as an associate professor at Yerkes Observatory
1964	Teaches at the University of California, San Diego (UCSD)
1964	Elected a Fellow of the Royal Society of London
1976-1978	Serves as president of the American Astronomical Society
1978	Elected to the National Academy of Sciences
1979-1988	Directs the Center for Astrophysics and Space Science at UCSD
1982	Receives the Catherine Wolfe Bruce Medal
1984	Receives the National Medal of Science
1988	Receives the Albert Einstein Medal

Early Life

Margaret Burbidge was born Eleanor Margaret Peachey in Davenport, England, on August 12, 1919. Her parents were Stanley John Peachey, a chemistry teacher at the Manchester School of Technology, and Marjorie Stott Peachey, a chemistry student at the school. In 1921, the family moved to London, where her father set up a laboratory to work on the chemistry of rubber. Burbidge was encouraged to study science from an early age and became interested in astronomy as a child.

She received a bachelor's degree with first-class honors from the University of London in 1939. During World War II, Burbidge was able to continue her studies while most of her male colleagues served in the military. She was awarded a Ph.D. for her study of astrophysics in 1943. In 1948, she married fellow astronomer Geoffrey Burbidge.

From 1948 to 1950, Margaret Burbidge worked as the assistant director of the University of London Observatory. From 1950 to 1951, she was the acting director. During this period, she was also the editor of *Observatory* magazine.

Fellowships in the United States

In 1951, Burbidge received a fellowship from the International Astronomical Union to work at Yerkes Observatory. This observatory, located in Williams Bay, Wisconsin, and owned and operated by the Department of Astronomy and Astrophysics at the University of Chicago, contained the largest refracting telescope ever built. In 1953, Burbidge returned to the United Kingdom.

A fellowship to the California Institute of Technology (Caltech), located in Pasadena, California, brought Burbidge back to the United States in 1955. In 1957, she was awarded a Shirley Farr Fellowship and returned to Yerkes Observatory. In 1959, she was made an associate professor at the observatory.

Nucleosynthesis, Galaxies, and Quasars

During the 1950's, Burbidge and her husband worked with the British astronomer Fred Hoyle and the American physicist William A. Fowler studying the evolution of stars. They studied the elements present within stars and concluded that these elements must have been created within the stars themselves. This process, known as nucleosynthesis, explains the existence of heavier elements in the universe. For their work, the Burbidges shared the Warner Prize, given by the American Astronomical Society, in 1959.

During the late 1950's and early 1960's, Burbidge studied the rotation of galaxies. The speed at which a galaxy spins reveals how much matter it contains and how that matter is distributed within the galaxy. Her pioneering work in this field would later lead American astronomer Vera Rubin to develop the concept of dark matter (invisible mass, in contrast to the bright objects astronomers usually study) to explain the way in which galaxies rotate.

In the late 1960's, Burbidge turned her attention to the recently discovered objects known as quasars. Quasars, also known as quasi-stellar objects, posed a mystery for astronomers. They seem to be extremely distant and yet ex-

Nucleosynthesis

Nucleosynthesis is the process within stars by which light elements such as hydrogen and helium are transformed into heavier elements such as carbon, oxygen, and iron. Burbidge's analysis of nucleosynthesis explains why the chemical elements present in the universe occur in the amounts that they do.

Astronomers can determine which chemical elements are present within stars by using spectroscopy. Spectroscopy is a process in which the light emitted by a star is first separated into its various colors. These colors are then compared with the colors produced by known samples of heated elements. In this way, astronomers can determine which elements are present in the star, and the brightness of the colors reveals how much of the element is present compared to all the other elements within the star.

Spectroscopy indicated to Burbidge a pattern of stellar evolution in which older stars contain more heavy elements than younger stars. This finding led her and her coworkers to conclude that heavy elements are created from lighter elements within stars as they age.

Most newly formed stars are composed almost entirely of hydrogen. In groups of four, these hydrogen atoms fuse to form helium atoms, releasing energy. Earth's sun undergoes this type of nuclear fusion to produce heat and light. As the star ages, the helium atoms fuse to form heavier elements such as carbon and oxygen. Then, the carbon and oxygen atoms combine to form such elements as magnesium, sodium, silicon, and sulfur. As the star grows older, complicated reactions among all these elements result in the production of even heavier elements, such as iron.

Nucleosynthesis within the star ends when the iron stage is reached. Elements that are slightly heavier than iron, such as nickel and cobalt, may be formed during this stage, but elements that are much heavier than iron cannot be obtained by this process because they are broken down by the star's heat as quickly as they are formed.

Elements that are considerably heavier than iron can be formed by a supernova explosion. A supernova occurs when a star several times larger than Earth's sun has reached the end of the iron stage. The star explodes, releasing the elements within it, as well as free neutrons. Elements heavier than iron are produced when lighter elements capture the free neutrons and stabilize.

An important consequence of a supernova explosion is the widespread distribution of elements heavier than iron throughout space. These elements may then come together with the more common lighter elements to form new stars. Earth's sun is considered to be an example of this type of star, and the existence of the solar system, with planets partly composed of elements heavier than iron, is explained by this theory of stellar evolution.

Bibliography

Principles of Stellar Evolution and Nucleosynthesis. Donald D. Clayton. New York: McGraw-Hill, 1968.

Stellar Evolution. Amos Harpaz. Wellesley, Mass.: A. K. Peters, 1994.

Stellar Interiors: Physical Principles, Structure, and Evolution. Carl J. Hansen. New York: Springer-Verlag, 1994.

(Archive Photos/Camera Press)

From 1976 to 1978, Burbidge served as the president of the American Astronomical Society. She also became a citizen of the United States at that time. In 1978, she was elected to the National Academy of Sciences.

Burbidge served as the director of the UCSD Center for Astrophysics and Space Science from 1979 to 1988. She was promoted to university professor in 1984 and professor emeritus in 1990.

Major awards presented to Burbidge during this time included the Catherine Wolfe Bruce Medal from the Astronomical Society of the Pacific in 1982, the National Medal of Science from President Ronald Reagan in 1984, and the Albert Einstein Medal from the World Cultural Council in 1988. She was also honored by being selected to serve on scientific committees involved in designing the Hubble Space Telescope, an orbiting observatory launched in 1990.

Bibliography

By Burbidge

"Synthesis of the Elements in Stars," *Review of Modern Physics*, 1957 (with Geoffrey Burbidge, William A. Fowler, and Fred Hoyle)

"The Life-Story of a Galaxy" in *Stars and Galaxies: Birth, Ageing, and Death in the Universe*, 1962 (Thornton Page, ed.)

Quasi-Stellar Objects, 1967 (with Geoffrey Burbidge)

About Burbidge

The Biographical Dictionary of Scientists: Astronomers. David Abbott. New York: Peter Bedrick Books, 1984.

The Continuum Dictionary of Women's Biography. Jennifer S. Uglow, ed. New York: Continuum, 1989.

Who's Who of American Women 1995-1996. Christina F. Moxley, ed. New Providence, N.J.: Marquis, 1995.

(Rose Secrest)

tremely bright. Either the methods used to measure astronomical distances were seriously flawed, or quasars rely on a source of energy far more powerful than anything previously known. Burbidge's careful measurements of quasars led astronomers to conclude that they are, indeed, very far away. Later, it was believed that they are distant galaxies with vast black holes at their centers releasing enormous amounts of energy.

Honors and Awards

In 1964, Burbidge began her career as a full professor in the Department of Astronomy at the University of California, San Diego (UCSD). The same year, she was elected a Fellow of the Royal Society of London. In 1968, the American Academy of Arts and Sciences also elected her a Fellow.

Jean Buridan

Areas of Achievement: Physics and science (general)
Contribution: Buridan was an important figure in the transition from the Aristotelean view of physics to the modern one. He advocated the interesting but erroneous impetus theory of moving objects.

c. 1295	Born in Béthune, France
c. 1314	Attends the University of Paris
c. 1320	Earns a master's of arts degree
1328	Appointed rector of the University of Paris
1340	Reappointed rector of the University of Paris
1345	Sent to Rome to defend the interests of the university
c. 1358	Dies in Paris, probably of the plague

Early Life

As with many individuals from the Middle Ages, little is known about the early life of Jean Buridan (pronounced "byoo-ree-DAHN"), not even his birth year. It is known that he was born in Béthune, France, toward the end of the thirteenth century and that he came to the University of Paris for his education. There, he studied the medieval curriculum, which included an emphasis on the works of Aristotle. It was only when he was appointed rector of the University of Paris in 1328 that there was any official documentation of his life.

The University of Paris

Buridan had a long and distinguished association with the University of Paris. Sometime in the second decade of the fourteenth century, he studied at the university under the famous English Scholastic philosopher William of Ockham, whose insights and methods had a profound impact on Buridan.

Upon the completion of his degree, Buridan remained at the University of Paris for the rest of his life—teaching, writing, and serving as rector. He became an influential member of the faculty and wrote commentaries on the works

Impetus Theory of Motion

Before Sir Isaac Newton's genius could revolutionize physics, Aristotle's theory of motion had to be discredited. One important step in the transition from Aristotle to Newton was supplied by Buridan and his impetus theory of motion, introduced to solve a problem faced by Aristotle's account of moving objects.

For Aristotle, terrestrial objects move not because of some external force acting on them (as Newton would say) but because of some internal principle intimately tied to the object's nature. He claimed that an object's natural state is rest (again contrary to Newton). If his theory were right, a thrown object should fall immediately to the ground once it has left the hand.

Buridan explains that the thrown object is impelled forward by the hand; that is, the object is given an impetus to continue the motion started by the hand. This impetus may be great or small and may be diminished by gravity and air resistance, but it comes from outside the object and is measurable. Buridan defined this impetus as the quantity of matter multiplied by its velocity, a definition that anticipates Newton's definition of momentum.

Buridan's insistence on an external source and the measurability of impetus gives his theory a modern flavor and makes it one of the primary steps on the road to the Newtonian understanding of motion.

Bibliography
"Ockham, Buridan, and Nicholas of Autrecourt." E. A. Moody. *Franciscan Studies* (June, 1947).
The Origins of Modern Science. H. Butterfield. New York: Macmillan, 1951.
The Science of Mechanics in the Middle Ages. Marshall Claggett. Madison: University of Wisconsin Press, 1959.

of Aristotle and textbooks that were still used as late as the seventeenth century. His main areas of expertise were moral and natural philosophy.

Commentaries on Aristotle

As was the custom for faculty at medieval scholastic universities, Jean Buridan published commentaries on and questions about the works of Aristotle, sometimes under his Latin name Joannes Buridanus. He is particularly noted for his commentaries on Aristotle's works that have to do with physics, which at that time was called "natural philosophy."

Two of Buridan's commentaries and questions stand out: those on the heavens and those on physics. In them, one finds the formulation of his impetus theory of motion, a theory that can best be seen as an intermediary between those of Aristotle and Sir Isaac Newton. Buridan offers an explanation of motion that overcomes objections raised against Aristotle's account of this subject.

"Buridan's Ass"

In the area of moral philosophy, Buridan was also concerned with motion, but it was of a different sort. He explored the relationship between will and reason and how this relationship leads to action. According to his theory, will can delay the actions of reason until further information is obtained.

Painter E. Tapissier depicts the dilemma of L'Ane de Buridan *(Buridan's ass).* (Roger-Viollet)

This situation presents a problem that has become known as "Buridan's ass," a parable demonstrating the consequence of his philosophical view that is ascribed to Buridan but not actually found in his writings. The story describes an ass (donkey) placed at a point equidistant between two bales of hay of equal size. Because it has no good reason to prefer one bale to the other, the animal is paralyzed by indecision and starves to death.

Later philosophers dismissed Buridan's theory, noting that negative consequences can impel the will to act even when reason cannot determine the best course of action.

Later Life

Just as not much is known about Buridan's birth, little is known about his death. It has been determined that he died around 1358 in Paris. There was a plague in Europe at that time, and it is generally surmised that he was a victim of it. His works were published many years later and had a great impact on the concept of modern mechanics.

Bibliography

By Buridan

Quaestiones in aristotelis ethica nicomachea, 1489

Sophismata, 1489 (*Sophisms on Meaning and Truth*, 1966)

Consequentiae, 1493 (*A Tract on Consequences Attributed to Buridan*, 1955)

Compendium totium logicae, 1499

Quaestiones super octo phisicorum libros aristotelis, 1509

Quaestiones super libris quattuor de caelo et mundo, 1509

About Buridan

The Encyclopedia of Philosophy. Paul Edwards, ed. New York: Free Press, 1967.

A History of Philosophy. Frederick Copleston. Vol. 4. Garden City, N.Y.: Doubleday, 1990.

Medieval and Early Modern Science. A. C. Crombie. Garden City, N.Y.: Doubleday, 1959.

(John H. Serembus)

Sir Frank Macfarlane Burnet

Areas of Achievement: Bacteriology, genetics, immunology, and virology

Contribution: Burnet, an accomplished virologist and theoretical immunologist, was best known for his work on the influenza virus and his theories on acquired immunological tolerance and clonal selection of antibody formation.

Sept. 3, 1899	Born in Traralgon, Victoria, Australia
1924	Earns an M.D. from the University of Melbourne
1928	Earns a Ph.D. from the University of London
1928-1931	Works as a bacteriologist at the Walter and Eliza Hall Institute
1932-1933	Works as a virologist at the National Institute of Medical Research in London
1934-1965	Serves as assistant director and then director of the Walter and Eliza Hall Institute
1949	Proposes the theory of acquired immunological tolerance
1951	Knighted
1957	Proposes the clonal selection theory of antibody production
1960	Awarded the Nobel Prize in Physiology or Medicine
1961	Named "Australian of the Year"
1965-1978	Serves as president of the Australian Academy of Science
Aug. 31, 1985	Dies in Melbourne, Victoria, Australia

(The Nobel Foundation)

Early Life

Frank Macfarlane Burnet was born in 1899 in the town of Traralgon, located in eastern Victoria, Australia. He lived there with his parents and six brothers and sisters until the age of ten, when his family moved to Terang in western Victoria.

As a child, Burnet was interested in nature and loved to spend time outdoors hiking and camping. He participated in Boy Scouts and developed a lifelong passion for collecting and studying beetles.

Burnet majored in biology and medicine at Geelong College in Victoria and then continued his education at Ormond College of the University of Melbourne, where he obtained a B.S. in 1922 and an M.D. in 1924.

Early Scientific Career

Burnet completed a medical residency in pathology at the Royal Melbourne Hospital and, in 1926, received a Beit Research Fellowship to the Lister Institute of Preventative Medicine in London, where he studied bacteriophages (viruses that infect bacteria). Based on his work at the Lister Institute, he was granted a Ph.D. degree from the University of London in 1928.

He then worked for several years as a bacteriologist at the Walter and Eliza Hall Institute in Melbourne, Australia, where he continued his work on bacteriophages and made many significant contributions to this field. In particular, he devised a classification system for bacteriophages and elucidated mechanisms by which these viruses replicate within bacterial cells.

In 1932, Burnet accepted a position at the National Institute of Medical Research in London, and his research interests changed from bacterial viruses to animal viruses, a topic that would dominate his scientific career for the next twenty-five years.

Animal Virology

Burnet returned to Australia in 1934 and worked at the Walter and Eliza Hall Institute until 1965, first in the position of assistant director in charge of the virus section and then as director.

After being named director, Burnet decided that all the research programs at the institute should be focused on animal virology, and, in time, the Walter and Eliza Hall Institute became a world-renowned center for virology research, attracting eminent scientists from Europe and America. Gaining the respect of the scientific community abroad was very important to Burnet, as he was fiercely patriotic. He had previously turned down positions at such prestigious locations as Harvard University in order to develop a world-class facility in Australia.

Burnet studied and published papers on a variety of viral diseases such as polio, Q fever, herpes simplex, psittacosis, and influenza. Among his numerous accomplishments were identification of the causative agent of Q fever and development of a method, using chicken embryos, for growing and enumerating viruses. He showed that more than one strain of polio virus exists and that new strains of influenza virus arise through genetic mutation. He also pioneered efforts to develop effective vaccines against the more potent strains of influenza.

Immunology

In 1957, Burnet's research interests changed again, this time to immunology (the study of the immune system). As an immunologist, his contributions were more theoretical than experimental, although he maintained an active research program.

Burnet had long been interested in understanding how the immune system defends against infectious or toxic agents (antigens) and, in particular, how it distinguishes between normal body components ("self") and potentially harmful foreign substances ("nonself"). Based on a variety of experimental observations, he proposed the concept of acquired immunological tolerance as an explanation of self-versus-nonself immunological recognition. He shared the 1960 Nobel Prize in Physiology or Medicine with Sir Peter Medawar for this theory.

The Clonal Selection Theory of Antibody Production

Every animal has a diverse array of lymphocytes, each with cell surface receptors specific for one antigen. When an antigen enters the body, it binds to the appropriate lymphocyte and triggers a clonal expansion of the selected lymphocyte.

Lymphocytes are cells that defend the body against harmful foreign substances (antigens), such as disease-causing microorganisms or toxins. B lymphocytes synthesize chemicals called antibodies that bind to and promote the destruction, neutralization, or elimination of antigens.

Any given antibody is specific for only one antigen, meaning that it will bind only to the antigen that stimulated its production. The immune system is capable of producing antibodies against virtually any foreign antigen that may be introduced into the body, even artificial substances that an individual would not normally encounter. With so many possibilities, how does the immune system know which antibody to produce in response to a given antigen?

Prior to 1955, scientists believed that antibody molecules were produced as generic proteins, all with the same structure initially but capable of being modified to react specifically with an antigen. Upon exposure to an antigen, the antibody would fold around the antigen to assume its final chemical structure. This theory, proposed by Linus Pauling in 1940, was known as the instructive or template theory.

In 1955, Niels K. Jerne postulated a selective theory of antibody production, which stated that every animal has a preexisting bank of circulating antibodies, each capable of binding to a different antigen. When an antigen enters the body, it binds to (selects) the appropriate antibody, which then signals lymphocytes to produce large quantities of antibodies with the same structural specificity. Then, in 1957, David Talmadge suggested that the antigen must also somehow trigger the multiplication of the cells responsible for making the matching antibody.

Burnet's clonal selection theory united the concepts of Jerne and Talmadge. According to Burnet, each individual possesses a diverse array of lymphocytes, each capable of producing a specific type of antibody and each carrying, on its cell surface, receptors with the same antigen specificity as the antibody that they are destined to produce. The antigen "selects" a lymphocyte bearing the appropriate receptor and binds to this receptor in a lock-and-key type of interaction. This stimulates the lymphocyte to proliferate (divide many times) and give rise to a large population of genetically identical daughter cells (clones), all of which synthesize and release antibodies specific for the original antigen.

The clonal selection theory is now universally accepted as an explanation of not only B lymphocyte but also T lymphocyte function. T lymphocytes also exhibit antigen specificity and clonal expansion, but, instead of producing antibodies, they destroy infected cells or tumor cells through direct, cell-to-cell contact.

Bibliography

"The Clonal Selection Theory." Gordon L. Ada and Sir Gustav Nossal. *Scientific American* 257 (August, 1987).

Essential Immunology. Ivan Roitt. London: Blackwell Scientific Publications, 1991.

Immunology: A Short Course. Eli Benjamini and Sidney Leskowitz. New York: Wiley-Liss, 1991.

He also proposed the clonal selection theory of antibody production, which he considered to be the most important accomplishment of his scientific career. This theory provides an explanation for the ability of the immune system to recognize and react against a limitless array of foreign antigens.

Retirement

In 1965, Burnet left the Walter and Eliza Hall Institute and retired from active research. He continued to write books and papers, ranging in scope from highly technical reviews of his research in virology and immunology to nontechnical books on cancer, aging, and human biology. He also served as president of the Australian Academy of Sciences until 1978. He died of cancer at the age of eighty-five in Melbourne, Australia.

Bibliography

By Burnet

Biological Aspects of Infectious Disease, 1940 (also as *The Natural History of Infectious Disease*, 1953)

The Production of Antibodies: A Review and Theoretical Discussion, 1941 (with M. Freeman, A. V. Jackson, and D. Lush)

Influenza: A Survey of the Last Fifty Years in the Light of Modern Work on the Virus of Epidemic Influenza, 1942

Virus as Organism: Evolutionary and Ecological Aspects of Some Human Virus Diseases, 1945

The Background of Infectious Diseases in Man, 1946

Viruses and Man, 1953

Principles of Animal Virology, 1955

Enzyme, Antigen, and Virus: A Study of Macromolecular Pattern in Action, 1956

The Clonal Selection Theory of Acquired Immunity, 1959

The Integrity of the Body: A Discussion of Modern Immunological Ideas, 1962

Autoimmune Diseases: Pathogenesis, Chemistry, and Therapy, 1963 (with I. R. MacKay)

Ciba Foundation Symposium: The Thymus, Experimental and Clinical Studies, 1965

Biology and the Appreciation of Life, 1966

Changing Patterns: An Atypical Autobiography, 1968

Immunological Surveillance, 1969

Self and Not-Self, 1969

Dominant Mammal: The Biology of Human Destiny, 1970

Genes, Dreams, and Realities, 1971

Walter and Eliza Hall Institute, 1915-1965, 1971

Auto-immunity and Auto-immune Disease: A Survey for Physician or Biologist, 1972

Intrinsic Mutagenesis: A Genetic Approach to Ageing, 1974

Biology of Ageing, 1974

Immunology, 1976

Immunology, Aging, and Cancer: Medical Aspects of Mutation and Selection, 1976

Uranium: For Good or Evil?, 1976

Endurance of Life: The Implications of Genetics for Human Life, 1978

Credo and Comment: A Scientist Reflects, 1979

Biological Foundations and Human Nature, 1983

About Burnet

The Nobel Prize Winners: Physiology or Medicine, edited by Frank N. Magill. Pasadena, Calif.: Salem Press, 1991.

The Seeds of Time: The Life of Sir Macfarlane Burnet. Christopher Sexton. Oxford, England: Oxford University Press, 1991.

(Darbie L. Maccubbin)

Melvin Calvin

Areas of Achievement: Botany, cell biology, and chemistry

Contribution: Calvin elucidated the path of carbon in photosynthesis, the biochemical process on which all life depends. For this work, he was awarded the 1961 Nobel Prize in Chemistry.

Apr. 8, 1911	Born in St. Paul, Minnesota
1931	Receives a bachelor of science degree from the Michigan College of Mining and Technology
1935	Earns a Ph.D. in chemistry from the University of Minnesota
1935-1937	Conducts research at the University of Manchester, England
1937	Appointed an instructor at the University of California, Berkeley (UCB)
1947	Promoted to full professor at UCB
1954	Elected to the National Academy of Sciences
1961	Wins the Nobel Prize in Chemistry
1963-1965	Appointed a member of the Presidential Science Advisory Committee
1967	Awarded a Guggenheim Fellowship
1967	Appointed associate director of the Lawrence Berkeley Laboratory
1972	Receives the Priestley Medal
1981	Awarded the National Medal of Science
1985	Named the first recipient of the Melvin Calvin Medal of Distinction, Michigan Technical College

Calvin with some of his molecular models. (The Nobel Foundation)

Early Life

Melvin Calvin was born in 1911 in St. Paul, Minnesota, the son of Russian immigrant parents. He was graduated with a bachelor of science degree from the Michigan College of Mining and Technology in 1931. Calvin then pursued his interests in organic molecular structure and the behavior of molecules at the University of Minnesota, where he earned his Ph.D. in chemistry in 1935.

For the next two years, he conducted research as a Fellow at the University of Manchester in England. During that time, he first developed an interest in exploring the mechanisms of photosynthesis, the process by which plants convert carbon dioxide and water to sugar in the presence of sunlight.

Upon his return from England, Calvin was appointed instructor at the University of California, Berkeley (UCB), where he stayed for the majority of his professional career, being promoted through the ranks to full professor. The

The Conversion of Carbon Dioxide to Sugar in Photosynthesis

Carbon atoms from atmospheric carbon dioxide are used to generate sugar molecules during the stage of photosynthesis called the dark reactions or the Calvin cycle.

Calvin used radioactively labeled carbon and biochemical separation processes called chromatography to determine experimentally the steps in the biochemical pathways that lead to the production of sugar in plants during photosynthesis. In the light reactions, light energy is harvested by plants. In the dark reactions, so called because they do not require light, the light energy is combined with carbon from atmospheric carbon dioxide to produce sugar. Calvin elucidated the steps in this biochemical cycle, which bears his name.

Calvin determined that three molecules of carbon dioxide entering the cycle are attached to three molecules of a five-carbon sugar called ribulose bisphosphate. Through a series of biochemical reactions that utilize the energy harvested during the light reactions, the three molecules of ribulose bisphosphate are converted into six molecules of the three-carbon sugar glyceraldehyde phosphate. One molecule of glyceraldehyde phosphate leaves the cycle, and the remaining five molecules are converted back into three molecules of ribulose bisphosphate. The cycle then begins again.

Two molecules of glyceraldehyde phosphate combine to form one molecule of the sugar glucose, the primary product of photosynthesis. Plants require both the light and the dark reactions in order to produce glucose.

All life on Earth is ultimately dependent on photosynthesis for survival. Knowledge of the biochemistry of this fundamental process has had a far-reaching impact on botany, agriculture, and environmental studies.

Bibliography

"The Control of Photosynthetic Carbon Metabolism." J. A. Bassham. *Science* 172 (1971).

"How Plants Make Oxygen." Govindjee and W. J. Coleman. *Scientific American* (February, 1990).

"Plant Life in a CO_2-Rich World." F. A. Bazzazz and E. D. Fajer. *Scientific American* (January, 1992).

---

one exception to that appointment was a few years during World War II in which he conducted work on the atomic bomb.

Photosynthesis

Until 1945, work on photosynthesis was quite difficult because no methods existed for following the pathways of the chemicals involved in this process. New and sensitive methods developed at this time, including radioisotopic labeling and chromatography, eased the way for Calvin to elucidate the role of carbon dioxide in photosynthesis. Radioisotopic labeling permitted the tagging of carbon dioxide, which then could be tracked during photosynthesis, and chromatography facilitated the separation and identification of chemical compounds.

Calvin was able to obtain a ready supply of radioactively labeled carbon 14 to conduct his first experiments at the Lawrence Radiation Laboratory of UCB in 1948. In the experiments, algae or green leaves were allowed to absorb radioactive carbon dioxide for a few seconds. Analyses were then performed to identify the fate of the radioactively tagged carbon in the products of photosynthesis. Having used radioactive phosphorous in other studies of photosynthesis, Calvin and his team knew that the carbon must combine with a phosphorous-containing compound. Testing proved that the molecule that accepted the carbon was phosphoglyceric acid.

A Cyclical Process

The results of the radioactive labeling experiments suggested that the "fixation" of carbon from carbon dioxide in the atmosphere into organic molecules in plants occurs in a cyclical fashion. An initial hypothesis about the specifics turned out to be incorrect, but further experimentation proved that the process is indeed a cycle.

This important stage of photosynthesis is when the light energy gathered from the sun during earlier chemical reactions combines with the carbon from carbon dioxide to form sugar. Because light is not necessary for this stage of photosynthesis to occur, these processes are known as the dark reactions of photosynthesis. To honor its discoverer, the process is commonly referred to as the Calvin cycle. As a result of his prodigious achievement of elucidating the fundamental process that supports life, Calvin was awarded the Nobel Prize in Chemistry in 1961.

Calvin's later work involved the production of synthetic catalysts, which could permit the construction of an apparatus that would use

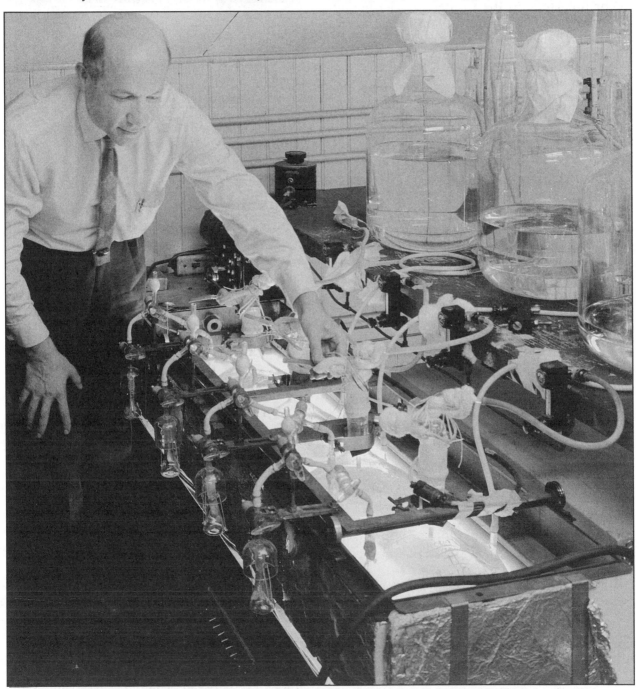

Calvin with an apparatus that he used to study photosynthesis. (Lawrence Berkeley National Laboratory)

light energy to produce oxygen from water and to convert carbon dioxide into a more usable form.

Legacy

Calvin's elucidation of the steps of carbon fixation into sugar during photosynthesis was a major milestone in the history of science and the understanding of how plants make food. Ultimately, all life on Earth is dependent on plants for food; even carnivores consume organisms that are ultimately dependent on plants in the food chain. Discovering the chemical details of the process opened the gates for further studies in plant productivity and the processes without which no life on Earth could exist.

Bibliography

By Calvin

The Theory of Organic Chemistry: An Advanced Course, 1941 (with Gerald E. K. Branch)

Isotopic Carbon: Techniques in Its Measurement and Chemical Manipulation, 1949

The Path of Carbon in Photosynthesis, 1949 (with J. A. Bassham)

Chemistry of the Metal Chelate Compounds, 1952 (with Arthur E. Martel)

The Photosynthesis of Carbon Compounds, 1962 (with Bassham)

Chemical Evolution: Molecular Evolution Towards the Origin of Living Systems on the Earth and Elsewhere, 1969

Following the Trail of Light: A Scientific Odyssey, 1992

About Calvin

How Did We Find Out About Photosynthesis? Isaac Asimov. New York: Walker, 1989.

"Melvin Calvin." In *The Nobel Prize Winners: Chemistry*, edited by Frank N. Magill. Pasadena, Calif.: Salem Press, 1990.

(*Karen E. Kalumuck*)

Annie Jump Cannon

Area of Achievement: Astronomy
Contribution: Cannon, a pioneer in stellar spectroscopy, developed a method of classifying stellar spectra.

Dec. 11, 1863	Born in Dover, Delaware
1884	Graduated from Wellesley College
1893	Returns to Wellesley to work for Professor Sarah Whiting
1895	Enrolls as a special student at Radcliffe College
1896	Hired by Edward Pickering to work for the Harvard College Observatory
1907	Earns an M.A. degree from Wellesley
1911	Becomes the curator of astronomical photographs at Harvard College Observatory
1918	Appointed an honorary member of the American Association of Variable Star Observers
1918-1924	Publishes "The Henry Draper Catalog"
1922	Discovers a nova while working in South America
1925	Awarded an honorary doctorate from Oxford University
1931	Elected an honorary member of the Royal Astronomical Society
1931	Given the Henry Draper Gold Medal by the National Academy of Sciences
1932	Awarded the Ellen Richards Research Prize
1938	Named William Cranch Bond Professor of Astronomy at Harvard
Apr. 13, 1941	Dies in Cambridge, Massachusetts

Spectral Classification of Stars

Stars may be categorized by analysis of their spectra. Cannon revised the way in which stellar spectral types are organized and categorized.

A careful analysis of light coming from stars indicates that certain wavelengths, known as spectral lines, are diminished in intensity. The study of these spectral lines is called spectroscopy. Many stars have similar spectra, and thus the idea arose to categorize stars based on this characteristic, a process known as spectral classification.

In an early spectral classification system at Harvard University, a letter of the alphabet was assigned to a star based on the spectral lines of hydrogen observed in that star's light. Cannon revised this system by limiting the letters used to only a few major categories. She then rearranged the letters in order of stellar temperature. Going from hottest to coolest, the spectral types used are O, B, A, F, G, K, and M. Several special types may also be used. Cannon subdivided each spectral type into ten parts; for example, the sun is spectral type G2.

This method of classifying stellar spectra provides astronomers with a tool for comparing different stars. Cannon's designation, even with comparatively few other parameters, can tell a student of astronomy much about a star and remains one of the most important pieces of information about it.

Bibliography

Discovering Astronomy. R. Robert Robins, William H. Jefferys, and Stephen J. Shawl. 3d ed. New York: John Wiley & Sons, 1995.

Introduction to Stellar Astrophysics. Erika Bohm-Vitense. Vol. 1. Cambridge, England: Cambridge University Press, 1989.

Observational Astronomy. D. Scott Birney. Cambridge, England: Cambridge University Press, 1991.

Early Life

Annie Jump Cannon was born in 1863 as the daughter of William Lee Cannon, a wealthy shipbuilder who served as lieutenant governor of Delaware during the Civil War. As a young student, Annie excelled in school, especially in mathematics. Her mother, Mary Elizabeth Jump Cannon, was an amateur astronomer who taught the young girl to love the stars.

Although few women in her day went to college, Cannon was encouraged to seek higher education because of her excellent scholastic record. She enrolled in Wellesley College, but she was not prepared for the harsh winters in Massachusetts and was sick often during her first year at college. These repeated illnesses left her partially deaf.

After her graduation, Cannon returned home and helped around the house until her mother died in 1893. Most of her friends had married while she was in school, and Cannon found that she had little in common with them anymore. She never married and thus was able to put all of her energies into her chosen career, astronomy.

(Library of Congress)

Life in Cambridge

In 1893, Cannon returned to Cambridge, Massachusetts, to work for Sarah Whiting, one of her professors at Wellesley. Cannon then enrolled in Radcliffe College in order to use the telescopes at the nearby Harvard College Observatory. Her work impressed Edward Pickering, the director of the observatory, enough for him to offer her a job analyzing stellar spectra. She moved into a small house within a block of the observatory, where she would live for the next four decades.

Cannon's early work involved the study of variable stars, an interest that she kept for the rest of her life. Her analysis of stellar spectra led Cannon to revise dramatically the way in which stellar spectral types were organized and categorized. Her new system of classification gained general acceptance by 1910 and remains the primary method of designating star types.

In her career, Cannon classified more than 350,000 stars, surpassing any other individual in history, and discovered more than 300 variable stars. Most of Cannon's stellar spectroscopy work appeared in "The Henry Draper Catalog," which was published in *The Annals of the Harvard College Observatory* from 1918 to 1924.

In reward for her meticulous and accurate work, Cannon was named the curator of the famed photographic plate collection at the Harvard College Observatory in 1911. She held this position until her death.

Recognition and Later Years

Women were rare in astronomy in Cannon's day and frequently were not well received. Nevertheless, her work was so spectacular that she received numerous awards and praises from her male colleagues, such as the Henry Draper Gold Medal in 1931 and the Ellen Richards Research Prize in 1932. In 1925, Cannon became the first woman ever to be granted an honorary doctorate from Oxford University. Although she received many awards from around the world, Harvard University did not grant her the same honors until 1938, when she was named the William Cranch Bond Professor of Astronomy.

Cannon never retired. She worked until the age of seventy-six, when heart problems forced her to take a leave of absence from the observatory. She died shortly thereafter.

Bibliography

By Cannon

"The Henry Draper Memorial," *The Journal of the Royal Astronomical Society of Canada*, 1915

"The Henry Draper Catalog," *The Annals of the Harvard College Observatory*, 1918-1924

"Astronomical Fellowships for Women," *Circular of Harvard College Observatory*, 1919

"The Henry Draper Extension," *The Annals of the Harvard College Observatory*, 1925-1936

"Sarah Frances Whiting," *Popular Astronomy*, 1927

About Cannon

"Annie Jump Cannon." Leon Campbell. *Popular Astronomy* 49 (1941).

Women Scientists. Nancy J. Veglahn. New York: Facts on File, 1991.

(Raymond D. Benge, Jr.)

George R. Carruthers

Areas of Achievement: Astronomy and physics

Contribution: Carruthers developed electronic imaging devices and techniques for photographing hydrogen molecules in space that help advance understanding of how stars are made and that can monitor carbon monoxide and other pollutants in the atmosphere above large cities.

Oct. 1, 1939	Born in Cincinnati, Ohio
1964	Earns a Ph.D. from the University of Illinois
1964	Joins the Naval Research Laboratory (NRL) as a research physicist
1969	Patents an electromagnetic radiation image converter
1971	Wins the Arthur S. Fleming Award for Scholarly Achievement from the Washington Jaycees
1972	Develops the ultraviolet camera deployed on Apollo 16
1972	Awarded the Exceptional Scientific Achievement Medal from NASA
1972	Develops the ultraviolet telescope on OAO 3 (Copernicus)
1973	His ultraviolet telescope is deployed on Skylab 4
1977	Wins the Samuel Cheevers Award from the National Technical Association
1980	Becomes the head of NRL's Ultraviolet Measurements Branch
1982	Becomes a senior astrophysicist at NRL
1982, 1991	Develops far-ultraviolet cameras flown on space shuttle missions

Early Life

George Robert Carruthers, who would become the most prominent African American in space science and work with the Naval Research Laboratory (NRL) in Washington, D.C., was born on October 1, 1939, in Cincinnati. He was the oldest of four children born to George and Sophia Carruthers.

As a young boy growing up in the Cincinnati suburb of Milford, George was inspired by reading Buck Rogers and other space-related comic books. His father, a civil engineer for the U.S. Air Force, encouraged his son's interest in astronomy. He insisted that George study all forms of science and mathematics and bought him many books. At the age of ten, Carruthers built his own telescope and saved money from his job as a delivery boy to purchase lenses from a mail order company.

When Carruthers was twelve, his father died and the family moved to Chicago, where his mother went to work for the post office. While attending Chicago's Englewood High School, he received additional encouragement from his science teachers. He built a bigger and better telescope that won for him first prize at a local science fair.

After being graduated from Englewood in 1957, Carruthers went to the University of Illinois at Urbana-Champaign, where he received a B.S. in aeronautical engineering and astronomy in 1961. He continued in graduate school at Illinois, earning an M.S. in nuclear engineering in 1962 and a Ph.D. in aeronautical and astronautical engineering in 1964. His dissertation title was "Experimental Investigations of Atomic Nitrogen Recombination."

The Naval Research Laboratory

After completing his doctorate, Carruthers received a National Science Foundation fellowship in rocket astronomy at the Naval Research Laboratory (NRL). Two years later, he became a research assistant in the E. O. Hurlburt Center for Space Research at NRL. He specifically worked in the fields of far-ultraviolet spectroscopy and photometry. Ultraviolet light is used by scientists to determine the atoms and molecules present in interstellar space.

In November, 1969, Carruthers was granted a patent for an "Image Converter for Detecting

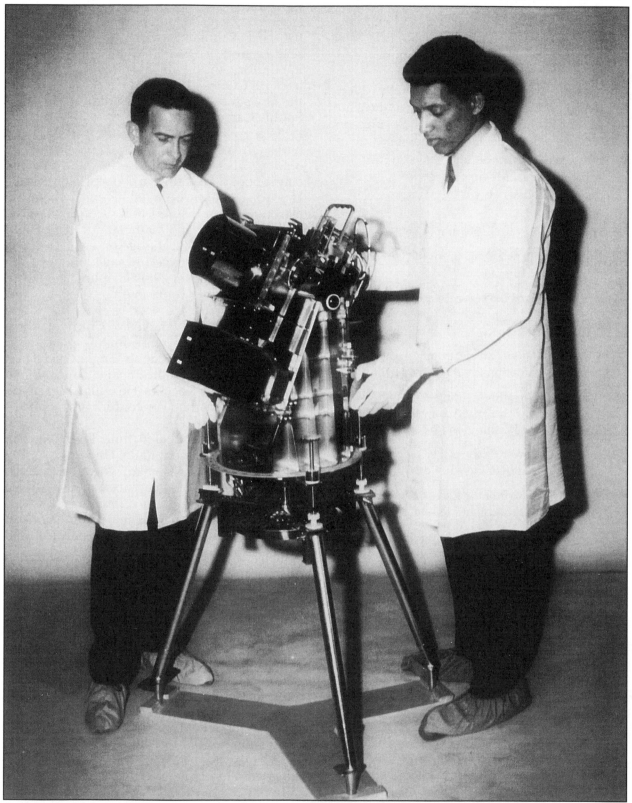

Carruthers (right) and W. Conway with the Apollo 16 lunar surface ultraviolet camera. (Archive Photos)

Far-Ultraviolet Astronomy from Space

Carruthers worked in developing electronic imaging devices and techniques for photographing hydrogen molecules in space that helped advance an understanding of how stars are made.

In April, 1972, an ultraviolet camera that Carruthers developed was carried to the moon on the Apollo 16 mission. His device was a semiautomatic combination spectrograph and camera with an electron intensifier. It had a Schmidt optical system that focused an image on a potassium bromide cathode that emitted electrons in proportion to the number of ultraviolet photons striking it.

Observing objects in wavelengths shorter than 1,600 angstroms, the camera created the first stellar observatory ever used on the moon and was the first instrument to photograph hydrogen bands around the earth up to 80,000 kilometers out in space, which helped monitor carbon monoxide and other pollutants in the atmosphere above large cities. It was also used to photograph the Great Magellanic Cloud, the closest galaxy to the Milky Way, among other objects, and it detected hydrogen molecules in deep space.

A modified version of the Apollo camera was carried on the Skylab 4 mission and deployed on the spacewalk of astronauts Eugene Carr and Bill Pogue on Christmas Day, 1973. It was used to photograph the hydrogen halo of Comet Kohoutek in the 1,050-to-1,600-angstrom-wavelength range. Carruthers also developed an ultraviolet telescope that was launched on the third Orbiting Astronomical Observatory (OAO 3, or Copernicus) in August, 1972.

One of his cameras, a cirris cryogenically cooled infrared telescope used to observe the earth's limb and rocket plumes, has flown aboard the space shuttle for the Strategic Defense Initiative (SDI). The first time was in June, 1982, on *Columbia* on mission STS-4; the project was classified at the time. It flew a second time in *Discovery*'s cargo bay on STS-39 in April, 1991. His far-ultraviolet imaging spectrograph (FUVIS), designed to study the ozone layer in near-earth space was scheduled to fly on a space shuttle mission as part of the Air Force Spartan-281 payload.

Bibliography

"Apollo 16 Far-Ultraviolet Camera/Spectrograph: Earth Observations." George Carruthers and T. Page. *Science* 177, no. 4051 (September 1, 1972).

"Astronomy with the Space Shuttle." George Carruthers. *Sky and Telescope* 48, no. 3 (September, 1974).

"Far-Ultraviolet Stellar Astronomy." George Carruthers. *Astronautics and Aeronautics* 7, no. 3 (March, 1969).

Electromagnetic Radiation Especially in Short Wave Lengths."

Carruthers married in 1973 but remained low-key about his private life. He became active in a program called Science, Mathematics, Aerospace Research and Technology (SMART), running workshops to train students and teachers, most of whom are members of minorities, in the Washington-Baltimore area. He also served as editor of the *Journal of the National Technical Association.*

In 1980, Carruthers became the head of NRL's Ultraviolet Measurements Branch, and, in 1982, he became a senior astrophysicist at NRL.

Over the years, he received numerous honors, such as the Arthur S. Fleming Award for Scholarly Achievement from the Washington Jaycees in 1971, the Exceptional Scientific Achievement Medal from the National Aeronautics and Space Administration (NASA) for his work with Apollo 16 in 1972, and the Samuel Cheevers Award from the National Technical Association for his work with minority students in 1977.

Bibliography

By Carruthers

"Far-Ultraviolet Stellar Astronomy," *Astronautics and Aeronautics*, 1969

"Far-Ultraviolet Photography of Orion: Interstellar Dust," *Science*, 1970 (with R. C. Henry)

"Apollo 16 Preliminary Science Report," 1972 (with others)

"Apollo 16 Far-Ultraviolet Camera/Spectrograph: Earth Observations," *Science*, 1972 (with T. Page)

"Sounding Rockets in Space Astronomy," *Sky and Telescope*, 1972

"Astronomy with the Space Shuttle," *Sky and Telescope*, 1974

"Far-Ultraviolet Rocket Survey of Orion," *Sky and Telescope*, 1977 (with C. B. Opal)

"Rocket-Ultraviolet Imagery of the North American Nebula," *Astrophysical Journal*, 1980 (with H. M. Heckathorn and T. D. Gull)

"Far-Ultraviolet Spectra and Flux Distribution of Some Orion Stars," *Astrophysical Journal*, 1981 (with Heckathorn and Opal)

"The Distribution of Hot Stars and Hydrogen in the Large Magellanic Cloud," *Astrophysical Journal*, 1981 (with Page)

"The Hydrogen Coma of Comet P-Halley Observed in Lyman Alpha Using Sounding Rockets," *Astronomy and Astrophysics*, 1992 (with others)

"Far-Ultraviolet Stellar Photometry: A Field in Monoceros," *Astrophysical Journal*, 1993 (with E. G. Schmidt)

"The Far-Ultraviolet Dust Albedo in the Upper Scorpius Subgroup of the Scorpius OB2 Association," *Astrophysical Journal*, 1994 (with others)

About Carruthers

American Men and Women of Science. 12th ed. Vol. 1. New York: Jaques Cattell Press, 1971.

Blacks in Science and Medicine. Vivian O. Sammons. Washington, D.C.: Hemisphere, 1990.

Blacks in Science: Astrophysicist to Zoologist. Hattie Carwell. Hicksville, N.Y.: Exposition Press, 1977.

Distinguished African American Scientists of the Twentieth Century. James H. Kessler et al. Phoenix, Ariz.: Oryx Press, 1996.

"Earth's Eye on the Moon." *Ebony* 28, no. 12 (October, 1973).

Notable Twentieth-Century Scientists. Emily J. McMurray, ed. New York: Gale Research, 1995.

(Derek W. Elliott)

Rachel Carson

Areas of Achievement: Biology, botany, and earth science

Contribution: Carson, a seminal figure in the environmental movement, made the public aware of the harmful effects of DDT and other pesticides in her landmark book *Silent Spring*.

May 27, 1907	Born in Springdale, Pennsylvania
1925	Attends the Pennsylvania College for Women (Chatham College) in Pittsburgh
1929	Receives a fellowship to study at the Woods Hole Marine Biological Laboratory for the summer
1932	Receives an M.A. in marine zoology from The Johns Hopkins University
1936	Joins the United States Bureau of Fisheries as a junior aquatic biologist
1941	Publishes *Under the Sea-Wind*
1947	Advances to editor in chief for the Fish and Wildlife Service
1950	Receives the Eugene F. Saxton Memorial Fellowship to pursue her writing career
1951	Publishes *The Sea Around Us* and receives the National Book Award
1955	Publishes *The Edge of the Sea*
1962	Completes *Silent Spring*
1963	Receives the Conservationist of the Year Award of the National Wildlife Federation
1963	Elected to the American Academy of Arts and Letters
Apr. 14, 1964	Dies in Silver Spring, Maryland

Early Life

Rachel Louise Carson was born in Springdale, Pennsylvania, in 1907. She grew up in rural Pennsylvania, where her mother instilled into her a love of the outdoors: birds, insects, and residents of streams. As a child, Carson also exhibited literary talent, even publishing stories in the *St. Nicholas Magazine*. She attended local public schools and in 1925 matriculated at the Pennsylvania College for Women (Chatham College) in Pittsburgh. She intended to major in English, but Mary Scott Sinkler, a professor of biology at the college, convinced Carson to pursue her interest in science as well.

Carson was graduated in 1929 as a biology major and was awarded a fellowship for summer study at the Woods Hole Marine Biological Laboratory, where she saw the ocean for the first time. In the fall, she began graduate studies at The Johns Hopkins University in Baltimore, Maryland.

While there, she studied genetics under Raymond Pearl and received her M.A. in marine zoology in 1932. She taught at The Johns Hopkins University in the summers and was a part-time assistant at the University of Maryland in the early 1930's.

Biology and Writing

To supplement her income, Carson wrote a series of feature articles on fisheries and related themes for the *Baltimore Sunday Sun*. In 1935, she obtained part-time work writing radio scripts for the series "Romance Under the Waters" sponsored by the United States Bureau of Fisheries. This assignment lead the following year to a permanent appointment as a junior aquatic biologist. With the encouragement of her chief, Elmer Higgins, Carson sent an article on the sea to the *Atlantic Monthly*; "Undersea" was published in 1937.

In 1941, Carson published her first book, *Under the Sea-Wind*, a natural history text in which the drama of the sea was seen through the lives of several creatures. During World War II, Carson continued her government work at the now-merged Fish and Wildlife Service. She wrote and edited pamphlets on conservation and was promoted to editor in chief in 1947.

In 1951, Carson received the Eugene F. Saxton Memorial Fellowship, which allowed her

Carson holds a copy of her influential book Silent Spring, *which sparked investigation into the widespread use of pesticides.* (AP/Wide World Photos)

A Call to Protect the Earth

In her fourth book, Silent Spring *(1962), Carson brought to the public's eye the harm that pesticides were doing to the environment.*

When her friend Olga Huckins wrote for help in stopping the aerial sprays that were destroying birds in her private sanctuary, Carson began to gather information on pesticides. She became increasingly appalled at her findings and realized that she must inform the public.

Silent Spring begins with a story, a fable in which people find themselves in a springtime when birds no longer sing. The people have brought the problem upon themselves. Carson goes on to delineate the deleterious effects of DDT (dichloro-diphenyl-trichloroethane) and other chlorinated insecticides to birds, ground water, and soil, which she then links to human diseases such as cancer. She cites hundreds of scientific articles and specialists. Carson synthesized the growing body of information about these substances in a way that galvanized the public to action.

In her final chapter, "The Other Road," she calls not for a ban on insecticides, as some have claimed, but rather for continued work on finding biological means to control pests. She tells of the elimination of screw-worms, which had been destroying livestock, by the release of sterilized, irradiated male flies in Florida. Carson describes the possibilities of using insect sex attractants and bacteria such as *Bacillus thurgiensis* to control specific pests. She advocates the use of the natural enemies of the insects rather than broad, nonspecific chemicals.

Carson knew that her book would meet with controversy. The publisher was threatened with a lawsuit and Carson was vilified, but her message was heard. Rachel Carson wanted her book to have a lasting influence on government policy. The environmental movement and the Environmental Protection Agency stand as tributes to the courage of this scientist-poet.

Bibliography
The Green Revolution: The American Environmental Movement, 1962-1992. Kirkpatrick Sale. New York: Hill & Wang, 1993.
The Recurring Silent Spring. H. Patricia Hynes. New York: Pergamon Press, 1989.
Since "Silent Spring." Frank Graham, Jr. Boston: Houghton Mifflin, 1970.

to pursue her writing career. In the best-seller *The Sea Around Us* (1951), Carson was able to incorporate the findings of oceanographic research done during World War II. She received a National Book Award and the John Burroughs Medal for a natural history book of outstanding literary quality. The film of her book won an Academy Award as the best full-length documentary in 1953.

Living by the Sea
The financial independence that Carson had achieved allowed her to devote her full attention to writing. A primary laboratory for her next book, *The Edge of the Sea* (1955), was the tidal zone in front of her Maine cottage. She traveled along the Atlantic coast of North America studying the variety of shore life. This book was also a best-seller, and Carson was praised for the poetry of her science.

Her article "Help Your Child to Wonder" was published in the *Woman's Home Companion* in 1956. In it, she writes of teaching her young nephew the mysteries of earth, sea, and sky. This work was published as *The Sense of Wonder* (1965) after her death in 1964.

A Time of Courage
While researching and writing her most important book, *Silent Spring* (1962), Carson first cared for her dying mother and then herself suffered from breast cancer. After the book's publication, she was surprised not so much by the controversy engendered by its warning against the dangers of pesticides such as DDT but by its popular reception. She received many awards, including election to the fifty-member American Academy of Arts and Letters. Carson was a scientist who exemplified the humanist traditions of the academy.

Her scientific work in *Silent Spring* was vindicated in 1963 when President John F. Kennedy's Science Advisory Panel called for legislation to safeguard against the harmful effects of pesticides and other toxins. Carson's mission was to change public policy toward the environment. She lived to see the beginnings of her effect.

Bibliography

By Carson
Under the Sea-Wind: A Naturalist's Picture of Ocean Life, 1941
The Sea Around Us, 1951
The Edge of the Sea, 1955
Silent Spring, 1962
The Sense of Wonder, 1965

About Carson
Always, Rachel: The Letters of Rachel Carson and Dorothy Freeman, 1952-1964—The Story of a Remarkable Friendship. Martha Freeman. Boston: Beacon Press, 1994.
The House of Life: Rachel Carson at Work. Paul Brooks. Boston: Houghton Mifflin, 1972.
Rachel Carson. Carol B. Gartner. New York: Frederick Ungar, 1983.
Women Champions of Human Rights: Eleven U.S. Leaders of the Twentieth Century. Moira Davison Reynolds. Jefferson, N.C.: McFarland, 1991.

(Helen M. Burke)

George Washington Carver

Areas of Achievement: Botany, chemistry, and invention

Contribution: Carver made important advances in soil-building, cotton cultivation, crop rotation, and uses of the peanut, the sweet potato, and clay.

1861?	Born on the Carver farm near Diamond Grove, Missouri
1875	Leaves the Carver farm to attend school in Neosho, Missouri
1880	Attends school in Minneapolis, Kansas
1885	Rejected from Highland College in Kansas because of his race
1890	Enrolls at Simpson College in Indianola, Iowa
1891	Transfers to Iowa State College
1894	Earns a B.S. from Iowa State College with a thesis entitled "Plants as Modified by Man"
1896	Receives a master's degree from Iowa State College
1896	Assumes a teaching position at the Tuskegee Institute in Tuskegee, Alabama
1915	Inducted into the Royal Society of London
1923	Given the Spingarn Medal for distinguished scientific service by the National Association for the Advancement of Colored People (NAACP)
1939	Awarded the Roosevelt Medal for his contribution to Southern agriculture
Jan. 5, 1943	Dies in Tuskegee, Alabama

Early Life

George Washington Carver was born to slave parents in Diamond Grove, Missouri, during the early 1860's. His exact birth date cannot be confirmed. His mother was kidnapped and taken to the Deep South during George's infancy. George, along with an older brother named Jim, was then reared by his mother's former owners, Moses and Susan Carver.

As a young child, George was enthralled by nature; locals referred to him as the "Plant Doctor." Being sickly as a youngster allowed him to avoid participation in the hard, time-consuming chores of the farm. He spent his free time learning to crochet, cook, and do housework. Susan Carver taught George to read and spell, while Moses Carver helped him with simple mathematics.

Education was important to George Washington Carver. Thus, he left the Carvers' home to attend school in a town about eight miles away. From there, he moved to various places across the Midwest seeking education and employment. Finally, at the urging of friends in

Carver in March, 1942, less than a year before his death. (Library of Congress)

Minneapolis, Kansas, Carver applied to Highland College, a Presbyterian college in Highland, Kansas. He was accepted in 1885, but, upon his arrival on campus, the offer of admission was revoked because of his race.

Discouraged, Carver's travels eventually took him to Iowa, where he was encouraged to apply to Simpson College in Indianola. He was accepted and began classes on September 9, 1890. Recognizing Carver's many talents, especially those in the sciences, Etta M. Budd, an art teacher, urged Carver to transfer to Iowa State College at Ames, which he did in May, 1891.

At Iowa State, Carver earned a bachelor of science degree in 1894 and a master of science degree in agriculture and bacterial botany in 1896. In 1896, Booker T. Washington offered him a teaching position at Tuskegee Institute, where Carver would remain an instructor until his death. He taught classes in chemistry and botany and initiated a popular Bible study class.

Helping Others Help Themselves

One of Carver's first projects upon his arrival at Tuskegee was to rejuvenate the campus' barren farm. Once he determined that the soil had been drained of nutrients, he enlisted the help of students to correct the problem. Carver and his students used compost, proper plowing techniques, and cover crops to rebuild the soil.

Carver experienced such success with the institute farm that local farmers became curious. Their interest inspired Carver to help organize the Farmers' Institute, a group that met monthly to receive agricultural advice from the staff of Tuskegee. Eventually, the Farmers' Institute spawned two-week "short courses" in agriculture and agricultural techniques, as well as a Farmers' Institute fair.

The Peanut Man

During Carver's tenure at Tuskegee Institute, an insect called the boll weevil became a major threat to the Southern cotton fields. Carver urged local farmers to switch crops from cotton to peanuts and sweet potatoes to prevent the spread of the pest and to provide farmers with an alternate source of income. Gradually, local farmers began following his suggestion.

The abundance of peanut crops presented a

The Peanut and Its Uses

Carver believed that the possibilities for synthesizing new products from various plants were endless. The plant for which he became most famous is the peanut.

Carver's main goal in the majority of his work was to develop products and agricultural techniques to make small-scale farming sustainable in the South and to allow the Southern small farmer self-sufficiency. Through the research of others, as well as his own experimentation, Carver recognized that the peanut had many characteristics that made it beneficial to accomplishing his goal.

Carver enumerated the multiple positive characteristics of the peanut in one of his bulletins, entitled *How to Grow the Peanut and 105 Ways of Preparing It for Human Consumption* (1916). As a nitrogen-fixing legume, the peanut enriches the soil for other crops. Based on an analysis of the composition of the peanut, Carver concluded that it had great value as a food staple for both humans and animals.

After determining that the peanut had the potential to be a profitable and beneficial crop, Carver turned his attention to instructing farmers on how best to raise peanuts. Among his suggestions was the use of a fertilizer consisting of compost, the components of which included "swamp muck, farmyard manure, leaves, and rich top earth."

The next step in Carver's work was finding ways of utilizing the peanut's beneficial properties. Carver developed a wide variety of products from the plant, including dyes, cosmetics, insulation, ink, stock feed, medicines, glue, soap, and peanut milk. In total, Carver was able to create approximately three hundred products from the peanut plant.

One of Carver's most interesting developments was peanut milk, described by Carver as an "emulsion of the oils, fats, carbohydrates, and some of the ash of peanuts." Peanut milk was prepared by adding two and a half quarts of water to one pound of peanuts. The mixture was then heated to 100 degrees Celsius for twenty minutes with constant stirring. Salt and sugar were added to taste, and the "milk" was refrigerated.

Carver was able to produce thirty-two types of peanut milk, which varied in fat, carbohydrate, and protein content. While all types looked like cows' milk and could be stored in the same manner, they varied widely in taste. Some "grades" of peanut milk tasted very similar to cows' milk, while others had a strong peanut flavor.

Peanut milk proved to be a very versatile product. Like cows' milk, it could be used to make cheese and cream or be condensed and dried. Unlike cows' milk, it could be consumed by those who were lactose-intolerant. Fruit juices could also be blended with the peanut milk without curdling. Unfortunately, like most of Carver's other inventions, peanut milk never became commercially viable.

Bibliography

How to Grow the Peanut and 105 Ways of Preparing It for Human Consumption. George Washington Carver. Tuskegee, Ala.: Tuskegee Institute Experiment Station, 1916.

The Peanut: Bulletin 44. George Washington Carver and A. W. Curtis, Jr. Tuskegee, Ala.: Tuskegee Institute Experiment Station, 1943.

new problem: What were the farmers supposed to do with their peanuts? Carver applied himself to the task of coming up with new uses for the peanut to make the crop profitable to farmers. By his death, Carver, dubbed the "Peanut Man," had invented more than three hundred uses. Unfortunately, few became commercially viable, but Carver's products provided farmers with a means of self-sufficiency.

Some biographers credit Carver's work with peanuts for saving and refurbishing the economy of the South. His work also triggered research into alternative uses for other crops. Carver is credited with nearly one hundred uses for the sweet potato and with developing paints from pigments derived from various clays. He also pioneered a method of food dehydration. Carver believed that "we can learn to synthesize materials for every human need from the things that grow."

Carver never ceased working until the day of his death. When he was not in the laboratory, he could be found helping students with their lessons or answering the thousands of letters asking for advice and expressing admiration that he received every day. He died on January 5, 1943, in his room at the Tuskegee Institute.

Bibliography

By Carver

Experiments with Sweet Potatoes, 1898

The Farmers' Manual and Complete Cotton Book, 1901 (rev. ed.; as editor, with J. L. Nichols)

Fertilizer Experiments with Cotton, 1901

Possibilities of the Sweet Potato in Macon County, Alabama, 1910

Some Possibilities of the Cow Pea in Macon County, Alabama, 1910

White and Color Washing with Native Clays from Macon County, Alabama, 1911

A Study of the Soils of Macon County, Alabama, and Their Adaptability to Certain Crops, 1913

A New and Prolific Variety of Cotton, 1915

How to Grow the Peanut and 105 Ways of Preparing It for Human Consumption, 1916

How to Grow the Tomato and 115 Ways to Prepare It for the Table, 1918

How to Make Sweet Potato Flour, Starch, Sugar Bread, and Mock Coconut, 1918

How to Build Up and Maintain the Virgin Fertility of Our Soils, 1936

About Carver

George Washington Carver: An American Biography. Rackham Holt. Garden City, N.Y.: Doubleday, Doran, 1943.

George Washington Carver: Man of God. Alvin D. Smith. New York: Exposition Press, 1954.

George Washington Carver: Scientist and Symbol. Linda O. McMurry. Oxford, England: Oxford University Press, 1981.

George Washington Carver: The Man Who Overcame. Lawrence Elliot. Englewood Cliffs, N.J.: Prentice Hall, 1966.

(Alvin M. Pettus)

Gian Domenico Cassini

Areas of Achievement: Astronomy, earth science, and physics

Contribution: Cassini discovered four satellites of Saturn and the structure of its system of rings and carefully charted the movements of the four brightest satellites of Jupiter. His determination of the astronomical unit established the distance scale for the solar system.

June 8, 1625	Born in Perinaldo, Imperia, Republic of Genoa (now Italy)
1650	Appointed a professor of mathematics at the University of Bologna
1668	Publishes tables of the positions of Jupiter's satellites
1669	Appointed the first director of the Paris Observatory
1671	Discovers Iapetus, the first known satellite of Saturn
1671-1673	Calculates the astronomical unit
1672	Discovers Rhea, a second satellite of Saturn
1673	Takes French nationality and changes his first names to "Jean Dominique"
1675	Observes that the ring around Saturn is divided into at least two concentric rings
1679	Completes a chart of the moon that is 3.6 meters in diameter
1684	Discovers Tethys and Dione, two additional satellites of Saturn
1693	Publishes improved ephemerides of Jupiter's satellites
1710	Becomes blind
Sept. 14, 1712	Dies in Paris, France

Early Life

Gian Domenico Cassini (pronounced "ka-SEE-nee"), the first of four generations of astronomers, was born in 1625 in Perinaldo, now in Italy. Little is known of his early training, but he seems to have distinguished himself as an industrious observer with telescopes. His mathematical talents and his remarkable breadth of knowledge in the sciences added to his reputation.

At the age of twenty-five, Cassini was asked to join the University of Bologna as a professor of mathematics to succeed Father Bonaventura Cavalieri, the first to have explained in his public lectures the Copernican system and the implications of the discoveries made by Galileo. Since at that time mathematics professors were required to teach Euclidean geometry and the Ptolemaic system of astronomy, the task to which the young Cassini was called assumed great importance.

During the nineteen years in which he remained at Bologna, Cassini considerably advanced astronomical studies with the modest means at his disposal. His duties at the university also included solving problems in hydraulics for the civil authorities and designing fortifications and road systems for the military.

Jupiter and Its System of Satellites

While at the University of Bologna, Cassini established a program of observations of the planet Jupiter and its four brightest satellites. The pronounced flattening of the planet indicated a rapid rate of rotation, and Cassini made carefully detailed maps of Jupiter's cloud belts and spots in an effort to measure the rotational period. His value of nine hours and fifty-six minutes is only five minutes longer than the best modern determinations. Cassini extended his methods to other planets—Mars, Venus, and Saturn—in attempts to determine their periods of rotation. He succeeded only with Mars, for which he also noted the changing face of the planet with the seasons.

Cassini was also greatly interested in the movements of the bright satellites of Jupiter. Occasionally, each of the satellites will pass through Jupiter's shadow and thus be eclipsed. Cassini worked steadily on compiling a set of tables that could be used to predict when such eclipses occur. The result was the renowned *Ephemerides bononienses mediceorum syderum ex hypothesibus, et tabules Io*, published in 1668. For the navigator, Jupiter and its system of satellites are a sort of celestial clock, offering a rough-and-ready way of determining longitude at sea. Cassini's tables were of immense commercial and military interest, for they improved travel across the seas by permitting accurate maps to be drawn.

Successes at the Paris Observatory

Cassini's work with Jupiter's satellites impressed Jean Picard, a French astronomer and an advisor to King Louis XIV of France. The king was building an observatory in 1669, and, at Picard's recommendation, the king appointed Cassini as the first director of the Paris Observatory.

Cassini's energy produced an almost uninterrupted stream of astronomical advances. Employing some novel developments in the construction and use of telescopes, he discov-

(Library of Congress)

The Scale of the Solar System

Through coordinated observations of the planet Mars from two widely separated stations on Earth, Cassini was able to determine the distance to that planet from Earth. With that distance known, the scale of the entire solar system was established.

The heliocentric models of the solar system developed by Nicolaus Copernicus and later modified by Johannes Kepler provided only the relative scale of the solar system. The distances separating the planets were known only in terms of the earth-sun distance, defined to be one astronomical unit (1 AU). The question addressed by astronomers then became "How long is 1 AU in terms of some standard length?"—for example, a meter or a mile.

The first successful measurement of the size of the astronomical unit was made by a team of astronomers headed by Cassini. Continued improvements in the performance and operation of telescopes made parallax measurements feasible for small angles. Such small parallactic shifts result when a relatively nearby object is viewed against a background of more distant objects. The nearby object's apparent position changes when it is measured from opposite ends of a baseline. The longer the baseline, the larger the apparent shift and the greater the parallax.

Cassini assigned Jean Richer the task of mapping the position of Mars relative to several bright stars at predetermined times. While Richer worked in Cayenne in the French colony of Guiana, Cassini and Jean Picard carried out similar measurements in Paris, 10,000 kilometers away. Mars was at the time in opposition, so that it was nearer the earth than at other times, as shown in figure 1. The principle of Cassini's method is illustrated in figure 2. One observer at

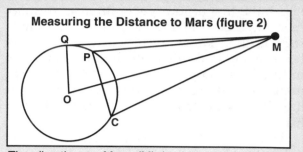

Measuring the Distance to Mars (figure 2)

The direction to Mars (M) is determined from two positions on the earth, Paris (P) and Cayenne (C). Knowing the distance between P and C allows all other relevant distances and angles to be determined. The position Q corresponds to an observer at M who would measure the maximum angle between the center of the earth (O) and Q. The angle OMQ is called the parallax.

Paris (P) observes the direction in which Mars appears, that is, the direction of line PM. The other observer at Cayenne (C) performs a similar measurement and determines the direction of line CM. The length of the line CP joining Cayenne and Paris is known geographically. Thus, two of the angles of triangle PCM and the length of one side are known, and so the lengths of all the other sides can be calculated. Knowing the positions of C and P on the earth's surface, the length of OM can be found. This represents the distance of Mars from the center of the earth (O), the distance EM in figure 1. Cassini found this to be 75 million kilometers.

The models of Copernicus and Kepler indicated that the distance from Mars to the sun was 1.52 AU; Earth's distance from the sun is defined to be 1 AU. Therefore, the distance that Cassini measured, EM, was equivalent to 0.52 AU. According to Cassini, 1 AU was then equivalent to 140 million kilometers. The scale of the sun's system of planets was now known. Future refinements would alter Cassini's result very little.

Bibliography

Coming of Age in the Milky Way. Timothy Ferris. New York: Doubleday, 1988.

The Planetary System. David Morrison and Tobias Owen. Reading, Mass.: Addison-Wesley, 1988.

The Space-Age Solar System. Joseph F. Baugher. New York: John Wiley & Sons, 1988.

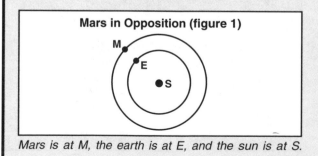

Mars in Opposition (figure 1)

Mars is at M, the earth is at E, and the sun is at S.

ered four new satellites of Saturn: Iapetus in 1671, Rhea in the following year, and Dione and Tethys in 1684.

In 1675, Cassini noticed a dark marking in Saturn's ring that separates it into two concentric rings. This division, which still bears Cassini's name, gave him an accurate idea of the constitution of the ring. He correctly surmised that the rings are formed by a swarm of very small satellites that could not be seen separately and that move around the planet with different orbital velocities.

While heading the Paris Observatory, he improved the theory that predicted the position of the sun in the sky, calculated new tables of atmospheric refraction that superseded the one published by Johannes Kepler, and issued, in 1693, a revised ephemeris of Jupiter's satellites, one whose accuracy was markedly better than his own tables of 1668.

Cassini also supervised several projects that brought him, his colleagues, and the observatory worldwide fame. He sent his assistant Jean Richer to Cayenne in the French colony of Guiana. They found that a pendulum of fixed length beat more slowly in Cayenne than in Paris, thus showing that the acceleration of gravity is smaller near the equator than at higher latitudes. This fact suggested that the earth is not a perfect sphere and served as the impetus for future investigations as to the shape of the earth. In another project, Richer's observations of the position of Mars in the sky, combined with observations made at the same time by Cassini and Picard in France, led to a much-improved estimate of the distance to Mars and ultimately to the distance scale of the solar system.

Cassini died in 1712 at the age of eighty-seven.

Bibliography

By Cassini

Ephemerides bononienses mediceorum syderum ex hypothesibus, et tabules Io, 1668

Connaissance des temps, 1679

Découverte de la lumière céleste qui paroit dans le Zodiaque, 1685

About Cassini

The History of Astronomy. Giorgio Abetti. New York: Henry Schuman, 1952.

History of Physical Astronomy. Robert Grant. New York: Jefferson Reprint, 1966.

Starseekers. Colin Wilson. Garden City, N.Y.: Doubleday, 1980.

Watchers of the Skies. Willy Ley. New York: Viking Press, 1963.

Worlds in the Sky. William Sheehan. Tucson: University of Arizona Press, 1992.

(Anthony J. Nicastro)

Henry Cavendish

Areas of Achievement: Chemistry and physics

Contribution: In addition to making the first accurate measurement of the gravitational constant, Cavendish also discovered the element hydrogen and carried out experiments on electricity and on gases.

Oct. 10, 1731	Born in Nice, France
1742	Enrolls at Dr. Newcome's Academy
1749-1753	Attends St. Peter's College, Cambridge University
1760	Elected a member of the Royal Society of London
1765	Writes an unpublished work on specific heat
1766	Reports the discovery and properties of hydrogen to the Royal Society of London
1767	Begins to study the composition of water
1771	Publishes a theory on the nature of electricity
1783	Publishes a study on the composition of air
1783-1788	Studies the freezing points of liquids
1784	Shows that the reaction of hydrogen with oxygen produces water
1785	Determines the composition of nitric acid
1798	Provides the first experimental determination of the gravitational constant and of Earth's mass
Feb. 24, 1810	Dies in London, England

Early Life

Henry Cavendish was born in Nice, France, in 1731. His parents were English aristocrats, and as a result Cavendish would be financially independent throughout his life. His father, Lord Charles Cavendish, was a member of the Royal Society of London and a noted experimental scientist. Lord Cavendish encouraged his son's interest in science, making his own scientific equipment available for his son's use.

At the age of eleven, Henry Cavendish enrolled at Dr. Newcome's Academy, a school for upper-class children. From 1749 to 1753, he attended St. Peter's College at Cambridge University. After leaving Cambridge, Cavendish moved to London, where he was to live for the remainder of his life.

(Library of Congress)

Early Scientific Work

Because Cavendish pursued his scientific investigations for his own pleasure, he was often careless in publishing his results. As a result, it has sometimes proven difficult to develop a chronology for his research. It appears, however, that his early research was in the areas of heat and the dynamics of moving bodies. Cavendish developed conservation laws for mechanical motion and in the early 1760's rediscovered the concept of specific heat.

Cavendish's first published work, appearing in 1766, concerned the properties of gases. He found differences in density between ambient air and gases produced by various chemical processes such as fermentation and the reaction of metals with strong acids or bases. In the course of his studies, Cavendish isolated a light gas that he identified as "phlogiston," the substance that was then believed to flow between objects during the transfer of heat. In fact, he had discovered a new chemical element, hydrogen.

In the early 1770's, Cavendish applied his knowledge of gas properties to develop a fluid model for electricity. He devised an experimental test to confirm the inverse square law for the interaction of charged objects. Cavendish carried out a number of additional experiments that anticipated later work by other researchers, including studies on the attractive and repulsive forces acting on charged bodies and on the relationship between charge and electrical potential for objects of various shapes and sizes. Most of this work did not appear during Cavendish's lifetime and only became available in 1879 when published by James Clerk Maxwell.

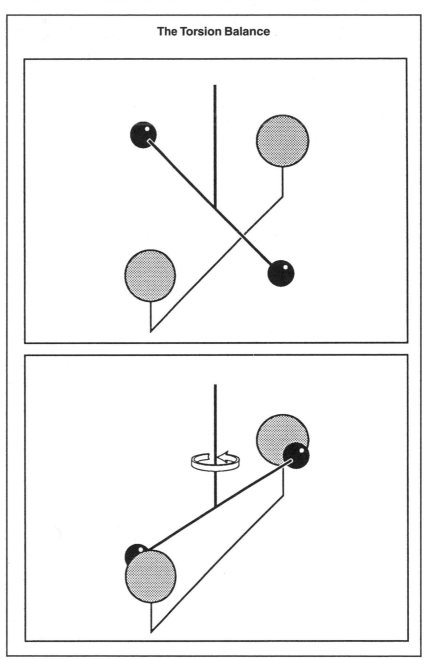

The Torsion Balance

Cavendish used a torsion balance to determine the gravitational constant.

The Chemistry of Gases and Solutions

In the 1780's, Cavendish returned to experimental work on the properties of gases. A paper in 1783 reported the results of his studies on the composition of air. The following year, he showed that the chemical reaction of hydrogen

The Determination of the Value for the Gravitational Constant

Cavendish used a modified torsion balance to determine the value for G, the gravitational constant.

Sir Isaac Newton discovered that the gravitational attraction between bodies follows an inverse square law of the form "$F = GM_1M_2/r^2$," where F is the force of attraction, M_1 and M_2 are the masses of the bodies that are interacting, and r is the distance between the centers of mass of M_1 and M_2. G, the constant of proportionality in the equation, is called the gravitational constant. Because of the weakness of the gravitational attractive force compared to that for electrostatic attraction, it proved difficult to obtain a value for the gravitational constant.

In 1798, Cavendish used a modified torsion balance to make the first accurate experimental determination of G. The apparatus consisted of two small spherical masses connected to opposite sides of a rod that was suspended from a thin wire. The movement of the rod as two large spheres were brought close to the masses and the change in the frequency in the oscillation of the rod allowed Cavendish to determine the force of attraction, from which G could be obtained.

The Cavendish experiment remains the most accurate method by which the gravitational constant can be found. It has also been used to search for small differences in G based on time or on the composition of the interacting bodies.

Bibliography

Gravitation and the Universe. Robert H. Dicke. Philadelphia: American Philosophical Society, 1970.

Gravity, the Universal Force. Don Nardo. San Diego: Lucent Books, 1990.

Great Experiments in Physics. Morris H. Shamos, ed. New York: Holt, Rinehart and Winston, 1959.

with oxygen produced water, thereby proving that water was a chemical compound and not an element, as had previously been thought.

In 1785, Cavendish carried out a series of experiments in which he passed an electrical discharge through air. When the product gases were bubbled through water, nitric acid was produced. During the course of these experiments, Cavendish found a component of air that would not combine with oxygen in the discharge. A century later, it was shown that this unreactive component of air was argon, a chemically inert element.

At the same time that he was investigating the properties of air, Cavendish also began a series of measurements on the freezing of liquids. He was able to show that mercury thermometers become unreliable at low temperatures because of the freezing of liquid mercury and the corresponding decrease in volume.

Gravitational Studies

During the last quarter century of his life, Cavendish gradually became interested in astronomy. While most of his astronomical research was of no importance, during this time he did conduct his most important scientific experiment: the determination of G, the gravitational constant.

Like electricity, gravitational attraction was known to follow an inverse square law. Because of the extraordinary weakness of gravitational attraction between small bodies, however, it proved difficult to determine the constant of proportionality governing the strength of gravitational attraction between objects. In 1798, Cavendish used a torsion balance to measure the force of attraction between two fixed masses attached to the balance and two larger movable masses. Based on the results from his experiments, he found the value for the gravitational constant. From this number, he was able to determine the mass and density of Earth.

Cavendish was extremely shy and had only limited contact with others. Nevertheless, during the last years of his life, he gradually gained recognition for his scientific achievements. Cavendish died in London in 1810.

Bibliography
By Cavendish
The Electrical Researches of the Honourable Henry Cavendish, 1879 (James Clerk Maxwell, ed.)

The Scientific Papers of the Honourable Henry Cavendish, F. R. S., 1: The Electrical Researches, 1921 (Maxwell, ed.; revised by Sir Joseph Larmor)

The Scientific Researches of the Honourable Henry Cavendish, F. R. S., 2: Chemical and Dynamical, 1921 (Sir Edward Thorpe, ed.)

About Cavendish

Henry Cavendish: His Life and Scientific Work. A. J. Berry. London: Hutchinson, 1960.

The Life of the Honourable Henry Cavendish. George Wilson. London: Cavendish Society, 1851.

Scientists of the Industrial Revolution. James G. Crowther. London: Cresset Press, 1962.

(Jeffrey A. Joens)

Anders Celsius

Areas of Achievement: Astronomy, mathematics, and physics

Contribution: A professor of astronomy, Celsius is most noted as one of the first to use the 100-degree centigrade temperature scale, which was named for him long after his death.

Nov. 27, 1701	Born in Uppsala, Sweden
1725	Becomes the secretary of the Uppsala Scientific Society
1730	Appointed a professor of astronomy at Uppsala University
1732-1736	Travels throughout Europe visiting astronomers and observatories
1733	Publishes 316 of his observations on the aurora borealis
1736	Advocates the introduction of the Gregorian calendar
1737	Participates in a French expedition to measure 1 degree of longitude in the polar region, proving Sir Isaac Newton's theory of Earth flattening at the poles
1740	Becomes the director of the newly finished observatory at Uppsala University, the first in Sweden
1741	Introduces his 100-degree thermometer scale
1742	Proposes that all scientific measurements of temperature be based on the boiling point and the freezing point of water, two nonvarying, naturally occurring points
1742	Moves into the new observatory at Uppsala
Apr. 25, 1744	Dies in Uppsala, Sweden

Early Life

Anders Celsius (pronounced "SEHL-see-us") was the son of a professor of astronomy at Uppsala University. As a boy, he was so intrigued with his father's work at the university that he decided to become an astronomer himself. Thus, when he entered college, he studied astronomy, mathematics, and experimental physics. At the age of twenty-four, Celsius became secretary of the Uppsala Scientific Society.

Field Research

Celsius first began teaching at Uppsala University as a professor of mathematics. In 1730, he was appointed professor of astronomy at the university, thereby achieving his goal of fol-lowing in his father's footsteps.

Beginning in 1732, Celsius traveled through Europe, visiting Berlin and Nuremberg in Germany. While in Nuremberg, he published his observations of the aurora borealis (northern lights).

He went next to Italy, then on to Paris. In Paris, he met Pierre-Louis Maupertuis and became affiliated with him in an expedition to measure longitude in the polar regions. In 1735, Celsius traveled to London to acquire needed scientific equipment for the journey. The French expedition to Tornea, Sweden (now Tornio, Finland), left Paris in 1736 and returned in 1737.

In Tornea, Celsius assisted in making meridional measurements supporting Sir Isaac

---

The Celsius Temperature Scale

Celsius developed a temperature scale based on the decimal system with fixed points separated by one hundred degrees, which renders it easy to use for scientific measurements.

In order to make quantitative measurements of temperature, it was necessary to devise scales with permanent sites at either end of the instrument, called fixed points. Celsius introduced a scale based on the decimal system with fixed points separated by one hundred degrees, making the Celsius scale easier to use than the other common scale devised by Gabriel Daniel Fahrenheit.

A Comparison of the Three Temperature Scales

Fahrenheit	Celsius (centigrade)	Kelvin	
212°	100°	373°	Boiling point
32°	0°	273°	Freezing point
–109°	–78°	195°	Solid CO_2
–297°	–183°	90°	Oxygen point
–460°	–273°	0°	Absolute zero

Celsius developed his temperature scale in 1742, twenty-eight years after the Fahrenheit scale was introduced. Initially, he assigned 100 degrees as the fixed point for melting ice and 0 degrees as the temperature at which pure water boils. Celsius achieved his ice point by stirring ice cubes in a container of water and inserting a thermometer. Later, another scientist, Carolus Linnaeus, inverted the scale so that 0 degrees represents the ice point and 100 degrees marks the boiling point of water. On the Celsius scale, 37 degrees is the normal human body temperature.

The scale introduced by Celsius was known as the centigrade scale until 1948. At that time, the Ninth General Conference of Weights and Measures officially changed the name from centigrade to Celsius.

Because the Celsius scale is based on one hundred degrees between the ice and boiling points, 1 degree Celsius is equal to 1.8 degrees Fahrenheit. Conversion from Celsius to Fahrenheit can be accomplished by employing the following formula: $°F = (1.8 × °C) + 32$.

Bibliography

The Atmosphere. F. K. Lutgens and E. J. Tarbuck. 5th ed. Engelwood Cliffs, N.J.: Prentice Hall, 1992.

Invention of the Meteorological Instruments. W. Middleton. Baltimore: The Johns Hopkins University Press, 1969.

Meteorology Today: An Introduction to Weather, Climate, and the Environment. C. Donald Ahrens. 4th ed. St. Paul, Minn.: West, 1991.

Newton's theory that a slight flattening of the earth's surface occurs in the polar regions.

Other Contributions

As an astronomer, Celsius was primarily considered a teacher and an observer. He attempted to determine the magnitude of the stars in the constellation Aries by filtering light through glass plates. In 1740, he published a paper on this work entitled *De constellatione Arietis* (the constellation of Aries).

He wrote a paper based on exact experiments to explain the falling water levels in the Baltic Sea entitled "Anmarkning om vatnets forminskande" in 1743. In another paper, *De observationibus profigura telluris determinanda in Gallia habitis, disquisitio* (1738), he had explained how to determine the size and shape of the earth accurately.

In 1742, Celsius moved into the new observatory built at Uppsala University, of which he had been named director two years earlier. On April 25, 1744, he died in Uppsala at the age of forty-two.

The Celsius Scale

Although Celsius was not the first to use the centigrade scale—based on a one-hundred degree interval between set points—he was the first to base the scale on two fixed points. He assigned 0 degrees to the boiling point of water and 100 degrees to the freezing point of water. Several years later, Carolus Linnaeus inverted Celsius' scale, changing it so that 100 degrees represents the boiling point of water and 0 degrees the freezing point of water.

In 1948, at the Ninth General Conference on Weights and Measures, the name "centigrade scale" was officially changed to "Celsius scale" and adopted in honor of Anders Celsius. Today, countries using the metric system employ the Celsius scale, and it is the preferred temperature scale worldwide for scientific use, especially in meteorology and climatology.

Bibliography

By Celsius

Dissertatio de nova methodo distantiam solis a terra determinandia, 1730

De observationibus profigura telluris determinanda in Gallia habitis, disquisitio, 1738

(Archive Photos)

De constellatione Arietis, 1740

"Observationer om twänne beständiga grader på en thermometer," *Kungliga Svenska vetenskapsakademiens handlingar*, 1742

"Anmärkning om vatnets förminskande," *Kungliga Svenska vetenskapsakademiens handlingar*, 1743

About Celsius

"Anders Celsius." In *Dictionary of Scientific Biography*, edited by Charles Coulston Gillispie. Vol. 3. New York: Charles Scribner's Sons, 1970.

"Anders Celsius." N. V. E. Nordenmark. In *Swedish Men of Science, 1650-1950*, edited by Sten Lindroth. Stockholm: Swedish Institute, 1952.

A History of the Thermometer and Its Use in Meteorology. W. Knowles Middleton. Baltimore: The Johns Hopkins University Press, 1966.

(Ralph D. Cross)

Sir James Chadwick

Area of Achievement: Physics
Contribution: Chadwick discovered the neutron, one of the fundamental subatomic particles.

Oct. 20, 1891	Born in Manchester, England
1911	Graduated from the University of Manchester with honors in physics
1913	Earns an M.S. from the University of Manchester
1913	Continues studies at the Physikalische-Technische Reichanstelt in Berlin
1914-1918	Interned in Germany during World War I
1921	Earns a Ph.D. from Cambridge University, England
1921	Appointed a Fellow at Gonville and Caius College, Cambridge
1923	Made assistant director of the Cavendish Laboratory
1927	Elected a Fellow of the Royal Society of London
1932	Discovers the neutron, a subatomic particle
1935	Awarded the Nobel Prize in Physics
1935-1948	Serves as a professor of physics at the University of Liverpool, England
1943	Leads the British science delegation in the United States that is developing the atomic bomb
1945	Receives a knighthood
1948-1958	Appointed master of Gonville and Caius College
July 24, 1974	Dies in Cambridge, England

Early Life

James Chadwick was born in Manchester, England, in 1891 as the son of John Joseph Chadwick and Ann Mary (Knowles) Chadwick. His father owned a small business. Chadwick attended the Manchester Grammar School, enrolled at the University of Manchester in 1908, and was graduated with honors in physics in 1911. While at Manchester, he studied under the famous physicist Ernest Rutherford and continued working with him after his graduation, receiving his master of science degree in 1913.

A scholarship allowed Chadwick to study in Germany, but, with the start of World War I, he found himself in an alien country. Considered a potential enemy, he was held in Germany against his will as a foreign national from 1914 to 1918. At the end of the war, he returned to England and again took up research with Rutherford, now at Cambridge University.

Studies in Radioactivity

Radioactivity, the spontaneous emission of particles and rays from selected chemical elements, was an unexplored area of science in the early twentieth century. Rutherford was a pioneer in this field, and Chadwick explored the effects of natural radioactive particles, called alpha particles, striking nonradioactive elements.

The Discovery of the Neutron

Chadwick and other scientists studying radioactive transitions had observed emissions that were inconsistent with the current knowledge of radioactivity. At the time, the proton and the electron were identifiable subatomic particles, and alpha particles, beta particles, and gamma radiation were the recognized atomic emissions. The divergent experimental results did not fit with the actions of these radioactive emissions.

Chadwick recalled that, some years before, Rutherford had postulated the existence of a different radioactive particle, a neutral particle similar in mass to the proton but without any electrical charge. Chadwick wondered if the strange emissions that he had detected could be secondary effects caused by the action of neutral particles on various materials. With

The Discovery of the Neutron

Chadwick proposed the existence of a neutral subatomic particle to explain certain experimental results involving radioactivity.

At the time that Chadwick began his studies on radioactivity, the basic ideas concerning the nature of individual atoms was well understood. Electrons and protons had been identified and their properties determined. Ernest Rutherford, with whom Chadwick studied, had identified the atomic nucleus as the central atomic mass. It was believed that the nucleus contained both protons and electrons. How else could one explain the close packing of protons, all with positive charges, in so confined a space? Yet, with all this knowledge, there were unexplained experimental observations that did not easily fit the developed theory.

Much of the early work undertaken by Chadwick and others dealt with observing the fragments and energies emitted when target substances are bombarded with radiation. Alpha particles, from naturally occurring radioactive sources, were the common particle type used to strike various target materials. The emissions of charged particles were detected by the amount of ionization that they produced in passing through air or another medium. Energy radiation, notably gamma radiation, could by detected photographically.

In 1930, German scientist Walther Bothe and coworkers reported a unique, unknown emission from beryllium when it was bombarded with alpha particles, but they did not investigate further. Another study at about the same time by the husband-and-wife team of Frédéric and Irène Joliot-Curie reported an increased and unexplained emission enhancement when beryllium bombarded with alpha particles was placed in contact with paraffin. Paraffin is a compound of large carbon and hydrogen molecules.

Chadwick repeated these experiments with beryllium, both alone and in the presence of paraffin, and observed the same results. He approached the explanation from the point of view that a neutral subatomic particle could be responsible for these events. Chadwick was fortunate to be associated with Rutherford, who had postulated a number of years earlier that a neutral subatomic particle could exist. No direct experimental verification of this hypothesis was forthcoming, however, as detection equipment for observing neutral particles was unavailable at the time.

Chadwick speculated that the direct emission from the alpha bombardment of beryllium was composed of neutrons and proposed the equation showing beryllium plus an alpha particle yields carbon plus a neutron.

$$^9_4Be + {}^4_2\alpha \rightarrow {}^{12}_6C + {}^1_0n$$

He later showed that boron, when bombarded by alpha particles, could also generate neutrons.

$$^{11}_5B + {}^4_2\alpha \rightarrow {}^{14}_7N + {}^1_0n$$

He explained the enhanced radiation from beryllium in the presence of paraffin as resulting from protons expelled from the paraffin when penetrated by neutrons from the beryllium-alpha interaction. He later calculated the atomic mass of the neutron, finding it to be nearly the same as that of the proton. Both the proton and the neutron are assigned a mass of one on the atomic mass scale.

Bibliography

Inquiry into Physics. Vern J. Ostdiek and Donald J. Bord. St. Paul, Minn.: West, 1991.

Inward Bound: Of Matter and Forces in the Physical World. Abraham Pais. Oxford, England: Oxford University Press, 1986.

Physical Science. Jerry S. Faughn, Jonathan Turk, and Amos Turk. Philadelphia: Saunders College Publishing, 1991.

World of Chemistry. Melvin D. Joesten, David O. Johnston, John T. Netterville, and James L. Wood. Philadelphia: Saunders College Publishing, 1991.

(The Nobel Foundation)

this concept in mind, he was able to justify the existence of a neutral subatomic particle, the neutron, and to determine its atomic mass. For his discovery of the neutron, he received the Nobel Prize in Physics in 1935.

The War Years

Following his discovery of the neutron, Chadwick accepted a position at the University of Liverpool, where funds were provided to build a cyclotron for further extensive study of radioactive interactions. Now that the existence of neutrons was established, the isotopic weights of elements, representing atoms of the same element but with different atomic masses, could be explained. They contained the same number of protons but different numbers of neutrons.

It was quickly recognized that neutrons are excellent probes for studying the effects of bombardment on other atoms. With no electrical charge, they easily penetrate target materials. This finding lead Chadwick to speculate that under the right conditions, neutron bombardment might split target atoms into various fragments. Nuclear fission, as it is called, was identified and proven experimentally by others.

It was soon realized that the tremendous energy release accompanying nuclear fission could have devastating effects. With World War II on the horizon, a race began between the Allied and Axis powers to be the first to develop an atomic bomb from the fission of uranium atoms. Chadwick lead a team of British scientists to the United States in 1943 to assist American scientists in the development of the first atomic bomb.

The Postwar Years

Following his return to England, having received various honors for his contributions to the war effort, Chadwick devoted himself to the development of peacetime uses of atomic energy and directed much of his work toward that goal. He also continued his theoretical studies on radioactive and nuclear interactions. In addition, as master of Gonville and Caius College, Cambridge, much of his time was spent in various administrative duties pertaining to the running of the college.

Chadwick was admired for his integrity and hard work. Although basically shy, he staunchly defended his positions pertaining to the directions that nuclear research should take and to the growth of that research effort. He moved to North Wales following his retirement from Gonville and Caius College, but he and his wife returned to Cambridge in 1969 to be nearer to the families of their twin daughters. Chadwick died in 1974.

Bibliography
By Chadwick
Radioactivity and Radioactive Substances, 1921
Radiations from Radioactive Substances, 1930
    (with Ernest Rutherford and C. D. Ellis)
"Possible Existence of a Neutron," *Nature*, 1932
"Existence of a Neutron," *Proceedings of the Royal Society of London*, 1932

Papers on the Neutron, 1932 (with Norman Feather and P. I. Dee)

About Chadwick
Asimov on Physics. Isaac Asimov. Garden City, N.Y.: Doubleday, 1976.
The Making of the Atomic Bomb. Richard Rhodes. New York: Simon & Schuster, 1986.
Notable Twentieth-Century Scientists. Emily J. McMurray, ed. Vol. 1. New York: Gale Research, 1995.
The Physicists. C. P. Snow. Boston: Little, Brown, 1981.

(Gordon A. Parker)

Subrahmanyan Chandrasekhar

Areas of Achievement: Mathematics and physics
Contribution: Chandrasekhar showed that not all stars end up as white dwarfs; those retaining a mass above a certain limit undergo further collapse. He also made contributions to hydrodynamics, hydromagnetics, and the mathematical theory of black holes.

Oct. 19, 1910	Born in Lahore, India
1930	Receives a B.A. from the University of Madras and formulates the Chandrasekhar limit
1933	Earns a Ph.D. in theoretical physics from Trinity College, Cambridge University
1936-1937	Conducts research at the Yerkes Observatory
1944	Elected a Fellow of the Royal Society of London
1952	Appointed a distinguished service professor at the University of Chicago
1952	Serves as managing editor of the *Astrophysical Journal*
1953	Awarded the Gold Medal of the Royal Astronomical Society
1962	Awarded the Royal Medal of the Royal Society of London
1966	Given the National Medal of Science from the United States
1971	Awarded the Henry Draper Medal from the National Academy of Sciences
1983	Awarded the Nobel Prize in Physics
Aug. 21, 1995	Dies in Chicago, Illinois

Early Life

Subrahmanyan Chandrasekhar (pronounced "chan-drah-SEEK-hahr") was born on October 19, 1910, in Lahore, India, to Chandrasekhara Subrahmanyan Ayyar and Sitalakshmi Ayyar. Sir Chandrasekhara Venkata Raman, a Nobel Prize-winning physicist, was his uncle. Taught at home until he was eleven, Subrahmanyan Chandrasekhar was admitted in 1921 into the Hindu High School in Triplicane, considered the best school in Madras. He was regarded as a prodigy, having mastered permutations and combinations, conic sections, coordinate geometry, calculus, and differential equations far ahead of his class.

At fifteen, he became a freshman at the Presidency College of the University of Madras. While studying for his B.A. honors degree, he was inspired by the example of Srini-

(The Nobel Foundation)

vasa Ramanujan, the mathematical genius who had died only a few years earlier.

Emergence as a Preeminent Astrophysicist

While Chandrasekhar was pursuing mathematical physics in college, his uncle's discovery in 1928 of the Raman effect, which received international acclaim, became a turning point in his life. Stimulated by a meeting with Arnold Sommerfeld in Madras in 1928, Chandrasekhar launched into a study of the new discoveries in atomic physics and statistical mechanics and in 1929 had his first paper published in the prestigious *Proceedings of the Royal Society of London*. Two other papers were ready to be published in the *Philosophical Magazine*, and several others were in progress.

In 1930, he received his B.A. honors degree and was offered a scholarship to study abroad by the government of India. On his way to England that year, he made the discovery that revolutionized stellar physics. Working on the theory of the evolution of white dwarf stars (such as the sun) from a relativistic standpoint, Chandrasekhar found that there is an upper limit to the mass of a star that will evolve into a white dwarf. A more massive star degenerates into a neutron star or a black hole. This limiting mass came to be known as the Chandrasekhar limit.

Cambridge and the Yerkes Observatory

Chandrasekhar spent the years between 1930 and 1935 at Trinity College in Cambridge University, where his research flourished in the company of mentors such as Edward Milne, Ralph Fowler, Paul A. M. Dirac, and the great astronomer Arthur Eddington. These years were stimulating and challenging, as well as extremely productive.

Despite their cordial personal relations, Eddington disagreed strongly with Chandrasekhar's conclusions vis-à-vis the fate of white dwarfs. Indeed, so great was Eddington's hold on the astronomical community that for many years Chandrasekhar received awards that carefully avoided citing his work on white dwarfs. Nevertheless, he continued his research on white dwarfs, despite repudiation by Eddington. During this period, Chandrasekhar also carried out research on a variety of sub-

The Chandrasekhar Limit

The Chandrasekhar limit is the mass that a star must have in order to end its life by contracting into an extremely dense white dwarf. A more massive star collapses into an object such as a neutron star or a black hole, which are smaller and denser than a white dwarf.

The evolutionary outcomes for high-mass and low-mass stars can be dramatically different. As a rule, every star eventually tries to generate a white dwarf at its core as it undergoes core contraction. During the 1920's, British physicist Ralph Fowler showed that a white dwarf has the peculiar property that the more massive it is, the smaller its radius. The explanation for this property is that a massive white dwarf has more self-gravity, so that more pressure is required to counter the stronger gravity. To increase the pressure, the degenerate electron gas constituting the white dwarf must be compressed until the pressure is strong enough to balance the gravitational force. This happens only at very high densities.

Chandrasekhar made a crucial modification to this hypothesis to accommodate Albert Einstein's special theory of relativity. Chandrasekhar showed that relativistic effects impose an upper limit on the mass of possible white dwarfs. This limit arises because electrons cannot move faster than the speed of light, and, for sufficiently massive stars, the internal degeneracy pressure cannot prevent the self-gravity of the star from crushing it to zero size. For likely white dwarf compositions, this limit is found to correspond to about 1.4 solar masses.

Suppose that a star attempts to exceed the Chandrasekhar limit, so that even after the initial envelope-mass loss, it has enough material to try to build a massive white dwarf. As the limit is approached, the core's outer boundary reaches arbitrarily small dimensions, generating enormous gravitational fields above it. To counteract the gravity, the pressure in the shell above the core must rise, yielding densities and temperatures that will drive all thermonuclear reactions to completion. Barring any other intervention, such a star suffers what is known as the iron catastrophe, whereby the envelope is expelled through a supernova explosion while the core turns into a large mass of hot neutrons or, in extreme cases, a black hole.

On the other hand, the final mass of the core in a low-mass star may end up well below the Chandrasekhar limit. The outer shell in such a star may still be dense and hot enough to allow nuclear fusion. The resulting heat will greatly distend its envelope, driving it to the red giant and the red supergiant phases. The surface gravity in these phases is too weak to hold the atmospheric mix of gas and dust, and the mixture is blown out as a stellar wind. Stars in this state are called planetary nebula. The white-hot core left behind is a bare white dwarf, composed mainly of carbon and oxygen.

Bibliography

The Internal Constitution of Stars. A. S. Eddington. Cambridge, England: Cambridge University Press, 1926.

"On Massive Neutron Cores." J. Robert Oppenheimer and G. M. Volkoff. *Physical Review* 55 (1939): 374-381.

jects, ranging from ionization in stellar atmospheres and the equilibrium of rotating gas spheres to distorted polytropes and relativistic degeneracy.

Between 1935 and 1936, Chandrasekhar spent several months lecturing at the Harvard Observatory. In 1937, he accepted an offer for a position as research associate at the Yerkes Observatory of the University of Chicago in Williams Bay, Wisconsin. Over the next ten years, his research encompassed stellar dynamics, dynamical friction, the negative hydrogen ion, and radiative transfer.

The Years at the University of Chicago

In 1952, Chandrasekhar became the Morton Hull Distinguished Service Professor of Astrophysics at the University of Chicago, a position that he held until 1986. During this time, his research shifted among such topics as stellar structure, energy transfer in stellar atmospheres, and black holes. Apart from his outstanding contributions to research, Chandrasekhar was also regarded as an exceptional teacher and an author of outstanding texts, many of which remain classics in their fields.

Chandrasekhar died in Chicago on August 21, 1995, at the age of eighty-four.

Bibliography

By Chandrasekhar
The Mathematical Theory of Black Holes, 1983
Truth and Beauty: Aesthetics and Motivations in Science, 1987
Selected Papers, 1989-1996 (7 vols.)

About Chandrasekhar
Chandra: A Biography of S. Chandrasekhar. K. C. Wali. Chicago: University of Chicago Press, 1991.
"Subrahmanyan Chandrasekhar." In *The Nobel Prize Winners: Physics*, edited by Frank N. Magill. Pasadena, Calif.: Salem Press, 1989.

(Monish R. Chatterjee)

Marquise du Châtelet

Areas of Achievement: Astronomy, chemistry, mathematics, and physics

Contribution: Châtelet translated Sir Isaac Newton's *Philosophiae Naturalis Principia Mathematica* (1687) into French; her translation was printed posthumously in 1759.

Dec. 17, 1706	Born in Paris, France
1712	Tutored in mathematics, languages, and music
1721	Translates her first book, Vergil's *Aeneid*
1725	Marries Florent-Claude, marquis du Châtelet and count of Lomont
1733	Begins a lifelong relationship with the writer Voltaire
1734	Her château in Champagne becomes a refuge for Voltaire, who is fleeing an arrest for having published the *Lettres philosophiques* without authorization
1737	Equips a small laboratory to carry out scientific experiments
1737	Submits the essay "Dissertation sur la nature et la propagation du feu" to the Académie des Sciences for a competition
1738	Publishes "Lettre sur les éléments de la philosophie de Newton"
1738	Turns to the study of Gottfried Wilhelm Leibnitz and his doctrine of the *forces vives*
1740	Publishes *Institutions de physique*
Sept. 10, 1749	Dies in Lunéville, Meurthe-et-Moselle, France
1759	*Principes mathématiques de la philosophie naturelle*, her translation of Newton's *Principia*, is published

Early Life

Gabrielle-Émilie le Tonnelier de Breteuil, the future marquise du Châtelet (pronounced "shaht-LAY"), was born to noble but not wealthy parents. Good fortune prevailed as her father, the baron de Breuteuil, was appointed to the post of chief of protocol at Louis XIV's court at Versailles in 1701. When Émilie was born, the fourth and youngest child, there was money to spoil her and to ensure her aristocratic upbringing.

Émilie was tutored in the arts, mathematics, and Greek, Latin, Italian, English, and French and was instructed in the correct behavior for an aristocratic young lady. Émilie was tall at five feet, nine inches, and very bright, neither of which was considered an advantage when looking for a husband. Her height and ungainly manner caused her parents anxiety as to their daughter's social prospects.

An Arranged Marriage

As was customary in the eighteenth century, young Émilie's parents chose her husband: Florent-Claude, the marquis du Châtelet, a man fifteen years her senior. An army colonel,

(Library of Congress)

he was rarely home, and thus the marquise enjoyed unusual freedom. Shortly after the birth of their third child, the couple moved to Paris, where the marquise led an active social life while pursuing her intellectual interests in mathematics and philosophy.

The Meeting of Minds

When the marquise du Châtelet met Voltaire in 1733, a new life of physical and intellectual companionship began for both of them. She had been studying mathematics with Pierre-Louis Moreau de Maupertuis and through him had met Alexis-Claude Clairault. Like Châtelet, Voltaire had written about the ideas of Sir Isaac Newton, and Maupertuis had a copy of those pages.

This interest sparked the fervor of Châtelet. Less than a year later, when the police wanted to imprison Voltaire for having published *Lettres philosophiques* (1733) without permission from the royal censure, the marquise proposed as a refuge Cirey, her château in Champagne.

Life at Cirey

Châtelet joined Voltaire later and eventually made Cirey into an intellectual capital to which only the most distinguished minds were invited. The marquise also helped Voltaire in his work on Newton while preparing her own essay on the nature and propagation of fire for submission to a competition by the Académie des Sciences. Neither she nor Voltaire won the prize, but he persuaded the academy to print both of their papers in the volume with the winning essays. Châtelet published a revised version of her essay in 1739.

Next, she turned to Newton's work on physics, perhaps because her teenage son could profit from such a study. This work was interrupted by her desire to learn about Gottfried Wilhelm Leibnitz's doctrine of the *forces vives*. Châtelet solicited the help first of Samuel König and then of Johann Bernouilli, but these relationships ended acrimoniously. Finally, she published her work addressing the subject, *Institutions de physique* (1740), anonymously.

Dedication to the *Principia*

Although the last years of her life were difficult emotionally, Châtelet continued her translation

Newton's *Principia*

Châtelet is remembered for her French translation of Sir Isaac Newton's groundbreaking text.

Newton's *Philosophiae Naturalis Principia Mathematica* (1687), known as the *Principia*, provided scientific and mathematical theories about the laws of motion that proved unintelligible to most of his contemporaries but that would be discussed for the next two hundred years. Not since Ptolemy had there been such revolutionary thought and such interest in the scientific community.

The *Principia* is divided into three books: The first two concern matter and the laws of motion, and the third uses the entire solar system to offer proof of his universal law of gravitation. The three main laws of motion are the center of the work.

The first law states that inertia is a property of matter that allows a body at rest to remain at rest and a body in motion to stay at the same speed and to continue traveling in a straight line until it meets a resistance from some outside source. The second laws states that when an external force presses on a body in motion, the body will travel in a straight line in the direction that the force is pressing, and the change in its rate of speed will be proportional to the amount of force being exerted. The third law states that whenever an external force presses on a body, the body will exert an equal amount of pressure in the opposite direction to that of the external force.

Bibliography

Introduction to Newton's Principia. I. Bernard Cohen. Cambridge, Mass.: Harvard University Press, 1971.

Isaac Newton, Adventurer in Thought. A. Rupert Hall. Cambridge, Mass.: Blackwell, 1992.

Isaac Newton, Mastermind of Modern Science. David C. Knight. New York: Franklin Watts, 1961.

Newton, the Father of Modern Astronomy. Jean-Pierre Maury. New York: Harry N. Abrams, 1992.

of Newton's *Philosophiae Naturalis Principia Mathematica* (1687) from the 1759 English edition. She was fortunate to have help from Clairault, who published the work ten years after her death during childbirth in 1749.

Bibliography

By Châtelet

Dissertation sur la nature et la propagation du feu, 1739

Institutions de physique, 1740

Principes mathématiques de la philosophie naturelle, 1759 (as translator, from an English edition of Sir Isaac Newton's *Philosophiae Naturalis Principia Mathematica,* 1687)

About Châtelet

The Divine Mistress: A Biography of Émilie du Châtelet. Samuel Edwards. New York: McKay, 1970.

An Eighteenth Century Marquise: A Study of Emilie du Châtelet and Her Times. F. Hamel. London: Paul, 1910.

"Emilie Du Châtelet, 1733-1749." Theodore Besterman. In *Voltaire.* Chicago: University of Chicago Press, 1976.

Madame du Châtelet. Esther Ehrman. Oxford, England: Berg, 1987.

The Romance of Mme du Chatelet and Voltaire. André Maurel. New York: Appleton, 1931.

(Patricia J. Siegel)

Pavel Alekseyevich Cherenkov

Area of Achievement: Physics

Contribution: Cherenkov undertook the comprehensive study of the light emitted by transparent substances placed near radioactive sources, discovering what is now called Cherenkov radiation.

July 28, 1904	Born in Novaya Chigla, Russia
1924-1928	Studies at the University of Voronezh
1928-1930	Teaches high school in Voronezh province
1930	Begins graduate studies at the Institute of Physics and Mathematics in Leningrad
1934	Begins to conduct experiments on the light emitted by transparent material placed close to radioactive sources
1937	Observes that the light is not emitted symmetrically
1946	Awarded the Stalin Prize, along with Sergei I. Vavilov, Ilya Frank, and Igor Tamm
1958	Awarded the Nobel Prize in Physics jointly with Frank and Tamm
1959	Appointed full professor at the Institute of Physics of the Academy of Sciences of the Soviet Union
1959-1990	Heads the Photo-Meson Laboratory at the P. N. Lebedev Institute of Physics in Moscow
1970	Elected a member of the U.S.S.R. Academy of Sciences
Jan. 6, 1990	Dies, probably in Moscow, the Soviet Union

Early Life

Pavel Alekseyevich Cherenkov (pronounced "chuh-REHN-kawf"), sometimes spelled Cerenkov, was born on July 28, 1904, to a peasant family in Novaya Chigla, in the Voronezh province of Russia. Because his family was poor, he had to work while going to school and was not able to start college until he was twenty years old. Cherenkov attended the University of Voronezh from 1924 to 1928 and was graduated in 1928 with a degree in physics and mathematics.

Cherenkov taught in a high school for two years, then moved to Leningrad in 1930 to begin graduate study in physics. He entered the Institute of Physics and Mathematics in Leningrad, where he studied under Sergei I. Vavilov, a well-known Russian physicist. Shortly afterward, the institute moved to Moscow, where it was renamed the P. N. Lebedev Institute of Physics, and Cherenkov moved there to continue his studies. He remained at the institute for the rest of his life.

The Discovery of Cherenkov Radiation

In 1932, Cherenkov, while a research student at the institute, began research project, supervised by Vavilov, on luminescence (or light emission) from liquids exposed to gamma rays. This light is very dim, and when the project began, Cherenkov had to observe it with his eyes. To sensitize his eyes to this light, he had to begin his day by spending between an hour and an hour and a half in a completely dark room, before conducting his experiments.

At the time, the phenomenon of fluorescence, in which an atom emits light of a single characteristic energy or color in response to an incident X ray, was understood. The question that Vavilov had posed to Cherenkov was to determine if the blue light emitted by liquids exposed to gamma rays was fluorescence. The first indication that this was a new phenomenon, not fluorescence, came when Cherenkov showed that the same blue light was produced when he changed the type of fluid. In the fluorescence process, the light emitted depends on the material that is activated.

Cherenkov himself was not able to explain why this blue light was emitted by the liquids that he was studying, and, without an explanation of the phenomenon, his project would not be complete. Two other physicists at the institute, Ilya Frank and Igor Tamm, became interested in Cherenkov's results. In 1937, Frank and Tamm developed a theory, using the principles of classical electromagnetism, that explained how the light was emitted and that predicted some of its properties. Consequently, Cherenkov went back into the laboratory to verify experimentally these predictions. By this time, sensitive photographic film was available, and Cherenkov was able to photograph the unusual, conical emission pattern of the radiation. In a series of elegant but simple experiments, he confirmed each of the predictions of Frank and Tamm's theory.

Cherenkov, along with Frank and Tamm, was awarded the Nobel Prize in Physics in 1958 for this work in understanding what became known as Cherenkov radiation.

Research Using High-Energy Electrons

In 1959, Cherenkov was appointed a full professor at the institute and went on to work in the field of high-energy physics, focusing his efforts on the interactions of high-energy electrons. He joined with Vladimir I. Veksler to construct a series of electron accelerators at the P. N. Lebedev Institute of Physics. They constructed first a bevatron, then a 200 million-

---

Cherenkov Radiation

Cherenkov conducted a series of experiments to measure the properties of the light emitted by particles traveling through transparent media at velocities greater than the local velocity of light. He established how the angle and intensity of the emission varies with the speed of the particle.

No material object can travel faster than the speed of light in a vacuum. However, the speed of light in any material substance—gas, liquid, or solid—is lower than the speed of light in a vacuum. Cherenkov demonstrated that when a particle exceeds the speed of light in the medium through which it is traveling, a bow wave, like the shock wave established by an aircraft exceeding the speed of sound in air, is established. Light is emitted in the forward direction θ to the path of the particle given by "$\cos \theta = c/nv$," where c is the speed of light in a vacuum, n is the index of refraction of the medium, and v is the velocity of the particle. The minimum velocity for which Cherenkov radiation is produced occurs when the emission is directly along the path of the particle, that is, $\theta = 0°$. This occurs for "$v_{min} = c/n$."

In a 1937 paper, Cherenkov had pointed out the possibility of using Cherenkov radiation to distinguish the velocities of relativistic particles. This feature of Cherenkov radiation has made it important in experiments in particle physics, where rare but interesting high-energy events are usually accompanied by a background of many low-energy particles. By carefully selecting a medium having the correct index of refraction, only particles having velocities greater than a chosen v_{min} are detected. In the discovery of the antiproton, Cherenkov detectors were employed to select only events exceeding the critical velocity predicted for antiprotons under the experimental conditions.

Cherenkov detectors are also employed by cosmic-ray physicists searching for rare heavy elements in a background of many protons and alpha particles. Signals from the Cherenkov detectors are used to establish that the velocity of each particle exceeds a critical v_{min}, and then a second detector determines the rate of energy loss by the particle.

The combination of these two measurements provides a unique identification of the particle charge and energy. Using this technique, cosmic-ray detectors on balloons and Earth-orbiting satellites have determined the relative abundances of the elements from hydrogen to uranium in cosmic rays.

Cherenkov was awarded the Nobel Prize in Physics in 1958 for his experiments to observe and quantify Cherenkov radiation.

Bibliography

"The Anti-Proton." E. Segrè and C. E. Wiegand. *Scientific American* no. 6 (1956).

Cerenkov Radiation. J. V. Jelley. New York: Pergamon Press, 1958.

(AP/Wide World Photos)

Rudolf Clausius

Area of Achievement: Physics
Contributions: Clausius formulated the second law of thermodynamics and introduced the term "entropy" to describe various thermodynamic processes.

Jan. 2, 1822	Born in Köslin, Prussia (now Koszalin, Poland)
1844	Receives a teaching certificate from the University Berlin and finds a position at the Fredrich Werder Gymnasium
1848	Receives a Ph.D. from the University of Halle
1850	Named a professor of physics at the Royal Artillery and Engineering School, Berlin
1850	Formulates the thermodynamic relation stating the equivalence of heat and work
1855	Teaches physics at Zurich Polytechnic, Switzerland
1859	Marries Adelhaide Rumpan
1865	Introduces the term "entropy" as a concept of thermodynamics
1867	Teaches physics at the University of Würzburg, Germany
1869	Teaches physics at the University of Bonn, Germany
1870	Organizes a student ambulance corps during the Franco-Prussian War
1875	His wife dies
1879	Receives the Copley Medal of the Royal Society of London
1880	Marries Sophie Sack
Aug. 24, 1888	Dies in Bonn, Germany

electron-volt synchrotron. In the 1970's, they constructed a 1.2 giga-electron-volt synchrotron, which served as a major research instrument of the institute for more than a decade.

Cherenkov's group collaborated with scientists at the Center for European Nuclear Research in Switzerland and the German Electron Synchrotron in Hamburg to study the electromagnetic interactions of high-energy electrons. Cherenkov died in 1990 while still on the faculty of the institute.

Bibliography
By Cherenkov
"Visible Radiation Produced by Electrons Moving in a Medium with Velocities Exceeding That of Light," *Physical Review*, 1937

About Cherenkov
Cerenkov Radiation. J. V. Jelley. New York: Pergamon Press, 1958.
"Pavel Alekseyevich Cherenkov." In *The Nobel Prize Winners: Physics*, edited by Frank N. Magill. Pasadena, Calif.: Salem Press, 1989.
"Pavel Alexeyevich Cherenkov." Alexander E. Chudakov. *Physics Today* (1992): 106-107.

(George J. Flynn)

(Library of Congress)

Early Life

Rudolf Julius Emanuel Clausius (pronounced "KLOW-zee-uhs") was the sixth of eighteen children born to the Reverend Carl E. G. Clausius and Charlotte W. (Schultze) Clausius. His early education was in a Lutheran school that his father directed and at the Gymnasium in Stettin, Germany (now Poland).

Clausius entered the University of Berlin in 1840 and, after four years, began teaching physics at the Fredrich Werder Gymnasium in Berlin. During this time, he also completed his doctoral studies at the University of Halle, Germany, receiving his Ph.D. degree in 1848. His dissertation dealt with the refractive nature of cloud particles on sunlight that causes the familiar red sunset often seen in the evening sky.

In 1850, Clausius accepted a teaching position as professor of physics at the Royal Artillery and Engineering School in Berlin, thus beginning a long and varied teaching career. His later teaching assignments were at Zurich Polytechnic, Switzerland; the University of Würzburg, Germany; and the University of Berlin.

Contributions to Thermodynamics

Early in his teaching career, Clausius investigated the relationship between heat transfer and mechanical movement, known as the study of thermodynamics. Previous studies by other scientists had illustrated the conservation of energy—the idea that energy can be neither created nor destroyed but only transformed from one form into another. This accepted principle, that energy is indestructible, is known as the first law of thermodynamics.

Previous work considered the addition of a certain amount of heat energy to a system, resulting in the performance of a certain amount of work (movement) by the system, which dissipates energy. Although correct in their overall analyses, these early explanations were based on the idea of heat as an invisible material substance. According to the theory, when this substance flowed from an object, heat was lost and the temperature dropped. When this substance was added to an object, heat was gained and the temperature rose.

Clausius and others rejected this caloric theory of heat and successfully explained the relations between heat and work based on molecular models. His theories form the basis for the modern understanding of thermodynamic principles. Clausius further postulated that heat can spontaneously flow from a warmer to a colder object but that the reverse process, heat flowing from a cooler body to one of higher temperature, is impossible unless other outside forces are employed.

He extended this concept to propose that in every energy transformation, a fraction of the energy (heat) transferred is lost and can never be recovered. He named this lost energy "entropy," after the Greek word for "transformation." His famous quotation about this subject, stated in 1865—"The energy of the world is constant. The entropy of the world tends towards a maximum"—remains as true as when it was first spoken. His concept of entropy is expressed today as the second law of thermodynamics—that is, for any spontaneous process, the entropy of the system increases.

The Kinetic Theory of Gases

A companion study to Clausius' thermodynamic investigations dealt with the properties of gases. The kinetic molecular theory of gases, the prediction of gaseous behavior based on the collective behavior of individual particles, was firmly established from his studies. These studies also supported the concept that certain gas particles must be diatomic, for only then could their observed experimental properties be explained by the kinetic molecular theory.

Clausius was the first to relate the thermodynamic properties of gases (their energies) with the kinetic properties of gases (those

Entropy and the Second Law of Thermodynamics

Clausius recognized that an overall decrease in available energy occurs during any transformation.

Certain changes in nature occur spontaneously—for example, ice melts, heated objects cool, and exposed metals rust if left unattended. The energy transformation required to cause a spontaneous process is inherent within the objects undergoing change. In order to reverse a spontaneous process, external energy must be supplied from an outside source. Water can be converted into ice by the energy used to operate the freezing compartment within a refrigerator. Plants assemble carbon dioxide and water from the environment and incorporate them in their growth structure, but only at the expense of the energy from the sun.

Clausius was the first to recognize fully that even within a spontaneous process, a portion of the available energy associated with change is irretrievably lost in the rearrangement of the molecules within the participating substances. This fact is shown most clearly in the conversion of heat energy into work as, for example, in the heat necessary to move a piston to propel an automobile. No real transformation is exactly 100 percent efficient, and, neglecting friction, a small energy loss is necessary for the rearrangement of the molecules undergoing change.

This transformation energy, as it was first called, was renamed "entropy" after the Greek work meaning "transformation." An overall decrease in available energy occurs during any transformation. Alternatively, one may state that for any process involving energy, the entropy of the system increases. This important principle is now known as the second law of thermodynamics.

Entropy is often described as an increase in the disorder of a system. Ice, with its rigid molecular structure, melts in a spontaneous process, and the molecules become more random in their movement, freely flowing over one another. Even those changes in which the orderly arrangement of particles increases will exhibit an increase in entropy if one considers the energy lost by whatever source drives the nonspontaneous process.

An interesting consequence of this concept is that, carried to its extreme and with a constant amount of energy available throughout the universe, an ever-increasing entropy implies an ever-decreasing amount of available energy for doing useful work. Over a period of time, might the amount of energy available for performing useful work decrease to zero? It is generally accepted that this will not occur even though this result could be predicted by extending the concept of the second law of thermodynamics.

An important consequence of the second law of thermodynamics is that certain energy transformations are forbidden. For example, objects cannot be made to roll up hill by themselves. A perpetual motion machine, one that supplies its own energy from internal sources without the assistance of any outside contributions, is impossible to construct.

Entropy considerations play an essential part in concepts and expectations regarding the utilization of energy in a world with increasingly demanding energy needs.

Bibliography

Inquiry into Physics. Vern J. Ostdiek and Donald J. Bord. St. Paul, Minn.: West, 1991.

"With Clausius from Energy to Entropy." Maximo Baron. *Journal of Chemical Education* 66, no. 12 (December 1, 1989).

The World of Physics. Arthur Beiser, ed. New York: McGraw-Hill, 1960.

based on their motion). He improved on the theory suggested by Benoit Pierre Émile Clapeyron relating the heat of vaporization of gases to gas pressure. The Clausius-Clapeyron equation appears in many general chemistry textbooks.

Particles in Solution

Clausius was among the first to suggest that some particles in solution break apart, or dissociate, into individual charged fragments. This idea was later developed by others into the important concept of electrolytic dissociation, the formation of charges particles (ions) from some crystalline materials when placed in a solution.

Later Years

The wounds suffered by Clausius during the Franco-Prussian War and the sudden death of his first wife during the birth of their sixth child placed a considerable weight on his energies during the latter part of his life. Nevertheless, he was able to remain active in teaching and research. He died in August, 1888, eight years after his second marriage.

Bibliography

By Clausius

"Über die bewegende Kraft der Wärme und die Gesetze welche sich daraus für die Wärmelehre sellost ableiten lassen," *Annalen der Physik*, 1850

"Über eine veränderte Form des zweiter Hauptsatzes der mechanischen Wärmetheorie," *Annalen der Physik*, 1854

"On the Discovery of the True Form of Carnot's Function," *Philosophical Magazine*, 1856

"Über die Art der Bewegung, welche wir Wärme nennen," *Annalen der Physik*, 1857

"Über die Wärmeleitung gasförmiger Körper," *Annalen der Physik*, 1862

"Über die Anwendung des Satzes von der Aequivalenz der Verwandlungen auf die innere Arbeit," *Annalen der Physik*, 1862

Abhandlungen über die mechanische Wärmetheorie, 1864

"Über die Zurückführung des zweiten Hauptsatzes der mechanischen Wärmetheories auf allgemeine mechanische Prinzipien," *Annalen der Physik*, 1871

"A Contribution to the History of the Mechanical Theory of Heat," *Philosophical Magazine*, 1872

"Über ein neues Grundgesetz der Elektrodynamik," *Annalen der Physik*, 1875

"Über den Satz vom mittleren Ergal und seine Anwendung auf die Molecularbewegungen der Gase," *Annalen der Physik*, 1876

"Über die Ableitung eines neuen elektrodynamischen Grundgesetzes," *Journal für die reine und angewandte Mathematik*, 1877

About Clausius

Dictionary of Scientific Biography. Charles Coulston Gillispie, ed. New York: Charles Scribner's Sons, 1971.

Historical Studies in the Physical Sciences. Russell McCormmach, ed. Philadelphia: University of Pennsylvania Press, 1970.

McGraw-Hill Encyclopedia of World Biography. Vol. 3. New York: McGraw-Hill, 1973.

Source Book in Physics. William F. Magie, Cambridge, Mass.: Harvard University Press, 1963.

(Gordon A. Parker)

Jewel Plummer Cobb

Area of Achievement: Cell biology
Contribution: Cobb researched the cytology of cancer, assessing the impact of new chemotherapeutic agents. She also supported opportunities for women and minorities in science.

Jan. 17, 1924	Born in Chicago, Illinois
1944	Earns a B.A. in biology from Talladega College
1947	Receives an M.S. in cell physiology from New York University
1950	Completes a Ph.D. in cell physiology at New York
1950	Begins a fellowship at the Harlem Hospital Cancer Research Foundation
1952	Joins the University of Illinois Medical School
1954	Marries Roy Raul Cobb and returns to Harlem Hospital
1960	Teaches full time at Sarah Lawrence College
1969	Named dean and professor of zoology at Connecticut College
1974	Made a member of the National Science Board
1976	Appointed dean of Douglass College at Rutgers University
1981	Named president of California State University, Fullerton
1990	Acts as trustee professor for the California State University, Los Angeles
1990	Works for the Southern California Science and Engineering ACCESS Center and the Network for Minorities in Science and Engineering

Early Life

The only child of an affluent African American family, Jewel Plummer was encouraged to pursue professional goals. Her father, a dermatologist, inspired her to study medicine. She also credited her teachers and Paul De Kruif's book *The Microbe Hunters* (1926) for stimulating her scientific interests.

Earning a B.A. from Talladega College, Plummer pursued graduate work at New York University. She completed an M.S. and a Ph.D. in cell physiology.

The National Cancer Institute financed a two-year postdoctoral fellowship at the Harlem Hospital Cancer Research Foundation. Plummer collaborated with Dr. Louis T. Wright, who was a pioneer in artificially producing folic acid to fight cancer.

Research

In 1952, Plummer joined the department of anatomy at the University of Illinois Medical School and concentrated on skin cancer research. At Illinois, she established and directed the first tissue culture laboratory. The National

(AP/Wide World Photos)

Cytology and Cancer

Cytology is the study of cells' life histories, including examinations of their structures, functions, and pathologies in diseases such as cancer.

In her research on the cytology of cancer, Cobb examined tissue cultures cultivated from cancerous tumor and melanoma cells, both human and animal, and developed strains of cancer in her test tube specimens. Particularly interested in the role of pigments and genetics in skin cancer, she focused on melanin.

Because cancer is a mass of uncontrolled, rapidly growing cells, Cobb studied the growth behavior of the cells. She wanted to understand the factors regulating cell growth and the role of genetic material in fostering cancerous growth.

She isolated individual cells grown in laboratory cultures to evaluate the impact of chemotherapeutic agents in the hope of discovering anticancer drugs to control cell growth. Among the pioneering cancer treatments that she investigated was synthesized folic acid.

Cobb realized that studying cells, the most basic physiological unit, was vital to securing successful chemotherapeutic formulas. Cytological studies of the effects of these anticancer drugs on cells provided a foundation for further advancements in the war against cancer.

Bibliography

"Advancing Current Treatments for Cancer." Samuel Hellman and Everett E. Vokes. *Scientific American* 275 (September, 1996).

"The Cell." Diana Willensky. *American Health* 14 (July/August, 1995).

"Gene Linked to Commonest Cancer." Elizabeth Pennisi. *Science* 272 (June 14, 1996).

Cancer Institute gave her a research grant, and, for the first time, she was an independent investigator. She planned experiments, growing tumor tissues from cancer patients in test tubes.

Returning to New York after her marriage to Roy Raul Cobb in 1954, Jewel Plummer Cobb received research funds from the National Institutes of Health (NIH) and the American Cancer Society. She studied the cytology of cancer, especially melanomas and human bladder cancer, at the Harlem Hospital.

Cobb utilized her expertise as a cell biologist to experiment with new drugs and to gauge their effectiveness in killing human cancer cells. During her career, she published articles about the factors influencing the rapid growth of cancer cells. She was especially interested in the role of genetics and pigmentation in cancerous cells.

Teaching

While conducting research in New York, Cobb also taught research surgery at the New York University Post-Graduate Medical School and lectured at Hunter College. She accepted a full professorship in biology at Sarah Lawrence College in 1960. Having studied melanomas in cell cultures and analyzing anticancer drugs, Cobb presented a paper at the Eighth International Cancer Congress in Moscow in 1962.

In addition to teaching, Cobb established research laboratories and wrote reports. She also gradually accepted administrative responsibilities.

Administration

In 1969, Cobb was named dean of Connecticut College and professor of zoology there. Now divorced, she concentrated on rearing her son and improving conditions for minority scientists. She established the Postgraduate Premedical and Predental Program for Minority Students. Cobb was the only minority member of the National Science Board, which created the Women and Minorities in Science Committee.

In 1976, Cobb accepted the position as dean of Douglass College at Rutgers University, where she became a professor of biological sciences. Five years later, she was named president of California State University, Fullerton.

A Leader in Science Education

Although she retired in 1990 as president emeritus, Cobb continued to lobby for opportunities for women and minorities in science. She became a trustee professor at California State University, Los Angeles, and served as principal investigator of the Southern California Science and Engineering ACCESS Center and the Network for Minorities in Science and Engineering.

Named to university, medical, business, and other boards of trustees, Cobb promoted the cause of science. She received numerous honorary degrees and awards, and several campus buildings were named in her honor.

Bibliography
By Cobb
The Comparative Cytological Effects of Several Alkylating Agents on Human Normal and Neoplastic Cells in Tissue Culture, 1960
"A Life in Science: Research and Service," *Sage: A Scholarly Journal on Black Women*, 1989

About Cobb
Contributions of Black Women to America. Marianna Davis. Columbia, S.C.: Kenday, 1982.
The Ebony Success Library: One Thousand Successful Blacks. Nashville: Southwestern, 1973.
"Jewel Plummer Cobb." Dona L. Irvin. In *Epic Lives: One Hundred Black Women Who Made a Difference*, edited by Jessie Carney Smith. Detroit: Visible Ink Press, 1993.

(Elizabeth D. Schafer)

Arthur Holly Compton

Area of Achievement: Physics
Contribution: Compton investigated the nature of X rays, eventually showing that they behave as discrete particles now called photons. He provided crucial evidence for the particle-like nature of light.

Sept. 10, 1892	Born in Wooster, Ohio
1913	Graduated from the College of Wooster
1916	Completes his doctoral degree at Princeton University
1916-1917	Teaches physics at the University of Minnesota
1917-1919	Works as an engineer at the Westinghouse Electric and Manufacturing Company
1919	Conducts research at the Cavendish Laboratory in England
1920	Appointed a physics professor at Washington University in St. Louis, Missouri
1923	Joins the faculty of the University of Chicago
1927	Given the Nobel Prize in Physics jointly with C. T. R. Wilson
1928-the late 1930's	Conducts research on cosmic rays and has a crucial role in the development of fluorescent lamps
1941	Chairs a committee exploring the possibility of a fission bomb
1942	Directs the construction of the first nuclear reactor, at the University of Chicago
1945-1954	Serves as chancellor of Washington University
Mar. 15, 1962	Dies in Berkeley, California

(The Nobel Foundation)

Early Life

Arthur Holly Compton was born to Elias and Otelia Compton in Wooster, Ohio. His father was a Presbyterian minister who also served as professor of philosophy and dean at the College of Wooster. Arthur was born into a family of achievers: The six members of the Compton family eventually received more than seventy earned and honorary degrees.

As a boy, Compton was interested in paleontology and astronomy, and he experimented with gliders. He and his siblings were all encouraged in their intellectual and athletic activities. Compton's biographers also note that the family's religious faith had a strong and positive influence on him.

Graduate Studies at Princeton

Compton's two older brothers had already received Ph.D.'s from Princeton University, and

Arthur entered graduate school there after obtaining his bachelor's degree from the College of Wooster in 1913. He advanced quickly, earning his master's degree in 1914 and a doctorate in 1916. Compton was an outstanding graduate student, and he maintained an active social life. He continued his athletic activities as well, especially tennis. His Ph.D. thesis began his interest in the study of X rays.

After completing his graduate studies, Compton married Betty McCloskey, whom he had known in his years at the College of Wooster. She became an active partner in all of his professional activities and a great support to him. After a year teaching physics at the University of Minnesota, Compton joined the Westinghouse Electric and Manufacturing Company as an engineer. In addition to his work there, Compton continued his X-ray studies.

Cambridge and Beyond

Following World War I, Compton was awarded a fellowship and spent a stimulating year at the Cavendish Laboratory at Cambridge University in England. He returned to the United States in 1920 as professor and head of the physics department at Washington University in St. Louis, Missouri.

Compton had done some experiments with gamma rays at Cambridge that suggested further experiments with X rays. Cambridge had no X-ray equipment, so at his permanent job in St. Louis, Compton built the needed equipment for X-ray experiments. He measured the shift in wavelength of X rays scattered from electrons in graphite, and he searched for an explanation to predict the change in wavelength.

A Revolutionary Theory

Compton eventually was forced to abandon the rules of classical physics for the momentum of X radiation. Reluctantly, he explored the photon model, in which X rays are seen as small packets of energy, each with a momentum that depends on the photon's energy. He then treated the X rays and the electrons that they hit as small particles and, in 1922, came up with his quantum theory for the process, which fit the experimental results perfectly.

The Compton Effect

The Compton effect provided striking evidence for the quantum model of light and for the validity of Albert Einstein's special theory of relativity.

When a beam of X rays, all having the same wavelength, strike a target such as a block of carbon, the X rays scatter from the electrons and nuclei within the target. When he analyzed the scattered X rays, Compton found that some were of the original wavelength but that a large fraction of these X rays had a longer wavelength than that of the incident beam. The change in wavelength also depended on the angle of scattering.

The accompanying diagram shows his apparatus. Scattered X rays were analyzed by a crystal that separated X rays according to wavelength, as discovered by William Henry Bragg. The angle of scattering is shown as θ.

In attempting to explain his observations, Compton was not naturally drawn to the quantum hypothesis. Einstein had earlier shown that light can be absorbed in packets, or quanta (later called photons). Although his experiment eventually confirmed the photon theory, Compton first tried several classical avenues of analysis, treating the X rays as electromagnetic waves, but none of these approaches worked.

Compton finally arrived at a solution (see figure). Within the carbon target, a photon collides with an electron; both are subsequently scattered. The electron is moving slowly enough that one can consider it practically at rest. A critical feature of this model is that the incident X ray is a wave packet, or photon, with energy E and a momentum given by E/c, where c is the speed of light. The energy is given by $E = hc/\lambda$, where h is Planck's constant and λ is the wavelength of the X ray. After the collision, the wavelength and direction of the photon are changed, and the electron flies off in a direction as illustrated.

Compton made the usual assumption that the total energy and momentum of the system are conserved quantities: They must be the same before and after the collision. He still could not make theory agree with experiment, however, until he related the electron's momen-tum and energy according to Einstein's theory of relativity, rather than using Sir Isaac Newton's classical expression. When he did so, he obtained an expression that accurately related the wavelength shift to the scattering angle θ.

The Compton effect thus offered strong evidence on behalf of a quantum approach to light and validated Einstein's special theory of relativity. The experiment was especially important in the development of quantum theory during the years 1924 to 1927.

The timing of Compton's finding was also significant because, almost at the same time, the electron was demonstrated to have a wave character, as proposed by Louis de Broglie in his doctoral thesis and confirmed by the experiments of Clinton Davisson and Lester Germer. Scientists eventually agreed that both light and massive particles have a dual nature: If one conducts an experiment "looking for" a wave, one finds a wave, but in other experiments, such as those showing the photoelectric effect or the Compton effect, one observes a particle-like nature.

Bibliography

The Compton Effect: Turning Point in Physics. Roger H. Stuewer. New York: Science History, 1975.

The Conceptual Development of Quantum Mechanics. Max Jammer. New York: McGraw-Hill, 1966.

In Search of Schrödinger's Cat: Quantum Physics and Reality. John R. Gribbin. New York: Bantam Books, 1984.

Modern Physics. Kenneth Krane. 2d ed. New York: John Wiley & Sons, 1996.

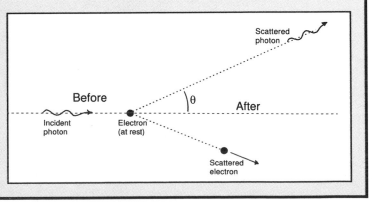

Most physicists did not at first accept Compton's theory. One reason was that it conflicted with Sir J. J. Thompson's theory of X-ray scattering, which was classically based. Furthermore, Compton had used Albert Einstein's special theory of relativity in developing his formulas, but this theory had not yet been generally accepted by physicists. At a scientific meeting in 1924 in Toronto, Canada, a special session was devoted to the controversy, and Compton was able to convince nearly everyone of his quantum model for X rays.

In 1923, Compton moved to the University of Chicago, where he spent twenty-two years. His research there extended his basic discoveries on X-ray scattering and further clarified his theory. In 1927, he shared the Nobel Prize in Physics with C. T. R. Wilson for these discoveries. That same year, he was elected to the National Academy of Sciences.

Studies with Cosmic Rays

In the 1930's, Compton became interested in cosmic radiation. These rays, which originate in deep space, were discovered in 1912 by Victor Franz Hess, but their nature remained a puzzle even in the 1930's. Accompanied by his wife, who loved to travel, Compton visited many parts of the world in order to measure cosmic-ray intensities accurately. He was able to show that the rays were most intense at the poles and weakest at the equator; this was strong evidence that cosmic rays were charged particles.

In 1941, President Franklin D. Roosevelt appointed a committee to explore the feasibility of developing a fission bomb. He asked Compton, then forty-nine, to chair the committee.

Eventually, Compton was involved in the Manhattan Project, which developed the bomb, and directed the construction of the world's first nuclear reactor, located at the University of Chicago.

When World War II ended in 1945, Compton accepted the post of chancellor of Washington University, which he held until 1954. He died of a cerebral hemorrhage in Berkeley, California, on March 15, 1962.

Bibliography

By Compton

X-Rays and Electrons: An Outline of Recent X-Ray Theory, 1926

X-Rays in Theory and Experiment, 1935 (with S. K. Allison)

The Freedom of Man, 1935

The Human Meaning of Science, 1940

Atomic Quest: A Personal Narrative, 1956

About Compton

"Arthur Holly Compton." Robert S. Shankland. In Dictionary of Scientific Biography, edited by Charles Coulston Gillispie. Vol. 3. New York: Charles Scribner's Sons, 1975.

Arthur Holly Compton. Samuel K. Allison. New York: Columbia University Press, 1965.

Nobel Prize Winners in Physics, 1901-1950. Niels H. Heathcote. New York: Henry Schuman, 1953.

Pioneers of Science: Nobel Prize Winners in Physics. Robert L. Weber. Edited by J. M. Denihan. New York: American Institute of Physics, 1980.

(Tom R. Herrmann)

James B. Conant

Area of Achievement: Chemistry
Contribution: Before he became the president of Harvard University in 1933, Conant played a major role in the development of physical organic chemistry with his research on hemoglobin.

Mar. 26, 1893	Born in Dorchester, Massachusetts
1910	Enters Harvard College
1916	Receives a Ph.D. in chemistry from Harvard and becomes a faculty member there
1933	Elected president of Harvard University
1940	Begins service on the National Defense Research Committee
1951	Publishes *Science and Common Sense*
1953	Appointed U.S. high commissioner to Germany
1955-1957	Serves as U.S. ambassador to West Germany
1959	Publishes *The American High School Today*
1961	Publishes *The Education of American Teachers*
1970	Publishes the autobiography *My Several Lives*
Feb. 11, 1978	Dies in Hanover, New Hampshire

Early Life

James Bryant Conant was born in Dorchester, Massachusetts, on March 26, 1893. From an early age, he showed an interest in chemistry and electricity. His parents realized that his interests would send him to a university one day, and they enrolled him in Roxbury Latin School, a college preparatory school that had a strong science program.

In 1910, Conant entered Harvard College,

where he studied chemistry. He also maintained his interest in electricity. In fact, he submitted two theses for his Ph.D., one in organic chemistry and one in electrochemistry. He continued his research at Harvard working under Theodore William Richards and Elmer Peter Kohler, and he joined the faculty there shortly after receiving his doctorate.

Scientific Contributions

Conant's main contribution to science was in clarifying the process by which hemoglobin combines with oxygen. He also conducted research on chlorophyll and synthetic rubber. His scientific research largely ended in 1933 when he became president of Harvard University. During the 1930's, Conant was active in

(Library of Congress)

bringing to Harvard a complement of young chemists who represented the best of the new chemistry: Paul D. Bartlett, George B. Kistiakowsky, and E. Bright Wilson.

Conant made significant contributions to the wartime effort during both world wars. In World War I, he worked with poison gases, as well as with chemicals and medicines. In World War II, he served on the National Defense Research Committee (NDRC). The NDRC supervised the research at various university laboratories and of other groups during the war, including the group that developed the atomic bomb. Conant's direct responsibility during this time was ensuring that the supply of synthetic rubber was adequate.

Educational and Diplomatic Contributions

Conant had always been interested in educational systems, and he visited universities in Europe to see how they were structured and administered. He also had an interest in public schools. During his career as the president of Harvard University, he devoted much energy to the Harvard Graduate School of Education. It was under his tenure that Harvard became coeducational, although he admitted that at first he believed that the disadvantages of having students of both sexes on campus outweighed the advantages.

Conant also served as a diplomat, being appointed by President Dwight David Eisenhower to serve as U.S. high commissioner to Germany. (The other countries with high commissioners were Great Britain and France.) After West Germany became a sovereign nation in 1955, Conant served as U.S. ambassador there until 1957.

After his diplomatic career, Conant concentrated on his interest in the public school system. He wrote several books about that system and also worked with the Educational Testing Service, which developed and administers the Scholastic Aptitude Test (SAT) and the Graduate Record Examination (GRE).

Conant died in Hanover, New Hampshire, on February 11, 1978, at the age of eighty-four.

Bibliography
By Conant
Science and Common Sense, 1951
The American High School Today, 1959

Research on Hemoglobin

Hemoglobin is the protein substance inside red blood cells (erythrocytes) that carries oxygen to body tissues and carbon dioxide away from them. There are about two hundred million molecules of hemoglobin in each erythrocyte.

Conant's work with hemoglobin combined his interest in organic chemistry and electrochemistry into the investigation of how hemoglobin combines with oxygen. By placing a pure solution of hemoglobin derived from horse blood into an electrical apparatus, he discovered that this combination was not an oxidation process, as had been thought.

Oxidation is a chemical reaction involving a loss of electrons. If hemoglobin is oxidized, however, methemoglobin is formed, which cannot combine with oxygen. Methemoglobin can be reduced back to hemoglobin by adding a reducing agent to the solution. This reduction, which is the opposite of oxidation, adds electrons and restores the hemoglobin's capacity to absorb oxygen.

Conant found that the reducing agent in this case involved a single hydrogen atom, rather than a pair as with other compounds that he had been studying. Because the hemoglobin molecule contains a single iron atom, Conant concluded that the state of oxidation of the iron atom was involved—that is, if the atom was in the oxidized state in methemoglobin, only one hydrogen atom would be needed to reduce it to hemoglobin.

Conant's observations cleared up the relationship between hemoglobin and oxygenated hemoglobin (both with iron in the reduced state) and methemoglobin (with iron in the oxidized state).

Bibliography
Hemoglobin: Molecular, Genetic, and Clinical Aspects. H. Franklin Bunn. Philadelphia: W. B. Saunders, 1986.

The Education of American Teachers, 1961
My Several Lives: Memoirs of a Social Inventor,
1970

About Conant
*James B. Conant: Harvard to Hiroshima and the
Making of the Nuclear Age.* James G.
Hershberg. New York: Alfred A. Knopf,
1993.
*The Teacher and the Taught: Education in Theory
and Practice from Plato to James B. Conant.*
Ronald Gross. New York: Dell, 1963.

(Todd A. Shimoda)

Nicolaus Copernicus

Areas of Achievement: Astronomy and cosmology

Contribution: Copernicus was the founder of modern astronomy. He taught that the sun, not the earth, is the center of the solar system, thus abolishing the ancient Ptolemaic theory of a geocentric universe.

Feb. 19, 1473	Born in Thorn, Prussia (now Toruń, Poland)
1483	Upon the death of his father, becomes the charge of his uncle, Lucas Waczenrode, bishop of Ermeland
1491-1494	Studies classics and mathematics at the University of Cracow
1496	Studies law and astronomy at the University of Bologna
Mar. 9, 1497	Makes his first recorded astronomical observations
1497	Named canon of the Frombork Cathedral
1500	Lectures on mathematics in Rome and studies law and Greek in Bologna and Padua
1503	Receives a doctorate in canon law at the University of Ferrara
1506-1512	Serves as personal physician and secretary to his uncle
1506	Returns to Poland and again serves as canon at the Frombork Cathedral
1513	Builds an observatory
1514	Privately circulates his revolutionary ideas on astronomy
1543	Publishes *De revolutionibus orbium coelestium*
May 24, 1543	Dies in Frauenburg, Prussia (now Frombork, Poland)

Early Life

The famed astronomer Nicolaus Copernicus (pronounced "koh-PER-nihk-uhs"), also known as Niklas Koppernigk or Mikolaj Kopernik, was born on February 19, 1473 in Thorn, Prussia (now Toruń, Poland), where he obtained his elementary education. Few of his teachers could have predicted his eventual impact on Western civilization, for Copernicus was part of a generation that revolutionized Europe's view of the world. What Christopher Columbus did for geography, Martin Luther and Ignatius Loyola did for theology, Dante Alighieri did for literature, Johann Gutenberg did for communications, and Michelangelo did for art, Copernicus did for astronomy.

Upon the death of his father in 1483 when Copernicus was only ten years of age, he became the ward of his maternal uncle, Lucas Waczenrode, who became the bishop of Ermeland. His uncle's patronage made it possible for Copernicus to attend the Cathedral School in Wloclawek. There, he was thoroughly prepared for his higher education, which began at the University of Cracow, where he was in residence from 1491 until 1494, concentrating on classics and mathematics.

(Library of Congress)

The Italian Years

Because Copernicus lived at the height of the Renaissance and seemed destined for a career in the Catholic Church, it was not surprising that his higher education included study for more than a decade in Italy. By 1496, Copernicus was at the world-famous University of Bologna, where he furthered his knowledge of canon and civil law and where he was introduced to the study of astronomy by D. M. de Novara.

On March 9, 1497, Copernicus made his first recorded observation of the heavens. At this time, his uncle named him a canon of Frombork (Frauenburg) Cathedral, a position that he held for the rest of his life and that gave him both an adequate income and the leisure to pursue his studies. Although a canon, Copernicus never took holy orders.

By 1500, Copernicus had lectured in Rome on mathematics and was studying law and greek at Padua. In 1503, he received a doctorate in canon law at the University of Ferrara. At Padua, he studied medicine, indicating that he was a true "universal man" of the Renaissance. Ironically, in his lifetime, Copernicus was more valued as a physician and lawyer than as an astronomer.

Contributions to Astronomy

Copernicus returned to his native land in 1506 and remained there until his death in 1543. For six years, from 1506 to 1512, he was employed as his uncle's personal physician and secretary.

The Heliocentric System

Copernicus taught that the sun, not the earth, is the center of the solar system. All planets, including the earth, rotate around the sun in regular orbits and according to predictable schedules. This view, the heliocentric system, became the basis of modern astronomy.

Until the time of Copernicus, the accepted cosmology (theory of the structure and evolution of the universe) was one based on the teachings of two celebrated Greek philosopher-scientists of antiquity: Aristotle and Ptolemy, or Claudius Ptolemaeus. Named the geocentric or Ptolemaic system, it had been in vogue for more than a millennium.

The work of Ptolemy, a brilliant geographer, mathematician, and astronomer working in Alexandria, had given the model great credibility among Muslim and Jewish scientists as well as among Christians. Ptolemy had done many amazing things, such as estimating the size of the earth, describing its surface, and locating places by longitude and latitude. His central hypothesis, however, was that the earth, as the center of the universe, was stationary and that the sun, the planets, and the stars, like the moon, orbited it. It was this central doctrine that Copernicus came to question.

Although Copernicus was not primarily an observational astronomer, he was a splendid mathematician and an inexhaustible scholar who was thoroughly familiar with the research done by others. On this basis, Copernicus came to have trouble with the Ptolemaic system. Too many facts could not be accommodated, and efforts to incorporate them simply made the Ptolemaic model more complex and unwieldy.

For example, the Ptolemaic system did not do justice to the simple phenomenon of the seasons, nor did it furnish good explanations for the movement of the then-known planets. The behavior of Mercury and Venus could only be understood if their orbits were inside that of Earth, which itself was rotating around the sun. The orbits of such outer planets as Mars, Jupiter, and Saturn became more understandable if they were seen as circumnavigating the sun outside Earth's own orbit. If, as Copernicus came to believe, the earth rotates on its axis and orbits the sun, then these other phenomena could be better explained, as well as the shifting star patterns in the night sky.

The Copernican cosmology was strongly opposed on two grounds. First, it went contrary to the accepted scientific views of the time. It was believed that the "ancients" were superior to the "moderns" in wisdom and that their authority was to be accepted passively. Second, it seemed contradictory to the religious teachings of Scripture and tradition. Making the earth only one of several planets circling the sun (and hence not at the center of the universe) was seen as diminishing the dignity and importance of humans as divine creations.

Although Copernicus' view faced opposition from both scholars and the public, it eventually prevailed for three reasons. First, it explained the behavior of the solar system better than any previous model. Second, it predicted where further findings in astronomy could be made, so it was instrumental in paving the way for Galileo, Tycho Brahe, and Johannes Kepler. Third, it had the value of simplicity, in keeping with the law of parsimony that the least complicated explanation that does justice to the data is to be preferred.

Without the pioneering work of Copernicus, the modern revolution in astronomy would have been impossible.

Bibliography

The Astronomical Revolution: Copernicus, Kepler, Borelli. Alexander Koyre. Translated by R. E. W. Maddison. Paris: Hermann, 1973.

The Grand Tour: A Traveler's Guide to the Solar System. Ron Miller. New York: Workman, 1993.

The Planets: Exploring the Solar System. Roy A. Gallant. New York: Four Winds Press, 1989.

Solar System Evolution: A New Perspective. Stuart Ross Taylor. Cambridge, England: Cambridge University Press, 1992.

Following the death of his uncle, Copernicus continued as a canon at Frombork Cathedral while also maintaining administrative, diplomatic, financial, and medical responsibilities.

On March 31, 1513, Copernicus finished the construction of an observatory, where he pursued his interests in the heavens. Although he was not primarily an observational astronomer—he probably never did more than one hundred observations—he did collect and reflect on the findings of others.

In 1514, he circulated privately and largely anonymously his brief text *De hypothesibus motuum coelestium a se constitutis commentariolus* ("The Commentariolus," 1939), in which he stated some of his revolutionary ideas. Copernicus believed that the cosmology inherited from Aristotle and Ptolemy could not do justice to the new discoveries.

Ptolemaic theory, developed in ancient times, held that the earth was the center of the universe (the geocentric model) and that the sun and the planets rotated around it. Copernicus taught that a heliocentric (or sun-centered) model better explained the evidence. It could account for the rotation of the earth on its axis and the movements of the planets, as well as the fluctuations of the earth's seasons.

A colleague and former pupil, George Joachim Iserin, or Rheticus, encouraged him to expand and publish his ideas in *De revolutionibus orbium coelestium* (1543; *On the Revolution of the Celestial Spheres*, 1939). Copernicus dedicated his work to Pope Paul III, hoping that this might forestall charges of heresy, because the Copernican view of the universe seemed to question the uniqueness of human beings as God's creations placed at the very heart of the cosmos.

Copernicus rightly predicted the impact of his teaching, for it would require major rethinking of the role of humans in the universe.

By postponing the publication of his research, he personally avoided controversy and a heresy trial. He saw his work in print only on his deathbed.

As anticipated, *De revolutionibus* was condemned for running contrary to scientific and religious orthodoxy. In 1616, it was placed on the *Index*, a list of books forbidden for Catholics to read, and it remained there until 1835.

Copernicus, one of the world's truly great scholars, died in Frauenberg (Frombork) on May 24, 1543, trusting his findings and reputation to the verdict of future generations. Building on his work, Galileo, Tycho Brahe, and Johannes Kepler proved Copernicus to be right and joined him in laying the foundations of modern astronomy.

Bibliography

By Copernicus

De hypothesibus motuum coelestium a se constitutis commentariolus, 1514 ("The Commentariolus" in *Three Copernican Treatises*, 1939)

De revolutionibus orbium coelestium, 1543 (*On the Revolution of the Celestial Spheres*, 1939)

About Copernicus

Copernicus: The Founder of Modern Astronomy. Angus Armitage. New York: T. Yoselaff, 1957.

The Eye of Heaven: Ptolemy, Copernicus, Kepler. Owen Gingerich. New York: American Institute of Physics, 1993.

Nicholas Copernicus: An Essay on His Life and Work. Fred Hoyle. New York: Harper & Row, 1973.

Nicolaus Copernicus and His Epoch. Jan Adamczewski. Translated by Edward J. Piszner. Philadelphia: Copernicus Society of America, 1970.

(C. George Fry)

BIOGRAPHICAL ENCYCLOPEDIA of SCIENTISTS

Index

In the following index, volume numbers appear in **bold face** type and page numbers appear in normal type. The names of scientists who are profiled in the encyclopedia are shown in **bold face**.